Third Edition

Money Troubles:

Legal Strategies to Cope with Your Debts

by Attorney Robin Leonard

NOLO PRESS BERKELEY

YOUR RESPONSIBILITY WHEN USING A SELF-HELP LAW BOOK

We've done our best to give you useful and accurate information in this book. But laws and procedures change frequently and are subject to differing interpretations. If you want legal advice backed by a guarantee, see a lawyer. If you use this book, it's your responsibility to make sure that the facts and general advice contained in it are applicable to your situation.

KEEPING UP-TO-DATE

To keep its books up-to-date, Nolo Press issues new printings and new editions periodically. New printings reflect minor legal changes and technical corrections. New editions contain major legal changes, major text additions or major reorganizations. To find out if a later printing or edition of any Nolo book is available, call Nolo Press at (510) 549-1976 or check the catalog in the *Nolo News*, our quarterly newspaper.

To stay current, follow the "Update" service in the *Nolo News*. You can get a two year subscription free by sending us the registration card in the back of the book. In another effort to help you use Nolo's latest materials, we offer a 25% discount off the purchase of any new Nolo book if you turn in any earlier printing or edition. (See the "Recycle Offer" in the front of the book.)

This book was last revised in: **January 1995**

Third Edition	JANUARY 1995
Editor	STEPHEN ELIAS
Illustrations	MARI STEIN
Cover Design	TONI IHARA
Book Design & Layout	TERRI HEARSH & JACKIE MANCUSO
Index	SAYRE VAN YOUNG
Proofreading	BOB WELLS
Printing	DELTA LITHOGRAPH

Leonard, Robin.
    Money Troubles : legal strategies to cope with your debts / by
Robin Leonard. -- 3rd ed.
        p. cm.
    Includes index.
    ISBN 0-87337-286-7
    1. Debtor and creditor--United States--Popular works.
    2. Collection laws--United States--Popular works. 3. Credit--Law
and legislation--United States--Popular works. I. Title.
KF1501 Z95L46 1995
346.73'077--dc24
[347.30677]   94-36930
                                                          CIP

DEDICATION

To Lee, who gives me more than money can buy and to whom I will always be indebted.

ACKNOWLEDGMENTS

The author gratefully acknowledges the following people for their support and creative contributions:

My delightful research assistants: **Karen Chambers**, who actually understands U.C.C. § 1-207; **Lisa Guerin**, who spent many hours breathing the fumes of her law school library; **Annie Tillery**, a researcher par excellence; **David Freund**, for his work on debtors' prisons; and **Tricia Bernens**, the funniest and most capable attorney in the state of Indiana. For research assistance with the second edition, **Katherine Jaramillo** was indispensable, finding every obscure citation I handed her. Thanks, too, to **Barbara Cowan** of Default Prevention—A Student Loan Service, located in Stone Mountain, Georgia, for her review of Chapter 7.

Lisa Goldoftas, who edited the book in its early stages and offered many creative suggestions, especially about organizing the material. **Steve Elias** and **Jake Warner**, brilliant editors who drove me slightly crazy sometimes, but that's what makes Nolo books as great as they are.

Terri Hearsh and **Jackie Mancuso,** for the layout and design.

All the **Noloids** who shared their debt problems with me.

Barbara Kate Repa, **Marcia Stewart**, **Mary Randolph** and **Albin Renauer**, my cohorts in the editorial department, whose support was more important to me than they will ever realize.

Sherri Conrad, **Amy J.D. Markowitz**, **Leslie Landau**, **Randy Michelson** and **Wendy Hannum**, friends from my lawyering days, who answered a never-ending string of questions, and offered lots of advice and good cheer.

Amy "AJ" Johnson, the best buddy a buddy could have, who made me realize that I should eat dinner when I thought I could write just one more section.

Diane and Pam, who run the DeHaven Valley Farm in Westport, California, and who know how to nurture a person when she needs it most.

CONTENTS

Chapter 3

NEGOTIATING WITH YOUR CREDITORS

Chapter 4

THE CONSEQUENCES OF IGNORING YOUR DEBTS

Chapter 5

WHEN THE BILL COLLECTOR CALLS

Chapter 8

CHILD SUPPORT AND ALIMONY

Chapter 9

IF YOU ARE SUED

Chapter 10

BANKRUPTCY—THE ULTIMATE WEAPON AND LAST RESORT

Chapter 11

PROPERTY YOU GET TO KEEP

Chapter 12

REBUILDING YOUR CREDIT

Chapter 13

HELP BEYOND THE BOOK

Appendix 1

GLOSSARY

Appendix 2

STATE AND FEDERAL EXEMPTION CHARTS

Introduction

BEING IN DEBT IS NOT AS BAD AS YOU THINK

The so-called debtor class ... are not dishonest because they are in debt.

—Grover Cleveland, 22nd & 24th President of United States, 1837-1908

IF YOU'RE IN DEBT, you probably feel very alone. But you shouldn't. All over the country, disposable incomes are down, savings are evaporating, and people are emerging from the recession of the early 90s deep in debt.

 Are You About to Lose—Or Have You Just Lost—Valuable Property?

If a creditor has threatened to garnish your wages, repossess property you desperately need, foreclose on your house, cut off your utilities or take other drastic action, turn to Chapter 10 and read about bankruptcy.

Filing for bankruptcy puts into action something called the "automatic stay." The stay immediately stops all collection efforts against you or your property by a creditor, collection agency or government entity—including the IRS.

Millions of honest, hard-working people—the ones who received credit offers almost daily in better economic times—are having problems paying their debts. Take a look at these statistics describing American consumers:

- Approximately 919,000 people sought assistance from Consumer Credit Counseling Service in 1992, and over one million people did in 1993. For the past several years, CCCS has been opening an average of 100 new offices *per year*.

- Over 900,000 people filed for bankruptcy in 1993. Although the number has dropped somewhat, it is still at record highs.

- Individuals incur approximately $4–5 billion a month in consumer debt. Collectively, they owe $1.3 trillion.

- Nearly 110 million consumers hold about one billion credit, charge, department store and gasoline cards, for an average of nine cards per person. The average balance per credit card in 1992 was $2,400, the average balance per retail card was $230, and the average interest rate on all cards was 17%. A typical consumer pays $440 per year in interest on credit, charge, department store and gasoline cards. In late 1994, American consumers added $5 billion to the nation's total credit card debt.

- Over 60% of recently-started small businesses have been unable to fill their capital needs. Nearly 40% of the companies have turned to credit cards to finance their business.

- The number of people behind on their car payments has risen almost 25% in the past few years.

Even though your situation is far from unique, being in debt may seem like the end of the world.

You may be afraid to answer your phone or open your mail. Your self-esteem may be shot. Your stomach, back and head probably ache. You may feel guilty, angry, depressed or all three. You may consider yourself a failure.

But there is good news. By knowing your legal rights and asserting them, you can get the bill collectors off your back and give yourself a fresh financial start. And often, you won't find it hard to fight back and affirmatively deal with your debt problems. One reason is that many creditors and bill collectors have modified their expectations and collections practices in response to mushrooming consumer debt. Debtors who assert themselves are getting more time to pay, late fees dropped and their debts settled for less than the full amount.

Money Troubles can help you take charge by:

Educating you about your legal rights. For example, *Money Troubles* explains in detail how to respond to a lawsuit, wage attachment, car repossession, foreclosure proceeding or property lien.

Helping you understand your debts. If you know how the law categorizes different kinds of debts, you'll know what kinds of collection efforts you can expect from, and negotiating ploys you can try with, different creditors.

Showing you how to avoid bankruptcy, if possible. Bankruptcy is a right way for many people to deal with their debt problems, but it's not for everyone. *Money Troubles* shows you the steps you can take to avoid bankruptcy when appropriate.

Giving you practical tips and information. *Money Troubles* contains over 20 sample letters and statements that can be used to get the bill collectors off your back, ask a creditor for more time to pay or to lower the amount of a bill. *Money Troubles* also includes over 300 addresses and phone numbers of places to lodge a complaint or ask for information, and nearly 75 charts of state laws.

Helping you evaluate your individual situation. *Money Troubles* includes several worksheets to help you figure out how much you earn, how much you owe, how much you spend and what you own. With these worksheets, you can prioritize your debts, determine if you are judgment-proof and decide if bankruptcy is appropriate. ■

Chapter 1

UNDERSTANDING YOUR DEBTS

Dreading that climax of all human ills,
The inflammation of one's weekly bills.

—George Gordon, Lord Byron, English poet, 1788-1824

A DEBT IS AN OBLIGATION to pay someone money. It may be a large obligation, such as a home mortgage or monthly rent, or a small obligation, like a monthly newspaper bill. If you don't pay, you usually suffer negative consequences. At the serious trouble end of the scale, if you don't pay your mortgage or rent, your house may be foreclosed or you may be evicted. At the minor inconvenience end, if you overlook paying your newspaper subscription, it will be canceled and you'll have to pick up the paper on your way to work.

The purpose of this chapter is to help you figure out the kinds of debts you have and exactly what your total debt burden is. Take the time necessary to do this. You can't negotiate with your creditors or prioritize your actions regarding your debts if you don't know where you stand.

You probably think of your debts in several different ways, such as:

- Debts you owe to people you know—such as a loan from your Aunt Muriel or a bill you owe Angelo, the owner of the local grocery store—versus debts you owe impersonal creditors—for example, a credit card company.

- Your regular monthly obligations—for instance, rent, phone bill or gas bill—versus debts you pay only when you buy something on credit.

- Debts for goods or services you are currently receiving—for example, a newspaper subscription or credit card bill—versus debts to repay money borrowed many years ago—such as a student loan.

- Debts you'd rather not pay and wonder if you really owe—for instance, back taxes—versus debts you don't have any reasonable grounds to object to paying—such as your rent.

Groupings such as these may be relevant in helping you decide how and in what order you will pay your bills. Legally, however, these categories are irrelevant. Instead, the law puts debts into two primary groups: secured and unsecured. To understand your debts and to intelligently decide what to do about each one, you must understand the difference. This point cannot be overemphasized. The consequences of not paying a secured debt differ tremendously from not paying an unsecured debt. (These consequences will be explained in great detail in Chapter 4.) If, after reading Sections A and B, you are still not sure you can tell a secured debt from an unsecured debt, re-read the sections.

A. Secured Debts

SECURED DEBTS ARE LINKED to specific items of property, called collateral. The collateral guarantees payment of the debt. If you don't pay, the creditor is entitled to take the property designated as the collateral. If you've ever had property, such as a car, repossessed when you failed to pay a loan, you already know a lot about how secured debts work. (See Chapter 4 for more on repossessions.)

Although the creditor has the right to take back your property, the creditor does not have to and can instead try other methods to collect the money you owe. For example, if you still owe $7,500 on your new car loan, but recently totaled the vehicle, the creditor won't repossess it—creditors want dollars, not dents.

There are two types of secured debts—those you agree to, called security interests, and those created without your consent.

1. Security Interests—Liens You Agree To

A security interest specifies precisely what property (collateral) can be taken by the creditor if you default. It also creates a "lien"—the creditor's legal right to take possession of the collateral in the event you don't pay. Security interests are of two kinds:

Purchase money. Here you pledge as collateral the property you use the loan proceeds to buy—

usually motor vehicles, furniture, large appliances or electronics equipment. This is the more common type of security agreement.

Nonpurchase money. Here you simply borrow a sum of money and pledge some property you already own as collateral. Personal loans from a bank and home equity loans are typical nonpurchase money agreements.

Some common examples of secured debts—both purchase money and nonpurchase money—include the following:

- Mortgages (sometimes called deeds of trust)—loans to buy or refinance a house or other real estate. The house or other real estate is collateral for the loan. If you fail to pay, the lender can foreclose.

- Home equity loans (sometimes called second mortgages) from banks or finance companies—such as loans to do work on your house. The house or other real estate is collateral for the loan. If you fail to pay, the lender can foreclose.

- Loans for cars, boats, tractors, motorcycles, RVs—the vehicle is the collateral. If you fail to pay, the lender can repossess the vehicle.

- Store charges with a security agreement—for example, when you buy furniture or a major appliance using a store credit card, a few stores require you to sign a security agreement in which you agree that the item purchased is collateral for your repayment. If you don't pay back the loan, the seller can come and take the property. Keep in mind that only a few store charges include security agreements. Most store purchases are unsecured. In fact, in New York, retailers are prohibited from taking a security interest in goods purchased and charged on a store credit card or any other revolving credit card.[1]

- Personal loans from finance companies—often your valuable personal property, such as a paid-off motor vehicle, is pledged as collateral.

2. Nonconsensual Liens—Liens Created Without Your Consent

A creditor can, in some circumstances, get a lien on your property without your consent. These liens are termed nonconsensual liens. In theory, a nonconsensual lien gives the creditor a right to force the sale of the property in order to get paid. In practice, however, few creditors (the IRS being the major exception) force a sale of property because of the time and expense involved. Instead, they wait to get paid until you sell or refinance the property, or another creditor sells the property after foreclosing on or repossessing it. There are three major types of nonconsensual liens.

- **Judicial liens.** A judicial lien can be imposed on your property only after somebody sues you and wins a money judgment against you. In most states, the judgment creditor then must record (file) the judgment with the county or state; the recorded judgment creates the lien on your real property. In a few states, a judgment entered against you by a court automatically creates a lien on the real property you own in that county—that is, the judgment creditor doesn't have to record the judgment to get the lien. In some states, judicial liens apply to personal, as well as real, property.

- **Statutory liens.** Some liens are created automatically by law. For example, in most states when you hire someone to work on your house, the worker or supplier of materials automatically gets a mechanic's lien (also called materialman's lien) on the house if you don't pay. So does a homeowners' association, in some states, if you don't pay your dues.

- **Tax liens.** Federal, state and local governments have the authority to impose liens on your property if you owe delinquent taxes.

---

[1] New York Personal Property Law § 413(12).

B. Unsecured Debts

WITH UNSECURED DEBTS there is no collateral. For example, when you charge a suit on your Visa card, you don't sign a security agreement specifying that the suit is collateral for your repayment. With no collateral, the creditor has nothing to take if you don't pay. This leaves the store owner only one option if he wants to be paid: to sue you, get a judgment for the money you owe and try to collect it. To try and collect, he can go after your wages, bank account or other property that can be taken under your state's laws to satisfy money judgments. (See Chapter 9.)

Most debts people incur are unsecured. Some of the more common ones are:

- accountants' bills
- alimony and child support
- church or synagogue dues
- credit and charge card cash advances
- credit and charge card purchases (Visa, Mastercard, American Express, Discover and the like)
- gasoline and most department store charges—a few department stores, however (particularly Sears), require you to sign a security agreement making the debt secured when you charge furniture and expensive appliances on your charge card
- health club dues
- loans from friends or relatives
- medical bills
- rent
- student loans
- union dues
- utility bills.

C. How Much Is Your Debt Burden?

NOW THAT YOU ARE confident that you can divide your debts into secured and unsecured, put the classifications aside (they will come up again throughout this book) and come to terms with your total debt burden. It may make you shudder. Some people with debt problems believe that the less they know, the less it hurts. They think, "I'm having trouble paying a lot of my bills. I can't stand the thought of knowing just how much I can't pay."

Happily, however, most debt counselors feel that people tend to overestimate their debt burdens. If your guess is that you owe $15,000, you may only owe $11,500. If you think you're over your head to the tune of $25,000, it may only be $15,000. This may bring little comfort to those of you who may find out that you owe more than you thought, but knowing the total amount of your debts will make a crucial difference in how you proceed.

To figure out your total debt burden, you need to compare what you bring in each month with what you (need to) spend each month on your monthly expenses (such as food, housing and utilities) and your other debts (for example, student loan payments).

Warning Signs of Debt Trouble

If you have panic attacks when you try to figure out your total debt burden, you'll feel better if you turn to the next chapter and come back to this material when you are better able to handle it. Before doing that, however, ask yourself the following questions. If you answer "yes" to any one of them, you are probably in or headed for debt trouble.

- Are your credit cards charged to the max?

- Do you use one credit card to pay another?

- Are you making only minimum payments on your credit cards while continuing to charge things?

- Do you skip paying certain bills each month?

- Have you taken out a consolidation loan? Are you considering doing so?

- Have you borrowed money or used your credit cards to pay for groceries, utilities or other necessities?

- Have you bounced any checks?

- Do your monthly loan and credit card payments—excluding your mortgage—exceed 30% of your take-home pay?

- Are collection agencies calling and writing you?

- If you lost your job, would you immediately have trouble making ends meet?

1. How Much Do You Earn?

To figure out how much you earn, spend and owe, we provide worksheets, below. If you are married or have jointly incurred most of your debts with someone other than a spouse, fill the worksheets out for both people.

Start by figuring out how much you earn each month. Complete Worksheet 1.

Worksheet 1: Monthly Income

Monthly Pay—In figuring out your monthly pay, you'll need to consider your net income; that is, your gross income (before deductions) less your mandatory deductions—federal, state and local taxes and FICA (Social Security tax). If your employer takes some money out of your paycheck and puts it towards a retirement fund or health insurance, or uses it to pay to your child support or credit union loan, don't subtract these deductions.

If you're paid weekly, multiply your net income by 52 and divide by 12.

If you're paid every two weeks, multiply your net income by 26 and divide by 12.

If you're paid twice a month, double your net income.

If you're paid irregularly, divide your annual net income by 12.

Job Income	You	Spouse or Joint Debtor	Total
Job 1			
Job 2			
Job 3			
Other Monthly Income			
Investment income			
Social Security			
AFDC or other public benefits			
Royalties			
Rent			
Pensions, dividends, etc.			
Other			
Total Income			

2 How Much Do You Owe?

In completing Worksheet 2, where you figure out your debts, do a thorough and complete job. Once Worksheet 2 is filled out, you'll know exactly how much you should be paying each month (to be current on all your bills) and how far behind you are.

Worksheet 2: Your Debts (combine for you and your spouse or other joint debtor)

1 Debts and other monthly living expenses	2 Outstanding balance	3 Monthly payment	4 Total you are behind	5 Is the debt secured? *(if yes, list collateral)*
Home loans—mortgages, home equity loans _____ _____ _____				
Rent _____ _____ _____				
Transportation expenses—car loans, car maintenance, gasoline, public transit _____ _____				
Education expenses—student loans, tuition expenses _____ _____				
Personal and other loans—bank loan, loan consolidator _____ _____ _____				
Total this page	$	$	$	

1 Debts and other monthly living expenses	2 Outstanding balance	3 Monthly payment	4 Total you are behind	5 Is the debt secured? *(if yes, list collateral)*
Totals from previous page	$	$	$	
Medical (doctors' and hospital) bills _____ _____ _____ _____				
Lawyers' or accountants' bills _____ _____ _____				
Department store or gasoline company charges _____ _____ _____ _____				
Credit and charge card bills _____ _____ _____ _____ _____				
Alimony or child support _____ _____				
Total this page	$	$	$	

1 Debts and other monthly living expenses	2 Outstanding balance	3 Monthly payment	4 Total you are behind	5 Is the debt secured? *(if yes, list collateral)*
Totals from previous page	$	$	$	
Back taxes _____ _____				
Utility bills _____ _____				
Child care _____				
Personal expenses—food, clothing, entertainment _____ _____ _____				
Insurance **Auto** _____ **Homeowners' or renters'** _____ **Health or disability** _____ **Medical or dental** _____				
Other unpaid bills _____ _____ _____ _____ _____				
TOTALS	$	$	$	

Column 1: Debts and other monthly living expenses. In Column 1, enter the type of debt or monthly expense. Don't enter a debt or expense more than once. If you charge your food purchases, for example, enter the debt under credit and charge cards, not under personal expenses.

If you are married, separated or recently divorced, you may not be certain which debts are yours and which are not. Most married couples think in terms of "us," however, and if your marriage is intact and you're together having financial problems, approach your debt problems as a team. That is, enter all your debts in Column 1. Similarly, if you live with someone else, combine your incomes and pay both of your debts with your joint funds; regardless of who actually incurred the debt, enter both partners' debts in Column 1.

Special Concerns for Separated or Divorced Debtors, or Married Debtors Where Only One Spouse Is Having Financial Problems

If you are separated or divorced, or you're married but only one spouse is having financial woes (for example, you owe back taxes from before your marriage, an old student loan and child support from a previous relationship), you'll want to figure out your debt problem from your perspective only. Although you may think of your economic lives completely combined, the law sometimes doesn't. While your spouse may emotionally suffer with you, she may not face the same financial liability.

If you live in a community property state (Arizona, California, Idaho, Louisiana, Nevada, New Mexico, Texas, Washington or Wisconsin) be sure to read the side bar on special rules for community property states.

Regardless of your state, that is, community property or not, keep in mind the following:

- In many states, each spouse is generally liable only for the debts that he or she incurs during marriage, except that both spouses are usually liable for all debts incurred with joint accounts, where the creditor was looking to both spouses for repayment, for the family's necessities (food, clothing and shelter) and for the children's education.

- Usually, debts incurred after the separation date but before the divorce is final are the responsibility of the spouse who incurred them and must be paid by that person. Again, however, there's an exception—both spouses are liable for debts to pay for the family's necessities and the children's education, regardless of which spouse incurred them.

- Spouses are generally not liable for the debts their mate incurred before they married or after their divorce became final.

- If you or your ex-spouse agreed to pay certain debts as part of a divorce settlement—or a divorce decree signed by a judge requires that one spouse pay the debts—the agreement or decree is binding only on you and your ex. Because you were married when the debts were incurred, the creditor has a right to collect from both of you. If you pay bills your ex-spouse agreed to or was ordered to pay, your only remedy is to try to get your ex to reimburse you. Complaints to the creditor will get you nowhere.

- Separate property is property owned prior to the marriage, property accumulated after divorce and property received during marriage by one spouse only, by gift or inheritance. In most non-community property states, separate property also includes wages earned by a spouse during marriage.

- Separate property of one spouse usually cannot be taken by a creditor to pay the separate debts of the other. Separate property of one spouse can be taken to pay joint debts, and separate property of one spouse is always available to pay that spouse's separate debts.

Although these last two items pertain to property owned by, and not debts incurred by, married people, they are included because debts and property are intricately linked. You may want to return to this information when you read Chapter 11, *Property You Get To Keep.*

Special Rules for Community Property States

The community property states are Arizona, California, Idaho, Louisiana, Nevada, New Mexico, Texas, Washington and Wisconsin. In those states, property acquired and debts incurred during marriage—called community property and community debts—are joint. For example, if one spouse buys a new kayak without consulting the other—and the other spouse objects—the objecting spouse is out of luck, meaning the debt is owed by both. Specifically:

- Both spouses are generally liable for all debts incurred during marriage, unless the creditor was looking to only one spouse for repayment. For example, if the spouse who bought the kayak put financial information only about himself—such as a bank account with funds containing money owned before marriage—on the loan application, his spouse would not be liable to pay for the kayak if he defaults.

- Spouses are generally not liable for the separate debts their mate incurred before marriage or after permanent separation. The debtor spouse's share of all community property (including the debtor spouse's half of the nondebtor spouse's income), however, can be used to pay the debtor spouse's debts incurred before marriage.

- Community property includes wages earned during marriage. In some community property states, community property does not include wages deposited into a separate deposit account and not mixed with any other community property.

- Separate property is limited to property owned prior to the marriage, property accumulated after divorce (after separation, in a few states) and property received during marriage by one spouse only, by gift or inheritance.

For more specific information on spousal debts, see the Spousal Obligations table at the end of the chapter.

Column 2: Outstanding balance. In Column 2, enter the entire outstanding balance on the debt. For example, if you borrowed $150,000 for a mortgage and still owe $125,000, enter $125,000 in Column 2. If you don't know what you owe, consider contacting the creditor. If you'd prefer that the creditor not hear from you, make your best guess. On debts where you make monthly payments that include both principal and interest, enter only the principal.

Columns 3 and 4: Monthly payment and total you are behind. In Columns 3 and 4, enter how much you currently owe on the debt. If the lender has not established set monthly payments, for example, a doctor's bill, enter the entire amount of the debt in Column 4 and leave Column 3 blank. If it is one for which you make regular monthly payments, such as your car loan or mortgage, enter the amount of the monthly payment in Column 3 and the full amount you are behind (monthly payment multiplied by number of months you haven't paid) in Column 4.

For credit card, department store and similar debts, enter the monthly minimum payment in Column 3 and your entire balance in Column 4.

Column 5: Is the debt secured? In Column 5, indicate whether the debt is secured or unsecured. Remember, a secured debt is linked to a specific item of property. You surely signed a security agreement giving the creditor this right or the creditor may have filed a lien against your property. If the debt is secured, specify the property—the collateral—that the creditor is entitled to if you default.

Add it Up

When you've entered all your debts onto the Worksheet, do the following:

- Total up Columns 2, 3 and 4. Column 2 represents the total balance of all your debts, even though some of it may not be due now; Column 3 represents the amount you are obligated to pay each month; and Column 4 shows the amount you would have to come up with to get current on all your debts.

- Compare the numbers at the bottom of Worksheet 2, Column 3 (the amount you are obligated to pay each month) and Column 4 (the amount you would have to come up with to get current on all your debts) to the figure at the bottom of Worksheet 1 (your net income).

The figures on Worksheet 2 may far exceed the figure on Worksheet 1. For example, your income and monthly payments both might be near $2,000, while the amount you need to pay to get current is $4,500. Or, your income might be less than half of how much you need to pay each month. Whatever is the situation, don't despair. The rest of this book gives you tips on prioritizing your debts, negotiating with your creditors and using other techniques to ease your burden. Use Worksheet 2 to guide you through the debt maze.

The information in this chart is subject to change. Before relying on the chart below, you may want to check the statute at a local law library for any amendments. See Chapter 13 for tips on doing legal research. (Note: Torts include negligence (such as car accidents), assault, battery, libel, slander and infliction of emotional distress.)

Obligations of Spouses

State	Code Section	Spousal Obligations
Alabama	Const. Art. X § 209	Wife's property owned before marriage and received during marriage as gift or inheritance is her separate property and not liable for any of her husband's debts.
Alaska	25.15.010	Separate property of one spouse isn't liable for the other's debts.
	25.15.050	Neither spouse is liable for the other's separate debts incurred before or during marriage.
Arizona	25-215	Separate property of one spouse is not liable for the other's separate debts.
		The portion of a spouse's community property that would have been separate property if that spouse were unmarried is liable for that spouse's debts incurred before marriage.
		Community property is liable for debts incurred outside the state during marriage if those debts would have been community debts had they been incurred in the state.
		Community debts are to be paid first by community property, then by the separate property of the spouse actually incurring the debt.
Arkansas	9-11-506	Neither spouse is liable to pay the other's debts incurred before marriage.
	9-11-507	Separate property of one spouse isn't liable for the other's premarital debts.
	9-11-508	Separate contracts entered into by a spouse where the creditor looks for payment only from that spouse's separate property does not bind the other spouse or the other spouse's property.
California	Family 910	Community property is liable for all debts incurred before or during marriage (marriage ends when the spouses move apart permanently) by either spouse.
	Family 911 (a)	The earnings of one spouse earned during marriage are not liable for the other spouse's debts incurred before marriage if those earnings are kept in a separate bank account to which the debtor spouse has no access, and those earnings are not mixed with other community property.
	Family 913 (a)	A spouse's separate property is liable for that spouse's separate debts incurred before or during marriage.
	Family 913 (b)(1)	A spouse's separate property is not liable for the other's debts incurred before or during marriage.
	Family 914	A spouse is liable for the other spouse's debts incurred during marriage for necessaries while they are living either together or apart.
	Family 916 (a)(1)	After divorce, a spouse's separate property is liable for all of that spouse's separate debts incurred before or during marriage, even if the other spouse agreed to pay that debt as part of the divorce settlement.
	Family 916 (a)(2)	After divorce, a spouse's separate property is not liable for any of the other spouse's separate debts incurred before or during marriage, unless that spouse agreed to pay that debt as part of the divorce settlement.

State	Code Section	Spousal Obligations
California (con't)	Family 1000	A spouse is not liable for injury or damage caused by the other spouse. Payment for injury, damage or death caused by a married person acting for the benefit of the community are to be paid first out of community funds and then out of the spouse's separate property. If the injury, damage or death happened when the spouse was not acting for the benefit of the community, payments are to be made first out the spouse's separate property and then out of community property.
Colorado	14-2-201	Wife's separate property is not liable for any of husband's debts.
	16-6-110	Both spouses are liable for family expenses and children's education.
Connecticut	46b-36	Neither spouse can acquire an interest in the other's property owned before or acquired after marriage.
		Separate earnings of wife are her separate property.
		Husband is not liable for wife's debts incurred before or during marriage.
	46b-37	If a spouse makes a purchase in own name, it's assumed to be a separate debt.
		Each spouse is liable to support the family—specifically to pay a physician, dentist or hospital; to pay rent; to pay for an item used for support or that benefits both spouses; and to pay for the wife's clothes in the event her husband abandons her.
		Spouse is not liable for other's separate debts incurred during separation if paying reasonable support.
Delaware	13 § 314	Wife's debts incurred before or during marriage shall be paid out of her separate property.
District of Columbia	30-201	Spouse or spouse's property is not liable for the other's debts, except that both spouses are liable for debts for necessaries for them or their dependent children.
Florida	708.05	Husband is not liable for wife's debts incurred before marriage.
Georgia	19-6-13	Both spouses are liable for shelter, food and necessaries for their children.
Hawaii	510-8	Separate property of spouse is liable for all of that spouse's debts.
		Marital property is liable for wife's separate debts, husband's separate debts or marital debts. Marital property should be used before separate property to pay marital debts.
		Husband and wife's earnings and separate property are liable for their own debts incurred before marriage. Separate property should be used to pay those debts before marital property is used.
		Husband and wife are obligated to support each other and the family, and to pay for all debts for necessaries during marriage. Marital property should be used to pay those debts before separate property is used.
	572-23	Neither spouse is liable for the other's separate debts.
	572-24	Both spouses are liable for debts incurred by the other for necessaries.

State	Code Section	Spousal Obligations
Idaho	32-910	Husband's separate property is not liable for wife's debts incurred before marriage.
	815 ILCS 505/2H	Creditor cannot try to collect a debt or loan from a spouse unless that spouse cosigned for the debt or loan.
Illinois	150-ICS ¶ 6515	Neither spouse is responsible for paying the other's separate debts incurred before or during marriage.
		Wages, property, and rents and profits of a spouse's property, cannot be taken to pay for other's separate debts.
	815 ICS ¶ 505/2H	Creditor cannot try to collect a debt or loan from a spouse unless that spouse cosigned for the debt or loan.
Indiana	31-7-10-3	Wife is liable for all torts committed by her.
	31-7-10-4	Husband is not liable for acts committed by wife.
Iowa	597.19	Spouse is not liable for torts committed by the other.
Kansas	23-201	Spouse's separate property remains that spouse's separate property and is not liable for the other spouse's debts.
Kentucky	404.010	Husband has no interest in wife's property owned before or acquired during marriage.
		During marriage, wife owns all her property separately; that property cannot be taken to pay for husband's debts.
		Wife's property is liable for her debts incurred before or during marriage.
	404.040	If wife gives property to husband, or husband receives property from wife by virtue of the marriage, husband is liable for wife's debts incurred before or during marriage to the value of property received.
		Husband is liable for wife's necessaries bought during marriage.
Louisiana	CC 2339	The following are community property when acquired during marriage: natural and civil fruits of a spouse's separate property; minerals from a spouse's separate property; bonuses, delay rentals and royalties; payments from a spouse's separate property mineral leases.
	CC 2345	Separate or community debt paid during marriage may be paid out of community property or separate property of the spouse who incurred the debt. If community property is used to pay a separate debt, the nondebtor spouse may ask a court to be reimbursed.
	CC 2360	Debt incurred by either spouse during marriage for the interest of both or the other is a community debt.
	CC 2363	Debt incurred before marriage or after divorce, or during marriage but for only one spouse's benefit is that spouse's separate debt.
Maine	19-164	Husband is not liable for wife's debts incurred before marriage, incurred in only her name or her torts in which he took no part.

State	Code Section	Spousal Obligations
Maryland	FL 4-301	Neither spouse is liable for the other's debts incurred before marriage. Spouse is liable for all his or her debts incurred before marriage.
		Husband is not liable for wife's debts incurred before marriage, nor for a court judgment against wife only.
		Wife's property owned before or acquired during marriage is not liable for husband's debts.
		Spouses cannot sell or give property to the other if it prejudices rights of creditors.
Massachusetts	209:7	Wife is not liable for husband's debts, except for husband's debts for necessaries to $100 if those necessaries were sold with her knowledge or consent. Wife is liable only if she has property of $2000 or more.
	209:8	Husband is not liable for wife's debts incurred before marriage or for court judgments against her.
	209:9	Wife's contracts made relative to her separate property or her own business are not binding on her husband and do not hold his property liable.
Michigan	26.165 (1)	Wife's property owned before or acquired during marriage remains her separate property and is not liable for husband's debts.
	26.165 (4)	Husband is not liable for wife's debts for breach of contract relating to her separate property.
Minnesota	519.02	Wife's property owned before marriage remains her separate property and is not liable for husband's debts.
	519.05	Husband is not liable for wife's debts except for necessaries furnished during marriage. If husband and wife live together, they are jointly liable for all necessaries used by the family.
Mississippi	93-3-13	If husband receives and uses wife's property or income, he becomes her debtor, but is accountable to her for only one year.
Missouri	451.250	Wife's property owned before or acquired during marriage remains her separate property and is not liable for husband's debts.
	451.260	Rents, profits, issues or sales proceeds of wife's real property is her separate property and is not liable for husband's debts except for his debts to provide necessaries for her and the family, or to improve her real property.
	451.270	Husband's property is not liable for wife's debts incurred before marriage.
Montana	40-2-106	Neither spouse is liable for the other's debts, however, both spouses are liable for debts for necessaries of family and children's education.
	40-2-201	Neither spouse has any interest in the other's property.
	40-2-209	Spouse's separate property is not liable for other's debts except for necessaries, or if the property is in the exclusive possession and control of the other and a creditor relied on that property for repayment, not knowing it didn't belong to that spouse.

State	Code Section	Spousal Obligations
Nebraska	42-201	Wife's property owned before or acquired during marriage is her separate property and is not liable for husband's debts except that 90% of her wages are liable for family's necessaries, although the creditors must seek payment from husband first.
	42-206	Husband is not liable for wife's debts incurred before marriage.
Nevada	123.050	Neither spouse is liable for the other's debts incurred before marriage.
	123.060	Neither spouse has any interest in other's property.
New Hampshire	460:1	Wife's property owned before or acquired during marriage is her separate property and is not liable for husband's debts.
	460:3	Husband is not liable for wife's debts incurred before marriage.
New Jersey	37:2-8	Wife is liable for her own torts.
	37:2-10	Husband is not liable for wife's debts incurred before or during marriage.
	37:2-12	Wife's separate property, and the rents, issues and profits from that property, remain her separate property.
	37:2-13	Wife's earnings, and investments on earnings, are her separate property.
	37:2-15	Husband cannot dispose of wife's separate property nor is it liable for his debts.
New Mexico	40-3-4	Neither spouse may enter into a contract of indemnity to obligate the community property.
	40-3-10	Separate debts are to first be paid with the following property: (1) debtor spouse's separate property, except for separate property that is a portion of joint tenancy or tenancy in common property with the other spouse; (2) debtor spouse's share of joint tenancy, tenancy in common or community property, except the residence; (3) debtor spouse's interest in residence. (Look at your deed to see if your property is held as joint tenancy or tenancy in common.)
		Neither spouse's community property or separate property is liable for the other spouse's separate debts.
	4-3-10.1	Court may declare a community debt incurred by one spouse while the spouses live apart to be a separate debt if it does not benefit both spouses or the spouse's dependents.
	4-3-11	Community debts are to be paid with the following property: (1) community property; (2) tenancy in common or joint tenancy property except the residence; (3) a tenancy in common or joint tenancy residence; (4) the separate property of spouse who incurred debt. If the spouses together incurred the debt, both spouse's separate property is liable.
New York	DRL 50	Wife's property owned before or acquired during marriage, as well as the rents and profits of that property, is her separate property and is not liable for husband's debts.
	GOL 3-305	Husband is not liable for wife's contracts.
	GOL 3-307	Husband who acquires some of wife's property owned before marriage by way of a contract with her is liable for her debts incurred before marriage to the value of the property received.

State	Code Section	Spousal Obligations
North Carolina	39-18	Every contract between a man and woman that transfers property in consideration of their marriage is not valid against their creditors.
	52-11	Neither spouse is liable for the other spouse's debts incurred before marriage.
	52-12	Neither spouse is liable for damages caused by the tort of the other or for criminal fines of the other.
North Dakota	14-07-03	Spouses must support each other out of their separate property and labor.
	14-07-04	Neither spouse has an interest in the other's separate property, however, neither can exclude the other from a separate property home.
	14-07-08	Neither spouse is answerable for the other's acts. Earnings of spouse are not liable for the other's debts. Earnings of spouse and a minor child residing with that spouse are the separate property of that spouse while the spouses live apart. Spouses are jointly liable for debts for necessaries contracted by either while they live together. Separate property of a spouse is not liable for the other's debts.
	14-07-10	Husband and wife are jointly liable to anyone who in good faith supplied articles necessary for their support.
Ohio	3103.03	Husband must support himself, wife and their minor children with his property or labor. If he can't, wife must assist insofar as she is able to.
	3103.04	Neither spouse has an interest in the other's property, however, neither can exclude the other from a separate property home.
	3103.08	Neither spouse is liable for the other's acts.
Oklahoma	43-202	Husband must support himself and wife out of his property or labor. Wife must support husband, if he has not deserted her, out of her property if he has no property and can't support himself.
	43-203	Except as under § 43-202, husband and wife have no interest in separate property of the other, however, neither can exclude the other from a separate property home.
	43-208	Neither spouse is liable for the other's acts. Separate property of wife is not liable for husband's debts, but is liable for her debts incurred before or during marriage.
Oregon	108.020	Neither spouse is liable for the other's separate debts incurred before or during marriage. The rent or income of property of one spouse is not liable for the other's debts.
	108.040	Both spouses are liable for the debts of the family and education of children. If creditor sues only the wife, creditor must sue within two years of when the debt becomes due. After divorce, wife is not liable for family expenses incurred by husband while they lived together.
	108.050	Wife's property owned before marriage or acquired during marriage by her own labor is not liable for her husband's debts.
	108.060	Spouses have no interest in each other's separate property and that property is not liable for debts of the other, except as provided in §108.040.

State	Code Section	Spousal Obligations
Pennsylvania	23-4101	Wife's property owned before marriage or acquired during marriage by will, descent, deed of conveyance or otherwise, is her separate property.
		Wife's separate property not liable for husband's debts.
		Husband is not liable for wife's debts incurred before marriage.
	23-4102	To obtain payment for debts for necessaries, creditors may look to all of husband's property and then separate property of wife if the creditor sued both spouses. Creditor cannot get a judgment against wife unless she contracted for the debt, or if the articles are for the support of husband and wife.
Rhode Island	15-4-9	If wife carries on her own business or trade, husband is not liable for her business debts.
	15-4-12	Husband is not liable for wife's debts incurred before marriage.
		Husband is not liable for wife's debts incurred during marriage unless he participated with her or coerced her to act.
		Wife is not liable for husband's debts.
South Carolina	20-5-30	Wife's property is not liable for husband's debts.
	20-5-40	Wife's earnings and income remain her separate property.
	20-5-60	Husband is not liable for wife's debts except for those necessary for her support and the support of their minor children residing with her.
South Dakota	25-2-6	Separate property of a spouse is not liable for the other's debts incurred before marriage.
	25-2-11	Spouses are jointly liable for all necessaries of life—food, clothing and fuel—purchased by either for their family while they live together as husband and wife.
	25-2-14	Neither spouse is liable for the other's acts.
Tennessee	36-3-502	No marital settlement agreement is valid against creditors if under the agreement wife receives more in debts than in property.
	36-3-503	Husband is not liable for wife's debts incurred before marriage.
	47-18-805	Spouse of credit applicant is not liable, except for necessities, if that spouse did not sign the application.
Texas	Fam. 4.031	Spouse is liable for the other's acts only if acting as agent or if spouse incurs debt for necessaries. In general, community property is not liable for debts arising from act of spouse.
	Fam. 5.61	Separate property of a spouse is not liable for the other's debts.
		Unless both spouses are liable under § 4.031, community property under one spouse's management and control is not liable for other's debts incurred before marriage or nontort debts incurred during marriage. Community property subject to one spouse's management and control is liable for that spouse's debts incurred before marriage. All community property is liable for tort debts of either spouse incurred during marriage.

State	Code Section	Spousal Obligations
Utah	30-2-1	Wife's property owned before or acquired during marriage is her separate property and is not liable for her husband's debts.
	30-2-5	Neither spouse is liable for other's debts incurred before or during marriage.
		Earnings of one spouse are not liable for other's separate debts.
	30-2-7	Husband is not liable for wife's torts.
	30-2-9	Both spouses are liable for family expenses and children's education.
Vermont	15-68	Wife's real property owned before marriage or acquired by gift or inheritance during marriage, is not liable for husband's debts. Rents and profits of wife's real property is liable for husband's debts for necessaries for wife and their family and for debts for improving her real property.
	15-69	Husband is not liable for wife's debts incurred before or during marriage unless debts incurred with husband's authority or at his direction.
Virginia	55-37	Wife's property is not liable for husband's debts.
		Neither spouse is liable for the other's debts incurred before or during marriage.
Washington	26.16.010	Husband's separate property is not liable for wife's debts.
	26.16.020	Wife's separate property is not liable for husband's debts.
	26.16.030	Either spouse may manage or control the community property.
		Neither spouse shall have a lien placed on, sell or give away the community property real estate without the other joining in; buy real estate without the other joining in or let a creditor take a security interest in household goods, furnishings, appliances or mobile home unless that item is being purchased.
	26.16.140	When the spouses live apart, their earnings and accumulations are separate property; minor child's earnings and accumulations are the separate property of the parent with whom the minor lives.
	26.16.190	If one spouse causes injuries to a third person, the injured person cannot recover against the other spouse's separate property.
		Neither spouse is liable for the other's separate debts.
		Spouse's earnings and accumulations are liable for own debts.
	26.16.200	No separate debt may be basis for claim against a husband or wife unless reduced to court judgment within three years of marriage.

State	Code Section	Spousal Obligations
West Virginia	48-3-1	Wife's separate property owned before marriage remains her separate property; rents, profits, issues of that property remain her separate property.
	48-3-14	Husband is not liable for wife's debts incurred before marriage.
	48-3-15	If spouse gives or sells property to the other in a prenuptial or marital agreement, creditors of original spouse owner may go after spouse who received the property to the value of the property received.
	48-3-16	Wife's earnings, and property purchased with her earnings, is her separate property.
	48-3-17	If wife runs her own business or carries on a trade or profession, the business is not liable for husband's debts nor subject to his control.
	48-3-20	Husband is not liable for wife's torts.
	48-3-22	A spouse is liable for all debts incurred in his or her name except both spouses are liable for services of physician, rent, support of family, and clothing if husband abandons wife. Husband's property is first liable and then wife's property.
Wisconsin	766.55	Debt incurred by a spouse during marriage is presumed to be in the interest of marriage or family and therefore both spouses are liable.
		A spouse's duty to support the other or their child must be paid from community property or the obligated spouse's separate property; a debt incurred by a spouse for the interest of family is to be paid from community property or the incurring spouse's separate property.
		A separate debt incurred before or during marriage may be paid only from that spouse's separate property or from community property that would have been that spouse's separate property but for the marriage.
		Any debt incurred by a spouse during marriage may be paid from that spouse's separate property or that spouse's interest in community property; for nontort debts, separate property must be used before spouse's interest in community property.
Wyoming	20-1-201	Spouse's property owned before marriage remains separate property; rents and profits from that property are separate property. Separate property is not liable for other's debts.
		Separate property is liable for necessary expenses of family and children's education.
	20-1-202	Spouse is not liable for the other's debts incurred before marriage.

■

Chapter 2

DEBTS YOU MAY NOT OWE

The buyer needs a hundred eyes, the seller not one.

—George Herbert, English poet, 1593-1633

THIS BOOK IS PRIMARILY about being over your head with debts you know you owe. I spend less space explaining your rights when you've been cheated by dishonest creditors or lenders, or when the merchandise you've purchased falls apart before you get a chance to use it. Those are the subjects for a book on consumer rights.

Nevertheless, it's important to focus some attention on debts you feel you shouldn't have to pay. Consumers' rights and debtors' rights are closely linked. If you bring something home and it falls apart before you use it, do you have to pay? If you want to cancel a door-to-door contract shortly after you signed it, can you? If you're sent unordered merchandise and a week later you get a bill, do you have to pay? These and similar questions are answered in this chapter.

> **Example:** Eric's new car has been to the repair shop several times. The engine has a serious problem and the dealer can't seem to fix it. Eric's car is probably a lemon, and Eric is most likely entitled to a refund or a replacement. (See Section B.)

 You Can Skip this Chapter if You Have No Disputes or Your Dispute Is Covered Elsewhere in the Book

Not everyone has bills they legitimately dispute. And, while some people will fight tooth and nail against any perceived injustice, others would rather try to work out a compromise with their creditors. If you really don't have anything to fight about—or if you aren't in a fighting mood—skip ahead to Chapter 3.

Also, certain types of "debts you may not owe" are covered in other chapters. See Chapter 1 for a discussion on debts incurred by your spouse, Chapter 6 for information on your rights as a cosigner and for information on credit card debts you may not owe, and Chapter 9 to see if the creditor has taken too much time to pursue the debt—that is, the statute of limitations has run.

A. The Seller Breaches a Warranty

A WARRANTY IS A GUARANTEE about the quality of goods or services you buy. Warranties are generally divided into two types: implied warranties and express warranties. An implied warranty is one that the law automatically entitles you to because it would be unjust for you to be without the protection.

An express warranty is different. You are not automatically entitled to an express warranty. The merchant or manufacturer must make a statement about the quality of its goods or services. An express warranty is usually written down, but it can also be stated by the seller when he talks to you about your purchase.

Is a Guarantee a Warranty?

Many manufacturers or sellers give guarantees with their products, not warranties. Is there a difference? No. If you receive a written (or oral) guarantee, it is the same thing as a warranty. The seller or manufacturer doesn't have to use the word "warranty" for you to get the protection.

The purpose of a warranty is to give you recourse if the item you buy turns out not to be what you thought it was. And if an item you buy does not conform to the warranty and you haven't yet paid for it, don't.

Let's take some more time to go into implied and express warranties.

1. Implied Warranties

Everything you buy comes with at least two implied warranties—one for "merchantability" and one for "fitness."

- Implied warranty of merchantability is an assurance by the seller that the item will work if you use it for a reasonably expected purpose. For example, if you buy a refrigerator and your food spoils because the refrigerator won't go below 55 degrees (a refrigerator should be about 45 degrees), you can safely assume there's a violation of the implied warranty of merchantability.

  If you buy a used item, the warranty of merchantability is a promise that the product will work as expected, given its age and condition. If a used refrigerator cools down to 45 degrees without any problem, but the door sticks or the light flashes every so often, this isn't a breach of the warranty of merchantability.

- Implied warranty of fitness applies when you buy an item with a specific (even unusual) purpose in mind. If you relate your specific needs to the seller—even a sales clerk who was hired the week before—the implied warranty of fitness assures you that the item will fill your need. For example, if you buy new tires for your bicycle after telling the store clerk you plan to do mostly off-road, mountain cycling, and the tires puncture every time you pass over a small rock, the tires don't conform to the warranty of fitness.

In some states, a seller can choose to eliminate implied warranties on new goods, but must do so in writing. This is called a written warranty disclaimer and must be very specific, usually using either the word "merchantability" or "fitness" to describe the warranty being disclaimed. For new goods, saying that the goods are sold "as is" or that "all warranties are disclaimed" isn't enough.

For used goods, however, the seller can legally eliminate implied warranties by selling products "as is" or by stating that "all warranties are disclaimed."

2 Express Warranties

Most written warranties state something like "the product is warranted against defects in materials or workmanship" for some specified time. Here are some examples of more specific express warranties:

- furniture—"We guarantee all furniture against defects in construction for one year. When a structural defect is brought to our attention, we will repair or replace it at our option."

- fabric shield—"We warrant that if this fabric becomes stained during its lifetime as a result of ordinary water or oil-based spills, we will service the stained area of the fabric at no cost to you."

- trash can—"If your new trash can cracks during normal usage within five years of the date of purchase, we will arrange for a replacement of the broken part."

- stereo speakers—"We warrant that these speakers will perform within two decibels of their advertised specifications for five years from the date of purchase."

- wrist watch—"We promise to repair or replace, at our option, your watch if it fails to function within its original tolerances of timing, that is, within 1–5 minutes per day, fast or slow, within one year of the date of purchase."

Most written warranties either come directly from the manufacturer or are included in the sales contract you sign with the seller. But a written warranty may be a feature in an advertisement or on a sign in the store ("all dresses 100% silk"). Or an express warranty may be oral. If a seller verbally describes a product's features or what the product will do, which you relied on when buying the item, the oral statement constitutes an express warranty.

Of course, oral warranties are hard to prove, as it becomes your word against the seller's. If the seller describes a feature about a product you are considering buying that makes your eyes light up, but the feature isn't in writing anywhere, ask the seller to jot it down.

If you purchase an item that comes with a written warranty, the seller or manufacturer—depending on who issued the warranty—must stand behind the writing. Again, the writing may consist of a sign in the store, an advertisement, the contract you sign or a separate warranty statement. But don't be ready to call absolutely everything written about an item an express warranty; retailers are allowed to "puff" a little when they advertise. For example, if you buy a used radio after reading an ad stating that it was "in great shape," that statement is not an express warranty. If the radio turns out to be complete junk, you may have recourse on the grounds of the implied warranty of merchantability, but not as an express warranty violation.

Many manufacturers and some sellers provide written warranties, but you don't have an automatic right to receive one. If you are given a written warranty, however, it must be clear and easy to understand. In addition, if you ask the seller if the item comes with a warranty, and it does, the seller must make it available for your inspection before you buy the item.

In addition, you must be told whether the written warranty is limited or full. A full warranty:

- usually, but not always, says "full warranty" on it

- does not disclaim the implied warranties

- covers any person who buys the product from you during the warranty period

- is free

- entitles you to a replacement or refund if the product is defective, usually for a year or two, and

- does not obligate you to do anything, other than notify the seller or manufacturer, to receive service.

Any other express warranty is a "limited warranty."

 ### Extended Warranties—Should You Buy One?

Many consumers are encouraged by merchants to buy extended warranties (also called service contracts) when they buy autos, appliances or electronic items. Service contracts are a source of big profits for stores, which pocket up to 50% of the amount you pay as a reward for just securing your business. In addition, the salesperson collects 15% to 20% of the value of the contract—almost double the commission on the sale itself—when you sign on the dotted line.

But do you need an extended warranty? Most of the time, no. Name-brand appliances usually don't break down during the first few years (and if they do they're covered by the original warranty), and often have a life span of eight to 15 years, depending on the product. The extended warranty usually lasts no more than five years, the period you're least likely to need it. Similarly, electronic equipment usually breaks immediately or within the first few months after purchase, and is thus covered by the original warranty. In fact, according to the president of the Professional Servicers Association, fewer than 3% of electronic goods actually break down during an extended warranty period.

If you're still toying with the idea of buying a service contract, call or write the Federal Trade Commission (see Chapter 12, Section B7, for a list of FTC addresses and phone numbers) and ask for a free copy of the pamphlet "Facts for Consumers—Service Contracts."

And be aware that a company that sells extended warranties may go out of business, leaving you out in the cold if you try to make a claim under the contract. To avoid this kind of problem, some states require that companies selling extended warranties post a bond.[1]

3. Enforcing Warranties

If a warranty is breached, you may be entitled to a refund or damages. In most states, an implied warranty lasts indefinitely. In a few states, however, the implied warranty lasts only as long as any written warranty that comes with a product. In either case, most states require that you sue the seller

[1]See, for example, General Statutes of North Carolina § 58-1-41; Code of Virginia § 59.1-437.

or manufacturer within four years of when you discovered the defect, if the seller or manufacturer won't make good under a warranty.[2] A thorough discussion of how to pursue your rights in the event of a breach of a warranty is in *Everybody's Guide to Small Claims Court*, by Ralph Warner (Nolo Press).

Most of the time, if an item you buy is defective, the defect will show up immediately and you can ask the seller or manufacturer to fix or replace it. If he won't, or he tries only once and the fixed or replaced version is still defective, you have to decide on your next step. In most cases, you should withhold any payments you haven't yet made, which may be welcome relief if you are over your head in debt.

If you are paying the seller directly (for example, you charged an item on a department store account), just stop paying. If you charged the item on a credit or charge card, you can normally withhold payment by following a specific procedure. See Chapter 6, Section A7 for the details. The merchant may sue you (see Chapter 9), but if you file an answer, show up in court and offer your side of the story, the judge may rule for you or at least reduce the amount you owe.

If you are uncomfortable withholding payments—for example, this debt takes priority because the merchant is providing you with absolute necessities—call the merchant and try to work out an arrangement. If the merchant refuses, try to mediate the dispute through a community or Better Business Bureau mediation program. (Prioritizing your debts is covered in Chapter 3, Section A.)

---

[2]The period of time you have to make a claim under the warranty may be extended. In California, for example, the time the product is back with the manufacturer or seller attempting to be repaired is not counted. California Civil Code § 1795.6. In Michigan, the time will be extended to cover any strike or work stoppage at the company's place of business. Michigan Compiled Laws Annotated § 19.418(3a).

If Your Product Breaks after the Warranty Expires

One common consumer story starts out "I bought this great _____ (fill in the blank) several years ago. It hardly gave me any trouble. But wouldn't you know it—the day after the warranty expired it died."

Most of us figure we're out of luck—but not necessarily. If your product gave you some trouble while it was under the warranty (and you had it repaired by someone authorized by the manufacturer to make repairs), many manufacturers will extend your original warranty for the amount of time the item sat in the shop. Call the manufacturer and ask to speak to the department that handles warranties. Any agreement you reach should be followed up by a letter from you confirming your understanding.

If your product was trouble-free during the warranty period, the manufacturer may offer a free repair for a problem that arose after the warranty expired if the problem is a widespread one. Many manufacturers have secret "fix it" lists—items with defects that don't affect safety and therefore don't require a recall, but that the manufacturer will repair for free. It can't hurt to call and ask. A few states have specific laws covering automobile "secret warranties." See Section B, below.

Also, in most states, the period of time you have to make a claim under the warranty is extended by the amount of time the product is with the manufacturer or seller for repair.

B. Your Car Is a Lemon

THE AVERAGE NEW CAR costs about $17,000. For that amount of money, you expect a safe and reliable product. Unfortunately, an estimated 150,000 vehicles each year (or 1% of new cars) are lemons. Buyers find themselves in and out of the shop month after month, with problems ranging from annoying engine "pings," to frequent stalls, to safety hazards, such as poor acceleration or carbon monoxide leaks.

To help consumers, every state except Arkansas and South Dakota has enacted some sort of "lemon law" which gives buyers the right to take the manufacturer to arbitration, and obtain a refund or replacement vehicle if a new car has a serious problem. A few states, including Connecticut, Massachusetts, New York and Rhode Island, have lemon laws for used cars as well.[3]

Here's how a lemon law for a new car typically works.

1. Your new car must have a "substantial defect" within the shorter of one year or a certain mileage period. (A few states extend this period to two years.) A substantial defect is one that impairs the car's use, value or safety, such as brakes or turn signals which don't work. Unfortunately, minor defects, such as loose radio and door knobs—even several minor defects or one that remains unfixed after many attempts—don't qualify.

2. The defect must remain unfixed after three or four repair attempts or after the car has sat in the shop a cumulative total of 30 days.

3. To get redress under a lemon law, you must notify the manufacturer of the defect. If you're not offered a satisfactory settlement, you can submit your dispute to arbitration which is free and designed to take place without a lawyer. The various auto makers use the following arbitration programs:

- in-house programs

- programs set up by the Better Business Bureau's Auto Line

- programs run by the American Automobile Association or the National Automobile Dealer's Association, and

- programs run through a state consumer protection agency.

Unfortunately, few consumers get to choose which program to use. If you have a choice, however, keep in mind that consumers who appear before a state consumer protection agency usually fare much better than those who use a manufacturer's in-house program or a private arbitration program run by the BBB, AAA or NADA.

At the arbitration hearing, the arbitrator hears both sides of the dispute. The arbitrator then has approximately 60 days to decide if the car is a lemon and if you are entitled to a refund or a replacement. Consumers who bring substantial documentation to the hearing tend to do better than those with little evidence to back up their claims. The type of documentation that can help includes:

- brochures and ads about the vehicle—an arbitration panel is likely to make the manufacturer live up to its claims, and

- service records showing every time you took the vehicle into the shop—if the mechanic or supervisor takes your complaint orally, make sure he writes up a repair order.

Manufacturers are typically bound by the arbitrator's decision, though consumers can usually go to court if they don't like the ruling. The arbitrator cannot award "consequential" damages such as the cost of renting a car while the lemon was in the shop. If you think your new car is a lemon, an excellent book to help you sort out your rights and remedies is the *Lemon Book,* by Nader & Ditlow (Center for Auto Safety). It includes a state-by-state breakdown of lemon laws.

---

[3]Connecticut General Statutes § 42-220 et seq.; Massachusetts General Laws Annotated § 90 ¶ 7N 1/4; New York General Business Law § 198-b; Rhode Island General Laws § 31-5.4-1 et seq.

Motor Vehicle "Secret Warranties"

Many automobile manufacturers have "secret warranty" (also called warranty adjustment) programs. Under one of these programs, a manufacturer makes repairs for free on vehicles with persistent problems after a warranty expires in order to avoid a recall and bad press.

Unfortunately, consumers aren't told of these secret warranties unless they come forward after the warranty has expired, complain about a problem and demand that the manufacturer repair it. And according to the Center for Auto Safety, at any given time there are a total of 500 secret warranty programs available through automobile manufacturers.

A few states, including California, Connecticut, Virginia and Wisconsin, now require manufacturers to tell eligible consumers when they adopt a secret warranty program, usually within 90 days of adopting the program.[4]

C. You've Been Defrauded

EVERY STATE AND THE FEDERAL government prohibit "unfair or deceptive trade acts or practices." This means that a seller can't deceive, abuse, mislead or cheat you. While 19th century business relationships were governed by the seller-protective doctrine "caveat emptor" or "let the buyer beware," the notion that a buyer-seller arrangement should be fair has generally gained ground in the 20th century.

For example, if you sign up for a low air fare only to be later told that to actually get the fare you must stay in a run-down hotel at a vastly inflated rate, you are being defrauded. If you sign a written contract with an electrician, authorizing her to rewire your kitchen for $250, but she uses the most expensive materials, rewires your entire house and charges you $1,500, you've been defrauded.

---

[4]California Civil Code § 1795.90; Connecticut General Statutes § 42-227; Code of Virginia § 59.1-207.34 et seq.; Wisconsin Statutes Annotated § 218.017.

If you think you've been cheated by anyone selling any service or product, don't pay a penny, and *immediately* let the appropriate federal, state and county government offices know. Although any investigation by a government office will take a few months (and possibly a few years), these agencies have the resources to help you and to go after unscrupulous merchants. Law enforcement in the consumer fraud area is not uniformly great around the country, but many hardworking investigators do their jobs superbly. The more agencies you notify, the more likely someone will take notice of your complaint and act on it.

Unfortunately, these agencies seldom are able to get you your money back. If the business is a reputable one, however, it may gladly refund your money when a consumer fraud law enforcement investigator shows up. It certainly can't hurt you to complain.

Begin by complaining to the appropriate federal agency:

Federal Trade Commission. Always complain to the FTC, which oversees the federal consumer product warranty law, as well as advertisers, door-to-door sellers, mail-order companies, credit bureaus and most retailers. If another federal agency is more appropriate, the FTC will let you know. Addresses and phone numbers are listed in Chapter 12, Section B7.

Consumer Product Safety Commission. Let them know about hazardous consumer products. CPSC, Washington, DC 20207, (800) 638-2772 ext. 999.

Federal Communications Commission. If you were defrauded by a telephone solicitor, or sucked in when a merchant aired a fraudulent advertisement on radio or television, tell the FCC. FCC, Complaints Office, Room 6202, 2025 M Street, NW, Washington, DC 20554, (202) 418-0200.

Department of Transportation. If you were cheated by an airline, contact DOT, Office of Consumer Affairs, I-25, Washington, DC 20590, (202) 366-2220.

U.S. Postal Service. If you were cheated by a mail-order company or any other seller who used the U.S. mail—including a magazine advertiser—contact a postal inspector. Look in the government listings of your telephone white pages for the local address. If you can't find one, notify the federal office, USPS, Inspection Services, 475 L'Enfant Plaza, SW, Washington, DC 20260-2100, (202) 268-4267.

One-Stop Fraud Complaining

The National Fraud Information Center, a project of the National Consumer's League, can also help you. NFIC provides the following services:

- assistance in filing a complaint with appropriate federal agencies
- recorded information on current fraud schemes
- tips on how to avoid becoming a fraud victim
- direct ordering of consumer publications.

Here's how to reach the NFIC:

Telephone	(800) 876-7060
Fax	(202) 347-0646
TDD	(202) 737-5084
Electronic BB	(202) 347-3189
Writing	NFIC c/o National Consumer's League 815 15th Street, NW, Suite 928-N Washington, DC 20005

You should also complain to state and local agencies. Addresses and phone numbers to make consumer complaints are in Chapter 13, Section D2. You may also want to complain to:

Local prosecutor (such as the District Attorney or State's Attorney) in the county where you live. Call and ask if there is a consumer fraud division.

State licensing boards for licensed professionals, such as contractors, lawyers, doctors and funeral directors. Never hesitate to file a complaint about a licensed professional. If, for example, you ordered a $500 pine coffin, and when you arrived for the funeral your mother was laid out in a $3,000 walnut coffin and the funeral director refused to make a change, report the director to your state's funeral industry licensing board. To find the address and phone number, call directory assistance for your state capitol. If that doesn't work, ask the local prosecutor for the address and phone number.

In addition, you'll want to contact the customer service department or even the chief executive officer for the main office of any major company you complain about. Most of these corporate addresses are in the *Consumer's Resource Handbook*, published by the U.S. Office of Consumer Affairs. It's free from the Consumer Information Center, Pueblo, CO 81009. Also, public libraries should have directories containing addresses and phone numbers of large companies.

When you send a letter to a government agency, be sure to attach copies (never the originals) of all receipts, contracts, warranties, service contracts, advertisements and other documents relating to your purchase. Keep a copy of your letter for your records.

Finally, contact your local newspaper, radio station or television station "action line." Especially in metropolitan areas, these folks often have an army of volunteers ready to try and right every consumer complaint.

D. Unconscionability—The Seller Took Advantage of You

UNCONSCIONABILITY MAY BE a mouthful to say, but it's a big remedy if you can prove it. Unconscionability basically means that the seller and buyer's bargaining positions were unequal—to the point that the seller took advantage of the buyer—perhaps because of the buyer's recent trauma, physical infirmity, ignorance, inability to read or inability to understand the language of an agreement. The taking advantage must be so severe that it is shocking to the average person.

Unconscionability is generally recognized as:

- the absence of any meaningful choice on the part of the buyer, and

- contract terms so one-sided that they unreasonably favor the seller.

For example, if you signed an agreement with a funeral home the day after your significant other died and agreed to pay the funeral home twice its normal fee without getting any extra services, a court would most likely declare the contract unconscionable. Or, if a home repair contractor showed up 45 minutes after your house was badly damaged in a fire, flood, hurricane, earthquake or similar devastation and got you to sign a very one-sided agreement, making an arrangement to repair your home for much more money than it should cost, you've probably been unconscionably taken advantage of.

If you believe you have a defense of unconscionability, don't make any payments on your debt and immediately let the seller or lender know why. Also, return any goods you purchased at once and tell any service providers that you don't want them to do any more work. You may find yourself sued (see Chapter 9), but you may be able to defend yourself just fine.

E. You Want to Cancel a Contract

YOU HAVE THE RIGHT to cancel certain consumer contracts you enter into, as long as you act quickly—most laws require that you cancel a contract within three days of signing. Even if you are not told of your right to cancel the contract, you can. And if you weren't told of your right, you may have longer than the standard three days to cancel. So if the day you took out a second mortgage you got laid off, and it wasn't too long ago, there may be hope.

1. Federal Laws Giving a Three-Day Right to Cancel

The Federal Trade Commission has a three-day cooling-off rule which lets you cancel, in person or by mail, two kinds of contracts, until midnight of the third business day after the contract was signed.[5] You must be given notice of the right to cancel and a cancellation form when you sign the contract. If you were not given a form, ask the seller to send you one. Your cancellation right extends until the seller sends it to you, even if it takes months.

The contracts you can cancel are:

- door-to-door sales contracts for more than $25, and

- a contract for more than $25 made anywhere other than the seller's normal place of business— for instance, at a sales presentation at a friend's house, hotel or restaurant, outdoor exhibit, computer show or trade show (public car auctions and craft fairs are exempted from coverage).

After canceling, the seller must refund your money within ten days. Then, the seller must either pick up the items purchased, or reimburse you within 20 days for your expense of mailing the goods back to the seller (many states give the seller 40 days). If the seller doesn't come for the goods or make an arrangement for you to mail them back, you can keep them. If you send them back but aren't refunded for your mailing costs, you can sue the seller in small claims court. The seller may keep 5% of the sales amount as a "cancellation fee," not to exceed $25 in Georgia and not to exceed the down payment in Wyoming.[6]

---

[5]16 C.F.R. § 429.1.

[6]Revised Code of Georgia Annotated § 10-1-6; Wyoming Statutes Annotated § 40-12-104.

State	Code Section	Additional State Protections For Contracts Covered by the FTC's Three-Day Cooling-Off Rule
Alaska	45.02.350	Buyer has until midnight of 5th business day to cancel sales contract of $10 or more.
Arizona	44-5002	Notice of cancellation and contract must be in same language as oral presentation.
California	CC 1689.7	Notice of cancellation and contract must be in same language as oral presentation.
Connecticut	42-135a	Notice of cancellation and contract must be in same language as oral presentation.
Delaware	6-4404	Notice of cancellation and contract must be in same language as oral presentation.
Hawaii	481C-2	Notice of cancellation and contract must be in same language as oral presentation.
	481C-2.5	If the seller is required to be licensed under state law and if not licensed, the right to cancel is extended to 30 days.
Iowa	555A.2	Notice of cancellation and contract must be in same language as oral presentation.
Kansas	50-640	Notice of cancellation and contract must be in same language as oral presentation.
Maryland	14-302	Notice of cancellation and contract must be in same language as oral presentation.
Massachusetts	93-48	Notice of cancellation and contract must be in same language as oral presentation.
Michigan	445.113	Notice of cancellation and contract must be in same language as oral presentation.
Nebraska	69-1604	Notice of cancellation and contract must be in English and same language as oral presentation.
Nevada	598.240	Notice of cancellation and contract must be in same language as oral presentation.
New Jersey	17:16C-61.6	Notice of cancellation and contract must be in same language as oral presentation.
New Mexico	57-12-21	Notice of cancellation and contract must be in same language as oral presentation.
New York	PP 428	Notice of cancellation and contract must be in same language as oral presentation.
North Carolina	25A-39	Notice of cancellation and contract must be in same language as oral presentation.
North Dakota	51-18-02	Buyer who is 65 or older has until midnight of 15th business day to cancel contract of $50 or more.
Ohio	1345.23	Notice of cancellation and contract must be in same language as oral presentation.
Texas	Civ. 5069-13.02	Notice of cancellation and contract must be in same language as oral presentation.
Vermont	9-2454	Buyer must be orally informed of the right to cancel contract.
Wisconsin	423.203	Notice of cancellation and contract must be in same language as oral presentation.
Wyoming	40-14-253	Notice of cancellation and contract must be in same language as oral presentation.

A second federal law, called the Truth in Lending Act, lets you cancel a home improvement loan, second mortgage or other loan where you pledge your home as security (except for a first mortgage or first deed of trust) until midnight of the third business day after you signed the contract.[7] You must be told of your right to cancel and given a cancellation form when you sign the loan papers.

2. Contracts You Can Cancel Under State Laws

Most states have their own laws that allow consumers to cancel, within a few days of signing, written contracts not covered by the FTC's three-day cooling-off rule or the Truth in Lending Act. This chart does not include state laws letting you cancel written contracts entered into with telephone solicitors. Those contracts are covered in Section G, below.

State	Code Section	Contracts You Can Cancel Under State Cancellation Laws	Time to Cancel
Arizona	44-1744	Dance lessons	15 days; must pay for lessons received
Arkansas	4-94-109	Health club	3 days
California	CC 1689.20	Seminar sales	3 days
	CC 1694.1	Dating service	3 days
	CC 1694.6	Weight loss	3 days
	CC 1695.4	Houses sold immediately before foreclosure sale	5 days, or until 8 a.m. of the day of the sale, whichever is earlier
	CC 1812.54	Dance lessons	180 days; must pay for lessons received
	CC 1812.303	Membership camping	3 days
	CC 2982.9	Motor vehicle financing from lender at a rate specified in purchase contract	
Colorado	6-1-105	Discount buying club	1 day
	6-1-105.5	Hearing aids	30 days
Connecticut	20-402a	Hearing aids	30 days; seller may keep 12% of purchase price

[7] 15 U.S.C. § 1635.

State	Code Section	Contracts You Can Cancel Under State Cancellation Laws	Time to Cancel
Delaware	2804	Membership camping	5 days
	2824	Time-share properties	5 days
	4205	Health club	3 days
District of Columbia	28-3817 28-3819	Health club Rental housing locators	15 days 30 days if locator fails to provide listings called for in the contract
Georgia	10-1-393	Membership camping	10 days
	10-1-393.2	Health club	7 days
Hawaii	486N-6	Health club	5 days
Illinois	815 ILCS 610/6	Dance lessons	Anytime; must pay for lessons received; after 30 days, seller may keep 10% of balance or $50, whichever is less
Indiana	24-5-9-28	Time-share properties; membership camping	72 hours
Kentucky	367.397	Discount buying club	30 days
	367.477	Recreational and retirement use land	5 days
Maine	33-589-A	Membership camping	7 days
Maryland	14-1802	For furniture or household appliance if goods aren't delivered within two weeks of date specified in contract	
	14-2402	Vacation club	10 days
Massachusetts	255-13K	Trade, vocational, technical or correspondence school or dance studio	5 days for a full refund, unless you have started studies; during first quarter, refund of 75% less reasonable costs; during second quarter, refund of 50% less reasonable costs; during third quarter, refund of 25% less reasonable costs
Michigan	19.418(31)	Sale of over $500 if you attended a promotion and received at least $25	3 days
Minnesota	153A.19	Hearing aids	30 days
Mississippi	75-83-5	Health club	5 days
Missouri	407.620	Time-share properties	5 days
	407.938	Foreclosure consultants	3 days
Nebraska	76-2112	Membership camping	3 days

State	Code Section	Contracts You Can Cancel Under State Cancellation Laws	Time to Cancel
Nevada	119A.410	Time-share properties	5 days
	119B.280	Membership camping	5 days
New Jersey	17:16C-99	Home repair	3 days
New Mexico	47-11-5	Time-share properties	7 days
New York	GBL 396-4	For furniture or household appliances and if goods aren't delivered within 30 days of date specified in contract	
North Carolina	66-118	Dance lessons, dating service, martial arts	3 days
Ohio	1345.43	Dance lessons, dating service, martial arts	3 days if contract exceeds $200 or 1 year
Pennsylvania	455.609	Time-share properties, membership camping	5 days
Rhode Island	5-50-2	Health club	10 days
	34-41-4.06	Time-share properties	3 days
South Carolina	27-32-40	Time-share properties	4 days
Tennessee	47-18-404	Membership camping	15 days
	66-32-114	Time-share properties	10 days (if buyer made on-site inspection before signing); 15 days (if buyer did not make on-site inspection before signing)
Texas	Prop. 221.041	Time-share properties	6 days
	Prop. 222.008	Membership camping	4 days if buyer did not make on-site inspection before signing
Utah	57-19-12	Time-share properties	5 days
		Membership camping	5 days
Virginia	55-79-88	Condominium sales	10 days
	55-376	Time-share properties	7 days
	59.1-297	Health club	3 days
	59.1-327	Membership camping	7 days
West Virginia	36-9-5	Time-share properties	10 days
	46A-2-138	Correspondence school; multiple magazine subscription	Anytime; you may get refund or cancel obligation for all goods and services not received
Wisconsin	707.41	Health club	3 days
		Time-share properties	5 days

Ambiguous Contracts

Connecticut, Delaware, Hawaii, Minnesota, Montana, New Jersey, New York, West Virginia and a few other states require that consumer contracts be written in "plain language." They must contain short sentences and paragraphs, be clear and coherent, use personal pronouns and words with everyday meanings and include captioned sections. Although you can't rescind the contract if it violates one of these requirements, you are entitled to actual damages (plus $50 in Montana and New York; times three in Delaware).

For example, if your contract had a cancellation clause which let you cancel without incurring any fee within 30 days, but for a $100 fee after 30 days, and the contract was so ambiguous that you didn't understand the difference, canceled on day 41 and were out $100, this law would let you collect the $100 actual damages.

For a seriously ambiguous contract, you may also have a claim of fraud or unconscionability. (See Sections C and D, above.)

3. How to Cancel a Contract

To cancel a contract under the FTC's cooling-off rule, the Truth in Lending Act or your state law, call the seller or lender and tell her you want to cancel the contract. If you call the seller, she can't claim she didn't know about your wish to cancel in the event your cancellation form is lost. But calling isn't enough. You still must sign and date one copy of the cancellation form you were given. Send it by certified mail so you have proof of the date you mailed it, or for immediate notice, fax it. If you were not given a form, and don't want to wait until you get the form in order to cancel the contract, write your own letter or telegram.

F. Canceling Goods Ordered by Mail, Phone, Computer or Fax

IF YOU ORDER GOODS by mail, phone, computer or fax (other than photo development, magazine subscriptions, goods ordered COD, or seeds or plants) and they don't arrive or they arrive late, you have some rights.[8] First, the seller must ship to you within the time promised ("allow 4–6 weeks for delivery") or, if no time was stated, within 30 days. This time is extended to 50 days if you are applying for credit to pay for your purchase.

If the seller cannot ship within those times, the seller must send you a notice with a new shipping date and offer you the option of canceling your order and getting a refund, or accepting the new date. If your financial picture has changed since you ordered the goods, cancel.

If you've already opted for the second deadline, but the seller can't meet this one, you must be sent a notice requesting your signature to agree to yet a third date. If you don't return the second notice, your order must be automatically canceled and your money refunded. But don't rely on the seller automatically canceling. Let the seller know you want your money back.

The seller must issue the refund promptly— within seven days if you paid by check or money order and within one billing cycle if you charged your purchase. If your credit or charge card was never billed, but the 30 days (or whatever time was promised for sending) have passed and you no longer want the goods, immediately telephone the company to cancel your order.

If the company doesn't cancel your order, don't pay the bill. See Chapter 6, Section A7, for your rights to cancel goods ordered and paid for by credit card.

---

[8]Federal Trade Commission's Mail or Telephone Order Rule. 16 C.F.R. 435.

Complaining About Mail-Order Companies

The Direct Marketing Association is a membership organization made up of mail-order companies and other direct marketers. If you have a complaint about a particular company, write Mail-Order Action Line, c/o DMA, 1101 17th Street, NW, Washington, DC 20036. DMA will occasionally contact the mail-order company and try to resolve your problem. If you want to be removed from direct marketing lists, write Mail Preference Service, c/o DMA, P.O. Box 9008, Farmingdale, NY 11735.

G. Canceling Goods Ordered from a Phone Solicitor

TELEPHONE SOLICITING IS A big business. Approximately 300,000 phone solicitors call 18 million consumers every day. Sales through telemarketing exceed $400 billion each year.

If a telephone solicitor calls you and you agree to purchase what he's selling, you may have the right to cancel your contract. You can cancel your purchase if the goods don't arrive within the time promised or 30 days. (See Section F, above.) In addition, if you use a credit or charge card, you can withhold payment if there's a problem with the purchase. See Chapter 6, Section A7.

You may also have the right to cancel a non-credit-card purchase under one of the below conditions. To find out if any of these laws have been adopted in your state, you can do some legal research. (See Chapter 13.) Also, try calling the state agency that regulates telephones, such as a Public Utilities Commission. Someone in the public information office should be able to help you.

Cooling-Off Rules. Some telephone solicitors are covered by state cooling-off rules. Typically, this requires that after you agree to purchase the goods, the phone solicitor must send you a written contract confirming your order. This contract must state that you are not obligated to purchase the item you ordered unless you sign the contract and return it to the seller.

Also, in some states, including Arizona, Florida, Illinois, Indiana, Maine, Maryland, North Carolina, Oregon and Washington, you have until midnight of the third business day following the day you signed the contract to cancel it. In addition, if you want to cancel a contract made over the telephone, argue that your phone is in your home and you therefore have an automatic three-day right to cancel. (See Section E, above.)

Prohibited Computer-Generated Calls. Computer-generated sales calls (sometimes referred to as calls generated by automatic dialing devices), are prohibited by in-state or out-of-state callers placing phone calls in several states, including Arizona, Connecticut, Michigan, North Carolina, Oregon, Virginia, Washington and Wyoming. If you live in one of those states and order something in response to a computer-generated sales call, not only shouldn't you pay for it, but you should report the company to your state Attorney General's Office, the Federal Communications Commission and the Federal Trade Commission.

Regulated Computer-Generated Calls. The federal Telephone Consumer Protection Act of 1991 prohibits telemarketing phone calls using automatic dialing devices or artificial or prerecorded voices if the seller doesn't have your prior consent.[9] If the caller has your consent, the message, at the outset, must identify the caller. At some point in the call, the message must give the caller's phone number. And if you hang up, the call must disconnect within five seconds.

---

[9] 47 U.S.C. § 227.

Stopping Telemarketing Calls

The Telephone Consumer Protection Act requires a telemarketer to keep a list of consumers who state that they do not want to be called again. The law also has some real teeth if companies ignore it—and many admittedly do. If you've told a telemarketer not to call you, but you get additional calls within 12 months, you can sue in Small Claims Court for $500 for each additional call. If the court finds that the telemarketer willfully or knowingly violated the law, the court can triple the amount.

For information on your rights under this law, send $3 to the Center for the Study of Commercialism, 1875 Connecticut Ave., NW, Suite 300, Washington, DC 20009; (202) 332-9110 and ask for a copy of "Stop the Calls: How Citizens call Sue Telemarketers."

If you order something after being called but not being asked if you consent to the call, and you later decide you don't want it, don't pay and return the item if you've already received it. Report the company to the Federal Communications Commission and the Federal Trade Commission.

Complaining About Phone Solicitors

The Direct Marketing Association (described in Section F, above), also takes complaints about phone solicitors and will remove your name from telephone lists used by national telemarketers. Write Telephone Preference Service, c/o DMA, P.O. Box 9014, Farmingdale, NY 11735-9014, (212) 768-7277. DMA will occasionally contact the mail-order company and try to resolve your problem.

H. Miscellaneous Remedies

IF YOU'RE BEING BILLED for merchandise you didn't order, you need not pay. And you may not owe the bill for goods you put on layaway or for an item you returned or tried to return.

1. Unordered Merchandise

You certainly don't owe any money if you receive an item you never ordered—it's considered a gift. If you get bills or collection letters from a seller who sent you something you never ordered, write to the seller stating your intention to treat the item as a gift. If the bills continue, insist that the seller send you proof of your order. If this doesn't stop the bills, notify the state consumer protection agency in the state where the merchant is located. (See Chapter 12, Section B7.)

If the unordered merchandise you're sent is the result of an honest shipping error (for example, you were sent 12 blankets instead of 2), you may have a legal right to keep the goods, but ethically you probably shouldn't. Write the seller (or call, especially if the seller has an 800 phone number) and offer to return the items provided that the seller pays for the shipping.

Give the seller a specific length of time—ten days is about right—to pick up the merchandise or arrange for you to send it back at no cost to you. Ask the business for its UPS or other delivery service shipping number. Let the seller know that if he doesn't retrieve the goods by the end of the ten days, you plan to keep the items or dispose of them as you see fit.

If you sent away for something in response to an advertisement claiming a "free" gift or "trial" period, but now are being billed, be sure to read the fine print of the ad. It may say something about charging shipping and handling; even worse, you may have inadvertently joined a club or subscribed to a magazine. Write the seller, offer to return the merchandise and tell him you believe his ad was misleading. Send copies of the letter to the agencies listed in Section C, above. Even if this doesn't work, the bill shouldn't be that much and in any event you should give it lowest priority. (Prioritizing your debts is covered in Chapter 3, Section A.)

Subscriptions to Magazines You Didn't Order

Your mailbox contains a promotion for a new magazine—"Free trial issue. No obligation necessary." You send for the trial issue and don't like the publication. A month later you get a bill.

Send the bill back, enclosing a note that you requested a free trial issue and you don't want a subscription, even if it is months after you requested the free trial issue. If that doesn't work, contact the Magazine Publishers Association, 919 3rd Avenue, 22nd Floor, New York, NY 10022, (212) 752-0055 and ask them to help you get the magazine company to stop billing you.

2. Layaway Goods

If you're purchasing an item on a layaway plan—where the seller keeps the merchandise until you fully pay for it—and you decide before you've finished paying that you no longer want it, read your written layaway agreement. Find out if you have the right to stop paying and get a refund of what you've paid. If you do, the seller may be able to keep a portion of your payments as a service fee. But this should be a small fee—the cost of storing your goods—and you should get the rest back.

If the contract is silent about your right to a refund, stop paying and ask for your money back. If the seller refuses and there's no law giving you a right to a refund, you're probably out of luck.

State	Code Section	Layaway Purchases Refund Rights
California	CC 1749	You are entitled to a refund if the goods aren't available in the same condition as when they were first sold.
Connecticut	42-125cc	Prior to accepting the goods, you can cancel the contract if the seller violates it, misrepresents the plan or the availability of the goods, delivers an unsatisfactory substitute, increases the price, substitutes lower quality goods, fails to deliver the goods after you've paid in full, or fails to send you a receipt each time you make a payment.
District of Columbia	28-3818	You may cancel the contract within 2 weeks after entering into it for full refund; after 2 weeks, seller may keep 8% of purchase price or $16, whichever is less.
Illinois	815 ILCS 360/4, 360/5	Prior to accepting the goods, you can cancel the contract if the seller violates it, misrepresents the plan or the availability of the goods, delivers an unsatisfactory substitute, increases the price, substitutes lower quality goods, fails to deliver the goods after you've paid in full, fails to send you a receipt each time you make a payment, or fails to deliver the goods within 30 days of original delivery date.
Maryland	CL 14-1104	You may cancel the contract within 7 days without incurring a penalty. If you cancel more than 7 days after the contract was signed, seller may keep 10% of price, or total amount paid, whichever is less.
New York	GBL 396-t	You must be given contract describing refund policy.

State	Code Section	Layaway Purchases Refund Rights
Ohio	1317.23	For contracts of $500 or more, you may cancel the contract within 5 days without incurring a penalty. If you cancel more than 5 days after the contract was signed, seller may keep $25 or 10% of price, whichever is less.
Rhode Island	6-32-3	You may cancel the contract until midnight of 10th day following signing of contract.

3. Cash Refund Rights

Unfortunately, a merchant doesn't have to have a refund policy. Many don't, but instead offer to exchange the goods. And some sellers have neither a refund nor an exchange policy. But four states do have refund laws.

State	Code Section	Cash Refund Rights
California	CC 1723	Merchants who do not allow full cash or credit refund, or equal exchange, within 7 days of purchase, must post store's refund-credit-exchange policy. If merchant doesn't post policy, buyer may return goods, for full refund, for up to 30 days after purchase.
Florida	501.142	If merchant has no refund policy, such a statement must be posted in store. If it isn't, buyer may return unused and unopened goods within 7 days for full refund.
New York	GBL 396-o	Merchants with cash refund policies must post policies and give cash refunds within 20 days. If merchants offer both refunds and exchanges, buyer decides which he'd prefer.
Virginia	59.1-17-200Q	Merchants must post refund or exchange policy unless they give cash refund or full credit for up to 20 days after purchase.

■

Chapter 3

NEGOTIATING WITH YOUR CREDITORS

Let us never negotiate out of fear, but let us never fear to negotiate.

—John F. Kennedy, 35th President of
the United States, 1917-1963

BY THIS TIME, YOU SHOULD HAVE a good grasp on how much you make, how much you owe, how much you can pay for your monthly expenses and how much (if anything) is left over to pay your other debts. This chapter helps you to prioritize your actions—to pay essential debts, ask for more time and negotiate. Chapter 4 explores the consequences of doing nothing.

If You're Considering Bankruptcy

If you think that filing for bankruptcy may be a viable option for you, read Chapter 10 before you make any payments on your debts. This is because it makes no sense to make payments on debts you will eventually erase (discharge) in bankruptcy. Also, some payments made during the 90 days before filing for bankruptcy—or one year for payments to, or for the benefit of, a relative or business associate—may be canceled by the bankruptcy court.

If, after reading Chapter 10, you decide that Chapter 7 bankruptcy is probable, put this book down and get a copy of either *How to File for Bankruptcy*, by Elias, Renauer and Leonard (Nolo Press), a detailed bankruptcy guide, or *Nolo's Law Form Kit: Personal Bankruptcy*, by Elias, Renauer, Leonard and Goldoftas (Nolo Press), a streamlined bankruptcy guide. Both contain all the forms and instruction necessary for filing your own Chapter 7 bankruptcy. If a Chapter 13 bankruptcy seems like the right approach, get a copy of *Chapter 13 Bankruptcy: Repay Your Debts*, by Robin Leonard (Nolo Press). Order information is in the back of this book.

A. Prioritize Your Debts

WHETHER OR NOT a particular debt is essential will ultimately be dictated by your situation. Nevertheless, some debts are more essential than others. Return to Chapter 1 and look at Worksheet 2: Your Debts. Then read the lists of common essential and nonessential debts, below. Using these lists as guidance only, figure out which of your debts are essential and which are nonessential. Consider the consequences of not paying each debt. If they are severe, paying the debt is essential. If they aren't, payment is less essential.

> **Example:** Josh is taking an experimental heart medication for which his health insurance only pays 50%. His outstanding bill to his pharmacist is currently $150. If he doesn't pay it, he won't be able to get the prescription refilled at that store. Because he has a poor credit history, he probably can't get credit elsewhere. This is an essential debt that Josh should pay.

Do not, under any circumstances, make payments on nonessential debts when you have not paid essential ones, even if your nonessential creditors are breathing down your neck. This advice may sound obvious, but when pressured by bill collectors, many people forget the obvious. For example, if you pay a few dollars on an old hardware store bill just because its collector is the loudest or most persistent, you may face eviction or have your heat turned off in mid-March because you won't have enough money left to pay for these essential services.

1. Essential Debts

An essential debt is one which you should make a top—or near top—priority in paying. If you let an essential debt slide, you could face serious, even life-threatening, consequences.

Rent or mortgage. Payments for a place to live are obviously essential. Many people get into serious debt problems—and find themselves on the streets—because they fail to stay current on their rent. Unless you know you are going to move and have a place to live, you'll probably want to make paying your rent a top priority. If your landlord is reasonable, ask for a reduction.

House payments are a little different. If you've lost your job and it looks long-term, your first thought should probably be to sell the place, get rid of a huge monthly debt, rent a moderately-priced place and use the excess from the proceeds to pay your other essential bills. If you have trouble selling your house and its value has come down considerably, one option is to simply walk away from it and deed it back to the lender.

If you decide to stay put, payments on a home equity line of credit or second mortgage are also essential because you can lose your house if you don't pay.

Utility bills. Being without gas, electricity, heating oil, water or a telephone is dangerous.

Child support. Not paying can land you in jail unless you convince the judge that you really couldn't pay (which is an uphill struggle). But if your income has dropped sharply, you may be eligible for a reduction of your child support obligation. See Chapter 8.

Car payments. If you need your car to keep your job, make the payments. If you don't, consider selling it to avoid repossession, which will inevitably occur if you fall behind on the payments. If you sell it yourself and repay the lender, you will have to make up any difference between what you owe the lender and what the sale brought in. But if the car is in reasonably good shape, this may not be that much. If you don't sell the vehicle yourself and it's repossessed, the seller will sell it at a fraction of its value and you'll owe the difference. (See Chapter 4, Section C, for a discussion on deficiencies.)

Other secured loans. Secured debts, you'll recall, are linked to specific items of property. You've already considered money owed on your house and car—both of these are secured debts. In addition, debts on furniture, boats, RVs and expensive electronic gear are likely to be secured. This means that the property (called collateral) guarantees payment of the debt. If you don't repay the debt, most states let the creditor take the property without first suing you and getting a court judgment. If you don't care if the property is taken or are confident that the creditor doesn't really want it—most creditors prefer the money, not the property—don't worry about missing a payment or two. If the property is something you cannot live without, however, and you think the creditor will take it, you'll need to keep that debt current.

Unpaid taxes. If the IRS is about to take your paycheck, bank account, house or other property, you'll want to negotiate to set up a repayment plan immediately. During the past few years, the IRS has become more flexible than it was previously and is now more willing than ever to set up repayment plans for virtually all taxpayers owing money. The best resource available to help you deal with the Internal Revenue Service is *Stand Up to the IRS*, by Frederick W. Daily (Nolo Press).

Essential or Nonessential?

Some debts may straddle the line between essential and nonessential. That is, not paying won't cause severe consequences in your personal life, but it could prove painful nonetheless. In deciding whether or not to pay these debts, consider your relationship with the creditor and at what stage the creditor is in his collection efforts.

Some of these debts include:

- Auto insurance. In some states, you can lose your driver's license if you drive without insurance.

- Medical insurance. Especially if you are currently under a physician's care, you'll want to continue making payments on your medical insurance. Also, if you have medical insurance through work and lose your job, you'll probably be able to keep your insurance coverage for 36 months, but you, not your former employer, will have to pay for it. If you let it lapse, you may have difficulty getting new insurance.

- Car payments for a car that is not essential for your job. The extreme inconvenience of not having a car may justify making these payments.

- Items your children need. Paying for a tutor for your child may not seem essential, but if the alternative is to have your child grow up unable to read, you probably want to keep paying for the help.

- Court judgments. Once you owe a judgment, a creditor can collect it by taking a portion of your wages or other property. If a particular judgment creditor is about to take some of your wages, the fact that the original debt may have been nonessential is irrelevant. Making payments to this creditor in exchange for him letting you keep all your wages may be essential.

2. Nonessential Debts

A nonessential debt is one where there are no immediate and devastating effects if you fail to pay. Paying these debts eventually is a desirable goal, but it is not a top priority.

Educational loans. Paying for an old student loan is rarely essential. The creditor may send you letters and call, but to collect it, the creditor will have to sue you and get a judgment. In one situation, however, paying the debt may become essential: if the IRS is about to intercept a tax refund to which you are entitled. Thus, if you're expecting a large refund which you plan to use to live on, it may be important to make payments until the refund arrives. (See Chapter 7.)

Credit and charge cards. If you don't pay your credit card bill, the worst that will happen before the creditor sues you is that you will lose your credit privileges. If you need a credit card, for example, to charge an upcoming medical operation or to rent a car on a business trip, keep—and pay the minimum on—one card, and put that card on your priority list.

Department store and gasoline charges. As with credit and charge cards, you'll probably lose your credit privileges and, if the debt is large enough, you may be sued.

Loans from friends and relatives. You may feel a moral obligation to pay, but these creditors—who probably seem the least like creditors of anyone—should be the most understanding with you.

Newspaper and magazine subscriptions.

Legal, medical and accounting bills.

Other unsecured loans. Remember, an unsecured loan is not tied to any item of property. The creditor cannot take your property. If you refuse to pay, the creditor can collect from you only by suing you and obtaining a court judgment. These other unsecured debts include money you borrowed from a finance company where you didn't sign a security agreement or money borrowed from friends or relatives.

3. Review Your Lists

Take a look at your essential and nonessential lists. At the end of each month, do you have enough to pay everything on the essential list? If you don't, read it over. Move the least essential debts on this list to the nonessential list, and keep moving debts until you can pay each month what is on the essential list. Remember—some things must go. You can't afford to pay for everything you'd like to. This doesn't mean you're a bad person. It just means you need to buckle down and tighten up your finances for a while.

 Bankruptcy Reminder

If you are in debt so far over your head that you are moving a lot of essential debts to the nonessential category, turn to Chapter 10 and read up on bankruptcy.

B. Cut Your Expenses

As you get ready to negotiate with your creditors, take some time to cut your expenses. Your creditors will want to know why you can't pay your bills and the efforts you've taken to live more frugally. The more expense-cutting measures you can honestly tell them you've undertaken, the more apt they will be to offer you reduced payments, drop certain fees and take other steps to help you through your financial crisis. Here are some suggestions:

- Shrink food costs by clipping coupons, buying on sale, purchasing generic brands, buying in bulk and shopping at discount outlets.

- Improve your gas mileage by tuning up your car, checking the air in the tires and driving less— carpool, work at home (tele-commute), ride your bicycle, take the bus or train, and combine trips.

- Conserve gas, water and electricity.

- Make long distance calls only when necessary and at off peak hours. Also, compare programs offered by the various long distance carriers to make sure you are getting the best deal.

- Carry your lunch to work; eat dinner in, not at restaurants.

- Buy secondhand clothing, furniture and appliances.

- Spend less on gifts and vacations.

C. Communicate with Your Creditors

 The Rest of This Chapter Gives Strategies for Contacting Your Creditors

Usually, staying in touch with them is a good idea—even if you can't pay anything. It doesn't always make sense, however. For example, if you just moved from Massachusetts to Arizona—to get a new start and, not incidentally, to get away from hounding creditors—and will probably file for bankruptcy before long, contacting your creditors is the last thing you should do.

MORE THAN ANYTHING, creditors hate it when debtors bury their heads in the sand and pretend that their debts don't exist or will go away. This forces them to institute collection proceedings, a process that usually turns the debtor into a former customer. To avoid the collection process and to keep customers, creditors often will reduce payments, extend your time to pay, drop late fees and make similar adjustments if they believe you are making an honest effort to deal with your debt problems.

As soon as it becomes clear to you that you're going to have trouble paying your bills, write to your creditors. Explain the problem—accident, job layoff, emergency expense for your child or aged family member, enormous back tax assessment or whatever. Be sure to mention any development that points to an encouraging financial condition— disability benefits beginning soon, job prospects improving, child finishing school and the like. Also, let the creditor know that you've taken many steps to cut your expenses. And, if it's an essential debt— or a nonessential debt and you have enough money to do so—send a token payment. This can't be emphasized enough. Sending a token amount tells the creditor that you are serious about paying but just can't now.

Your success with getting creditors to give you time to pay will depend on the types of debts you have, how far behind you are and the creditors' policies toward arrearages. The following sections give you a general idea of what you can expect.

Tips on Negotiating

This isn't a book on negotiating. Although many are available, few are worth reading. No formula approach will teach you to be a great negotiator in six steps. Nevertheless, here are some basic guidelines:

- Identify your bottom line. If you owe a doctor $1,100 and are unwilling to pay more than $600 on the debt over six months time, don't agree to pay more.

- Try to identify the creditor's bottom line. If a bank offers to waive two months interest as long as you pay the principal on your car loan, that may mean that the bank will actually waive three or four months of interest. Push it.

- Bill collectors lie a lot. If they think you can pay $100, they will vow that $100 is the lowest amount they can accept. Don't believe them.

- Use bargaining chips. If a creditor will settle at 50% of the total debt if you pay in a lump sum, but will insist on 100% if you pay over time, consider a way to get the money to pay the half and settle the matter. Perhaps a parent will help; if the amount is large enough, take it out of your eventual inheritance. If you settle the debt, or are put on a new payment schedule, insist that associated negative information in your credit bureau file be removed and that your account be re-aged, that is, reported as current as long as you make the payments on the new schedule. See Chapter 12.

- Don't split the difference. If you offer a low amount to settle a debt and the creditor proposes that you split the difference between his higher demand and your offer, don't agree to it. Treat his split-the-difference number as a new top and propose an amount between that and your original offer.

If you don't feel comfortable negotiating—for example you hate bargaining at flea markets and would rather sell your used car to a dealer than find a buyer yourself—ask a friend or relative to negotiate on your behalf. This can often work well for you. As long as your negotiator knows and will keep to your bottom line, it will be hard for the creditor to shame or guilt her into agreeing that you will pay more.

1. Rent Payments

Few landlords will reduce the monthly rent. But it never hurts to ask. If the landlord knows he'd have a hard time re-renting your place, he may agree to accept a partial payment now and the rest later or temporarily lower your rent, rather than have to evict you. He might even agree to let you make up any back rent you owe a little bit each month.

If your landlord agrees to a rent reduction or lets you make up the back payments, send the landlord, by certified mail, a letter confirming the arrangement. (See sample letter, below.) Be sure to keep a copy for yourself. Once the understanding is written down, the landlord will have a hard time evicting you for not paying the rent, as long as you make the payments under your new agreement.

Sample Letter to Landlord

```
                    Frank O'Neill
                    1556 North Lakefront
                    Minneapolis, MN 67890
                    September 22, 19__

Dear Frank:

Thanks for being so understanding about my
being laid off. This letter is to confirm
the telephone conversation we had yesterday.

My lease requires that I pay rent of $550
per month. You agreed to reduce my rent to
$400 per month, beginning October 1, 19__,
and lasting until I find another job, but
not to exceed three months. That is, even if
I haven't found a new job, my rent will go
back to $550 per month on January 1, 19__.

Thank you again for your understanding and
help. As I mentioned on the phone, I hope to
have another job shortly, and I am following
all leads in order to secure employment.

Sincerely,


Leslie Landsberg
```

2. Mortgage Payments

If you want to keep your house and you've missed a payment or two, most mortgage companies will let you make up the delinquency through a repayment plan, but most will insist that you do it within four months. If, for example, your mortgage is $1,000 a month and you missed one payment, the lender will probably let you make it up by tacking an extra $250 onto your regular $1,000 payment for four months. A few lenders will drop late charges to help you get current.

If you know that you're going to have trouble making the payments for a certain period of time, the lender may:

- defer or waive late charges

- have you pay only interest for a while

- apply any prepayments you have made to the current debt, or

- temporarily reduce or suspend payments.

If your problem looks long-term, the lender may let you refinance the loan to reduce the amount of the monthly payments, assuming you can convince the lender that you have enough income to make the reduced payments. Typically, a lender looks at the ratio of your total monthly debt burden to your monthly income. If the ratio is between 25% and 33%, you'll probably qualify for the refinancing. If your ratio is higher the lender may balk, unless the lender thinks it will be hard to resell your house at a profit if it foreclosed.

Any newly refinanced loan may have unfavorable features, such as:

- Rapidly increasing interest. For example, the interest begins low (such as 3%), so that you qualify for the loan, but after six months or a year, the interest rises to the prime rate (closer to 7%) and then every six months or year after, the interest rate rises a point or two above the prime rate.

- Large balloon payment. A jumbo payment at the end of the loan term. Balloon payments are often many thousands of dollars. Few people can afford them and often must refinance the loan—or take out yet another loan—to pay the balloon payment.

- Negative amortization. Because your interest rate is so low, your monthly payment doesn't actually cover what you owe. The amount you are short each month is added to your entire loan balance, which means while you are paying off your loan, the balance actually increases, not decreases.

If refinancing your loan is the only way you can afford to keep your house, consider it, but be sure you clearly understand the terms of your new loan agreement.

Alternatively, you may find another lender who will lend you money to pay off all or some of your first loan. If you've missed only a few payments, you can prevent foreclosure simply by paying what you missed and then obtaining the new loan. If the original lender has accelerated the loan—declared the entire balance due because you've missed several payments—you'll have to refinance the entire loan to prevent foreclosure.

> **Example:** Sherri owes $113,000 on her mortgage, which has monthly payments of $850. She has missed four payments and received a letter from the lender stating that it had "accelerated" the mortgage as permitted under the loan agreement. All $113,000—not merely the $3,400 in missed payments—is due immediately. For Sherri to save her house, she will need to get a loan from a second lender to cover the full $113,000, unless the original lender agrees to reinstate her loan.

In this situation it may be difficult for you to get a new loan. The new lender will do a credit check. If your original lender has reported your mortgage delinquency, it will show up on the credit check. You'll have to convince the new lender that you won't default on the new loan.

Insurance to Pay Your Mortgage When You Can't

For many years, some banks and savings and loans have offered to sell home buyers mortgage payment protection insurance. Usually, this insurance will cover the amount of your mortgage payments if you lose your job—laid off, terminated or locked out in a labor dispute. The insurance probably has some limitations, however, such as the number of months it will pay out (often up to six) or the maximum amount it will pay each month. (Mortgage payment protection insurance is different from private mortgage insurance, often referred to as PMI, which lenders require home buyers putting under 20% down to buy.)

Occasionally, a bank or savings and loan might offer mortgage payment protection insurance for free as an incentive for home buyers to borrow from that institution. If you are considering refinancing your mortgage or taking a new loan and paying off the first, ask about mortgage payment protection insurance, especially if you've been in and out of work lately. When mortgage rates are competitive, you may find a lender offering the insurance for free.

If you don't want to keep your house or you've come to the painful conclusion that you can't, you're probably best off selling your house and trying to cut your losses. In that case, you can probably stop making mortgage payments. If the lender chooses to foreclose, it may take up to 18 months, and if you're willing to take any reasonable offer, you can probably sell your house much sooner.

If you have trouble selling your house or the value has dropped so substantially you owe far more than it's worth, your other option is to simply walk away from your house. Don't, however, just send the keys back to the lender.

Instead, call the lender and ask if he'll accept your deed in lieu of foreclosing. Many will. Some, however, won't, especially if any liens have been recorded against your property. If your lender won't accept your deed in lieu of foreclosure, you can prepare what's called a quitclaim deed—you "quit" your interest in the property—transferring ownership to your lender. Be sure to write DEED IN LIEU OF FORECLOSURE in block capital letters across the top of the deed. You pay any transfer fee and record the quitclaim deed where you recorded your ownership deed. Then mail a copy of the recorded quitclaim deed to the lender. Virtually all lenders will keep the property without quitclaiming it back to you. And you've avoided foreclosure and owing any other money you would have owed your lender had he foreclosed.

3. Utility Bills

If you miss one month's utility bill—including a bill for heating oil or gas deliveries—you probably won't hear from the company, unless you have a poor payment history. If you ignore a few past due notices, however, the company will threaten to cut off your service. You want to communicate with the company before their threats become dire. Most utility companies will let you get two or three months behind as long as you let the company know when you'll be able to make it up. If your service has been shut off, the company will most likely require that you make a security deposit—usually for about three times the average of your monthly bill—before it reconnects you. The deposit rates following disconnects are regulated in some states. You may want to call a Legal Aid or Legal Services Office (see Chapter 13) to find out.

Many utility companies offer reduced rates and payment plans to elderly and low income people. To find out if you qualify, call the utility company and ask. If you do, you'll be able to get future bills reduced—and may be able to spread out payments on past bills.

4. Car Payments

Handling car payments depends on whether you are buying or leasing your vehicle.

a. Purchase Payments

If you suspect you'll have trouble for several months making your car payments, your best bet is to sell the car, pay off the lender and use whatever is left to either pay your other debts or buy a used car that can get you where you need to go.

If you want to hold onto your car and you miss a payment, immediately call the lender and speak to someone in the customer service or collections department. Don't delay. When an owner misses a payment, cars are more quickly repossessed than any other type of property. One reason for this is that the creditor doesn't have to get a court judgment before seizing the car. (See Chapter 4, Section C.) Another reason creditors grab cars so fast is that cars lose value fast—if the creditor has to auction it off, it wants the largest possible return.

Finance companies are most likely to grab a car as soon as you miss a payment. Banks will often wait a little while longer, unless they have some information about you that indicates they should come and grab the car right away. For example, a bank will probably show up ASAP if it hears from your soon-to-be-ex-spouse that you just got laid off. Credit unions can be quite patient, especially if you explain your situation.

If you present a convincing explanation of why your situation is temporary, the lender will probably grant you an extension, meaning the delinquent payment can be paid at the end of your loan period and your account is brought up-to-date. The lender probably won't grant an extension unless you've made at least six payments. Also, most lenders charge a fee for granting an extension, and don't grant more than one a year. Fees for extending car loans vary tremendously. Some lenders charge a flat fee, such as $25. Others charge a percentage (usually 1%) of the outstanding balance. Others charge you one month's worth of interest. Be sure to call your lender and ask.

Instead of granting an extension, the lender may rewrite the loan to reduce the monthly payments. This means, however, that you'll have to pay longer and you'll have to pay more total interest.

b. Lease Payments

A growing number of people have chosen to lease, rather than purchase, automobiles. The reasons are many—but most people like the low monthly payments which accompany vehicle lease contracts.

If you can't afford your lease payments, your first step is to review your lease agreement. If your total obligation under the lease is less than $25,000 and the lease term exceeds four months (virtually all car leases meet these two requirements), the federal Consumer Leasing Act requires that your lease include the following:[1]

- A written statement of costs, including:

  ✓ the amount of any "advance" payments, including the down payment and any security deposit

  ✓ the number, amount and dates of your regular payments as well as the total amount of all payments, and

  ✓ the amount you must pay for license, registration, taxes and other fees such as maintenance.

- Other terms under the lease, such as the kinds of insurance you must have, any extended warranty you are required to purchase, the penalty for defaulting or how to terminate the lease early.

- Whether your lease is closed-ended or open-ended. A close-ended lease means that the monthly payments are all you are obligated to pay. At the end of the lease term, you simply return the vehicle and have no additional liability. An open-ended lease means usually lower monthly payments than a close-ended lease, but also usually requires that you pay a "balloon payment" at the end of the lease term.

If you want to cancel your lease and it includes the above, look carefully at the provisions describing what happens if you default and how you can terminate the lease early. Many of these provisions include claims that you'll owe a ridiculous sum of money or complex formulas difficult to understand. For example, the lease agreement might say that if you terminate early, you'll owe the total of the remaining payments, plus several other fees minus the wholesale value of the car and some other fees.

If a formula is unreasonable or not fully disclosed to you, assert your right to cancel the lease. Write to the dealer stating that you want to terminate the lease early. (Keep a copy of the letter.) The dealer will write back or call telling you that you owe a certain amount of money, based on the formula. You should now write a second letter stating that the formula in the lease agreement is unreasonable and was not fully disclosed to you. State further that you know you are entitled to sue for damages because of the dealer's failure to fully disclose the formula or failure to use a reasonable formula. Finally, state that you are willing to waive your right to sue if the dealer will drop his claim against you. If the dealer refuses to back off, consider hiring a lawyer to write some letters. The lawyer won't really say anything different than what you said, but the lawyer's letter-head carries clout. (See Chapter 13.)

5. Secured Loan Payments

If a personal loan or store agreement is secured—for example, you pledged a refrigerator or couch as security for your repayment—the lender probably won't reduce what you owe. Instead, the lender may threaten to send a truck over and take the property if you don't make reasonable payments. Some states require that the lender have a court judgment before taking your personal property other than a car. (See Chapter 4, Section C.)

But few lenders take non-vehicle personal property. The resale value of used property is low. Most items bought through security agreements are furniture, appliances and electronics equipment, which depreciate fast. The lender is not in the used furniture business and doesn't want your dining room table or stereo. Almost always the lender values the debt—even if it is hard to collect—as being worth more than the property. Also, the

---

[1]15 U.S.C. §§ 1667-1667e.

lender can't get into your house to get the property unless he has a court order or you let him in. Few lenders ever go to the expense of getting a court order.

The lender may extend your loan or rewrite it to reduce the monthly payments. Be prepared to disclose your complete financial situation to your lender, however.

6. Insurance Payments

You may consider your medical, homeowner's or auto insurance payments to be fairly essential debts. At the same time, your life or disability insurance payments probably aren't, unless you or other members of your family are very, very ill. Use this discussion to help you decide what to do about your various insurance policies.

Most policies have 30-day grace periods—that is, if your payment is due on the 10th of the month and you don't pay until the 9th of the following month, you won't lose your coverage. A few companies may let you get away with 60 days, but don't count on it. After 60 days, your policy is sure to lapse.

If you want to keep your insurance coverage, contact your insurance agent. If you don't have an agent, or the agent has left the company, call the office and ask to speak to the general manager. Describe the kind of insurance you have, tell the manager a little bit about yourself and ask to be given an agent who will be responsive to your particular needs.

Your insurance agent probably can't let you reduce your premium payments, or spread out back payments over a few months. But you can reduce the amount of your coverage and increase your deductible, thereby reducing the overall amount you pay, including the premium payments. This can usually be done easily for auto, medical, dental, renter's, life and disability insurance. It will be harder for homeowner's insurance, because you'll probably have to get authorization from the lender, who won't want your house to be underinsured.

If you have a life insurance policy with a cash value that you really want to keep, you usually can apply that money toward your premium payments. And if the cash value is large enough, consider taking the money and putting it toward other debts. You can ask the company to use the cash reserves as a loan. Your policy's cash value won't decrease, but you are theoretically required to repay the money. (If you don't repay it, when you die the proceeds your beneficiaries receive will be reduced by what you borrowed.) Or you can simply ask that the cash reserves be used to pay the premiums. This will reduce your cash value, but you won't have to repay it.

Another way to keep life insurance coverage but to reduce the payments is to convert a whole or universal policy (with relatively high premiums and a cash value build-up) into a term policy (with low premiums and no cash value.) You may lose a little of the existing cash value as a conversion fee, but if you believe life insurance coverage is essential, losing a few dollars may be worth it in exchange for getting a policy which will cost far less to maintain.

If your insurance policy—life or otherwise—has lapsed, and your financial picture is improving, many insurance companies will let you reinstate your policy if you pay up what you owe within 60 days of when the premium payment first became due. You may also have to pay interest on your back premiums, usually between 5%–10%. After 60 days, the company will probably make you reapply for coverage. If your risk factors have increased since you originally took out the insurance—for example, you took out auto insurance two years ago, have since had a car accident and a moving violation and your insurance just lapsed—you may be denied coverage or offered coverage at a higher rate.

7. Medical, Legal and Other Service Bills

Before assuming that your bill is correct, review it carefully and be sure that you understand and agree with every charge. With hospital bills in particular, ask for specific itemization if the bill only gives broad categories. And if the bill is filled with indecipherable codes, make someone in the hospital billing office explain to you what every code means.

Once you understand what each charge is, look for mistakes. The federal General Accounting Office estimates that 99% of all hospital bills contain overcharges, and one insurance company stated that the average hospital bill contains almost $1,400 of mistakes. The types of errors include inflated charges (such as $5 per aspirin tablet), charges for items never received by the patient (for example, an extra pillow) and double billing.

Assuming you do owe the full amount of the bill or can't afford the corrected bill, many doctors, dentists, lawyers and accountants will accept partial payments, reduce the total bill, drop interest or late fees and delay sending bills to collection agencies if you clearly communicate how difficult your financial problems are and try to get their sympathy. Some doctors, especially, won't spend too much effort in collecting the outstanding bills of long-time patients who suddenly find themselves unable to pay.

Before deciding whether or not to pay a doctor, dentist, lawyer or accountant, assess how necessary that person's services are. Pay the bill to your dentist if your child desperately needs dental care before you pay the lawyer who you consulted once and who didn't help you resolve your problem.

If your problem is that your insurance will eventually cover all or most of your medical bill, but the medical provider is pursuing you because it hasn't yet been paid by your insurance company, you'll have to take a different approach. Gather together evidence of:

- your submission of the bill to your insurance company, and

- your insurance company's coverage for the specific medical care you (or your other family member) received.

Armed with this information, call the doctor or hospital's collections department and ask for an appointment. At the meeting, provide the collector with copies of your documentation and plead with the person to cease collection efforts against you. Let the collections representative know that your medical condition may worsen if the stress of the collection calls and letters doesn't stop. If you get nowhere with the collections representative, make an appointment to see the department supervisor. Also, if the bill is from a hospital, see if the facility has an "ombudsman"—many do. An ombudsman works at a hospital to help resolve disputes between patients and the institution.

8. Child Support and Alimony Payments

No matter what your hardship, your duty to pay child support or alimony won't go away. You must take affirmative steps to legally reduce your payment obligation. Because a court ordered you to pay child support or alimony, only a court can reduce the amount. Thus, when your income drops, immediately file a paper (usually called a motion or petition) with the court asking that your future child support or alimony payments be reduced, at least temporarily.

The court cannot retroactively reduce child support or alimony, however. The court can set up a payment schedule, but if you miss payments before you ask for a reduction, it can't erase your debt. See Chapter 8 for a thorough discussion on reducing child support or alimony.

9. Income Taxes

You have several strategies for dealing with the IRS. For example, if you haven't recently been in trouble with the IRS, you will be given an installment agreement to pay your taxes if you owe under $10,000. Another option, if you are unable to afford an installment agreement, is to make an "offer in compromise." This means that you make a lump sum offer to the IRS to settle what you owe. Your offer must be at least the value of your nonnecessary property. Finally, you may be able to eliminate, reduce or spread out your IRS debt by filing for bankruptcy. (Bankruptcy is covered in Chapter 10.) For a complete discussion of your options with the IRS, see *Stand Up to the IRS*, by Frederick W. Daily (Nolo Press).

10.   Student Loan Payments

You can probably get your student loan payments deferred (postponed) if you have a good reason for not being able to pay. The maximum deferment, if you are temporarily totally disabled, unemployed but looking for work, or are suffering from economic hardship, is three years. See Chapter 7, Section D, for the details.

11.   Credit and Charge Card Payments

If you can't pay anything on your credit or charge card, and have decided that keeping the card isn't essential, don't pay. You will lose your credit privileges. You may also be sued, but that will take some time.

If you want to keep the card, most card companies insist that you make the monthly minimum payment. But if you can convince the company that your immediate financial situation is truly difficult, your payments may be further reduced to 2% to 3% of the outstanding balance and you won't be charged late fees while you're paying what you owe. It's almost impossible to get a credit or charge card company to reduce interest charges. Some will stop interest charges, however, if you get assistance from a Consumer Credit Counseling program. (See Chapter 13.) Bear in mind that this should be a temporary solution. The longer you pay only a small amount on your credit card, the quicker your balance will increase due to interest charges.

Below is a sample letter you can modify and send to your creditors to request a reduction, extension or other repayment program. It often helps to send a copy to the company president.

Sample Letter to Creditor

```
                    Collections Department
                    Big Bank of Bismark
                    37 Charles Street
                    Bismark, ND 77777

                    August 19, 19__
```

Re: Amy and Robert Grange
        Account 411-900-LOAN

To Whom It May Concern:

On June 5, 19__, your bank granted us a three-year $3,300 personal loan. Our agreement requires us to pay you $125 per month, and we have diligently made those payments since July 1, 19__.

We now, however, face several emergencies. Robert had a heart attack last April and has been out of work ever since. His doctors do not believe that he'll be able to work again until this November. On top of that, Amy's company filed for bankruptcy and laid her off last week. She expects to receive a small unemployment check and is looking for work. Unfortunately, though, many industries in our town have closed down, and the prospects for a 46-year old semi-skilled worker are few. Amy may be able to work in her uncle's office, but it's a 90-minute drive each way and she can't afford the time while Robert is recovering.

We cannot pay you more than $20 a month right now. We expect to resume the full $125 per month payments this November. We ask that you please accept our $20 a month until then, and just add the balance we miss to the end of our loan and extend it the few months necessary.

Thank you for your understanding and help. We expect a response within 20 days. Please call (701) 555-8388 in the evenings and ask for Amy.

Sincerely,

Amy and Robert Grange

cc: Leonard O'Brien,
    President, Big Bank of Bismark

D. If the Creditor Has a Judgment Against You

IF YOU DON'T PAY A DEBT, the creditor may sue you. Once a creditor has a judgment against you, she also has an expanded arsenal of collection techniques. She can put a lien on your house, empty your bank accounts and attach a portion of your wages, to name a few. A nonessential debt may move into the essential category very fast once it is turned into a judgment. Chapter 9 gives you strategies for dealing with judgment creditors.

E. Get Some Money to Pay Your Debts

YOU MAY BE CONSIDERING several methods of raising cash to pay your debts. Before doing so, ask yourself again if bankruptcy is a serious option for you. (Chapter 10 can help you answer the question.) If it is, raising cash to pay debts you will ultimately erase in bankruptcy is a waste of your time and already stretched resources.

Below are several different methods of raising cash. Most have costs associated with them—penalties, interest, fees and the like. A few may cost you more money than the cash raised is worth. So read on, but read on cautiously.

1. Sell a Major Asset

One of the best ways you can raise cash and keep associated costs to a minimum, is to sell a major asset, such as a house or car. With the proceeds of the sale you'll have to pay off the lender and any secured creditor to whom you pledged the asset as collateral. Then you'll have to pay off any liens placed on the house by your creditors. You can use what's left to help pay your other debts. Even if nothing is left, getting rid of large monthly payments may be what you need to afford your other bills.

Example: Ellie owes her mortgage lender $130,000 and a finance company, from whom she took out a second mortgage, $25,000. Two liens have been filed against her house—one for $15,000 by a contractor who wasn't paid for work he did, and the other for $24,000 by the Department of Education when it got a court judgment for an outstanding student loan.

If Ellie sells her house, she'll get about $220,000. The sales cost will be about $10,000. After paying off the lenders and liens, Ellie will pocket about $15,000, enough to make it worth her selling.

2. Cash In a Tax-Deferred Account

If you have an IRA or other tax-deferred account into which you've deposited money, consider cashing it in. You'll have to pay the IRS a penalty—10% of the money you withdraw—and you'll owe income taxes on the money you take out. But paying these penalties to the IRS, especially if you have been laid off or face a major medical emergency, is probably better than losing your house.

You may also be able to tap your 401(k) plan. Again, you'll owe taxes on the money withdrawn and a 10% penalty if you're under age 59-1/2. But there is a bit of good news: Not only can you withdraw money to cover your emergency expenses, but you can also withdraw enough to cover the taxes and penalty. And, as mentioned in Section B6, above, you may be able to borrow the cash value of any life insurance policy you own.

3. Obtain a Home Equity Loan

Many banks, savings and loans, credit unions and other lenders offer home equity loans, also called second mortgages. Lenders who make home equity loans establish how much you can borrow under the following formula: a percentage, usually between 50% and 80% of the market value of your house, less what you still owe on it.

Example: Winnie's house is worth $200,000 and she owes $120,000 on her first mortgage. A bank has offered her a home equity loan at 75%, that is, for $30,000. The lender figures it like this: 75% of $200,000 is $150,000. $150,000 less $120,000 is $30,000.

Obtaining a home equity loan has its advantages and disadvantages. Be sure you understand all the terms before you sign up for one.

Advantages

- You can obtain a closed-end loan. You borrow a fixed amount of money and repay it in equal monthly installments for a set period. Or you can obtain a line of credit—you borrow as you need the money, drawing against the amount granted when you opened the account. Be sure you understand the difference.

- The interest you pay is fully deductible on your income tax return.

- Federal law requires that lenders cap the interest rates on home equity loans with adjustable interest rates.

Disadvantages

- You are obligating yourself to make another monthly or periodic payment. If you are unable to pay, you may have to sell your house, or even worse, face the possibility of the lender foreclosing. *Before you take out a home equity loan, be sure you can make the monthly payment.*

- While interest is deductible and capped for adjustable rate loans, it's often high—up to 19% per year.

- You'll have to pay an assortment of up-front fees for such costs as an appraisal, credit report, title insurance and points. These fees can run close to $1,000. In addition, many lenders charge a yearly fee of $25 to $50.

Before obtaining a home equity loan, carefully evaluate your situation. You want to take steps to help you pay your debts; you don't want to make your debt burden worse.

Canceling a Home Equity Loan

Under the federal Truth in Lending Act, you have the right to cancel a home equity loan or second mortgage until midnight of the third business day after you sign the contract. You must be given notice of your right to cancel and a cancellation form when you sign the contract. The details are spelled out in Chapter 2, Section E1.

---

4. Use the Equity in Your Home if You Are Elderly

A variety of plans are designed to help older homeowners make use of the accumulated value (equity) in their homes without requiring them to move, give up title to the property or make payments on a loan. The most common types of plans are reverse mortgages and deferral loans for property tax and home repair.

These plans can raise a senior citizen's standard of living and help an older person maintain independence by providing cash for everyday living expenses, home maintenance and repair, or to finance in-home care.

a. Reverse Mortgages

Reverse mortgages are loans against the equity in the home that provide cash advances to a homeowner and require no repayment until the end of the loan term or when the home is sold. The borrower can receive the cash in several ways—a lump sum, regular monthly payments, a line of credit or a combination.

To qualify, you must be at least 62 years old and own your home free and clear or have a very small mortgage that can be paid off with an initial lump sum payment from the reverse mortgage.

All reverse mortgages will cost you money— closing costs (title insurance, escrow fees and appraisal fees), loan origination fees, accrued interest, and in most cases, an additional charge to offset the lender's risk of you not repaying.

There are three basic types of reverse mortgages:

- **Fixed Term Reverse Mortgages.** You receive monthly advances for a specified period of time. At the end of the period, the advances stop and you must repay the loan.

- **Tenure Reverse Mortgages.** You receive monthly advances as long as you stay in your home. Once you leave (for example, sell your house), you must repay the loan.

- **Portable Reverse Mortgages.** You receive an advance in order to purchase an annuity that will pay you a fixed amount as long as you are alive, no matter where you live.

b. Deferral Payment Loans

Deferral payment loans are need-based loans used for a special purpose—to make property tax payments or to pay for home repairs. The cost of these loans is very low and repayment is deferred as long as you live in your home. Deferral payment loans are generally available through state or local government agencies.

There are two types of deferral payment loans:

- **Property Tax Deferral Loans.** Many states will provide vouchers to approved applicants to pay their property taxes. Contact your tax assessor to see if such a program is available in your county.

- **Home Repair Deferral Loans.** These are loans for home repairs at no or very low interest.

c. Other Options to Tap the Equity in a Home

Several other options exist for older people who want to use the equity in their homes. These include:

- **Sale-Leaseback.** You sell your home and rent it back from the buyer for the rest of your life. The rental payments are deducted from the mortgage payment, giving you a monthly check for the difference.

- **Life Estate Sale.** You sell your home at a discounted price which reflects your right to live in the house for the rest of your life. The price is based on the home's value and your age and life expectancy. Usually, the entire amount of money is given at the closing of the transaction.

- **Hospital Foundation Loans.** These programs (tied in with charitable gifts) are fixed term reverse mortgages but usually have a maximum time limit of ten years. You will have to check with various hospitals to see if they have such a program.

- **Deed/Annuity or Remainderman Interest Sale.** Some universities, religious organizations and hospitals have programs under which you transfer title to the institution in exchange for income and the right to stay in the home for your lifetime. Contact the various institutions to see if they have such a plan.

d. Additional Resources

The following brochures are free:

- *Reverse Mortgages*, Federal Trade Commission, Office of Consumer Education, Washington, DC 20580.

- *Homemade Money*, American Association of Retired Persons (AARP), Home Equity Information Center, Consumer Affairs Division, 601 E Street NW, Washington, DC 20049.

- *Money From Home: A Consumer's Guide to Home Equity Conversion Mortgages*, Fannie Mae, Consumer Education Group, 3900 Wisconsin Avenue NW, Washington, DC 20016-2899.

- *Retirement Income on the House*, by Ken Scholen, National Center for Home Equity Conversion, 7373 147th Street West, Suite 115, Apple Valley, MN 55124.

Also available for $20 is a video, *Reverse Mortgages—Cashing in on Your Home*, put out by the

Human Investment Project, Inc., 364 S. Railroad Avenue, San Mateo, CA 94401, (415) 348-6660.

5. Borrow From Family or Friends

In times of financial crises, some people are lucky enough to have friends or relatives who can and will help out. Before asking your college roommate, Uncle Paul or someone similar, consider the following:

- Can the lender really afford to help you? If the person is on a fixed income and needs the money to get by, your taking the money could really hurt him.

- Do you want to owe this person money? If the loan comes with emotional strings attached, be sure you can handle the situation before taking the money.

- Will the loan help you out or will it just delay the inevitable (most likely, filing for bankruptcy)? Don't borrow money to make payments on debts you will eventually discharge in bankruptcy.

- Will you have to repay the loan now or will the lender let you wait until you're back on your feet? If you have to make payments now, you're just adding another monthly payment to your already unmanageable pile of debts.

- If the loan is from your parents, can you treat it as part of your eventual inheritance? If so, you won't ever have to repay it. If your siblings get angry that you are getting some of mom and dad's money, be sure they understand that your inheritance will be reduced accordingly.

6. Borrow From a Finance Company

A few consumer finance companies—the three biggest nationwide are Beneficial Corp., Household International Inc. and ITT—lend money to consumers usually in the form of consolidation loans. Finance companies make secured consolidation loans, usually requiring that you pledge your house or car as collateral. These are just second mortgages or secured vehicle loans, and you'll usually be charged interest between 10% and 15%. If you default on the loan, the finance company can foreclose on your home or take your car.

Finance companies, banks, credit unions and similar lenders also make unsecured consolidation loans—that is, they lend you some money without requiring that you pledge any property as a guarantee that you'll pay.

But the interest on these loans, especially from finance companies, often reaches 25%. They also charge all kinds of fees—many not disclosed—bringing the true interest rate closer to 50%.

If you still want to take out a consolidation loan, you are better off borrowing from a bank or credit union than a finance company. Many finance companies engage in illegal or borderline collection practices if you default, and are not as willing as banks and credit unions to negotiate if you have trouble paying. Furthermore, loans from finance companies are viewed negatively by potential creditors who see them in your credit file. They often imply prior debt problems.

7. Get Your Tax Refund Fast

Sometimes, getting a tax refund quickly will help you through a crisis, especially if the IRS owes you a lot. You essentially have two ways of getting your refund fast—contacting the IRS directly or paying someone for help.

Contact the IRS directly. The IRS's Problem Resolution Program (PRP) is set up to give assistance to taxpayers. Each IRS district office has a PRP; the offices handle about 400,000 calls each year. Most callers are seeking help in getting their refund early. To contact a local office, check the government listing of your phone book for the PRP office in your region, or call the Washington, DC office at (202) 566-6475.

Pay someone to help you. Beneficial Corp., the consumer finance company, and H & R Block, the income tax return preparation company, provide a service for taxpayers to get the amount of their tax refunds quickly. For a fee usually under $50, you file your tax return electronically through H & R Block. Within two days, Beneficial cuts you a check for the size of your refund. When your actual refund comes in, Beneficial keeps it.

You obviously want to try the PRP before paying someone to get you the amount of your refund fast.

8. Visit a Pawnshop

Visiting a pawnshop should be one of the last ways you consider raising cash. Using a debt consolidator, described just below, should probably be the last. At a pawnshop, you leave your property—the most commonly pawned items are jewelry, electronics and photography equipment, musical instruments and firearms. In return, the pawnbroker lends you approximately 50% to 60% of the item's resale value; the average amount of a pawnshop loan is $50.

You are given a few months to repay the loan, and are charged interest, often at an exorbitant rate. Although you borrow money for only a few months, paying an average of 10% a month interest means that you are paying an annual interest rate of 120%. You might also be charged storage costs and insurance fees.

If you default on your loan to a pawnshop, the property you left at the shop to obtain the loan becomes the property of the pawnbroker. You are usually given some time to pay up your debt and get your property back; if you don't, the pawnbroker will most likely sell it. In about a dozen states, if the sale brings in money in excess of what you owe on the loan, storage fees and sales costs, you're entitled to the surplus. But don't count on getting anything.

9. Use a Debt Consolidating Company

Debt consolidating, debt pooling, budget planning, debt adjusting or debt prorating companies produce poor results. They siphon off your limited resources in debt consolidation charges, pay a few creditors and jeopardize much of your property. These companies are often merely a front for loan sharking. Some charge outrageously high interest; others charge ridiculously high fees.

Debt consolidating is either regulated or prohibited in most states. (See the chart, below.) These laws usually don't apply to nonprofit organizations, lawyers and merchant-owned associations claiming to help debtors.

State	Code Section	State Debt Consolidating Regulations
Alabama	5-19-22	Debt consolidation companies must be licensed.
Arizona	6-710	Debt consolidation companies must be licensed and cannot accept an account unless it reasonably appears that the debtor can make the payments.
Arkansas	5-63-302	Debt consolidating prohibited.
California	Finance 12200.5, 12314	Debt consolidation companies must be licensed; debt consolidation companies cannot charge more than 12% for first $3,000 owed; 11% for next $2,000 and 10% for balance.
Colorado	12-20-103	Debt consolidation companies must be licensed.
	12-20-108	Debt consolidation contracts must be in writing and cannot last more than 24 months.
Connecticut	36-376	Debt consolidation companies must be licensed.
Delaware	11 § 910	Debt consolidating prohibited.
District of Columbia	22-3426	Debt consolidating prohibited.
Florida	559.11	Debt consolidating prohibited.
Georgia	18-5-1	Debt consolidating prohibited.
Hawaii	446-2	Debt consolidating prohibited.
Illinois	Ch. 32 ¶ 360.1	Debt consolidating prohibited.
Iowa	533A.8	Debt consolidation companies must be licensed; debt consolidation contracts must be in writing, cannot last more than 36 months and must state total charges.
Kansas	21-4402	Debt consolidating prohibited.
Kentucky	380.020	Debt consolidating prohibited.
Louisiana	14:331	Debt consolidating prohibited.
Maine	17-701	Debt consolidating prohibited.
Maryland	27-79A	Debt consolidating prohibited.
Massachusetts	221-46C	Debt consolidating prohibited.
Michigan	23:630(38)	Debt consolidation companies must be licensed and debt consolidation contracts cannot charge more than 15% of debt and cannot last more than 24 months.

State	Code Section	State Debt Consolidating Regulations
Minnesota	332.28	Debt consolidation companies must be licensed.
Mississippi	85-9-3	Debt consolidating prohibited.
Missouri	425.020	Debt consolidating prohibited.
Montana	31-3-202	Debt consolidating prohibited.
Nebraska	69-1203	Debt consolidation companies must be licensed.
Nevada	676.110	Debt consolidation companies must be licensed.
New Hampshire	399-D:13	Debt consolidation companies must be licensed; debt consolidation contracts must be in writing and cannot last more than 24 months.
New Jersey	17:16G-2	Debt consolidating prohibited.
New Mexico	56-2-2	Debt consolidating prohibited.
New York	GBL 456	Debt consolidating prohibited.
North Carolina	14-424	Debt consolidating prohibited.
North Dakota	13-06-02	Debt consolidating prohibited.
Ohio	4710.02	Debt consolidating prohibited.
Oklahoma	24-15	Debt consolidating prohibited.
Oregon	697.662	Debt consolidation contract cannot contain blanks after debtor signs it; debt consolidation companies cannot accept any negotiable instrument except a check and cannot take a judgment against a debtor.
Pennsylvania	18-7312	Debt consolidating prohibited.
Rhode Island	5-66-2	Debt consolidating prohibited.
South Dakota	22-47-2	Debt consolidating prohibited.
Tennessee	39-14-142	Debt consolidating prohibited.
Texas	Civ. 5069-9.02	Debt consolidating prohibited.
Vermont	8-4862	Debt consolidation companies must be licensed.
Virginia	6.1-363.1	Debt consolidating prohibited.
Washington	18.28.020	Debt consolidation companies must be licensed.
West Virginia	61-10-23	Debt consolidating prohibited.
Wyoming	33-14-102	Debt consolidating prohibited.

F. Try to Pay Off a Debt for Less Than the Full Amount

IF YOU OWE A CREDITOR $750, you may be tempted to send a check for $450 and state on the check that "cashing this check constitutes payment in full." This is especially true if you don't feel you really owe all the money. Before sending a "payment in full" or "full payment" check, however, be sure that your state recognizes this legal concept.

 If the Creditor Shows There's No Real Dispute, He Can Cash the Check and Sue You for the Balance

Cashing a full payment check only satisfies a debt if you and the creditor dispute how much you owe. If there's no dispute—you borrowed $1,500 from your neighbor, spent it and admit that you owe that amount—the creditor can cash your "payment in full" check and sue you for the rest.

So before you send a full payment check, make sure there is a dispute. If you haven't paid the dress shop yet, look carefully at the dress. Is it fading or fraying unusually fast?

In general, if a creditor deposits a full payment check, even if she strikes out the "payment in full" notation or writes some kind of protest on the check such as "I don't agree" before cashing it, she can't come after you for the balance. Once she cashes it, you are free and clear.[2]

Unfortunately, several states have modified this rule.[3] In those states, if a creditor cashes a full payment check and explicitly reserves his right to sue you—by writing "under protest" or "without prejudice" with his endorsement—he can come after you for the balance. But he must use those words. If he writes "without recourse," communicates with you separately, notifies you verbally or writes on the check that it is accepted as partial payment, it is not enough.

One other state—California—lets creditors cross out the full payment language and sue you for the balance.[4] California is the only state where a legislative bill gave creditors this right. In all other states, a creditor's right to cross out the full payment language was established by courts. When the California legislature enacted the law, it also enacted a procedure to let debtors get around it, if they follow very specific steps and use certain language.

How Californians Can Get Around Their Full Payment Law

1. Send a letter to the creditor stating that you intend to send a full payment check.

2. Wait 15–90 days to give the creditor time to object.

3. Send the check with a letter stating that the check constitutes payment in full.

Sample letters are below.

---

[2]States that specifically bar creditors from suing you for the balance after they cash a full payment check—even if the creditor crosses off the full payment language—include Alaska, Arkansas, Colorado, Connecticut, Georgia, Kansas, Louisiana, Maine, Michigan, Nebraska, New Jersey, North Carolina, Oregon, Pennsylvania, Texas, Utah, Vermont, Virginia, Washington and Wyoming.

[3]Alabama, Delaware, Massachusetts, Minnesota, Missouri, New Hampshire, New York, Ohio, Rhode Island, South Carolina, South Dakota, West Virginia and Wisconsin.

---

[4]California Civil Code § 1526.

Sample Letter *Before* Sending Full Payment Check (California Only)

> Hermann's Helpful
> Hardware
> 1145 North Francisco
> Blvd.
> Chico, CA 90000
>
> July 17, 19__

Re: Philip Van Bugle

Account Number: PVB-92-4545

Dear Mr. Hermann:

This letter concerns the money I owe you. For the past three months, I have received bills from you stating that I owe $300 for a three-day rental of your New-Finish-Now hardwood floor finisher. As you will recall, I rented the finisher on a Friday evening intending to return it on Sunday, for a total of two days rental. When I came to your store on Sunday, it was closed and I could not return the finisher until Monday. I believe that I owe you no more than $200, and it is obvious that there is a good faith dispute over the amount of this bill.

To satisfy this debt, I will send you a check for $200 with a restrictive endorsement and if you cash that check, it will constitute an accord and satisfaction. In other words, you will receive from me a check that states "cashing this check constitutes payment in full." If you cash it, that check will take care of what I owe you.

Sincerely,

Philip Van Bugle

After sending the letter, wait at least 15 days, but not more than 90 days, before sending the check and a second letter. Below is a sample of the second letter to send.

Sample Letter *When* Sending Full Payment Check (California Only)

> Hermann's Helpful
> Hardware
> 1145 North Francisco
> Blvd.
> Chico, CA 90000
>
> August 3, 19__

Re: Philip Van Bugle

Account Number: PVB-92-4545

Dear Mr. Hermann:

Enclosed is a check for $200 to cover the balance of account PVB-92-4545. This check is tendered in accordance with my letter of July 17, 19__. If you cash this check you agree that my debt is satisfied in full.

Sincerely,

Philip Van Bugle

Enclose your check and write on the check—on the front along the top or bottom—the exact language you used in the second letter: "This check is tendered in accordance with my letter of _____ (date). If you cash this check you agree that my debt is satisfied in full."

G. Don't Write a Bad Check

PEOPLE WHO ARE BROKE and desperate are often tempted to write bad checks. If you're faced with the prospect of no food or the electricity being cut off, writing a bad check can seem like a reasonable solution. It isn't. In every state, writing a bad check when you know you don't have the money to cover it is a crime. Aggressive district attorneys don't hesitate to prosecute, especially given that an estimated 450 million rubber checks are written each year. It is not a crime, however, if you stopped payment because of a good faith dispute you are having with a merchant. (See Chapter 2, *Debts You May Not Owe.*)

If you are prosecuted, you may be able to avoid the ordeal of a trial if your county has a "diversion" program. Instead of being tried, you are given the option of attending classes—anywhere from 4 hours to 20 months—for bad check writers. If you choose to go, you must pay the tuition, which usually ranges from $40 to $125 per session, and you must make restitution, that is, make good on the bad checks you wrote.

Even if you escape criminal prosecution, you'll be charged a bad check "processing" fee by your bank. Many banks charge as much as $20 or $30, when the actual cost to the bank to process your bounced check is between $0.12 and $0.35—that's a profit of at least 5,600% to the bank.

If $20 or $30 is all you have to pay, you'll be lucky. Most creditors who receive a bad check—or one where a stop payment was later ordered—can sue for damages. And like the criminal sanctions for writing a bad check, these laws don't apply if you stopped payment because of a good faith dispute you are having with a merchant.

Before suing you, the creditor usually must first make a written demand that you make good on the bad check. If you don't within approximately 30 days, the creditor can sue you.

State	Code Section	Maximum Damages Under State Bad Check Laws
Alabama	6-5-285	Actual and punitive damages (meant to punish), and reasonable attorneys' fees.
Alaska	09.65.115	$100 or three times the amount of the check, whichever is greater, not to exceed the amount of the check by more than $1,000. If you pay before trial but after suit filed, creditor is entitled to amount of check plus $150.
Arizona	13-1809	Twice the amount of the check or $50, whichever is greater, plus costs and reasonable attorneys' fees.
Arkansas	4-60-103	Two times the amount of the check, but in no case less than $50.
California	CC 1719	Three times the amount of the check, not less than $100 nor more than $500, plus costs.
Colorado	13-21-109	Three times the amount of the check, not less than $100.
Connecticut	52-565a	Damages set by the court. If you wrote check for which there was no account, damages not to exceed the face amount of the check or $750. If you wrote check on account with insufficient funds, damages not to exceed the face amount of the check or $400.
Florida	68.065	Three times the amount of the check or $50, whichever is greater, plus costs and reasonable attorneys' fees.
Georgia	13-6-15	Two times the amount of the check, but in no case more than $500.
Hawaii	490:3-506	Three times the amount of the check or $100, whichever is greater, but not more than $500.
Illinois	720 ILCS 5/17-1a	Three times the amount of the check or $100, whichever is greater, but not more than $500.
Indiana	28-2-8-1	Three times the amount of the check, but not more than $500.
Iowa	554.3806	Three times the amount of the check, but not more than $500.
Kansas	60-2610	Three times the amount of the check or $100, whichever is greater, but not more than $500.
Louisiana	9:2782	Twice the amount of the check or $100, whichever is greater, plus reasonable attorneys' fees and costs.
Maine	14-6071	Face value of check, or court costs, service costs, collection and processing costs not to exceed $40, whichever is less, plus interest at 12% per year.
Maryland	CL 3-512	Twice the amount of the check, not to exceed $1,000.
Massachusetts	93:40A	Damages determined by court, not less than $100 and not more than $500.
Michigan	27A.2952	Two times the amount of the check or $50, whichever is greater, but not more than $500.
Minnesota	332.50	$100 plus interest and reasonable attorney's fees.
Mississippi	11-7-12	For checks up to $25, the face amount of the check; for checks between $26 and $200, 50% of face amount, not to exceed $50 nor to be less than $25; if check is over $200, 25% of face amount.
Missouri	570.123	Three times the amount of the check or $100, whichever is greater, but not more than $500.

State	Code Section	Maximum Damages Under State Bad Check Laws
Montana	27-1-717	Three times the amount of the check or $100, whichever is greater, but not more than $500.
Nevada	41-620	Three times the amount of the check, not less than $100 nor more than $500, plus costs.
New Hampshire	544-B:1	Court, service and collection costs; if you fail to pay judgment, you may be fined $10 per business day up to $500, from date of judgment until debt paid.
New Mexico	56-14-1	Three times the amount of the check or $100, whichever is greater, but not more than $500.
New York	GOL 11-104	If you wrote check for which there was no account, two times the amount of the check or $750, whichever is less. If you wrote check on account with insufficient funds, two times the amount of the check or $400, whichever is less.
North Carolina	6-21.3	Three times the amount of the check or $500, whichever is less, but not less than $100.
North Dakota	6-08-16	Three times the amount of the check or $100, whichever is less.
Oregon	20.090, 30.700	Three times the amount of the check or $100, whichever is greater, but not more than $500; attorney's fees.
Pennsylvania	42-8304	Three times the amount of the check or $100, whichever is greater, but not more than $500.
Rhode Island	6-42-3	Three times the amount of the check, no less than $200, no more than $1,000.
South Carolina	34-11-75	Three times the amount of the check, not to exceed $500.
Tennessee	47-29-101	Three times the amount of the check, not to exceed $500.
Vermont	9-2311	Costs of servicing returned check, the amount of the check, bank fees, interest, attorneys' fees and damages to $50.
Virginia	6.1-118.1	$10 to cover the returned check fee, the amount of the check and lost wages, to a total of $250.
Washington	62A.3-515	Three times the amount of the check, not to exceed $300.
Wisconsin	943.245	Actual damages; three times the amount of the check and attorneys' fees, not to exceed $300.
Wyoming	1-1-115	Two times the amount of the check, not less than $50, and for interest, costs and attorneys' fees.

Stale Checks—How Long Will a Check Be Honored?

If you wrote a creditor a check several months ago, but the creditor has not yet cashed it, can you add the balance back into your checkbook—that is, has the creditor taken too much time?

Perhaps, but not necessarily. A bank, savings and loan or credit union is not required to honor a check presented for cashing more than six months after the check was written. Most banks do, however, unless the check has an express notation on it "not valid after six months."

What does this mean for you? If you wrote a check more than six months ago and the creditor still hasn't cashed it, you can call your bank and put a stop payment on it. The debt, however, does not go away. Be prepared for the creditor to try and collect, arguing that your stop payment was not in good faith. You should respond that you gave the creditor six months, and if a bank isn't obligated to honor a check that old, you shouldn't be either.

H. Writing a Post-Dated Check Is a Bad Idea

MANY AGGRESSIVE BILL collectors will try to pressure you into sending them a post-dated check—a check dated with a future date. Sending a post-dated check is usually a bad idea. When you write a post-dated check you are committing yourself to having the money in your checking account when the date on the check arrives. If you are already having debt problems, this is a commitment you can't realistically make.

If for some extremely important reason you decide to send a creditor a post-dated check, it's legal to do so. Many creditors are used to receiving them and usually won't deposit them until the date written. This is because banks won't usually accept a post-dated check until the date written on the check itself.

Example: Greg has never been financially disciplined and found himself owing several creditors. He received a moderate-sized inheritance to be paid in six monthly installments. Greg sent each of his creditors six post-dated checks (one for the present month, one for the month following, one for the month after that, etc.) to cover that creditor's bill. Once he sent the checks, his creditors left him alone. As Greg received his inheritance each month he deducted the amount of his already-sent checks from his checking account and each creditor deposited the check written for that month. Greg paid off his debts in six months.

I. Beware of the IRS If You Settle a Debt

AN IRS REGULATION WHICH TOOK EFFECT IN 1994 could cost you money if you successfully settle a debt with certain creditors. Under the regulation, certain debts that you negotiate with your creditors not to pay are treated as income to you. Specifically, any bank (this includes banks that issue credit cards), credit union, savings and loan or other financial institution that forgives a debt or part of a debt of yours for $600 or more must send you and the IRS a Form 1099 at the end of the tax year. A Form 1099 is a report of income, which means that when you file your tax return for the tax year in which your debt was forgiven, the IRS will make sure that you report the amount on the Form 1099 as income.

The only times the financial institution doesn't have to issue a Form 1099 (and therefore you don't have to report the "income") is when:

- you discharge the debt in bankruptcy

- you are no longer obligated to pay the debt because the time limit (called the statute of limitations) has expired, or

- the amount forgiven is for late fees, interest and other amounts that don't include the principal of the debt.

Example: Your Visa debt is $2,000 and you can't afford to pay nearly that amount. After several conversations with your bank's collections department, you agree to pay $1,100 to settle the entire bill. The January after the bank gets your check, it sends you (and the IRS) a Form 1099 showing that you "earned" $900—the amount your bank forgave you to settle the debt. When you file your tax return that April, you must include the $900 as income.

If your debts are enormous and your bank or other financial institution is willing to settle for less than you owe, it could cost you a lot in the end. Before taking the deal, have a tax preparer calculate your tax liability including your likely Form 1099 income. If your tax bill will be too high, you may be better off filing for bankruptcy and discharging the entire debt. ■

Chapter 4

THE CONSEQUENCES OF IGNORING YOUR DEBTS

Where everything is bad it must be good to know the worst.

—Francis Herbert Bradley,
English philosopher, 1846-1924

WHAT ARE THE CONSEQUENCES of ignoring your creditors completely? While this is not the strategy I normally recommend, it's one many people follow— at least for a while—so you need to know what could happen. Before I get into the details of what happens if you fail to pay various types of debts, here's a brief overview.

If you ignore your creditors long enough, they will probably take legal action to try and get either the money you owe or the secured property you pledged to guarantee repayment. You may lose some property, including your house, car and a portion of your wages. But because exemption laws (see Chapter 11) protect you from having your essential property taken, you won't lose your clothing, public benefits, most personal property, and for the majority of debts, most of your wages. And most important, for all debts (except possibly child support) no matter how much you owe, you won't lose your liberty unless you do something foolish that infuriates a judge such as deliberately disobeying her order or lying in a court document.

A. Eviction

 Landlord-Tenant Rules Vary Throughout the Country

Landlord-tenant rules are state- and sometimes city-specific, and vary tremendously from one place to the next. If paying your rent becomes a problem, seriously consider getting some help from a tenants' advocacy or other consumer group. See Chapter 13.

IF YOU DON'T PAY YOUR RENT, your landlord can evict you. In many populous states, such as New York, California and Massachusetts, an eviction can take as long as a month or two. The landlord must first give you notice to get out and then file a lawsuit and serve it on you. You then have a set number of days to respond (five is common), and then a week or two later the court holds a hearing.

Even if you ignore the suit and the landlord gets an automatic (default) judgment against you, the landlord must take that judgment to the local sheriff. The sheriff, whose primary job is evicting people, must fit you into the schedule. Many states require that the sheriff give you a week's advance notice of when the eviction is scheduled. If you're not out of the house or apartment on the selected day, the sheriff comes and gives you the boot.

Evictions don't always take a month, however. In states—or even towns and counties—with few protections for tenants, an eviction can take place fast. The landlord gives you just a few days notice to pay what you owe—or defend in court—or be on the street. And no matter where you live, if you're evicted, a landlord can sue you for the back rent you owe.

In addition to eviction, in several states if you don't pay your rent, the landlord gets an automatic lien on your personal property to secure payment. A lien is a notice, filed at a county office, telling the world that the landlord claims you owe her some money. Having a lien on property makes it difficult to sell that property. Most landlord liens begin when you don't pay your rent and last for a few months. In a few states, the lien lasts up to a year. Some landlords, especially in states which don't have automatic landlord liens, require that you put down one or two month's rent when you move in. That deposited money covers the rent if you are evicted or leave.

If the landlord gets a lien, the landlord can't simply enter your apartment while you're away and take your property. The landlord must notify you that she plans to sell your property if you don't pay your rent. At this point, you can pay up or move out. If you don't do either, the landlord can hire a sheriff to enter your dwelling, take certain personal property and sell it to satisfy your outstanding rent.

In every state, certain property can't be taken as a matter of law by creditors including your landlord. This property is called your exempt property and usually includes your clothing, personal effects, furniture, small electronic equipment and food. (See Chapter 11 for more details.)

State	Code Section	Property Landlord May Attach; Restrictions on Attachments
Alabama	35-9-60	Tenant's goods, furniture and personal effects. Landlord cannot seize property whose value exceeds amount owed.
Arizona	33-361	Tenant's property found on the premises, except household possessions. Landlord must obtain court judgment before seizing property and must wait 60 days after seizing to sell.
Colorado	38-20-102	All of tenant's personal property, except necessaries—food, clothing, fuel—found on the premises. Landlord cannot "substantially interfere" with tenant's right to reasonably occupy and enjoy the premises.
District of Columbia	45-1413	Tenant's personal property found on the premises. Lien cannot exceed 3 months' rent.
Florida	85.011	All of tenant's personal property found on the premises. Landlord may record notice of lien with county recorder's office. If landlord doesn't, landlord cannot enforce lien after 12 months.
Georgia	61-201	All of tenant's personal property.
Kentucky	383.010	Tenant's fixtures, household furniture and other personal property.
Louisiana	9:3241	All of tenant's property that is not affixed (light fixtures, draperies and other attached items are considered affixed) found on the premises.
Mississippi	89-7-51	All of tenant's personal property found on the premises. If landlord "verily believes" that tenant will leave town without paying rent, landlord can seize property even before rent is owed.
New Jersey	2A:42-1	Tenant's goods found on the premises. Lien lasts for 1 year.
New Mexico	48-3-5	All of tenant's property found on the premises.
Oregon	87.162	All of tenant's property found on the premises, except clothing. Lien attaches 20 days after rent becomes due.
Pennsylvania	68-321	All of tenant's personal property. Landlord must obtain court judgment for the rent due in order to enforce the lien. Amount of the lien cannot exceed 1 year's rent.
South Carolina	27-39-210	Tenant's property, except certain household articles, on the premises.
Texas	54.041	All of tenant's property found on the premises.
Utah	38-3-1	All of tenant's property found on the premises up to 30 days after tenant moves out.
Virginia	55-227	All of tenant's property found on the premises.
Washington	60.72.010	All of tenant's personal property found on the premises for up to 2 months' rent.

Although many people have little or no non-exempt property, few people relish the idea of their landlord sifting through their belongings. If the sheriff takes some property, before it's sold you get the chance to reclaim it by paying the rent or claiming that the property is exempt under your state law. In addition, you may be able to claim that you need the property for your survival.

B. Foreclosure

IF YOU MISS SEVERAL MORTGAGE or home equity loan payments, the lender has the right to foreclose—forcing a sale of your house—to recover what you owe. Approximately 1% of homeowners default on their loans to the point of foreclosure. But mortgage lenders don't always foreclose, even if they have the right to. They generally don't like to force collection of their debts. Especially in parts of the country with depressed economies, foreclosing is expensive and time-consuming, and when the house is resold it usually only brings in a part of what is owed.

The entire foreclosure process can take up to 18 months, depending on the state and type of loan. Here is a general overview of how it works.

After you miss a payment or two, the lender will send you a letter reminding you that your payment is late and imposing a late fee—often 5% or 6% of the payment. If you still don't pay up, the lender will send more letters and call, demanding payment.

If, about 60–90 days after the last letter or phone call from the lender, you still haven't paid or contacted the lender to discuss your situation, the lender will send you a formal notice telling you that it has declared your loan in default. This notice, often called a Notice of Default, states that foreclosure proceedings will begin unless payment is received.

After the lender sends you the notice of default, you usually have approximately 90 days to "cure" the default and reinstate the loan—pay all your missed payments, late fees and other charges. You can avoid the actual foreclosure (and often minimize the damage to your credit rating) by selling the house during this period. Many buyer-investors purchase houses about to go into foreclosure, but they are not willing to pay—and you shouldn't expect to get—top dollar. They will pay enough to cover what you owe your lender—and maybe a little more—but you are likely to lose whatever equity you have in your house.

If you don't cure the default or sell the house during the 90-day period, the lender applies to a court for an order allowing it to sell your house. In California, obtaining prior court approval is unnecessary.

Once it has the court order (or if the lender is in California), the lender publishes a notice of the sale in a newspaper in the county where your house is located. The notice includes information about the loan and the time and location of the sale—in most states, the sale must take place at least three to five weeks after the notice is published.

Between the dates when the notice is published and the sale takes place, most lenders allow you to reinstate the loan by making up the back payments and paying some penalties. But if interest rates have gone up since you took out your loan, the lender may refuse to let you reinstate the loan, preferring to foreclose and resell it at a higher interest rate. Also, many investors, looking for a good bargain, will buy houses at this time. Again, those investors won't pay top dollar. They will usually pay enough to cover what you owe the lender, but not your equity.

Example: Sue obtained a mortgage three years ago at 9% interest. Her monthly payments are $725. She has missed four payments and the lender has started to foreclose. Sue's mother just offered to give her $3,190 to pay what she owes—$725 x 4 = $2,900 plus a 10% penalty of $290. Although interest rates are up to 10%, the lender lets Sue reinstate the loan, figuring the 1% increase in interest isn't worth the time and expense of foreclosing and reselling the house.

If you haven't reinstated the loan or sold the house by the date of the foreclosure sale, the lender will accelerate the loan. This means you no longer can reinstate the loan. The only way you can keep your house is by paying the entire balance immediately.

At the foreclosure sale, anyone with a financial interest in your house will probably attend. This includes the first, second and even third mortgage (deed of trust) holders and any creditor, such as the IRS or a construction worker who has placed a lien on your house. Investors who like to purchase distressed (real estate lingo for foreclosed on) property will also be present. The foreclosure sale will probably take place in the foreclosing lender's lawyer's office.

The lender who foreclosed—usually the holder of the first mortgage, but sometimes a home equity lender—makes the first bid, usually for the amount owed him, but often, especially in depressed economies, for less. It may seem like the lender is bidding to buy the house from itself. Both you and the lender have ownership interest in the house, however, and so by bidding, the lender is essentially buying you out. If the sale is for more than you owe your creditors who have a security interest in your house, you're entitled to the excess. But the foreclosing lender first gets to deduct the costs of foreclosing and selling, usually a few thousand dollars.

Any other lender or lienholder will get worried if that is the only bid because the amount covers only what is owed the foreclosing lender. If the sale goes through at that price, the holders of the other mortgages get nothing from the sale. Thus, if the property is worth more than the amount the foreclosing lender bid, another lender or lienholder may bid to protect her interest. So might a buyer who sees that the property's value far exceeds the amount owed the lenders and lienholders. The house is sold to the highest bidder.

> **Example:** Steve's house is worth $210,000, though he paid only $120,000 for it ten years ago. He has now hit hard times. He owes the original lender $74,000. A few years back he took out a home equity loan and owes that lender $35,000. He also owes the IRS $43,000 in back taxes,

interest and penalties. Thus, Steve's lenders are owed $152,000.

The foreclosing lender started the bidding at $74,000. The holder of the home equity loan then bid $109,000 (the amount of the original loan plus the home equity loan). The successful bid was by an investor for $165,000, $45,000 less than the house is worth, but enough to pay off Steve's creditors who have a security interest in his house. Steve gets the $13,000 balance.

If no one bids above the foreclosing lender at the sale, the house reverts to the lender for the amount of its bid. In some states, the successful bidder doesn't actually get title to the house for a period of time, from several days to several months. During that period, you can "redeem" the property, that is, pay off the foreclosing lender the entire balance of what you owe that lender and get your house back. This is the likely scenario in very depressed markets. In stronger markets, however, investors or other buyers will probably bid.

 Watch Out for Deficiency Balances

A deficiency balance is the difference between the amount you owe the foreclosing lender and the value of the property. In most states, if the value doesn't cover what you owe, the lender is entitled to a deficiency for the difference. The lender usually must schedule a court hearing and present evidence of the value of the property to obtain the deficiency.

A lender with a deficiency can use the collection techniques covered in Chapter 5, and will often accept less than the full amount if you can offer a lump sum settlement. If you owe a lot of money or there's any easy target for collection (such as a large bank account or monthly wages), the lender is likely to pass your debt onto a collection agency or a lawyer (to sue you).

One possible way to avoid a deficiency balance is to deed the property back to the lender in lieu of foreclosure. (This strategy is discussed in Chapter 3, Section C2.) If the lender agrees to accept the deed, the lender is essentially agreeing that the amount you owe equals the current value of the property, eliminating any deficiency balance.

State	Code Section	Limits on Deficiency Balances After Foreclosure
California	CCP 580d	If a house is foreclosed on by a lender from whom you borrowed money to finance the purchase of the house, the lender is not entitled to a deficiency. If any other creditor forecloses, such as the holder of a refinanced loan or a creditor with a lien, the creditor will be entitled to a deficiency if the sale doesn't cover what you owe.
Massachusetts	244-17A	Lender has only two years to collect deficiency.
Minnesota	582.30	If the foreclosure has a redemption period of at least six months, the lender is not entitled to a deficiency. If a house is foreclosed on by a lender from whom you borrowed money to finance the purchase of the house, the lender is not entitled to a deficiency.
Montana	71-1-232	If a house is foreclosed on by a lender from whom you borrowed money to finance the purchase of the house, the lender is not entitled to a deficiency.
North Carolina	45-21.38	If mortgage includes any part of purchase price, lender is not entitled to deficiency judgment.
Ohio	2329.08	Lender is limited to 2 years to collect a deficiency on a 2-family or smaller home that was claimed as a homestead. (See Chapter 13.)
Washington	61.24.100	Deficiency is prohibited unless real estate was not purchased—or lien created by creditor with debt—for family, personal or household use.

C. Repossessing or Taking Property Securing a Debt

AS EXPLAINED IN CHAPTER 1, a secured debt is one linked to a specific item of property—called collateral—that guarantees payment of the debt. On secured debts of personal property, if you don't pay, the creditor can simply take the personal property pledged as collateral for the loan.

The most common type of loans that let a secured creditor take your personal property if you miss a payment are:

- motor vehicle loans for cars, trucks, RVs, tractors, mobile homes, boats and the like

- department store charges for items such as furniture, rugs, electronic equipment, computers or appliances when you pledge the item purchased as collateral by signing a security agreement, and

- personal loans from banks where you pledge valuable existing personal property, such as your car, as security.

Limitations on Secured Loans

The federal government has recognized the inherent problems of having consumers' household goods and personal effects repossessed by lenders when they default on secured loans. Thus, unless you are actually buying the item, a lender cannot take a security interest in your clothing, personal effects, furniture, appliances, linens, china, crockery, kitchenware, one radio and one television or wedding ring. [1]

---

[1] Credit Practices Rule, 16 C.F.R. § 444. A few states have additional prohibitions. See Chapter 6, Section C3h.

1. What Constitutes a Default?

If you miss even one payment, you have defaulted on your loan and, under most security agreements, the creditor is entitled to take the goods. If you make your payments but otherwise don't comply with an important term of the security agreement, the creditor can declare you in default and take the property on that ground. Be sure you read the security agreement's fine print terms carefully. Lenders often have the right to declare a secured debt in default, even if you're all paid up, if:

- you sell the collateral (your security agreement may bar you from "hypothecating," "alienating" or doing something else not necessarily written in English to the property, which generally means you can't sell it)

- the collateral is destroyed or stolen, or its value substantially depreciates

- you let required insurance lapse—some lenders require that you have collision and comprehensive insurance on motor vehicles, or that you buy credit life or credit disability insurance

- you are sued by another creditor for failure to pay a debt or the collateral is attached by another creditor

- you become insolvent (as defined by your lender) or file for bankruptcy

- you refuse to let the creditor examine the collateral at his request, or

- the creditor has a "feeling" that the prospect of your paying is uncertain. In Louisiana, this one does not have to be spelled out in the loan agreement—a creditor may annul any contract if she believes that the contract causes or increases your insolvency. [2]

---

[2]Louisiana Civil Code § 2306.

2. When You Have Defaulted

In general, a creditor does not have to give you advance warning or obtain a court order to take your property pledged as collateral (more likely, to send a hired "repo" person to take the property). Creditors in Louisiana and Wisconsin, however, must get a court order before taking any item of personal property. And in California, creditors need a court order to take any item other than a motor vehicle (car, truck, motorcycle, RV).

But even outside of Louisiana, Wisconsin and California, a creditor is unlikely to go ahead and take your property unless you have defaulted in the past, have missed several payments or are uncooperative, or if the creditor has learned something worrisome about your finances—for example, your wife calls the finance company to say that she has left you because you were arrested.

You can, of course, voluntarily return the collateral to the creditor or repossessor, but she doesn't have to take it. And she probably won't if it's worth far less than you owe. If you want to give the property back, first call the creditor—ask to speak to someone in the collections department—and find out if your entire debt will be canceled when the collateral is returned. If it isn't canceled, there probably isn't much point in returning the item, as you'll be liable for the difference between what the collateral sells for and what you owe. (See Section 4, below.)

a. How Motor Vehicles Are Repossessed

The first property most lenders and repossessors go after is a motor vehicle—especially if the loan agreement was to finance the purchase of a new car or truck as opposed to a personal loan agreement where you pledge your existing car as collateral. In a number of states, however—including Colorado, Iowa, Kansas, Maine, Massachusetts, Mississippi, Missouri, New Hampshire, South Carolina, West Virginia, Wisconsin and the District of Columbia— the lender must first send you notice of the default and give you the right to make up the payments (called a right to "cure") before repossessing your car.

In addition, a repo person can't use force to get to your vehicle—repossessions must occur without any "breach of the peace."

Unfortunately, breach of the peace lets a repo person grab your vehicle almost anytime you're not in it or standing guard. It's legal to hotwire a car. It's legal to use a duplicate key and take a car. It's legal for her to remove a car from a carport or open (meaning the door is up) garage. In most states, it's legal to take a car from a garage where the door is closed but unlocked, but a few cautious repossessors won't do this. It's illegal to break into a locked garage, even by using a duplicate key. But a repossessor might anyway, especially in parts of the country where the repossession won't be nullified and all the lender will be required to do is fix the lock.

The repossessor can't take your car until she finds it. The lender will supply her with your home and work addresses, and any other useful information such as where you attend graduate school. Then the repossessor starts looking. If she finds the car in your driveway or on the street in front of your house, she'll wait until you're asleep or out, use a master key or hotwire it, and then drive away.

If the car isn't near your house, the repossessor will search the neighborhood. Many debtors, fearful of having their car repossessed, park it about three blocks from their home. This is the distance they figure is far enough away to be hard to find, but close enough to still be convenient to use. Repossessors know this trick, however, and often find a car within ten minutes after starting to search. Knowing this, some people leave their car in a neighbor's locked garage, an approach that will frustrate the repo person at least for a little while. In most states, however, if you hide your car and the repossessor finds it, you lose your right to get it back. (See Section 3, below.)

b. How Other Property Is Taken or Repossessed

Most creditors don't hire repossessors to take back personal property other than cars, trucks, motorcycles and the like because:

- the loan is often only a few thousand dollars or less
- the property may be worth far less than you owe, and
- the repossessor will have a hard time getting in your house.

A few major department stores, however, especially Sears, encourage debtors to return property bought with a security agreement. If the property is less than a year old, Sears will usually credit your account for 100% of what you owe.

If the lender hires a repo person to take back your property, you don't have to give the property back or let the repo person in your house unless a sheriff shows up with a court order telling you to do so. If, however, your property is sitting in the back yard— for example, the repo person has come to take your new gas barbecue and lawn furniture—it's generally fair game. But the repo person can't use force to get into your house or to take your back yard furniture—for example, you can't be thrown out of a lawn chair. As stated above, repossessions must occur without any breach of the peace.

If you or a member of your family ask the repossessor to leave your property, and she doesn't, it is probably a breach of the peace. So is using abusive language or showing up with a gun-carrying sheriff in an effort to intimidate you. But lying isn't a breach of the peace.[3]

Entering your house when you are away with a duplicate key to take your refrigerator or living room sofa is seldom done by repo people because it

---

[3]A few courts have held that a breach of the peace occurs only when the repossessor uses violence. See, for example, *K.B. Oil Co. v. Ford Motor Credit Co.*, 811 F.2d 310 (6th Cir. 1987).

is illegal. Only the rarest of repossessors would take this risk.

3. Can You Get the Vehicle or Other Property Back?

If your car or other property is taken, you have a short time during which you can get it back by redeeming it. Redeeming it means paying the balance due. The lender may let you redeem the property by reinstating the contract.

Reinstating the contract—getting the property back and resuming the payments under the same terms of the original agreement—requires that you pay all the past due installments and late fees, as well as the costs the lender has incurred in taking and storing the property (often a few hundred dollars). This right of reinstatement is limited, however, and you probably can't get the property back if you:

- had the contract reinstated in the past
- lied on your credit application
- hid the property to avoid repossession
- didn't take care of the property and its value has substantially diminished, or
- have committed violence against the lender or repossessor.

The lender must give you a notice of your right to redeem the property after repossession, even if the lender thinks you have given up the right. If the lender doesn't, you may have the right to get the property back for nothing—but you will have to resume making payments on your loan. If you have been given notice and want to try to reinstate the contract, contact the lender as soon as possible to work out an agreement.

If you don't redeem the property within the time permitted by the agreement, the lender will send you a formal notice of its intent to sell the property.

Personal Property in Repossessed Cars

If the repo person takes your car, you're entitled to get back all your personal belongings not attached to, but inside of, the car when it was repossessed. This means that you can probably get back your gym shorts but not your $500 stereo system (assuming it was installed). Also, make sure you look at your loan agreement. Some say that you must make that request within 24 hours of the repossession. To be safe, promptly contact the lender after your car is repossessed and ask that your property be returned. If he is uncooperative—which is unlikely—consider suing in small claims court. (See Chapter 9.)

4. Beware of Deficiency Balances

If your inclination is to not cure the default and redeem the property, you may change your mind once you read this section. If you don't redeem the property within the time provided in the lender's notice of its intent to sell the property, the property will be sold. If the proceeds don't cover the total of what you owe—and they never do—you may be liable for the balance, called a deficiency. Often that balance is a lot.

Bankruptcy note. If you're planning to file for bankruptcy, you probably don't have to worry about any deficiency—it will likely be wiped out in your bankruptcy case.

Are You Always Liable for a Deficiency?

In nearly half the states (see chart, below), you won't be liable for a deficiency balance if the amount you originally paid is less than a few thousand dollars. This means you will almost always be liable for a deficiency if your car, truck or motorcycle is taken. Also, most states bar creditors from collecting a deficiency if:

- the creditor has repeatedly accepted late payments and then suddenly repossesses the property without telling you

- you are not notified of your right to cure the default or redeem the property

- you are not notified of the sale, or

- the sale is not commercially reasonable or the sale price was unfair—you'll have a hard time showing this.

When the lender sends you a notice announcing that the property will be sold, you'll see that the sale is one of two kinds. If it will be a public sale—open to anyone—you must be told the date, time and place of the sale. If it's a private sale—the lender tells certain people who it feels might be interested in the sale—you might just be told of the date.

In most states, the creditor chooses whether to have a public or private sale. A private sale can only be held if the item "is of a type customarily sold in a recognized market" or "is the subject of widely distributed standard price quotations." Cars are frequently sold at private sales to which used car dealers and others who regularly buy repossessed cars are invited.

The lender must conduct a "commercially reasonable" sale, but no one knows quite what that means. In fact, it often includes sales where only dealers are invited, all who have a motive to keep the bids very low. This is one reason why most property sold at repossession sales bring in far less than what is owed the lender. For instance, a car valued at $12,000 might sell for $5,000, and a refrigerator worth $800 might sell for $250. And even though you could have sold the item for twice as much, this sale will be considered "commercially reasonable."

Should you care what the sale brings in? Yes, because after the item is sold, the sale price is subtracted from what you owe the lender. Then, the cost of repossessing, storing and selling the property is added to the difference. Nine times out of ten, you are liable for that balance—the deficiency balance. To collect, the lender can send you letters and call you. If you still don't pay, the lender can sue you.

State	Code Section	Limitations on Repossessions and Deficiency Balances
Alabama	5-19-13	If lender repossesses an item where the price you originally paid was $1,000 or less, you are not liable for any deficiency.
Arizona	44-5501	If lender repossesses an item where the price you originally paid was $1,000 or less, you are not liable for any deficiency. If lender sues you instead of repossessing the item, lender cannot repossess after obtaining a judgment.
California	CC 1812.5	Lender cannot repossess any consumer goods (except motor vehicles) without a court order. If lender repossesses a non-motor-vehicle consumer good after obtaining a court judgment, you are not liable for any deficiency.
	HS 18038.7	Lender is not entitled to deficiency upon sale of mobile home, manufactured home, commercial coach, truck camper or floating home.
Colorado	4-9-503	Lender cannot repossess mobile home or trailer unless you have vacated or abandoned the property or the lender has a court judgment.
	5-5-103	If lender repossesses an item where price you originally paid was $2,100 or less, you are not liable for any deficiency. If lender sues you instead of repossessing the item, lender cannot repossess after obtaining a judgment.
Connecticut	42-98	If lender repossesses, you are not liable for any deficiency except for cars with cash price over $2,000 if fair market value is less than the balance on the contract.
District of Columbia	28-3812	If lender repossesses an item where the price you originally paid was $2,000 or less, you are not liable for any deficiency. If lender sues you instead of repossessing the item, lender cannot repossess after obtaining a judgment.
Florida	516.31	If lender repossesses an item where the price you originally paid was $2,000 or less, you are not liable for any deficiency.
Idaho	28-45-103	If lender repossesses an item where the price you originally paid was $1,000 or less, you are not liable for any deficiency. If lender sues you instead of repossessing the item, lender cannot repossess after obtaining a judgment.
Indiana	24-4.5-5-103	If lender repossesses an item where the price you originally paid was $2,800 or less, you are not liable for any deficiency. If lender sues you instead of repossessing the item, lender cannot repossess after obtaining a judgment.
Kansas	16a-5-103	If lender repossesses an item where the price you originally paid was $1,000 or less, you are not liable for any deficiency. If lender sues you instead of repossessing the item, lender cannot repossess after obtaining a judgment.
Louisiana	13:4106	If seller repossesses, you are not liable for any deficiency if seller did not obtain appraisal before the sale.
Maine	9A-5-103	If lender repossesses an item where the price you originally paid was $2,800 or less, you are not liable for any deficiency. If lender sues you instead of repossessing the item, lender cannot repossess after obtaining a judgment.

State	Code Section	Limitations on Repossessions and Deficiency Balances
Massachusetts	Ch. 255 ¶ 13J	If lender repossesses an item where the price you originally paid was $1,000 or less, you are not liable for any deficiency. If lender sues you instead of repossessing the item, lender cannot repossess after obtaining a judgment.
Minnesota	325G.22	If lender repossesses an item where the price you originally paid was $4,800 or less, you are not liable for any deficiency. If lender sues you instead of repossessing the item, lender cannot repossess after obtaining a judgment.
Missouri	408.556	If lender repossesses an item where the price you originally paid was $500 or less, you are not liable for any deficiency.
Oklahoma	14A-5-103	If lender repossesses an item where the price you originally paid was $2,500 or less, you are not liable for any deficiency. If lender sues you instead of repossessing the item, lender cannot repossess after obtaining a judgment.
Oregon	83.830	If lender repossesses an item where the price you originally paid was $1,250 or less, you are not liable for any deficiency. If lender sues you instead of repossessing the item, lender cannot repossess after obtaining a judgment.
South Carolina	37-5-103	If lender repossesses an item where the price you originally paid was $1,500 or less, you are not liable for any deficiency. If lender sues you instead of repossessing the item, lender cannot repossess after obtaining a judgment.
Utah	70C-7-101	If lender repossesses an item where the price you originally paid was $3,000 or less, you are not liable for any deficiency. If lender sues you instead of repossessing the item, lender cannot repossess after obtaining a judgment.
West Virginia	46A-2-119	If lender repossesses an item where the price you originally paid was $1,000 or less, you are not liable for any deficiency. If lender sues you instead of repossessing the item, lender cannot repossess after obtaining a judgment.
Wisconsin	425.209	If lender repossesses an item where the price you originally paid was $1,000 or less, you are not liable for any deficiency. If lender sues you instead of repossessing the item, lender cannot repossess after obtaining a judgment.
Wyoming	40-14-503	If lender repossesses an item where the price you originally paid was $1,000 or less, you are not liable for any deficiency. If lender sues you instead of repossessing the item, lender cannot repossess after obtaining a judgment.

If the lender or bill collector comes knocking to collect a deficiency, review how your repossession was handled. If the lender didn't tell you of your right to cure the default or redeem the property, or didn't sell the item in a commercially reasonable manner, resist paying. If the lender sues you, file your answer with the court and tell the court of the violation. If you'd rather take the offensive, you can sue the lender for wrongful repossession. For large items, such as cars, you'll probably need a lawyer. But for smaller items, you can probably represent yourself in small claims court. (See Chapter 9.)

Suggestion: If your property, especially a car, is about to be repossessed, cure the default or redeem the property and ask for a contract reinstatement just to get the car back so you can sell it yourself. Even if you get $7,000 for a $9,000 car, it's better than the lender repossessing it and selling it for $3,000. You can use the $7,000 to pay off your car lender and will owe only $2,000 more, far less than the $6,000 you'd owe if the lender sold it through repossession.

D. Taking Property Before a Court Judgment (Pre-Judgment Attachment of Unsecured Property)

A PRE-JUDGMENT ATTACHMENT IS a legal procedure which lets a creditor tie up property before obtaining a court judgment. It is the *unsecured creditor's* way of telling the world that you owe him some money and that the property covered by the attachment can be used to pay the creditor if he wins in court. *Secured creditors* can, under the terms of the security agreement, take your property if you don't pay without suing you. (See Section C, above.) They don't need to attach your property.

Because a pre-judgment attachment can make it easy for a creditor to collect what he is owed if he eventually sues you and gets a judgment, a creditor may use one against your property if you live out of state, have fled the state or the creditor believes you are about to spend, sell or conceal your property.

In most states, a pre-judgment attachment works like this. As the creditor is about to sue you, she prepares a special document called a "writ of attachment" which lists your property that she believes is being held by others. The writ of attachment must be approved by a judge or court clerk, and then the creditor serves it on you and on everyone she thinks has some of your property. Serving means making sure you get a copy. Usually, you must be hand-delivered a copy, but in some cases the creditor can just mail it to you. The most common property to attach is deposit accounts—savings, checking, money markets, certificates of deposit and the like.

The serving of the writ freezes your property—the holder of your property can't let you sell it, give it away or, in the case of deposit accounts, make withdrawals. You must be given the opportunity to have a prompt court hearing—this isn't the trial where you argue whether or not you owe the debt. This hearing pertains to only the attachment, and you'll want to argue that the attached property is exempt (see Chapter 11), you need the property to support yourself and your family or the value of the property attached exceeds what you owe.

If you don't show up (or you do show up but lose the court hearing), the court will order that the attachment remain on your property pending the outcome of the lawsuit. You won't be able to withdraw or otherwise dispose of any of the attached property. You can get the attachment released by filing a bond for the amount of money you owe. But if you don't file a bond, and the creditor wins the lawsuit, she's almost certain to be paid out of the attached property.

E. Lawsuit

IF YOU DON'T PAY a debt, the most likely consequence is that you will be sued, unless the creditor thinks you are "judgment proof" and will be for the foreseeable future. Being judgment proof means that you don't have any money or property to pay the debt and aren't likely to get any soon. But because most court judgments last many (up to 20) years, and in some states can be renewed indefinitely, people who currently are broke (especially younger people) may nevertheless be sued on the assumption that they'll come into some money or property eventually.

Being judgment proof doesn't mean that you have no money or property at all. Even if you are sued and the creditor obtains a court judgment, you are allowed to keep certain items of property—called exempt property. (Exempt property is covered in detail in Chapter 11.) Suffice it to say that if you receive no income except government benefits, such as Social Security or unemployment, and have limited personal property and no real property, you are judgment proof, at least right now.

If a creditor sues you in regular court (as opposed to small claims court) and you fight it, the lawsuit can take time—often several years—to run through the court system. If you don't oppose the lawsuit, or let the court automatically enter a judgment against you (called a default judgment), however, the case could be over in 30 to 60 days from the time the papers are served on you.

If the creditor gets a judgment, he has a number of ways to enforce it. If you are working, the most common method is to attach your wages, meaning a portion of what you earn is removed from your paycheck and sent to the creditor before you ever see it. Next most common is to attach your bank account. See Chapter 9 for more details on getting sued and defending against judgment collections.

F. Lien on Your Real Estate

A LIEN IS A NOTICE ATTACHED to your property telling the world that a creditor claims you owe her some money. Liens on real property are a common way for creditors to collect what they are owed. To sell any real estate, you must have "clear title." A lien on your house, mobile home, farm or other real estate makes your title unclear. To clear up the title to be able to sell your house, you must pay off the lien. Thus, creditors know that putting a lien on real estate is a cheap and almost guaranteed way of collecting what they are owed—sooner or later.

Most creditors can place a lien on your real property as soon as they receive a court judgment. But many creditors need not wait that long. Here are examples of other property liens:

- If you don't pay your property taxes, the local government can place a lien on your house. When you sell your house—or a lender forecloses on it—the government will stand in line and get paid out of the proceeds of the sale.

- If you fail to pay back taxes after receiving a series of notices from the IRS, it may place a lien on your real property, especially if you don't have regular wages to attach—you're unemployed, self-employed or sporadically employed. While many creditors who place liens on real property—except mortgage or home equity lenders—will simply wait until the house is sold or refinanced to get paid and won't force a sale, the IRS doesn't like to wait. For more information on dealing with tax liens, see *Stand Up to the IRS*, by Frederick W. Daily (Nolo Press).

- If you owe a lot in child support or alimony, the recipient may put a lien on your house. The lien will stay until you pay the support you owe or until you sell your house, whichever happens first. (See Chapter 8.)

- If a contractor works on your house or furnishes construction materials to be used on your house, and you don't pay him, he can record—in the county office where your property deed is recorded—a lien on your property called a "mechanic's lien." In most states, he must record the lien within one to six months of when he wasn't paid. He then must sue you to enforce the lien within about one year (the range, depending on the state, is one month to six years) of when he recorded it. If he wins his lawsuit, he can force the sale of your home to be paid.

G. Jail

JAILING SOMEONE FOR not paying a debt is prohibited in most instances. In a few situations, however, you could land behind bars.

- If you willfully violate a court order. This comes up most frequently when you fail to make court-ordered child support or alimony payments, the recipient requests a hearing before a judge and the judge concludes that you could have paid, but didn't. (See Chapter 8.) But imprisonment for willful violation of a court order is not limited to child support or alimony situations.

- If you are convicted of willfully refusing to pay income taxes.

- If you fail to show up for a debtor's examination. A debtor's examination is a procedure where a judgment creditor, with court approval, orders you to come to court and answer questions about your property and finances. (See Chapter 9, Section F5.)

- If you are about to conceal yourself or your property to avoid paying, and a creditor who has a judgment against you presents evidence to a court showing as much.

- If you live in Rhode Island or Wisconsin, which still have debtors' prisons. In Wisconsin, you may be jailed only if a creditor has a judgment against you for a tort—such as negligence (such as causing a car accident), assault, battery, infliction of emotional distress, false imprisonment, libel and slander—you committed and you refuse to pay. In both states, poor debtors, after going to jail, may request a hearing before a judge, swear that they have no money or property and get out of jail. [4]

---

[4]See General Laws of Rhode Island § 10-13-1 and Wisconsin Statutes Annotated § 898.01. I found no case interpreting the Wisconsin statute. In a Rhode Island case, however, the court held that a debtor who was imprisoned for not paying a $3,100 judgment on a promissory note could be released after swearing that he had no money or property. *White v. Tenth District Court*, 251 A.2d 539 (1969).

Debtors' Prisons—A Little History

The mere thought of debtors' prison probably sends shivers up your spine. It should. As unusual and cruel as it seems today, debtors' prison was a major collection method in the 18th and mid-19th centuries of our republic, and for many centuries before that in Europe. Creditors who were owed money could simply ask the sheriff to arrest the debtor and throw him (literally him—women were not allowed to own property and therefore couldn't get into debt trouble) in jail. If he couldn't raise the bail, and most couldn't as they had no money, he sat in his cell until someone paid his bill or bailed him out.

Many creditors felt the humiliation of jail was too much to impose on a debtor without first giving him a chance to pay what he owed. Those creditors, rather than having the debtor arrested, sued to obtain a judgment entitling them to payment. If the debtor didn't pay after a judge ordered him to, the creditor then asked the sheriff to arrest the debtor and toss him into the slammer.

Judicial attitude toward debtors and debtors' prison is reflected in one 17th century English case:

"If a man be taken in execution, and lie in prison for debt, neither the plaintiff at whose suit he is arrested, nor the sheriff who took him is bound to find him meat, drink or clothes, but he must live on his own, or on the charity of others; and if no man will relieve him, let him die, in the name of God, says the law; and so say I." *Manby v. Scott*, 1 Mod. 132, 84 Eng. Rep. 781 (1659).

Local businesses, preachers, butchers and market keepers often felt sorry for these prisoners and would try to help them out, but most sat in their cells until someone paid their debts. Even royalty felt compassion for many imprisoned debtors. Just outside of the Palace at Holyrood in Edinburgh, Scotland, there was (and still is) a small triangular-shaped area in which debtors could stay free from their creditors.

In 1830, an American Indian prisoner lamented on the absurdity of his being imprisoned as punishment for not delivering the payment of beaver skins. "If I was put there to compel me to perform my agreement, my prosecutors have selected a poor place for me to catch beavers."

Public indignation with debtors' prisons found a voice in Silas M. Stillwill, a New York lawyer. In 1831 he introduced the Act to Abolish Imprisonment for Debt, and by 1900, virtually all states outlawed debtors' prisons. But the fact that we had debtors' prisons in this country is an indication of an early attitude supporting payment of debts at virtually any cost.

H. Bank Setoff When You Owe Money to a Bank

A BANK SETOFF happens when a bank, savings and loan or credit union where you have a loan removes money from your deposit account—checking, savings, certificate of deposit, money market or the like—to cover a payment you missed on that loan.

There are a few limitations. First, at the time you take out the loan, the bank must disclose in writing its right to use a setoff. If it doesn't, and later takes funds out of your account, it has probably violated the Federal Truth in Lending Act. (See Chapter 6, Section C1.) You can sue for damages—the amount taken out of your account and any other damages you suffer, such as bounced check fees.

Second, the bank cannot take money out of your account to cover a missed credit card payment. If you have a checking account with the same bank that issued your Visa card, for example, the bank can't touch your deposits.[5]

Third, most states will not let the bank take money derived from unemployment compensation, disability benefits or other property exempt under state or federal law. (See Chapter 11 for information on exempt property.)[6]

In addition, California prohibits bank setoffs if the aggregate balance of all your accounts with that financial institution is under $1,000. And in Maryland, all bank setoffs are prohibited unless you have explicitly authorized the setoff or a court has ordered one.[7]

I. Collection of Unsecured Debts from Third Parties

IF A THIRD PERSON holds property for you or owes you money, most states give creditors the right to sue those third parties to reach your property or the money. Sometimes that third person is a financial institution—bank, savings and loan or credit union—where you have a deposit account. Or, it may be a landlord or utility company to whom you've made a security deposit. Or, it could be a financial adviser, such as a stock broker, with whom you've deposited funds to invest on your behalf.

In some states, for a creditor to pursue the third person, the creditor must first obtain a court judgment against you and have been unable to collect it. In most states, however, the creditor can sue the third person even before getting a judgment against you. If that happens, you will have to be notified of the suit and allowed the opportunity to contest the debt.

J. Interception of Your Tax Refund

IF YOU OWE BACK student loan payments, income taxes or child support, the agency trying to collect can request that the IRS intercept your federal income tax refund and apply the money to your debt. (See Chapters 7 and 8.)

Before your money is actually taken, the agency must notify you that the IRS proposes to intercept your refund. You are given the opportunity to present written evidence or to have a hearing to show that the amount proposed to be taken has been paid, is more than you owe or is not legally enforceable. If you are married and the amount to be taken out is for child support from a previous relationship, your spouse can file a claim for her share of the refund.

---

[5]See 15 U.S.C. § 1666h; Regulation Z of the Truth In Lending Act, 12 C.F.R. § 226.12(d).

[6]The leading case in this area is *Kruger v. Wells Fargo Bank*, 11 Cal.2d 352 (Calif. 1974).

[7]California Finance Code § 6660; Maryland Commercial Law § 15-702.

K. Loss of Insurance Coverage

IF YOU MISS YOUR payments on any insurance policy you have, your coverage will end. Most insurance companies will give you a 30-day grace period—that is, if your payment is due on the 10th of the month and you don't pay until the 9th of the following month, you won't lose your coverage. A few companies may let you get away with 60 days, but don't count on it. After 60 days, your policy is sure to lapse.

If your policy has lapsed, and your lender required you to obtain the insurance as a condition of your loan, you could face more than a canceled insurance policy. Because usually only lenders who make secured loans require insurance coverage— auto, homeowner's, or credit life or disability—the lender could declare you in default of your loan and either repossess your personal property or foreclose on your house. Alternatively, the lender could pay for the insurance and bill you for it.

L. Loss of Utility Service

IF YOU MISS PAYMENTS on your utility or telephone bill, the utility company will cut off your service. If the utility company is publicly owned, it must give you notice of the disconnect and the opportunity to discuss it with a representative of the utility company.[8] In most states, except California and a few others, a private utility company doesn't need to give you any notice.

M. Take a Deep Breath

THIS CHAPTER HAS just described the worst-case scenarios for all of your debts. If you ignore all your creditors, have some property and a job, some of these things will happen to you. This is why I don't recommend sticking your head in the sand. Pull out your list of essential and nonessential debts. After reading this chapter, you should know where you are most vulnerable—that is, where you are most likely to lose some property. If not paying a debt you considered nonessential means you'll probably lose your bank account, move that debt to the essential list and rethink your strategy.

Most important, focus on finding a solution. ■

---

[8]This is because a publicly owned utility company cannot deprive you of due process of the law, according to the U.S. Supreme Court. See *Memphis Light, Gas & Water Div. v. Craft*, 436 U.S. 1 (1978).

Chapter 5

WHEN THE BILL COLLECTOR CALLS

The most trifling actions that affect a man's credit are to be regarded. The sound of your hammer at five in the morning, or nine at night, heard by a creditor, makes him easier six months longer; but if he sees you at a billiard table, or hears your voice at a tavern when you should be at work, he sends for his money the next day.

—Benjamin Franklin, American statesman,
philosopher & inventor, 1706-1790

AS RECENTLY AS 20 YEARS ago, bill collectors regularly threatened, scared, lied to, harassed, intimidated and otherwise abused debtors. Debtors were told they'd go to jail for not paying their bills, friends and relatives were often interrogated and threatened with financial and bodily harm if they didn't tell where runaway debtors were living, and bill collectors published lists of people who didn't pay their debts.

The federal Fair Debt Collection Practices Act (FDCPA), passed in 1977, outlaws unfair collection practices including debtor harassment. This law has greatly improved conditions for debtors, although an unfortunate number of collectors still resort to abusive practices—especially with debtors whose first language is not English or with debtors who are not U.S. citizens.

Shame, Guilt and Maybe a Little Fear

When the Fair Debt Collection Practices Act was passed, bill collectors changed their main approach from abuse to fear. But the fear tactic of the 1980s became less and less effective as debtors learned their rights. In the early 1990s, most bill collectors abandoned their fear tactics and instead worked on debtors' guilt and shame.

Today, however, many debtors don't react to the shame and guilt tactics. And so a few debt collectors again try to instill fear. As one debt collector told me recently, "We like debtors to think that we're going to break their knees if they don't pay."

In dealing with a bill collector, adopt a plan and stick with it. One choice—if you have no money, plan to file for bankruptcy or just don't feel like paying right now—is to not talk to the collector. As explained in Section E1, below, under the FDCPA you can request that a collection agency stop contacting you. Another option, if you really need more time to pay, is to contact the bill collector to negotiate a payment schedule.

If you do contact a bill collector, realize that as nice as a bill collector appears, he is not your friend and does not have your best interest at heart. HE WANTS YOUR MONEY. To get it, he may ask you to take him into his confidence regarding your personal problems, or he may claim that he's trying to save you from ruining your credit. Don't believe him. He doesn't really care about your problems or your credit rating. His only goal is to get you to send him some green bills. Stick to your plan. If you want extra time to pay or to lower your payments, insist on it. If you want the bill collector to go away, tell him not to contact you.

 This Chapter Assumes You Have Not Been Sued

This chapter focuses on pre-judgment collection efforts. If the creditor or a collection agency has sued you and obtained a court judgment, his collection options increase and you will want to read Chapter 9.

A. Original Creditor or Collection Agency?

LET ME EMPHASIZE the difference between the original creditor and a collection agency. As we go along, this distinction will be important, primarily because the federal law regulating collection agencies doesn't apply to original creditors. Here are the key terms.

Original creditor. An original creditor is a business or person (such as an owner of a local store, a large-chain department store, a credit card company or a bank that gave you a loan) who first extended you credit. Sometimes original creditors are called credit grantors.

Collection agency. A collection agency is a company hired by an original creditor to collect the original creditor's debt for it. Under the Fair Debt Collection Practices Act (FDCPA), a collection agency also includes:

- an original creditor who sets up a separate office (operated under a different name) to collect its debts, and

- a lawyer, who does not work as an employee of the original creditor, but who has been hired by an original creditor to help the original creditor collect its bills. More and more lawyers are getting into collections work, which means you could be sued more quickly than if the debt goes to a collection agency first.

Form Letters From an Attorney

If you get what appears to be a form collection letter with a lawyer's mechanically reproduced signature at the bottom (and perhaps her letterhead at the top), the lawyer may be violating the FDCPA—and you may have a grounds for suing for $1,000.

Under the FDCPA, a lawyer must review each individual collection case before her name appears on any collection letters. She can't authorize a form letter and then let the bill collector mail out letters bearing her signature without reviewing each particular debtor's file. [1]

Bill collector or debt collector. The term bill collector or debt collector can refer to either an original creditor or a collection agency. Be sure you know who you are dealing with.

As mentioned, the difference between an original creditor and a collection agency is important. Original creditors *are not* governed by the FDCPA. Several states, however, have fair debt collection laws that apply to both original creditors and collection agencies. (These are outlined in Section D4, below.) Also, many states have laws that refer to collection agencies. To the extent that those laws more strictly regulate collection agencies, they—not the FDCPA—apply.

Efforts to collect past-due bills usually follow a standard pattern. Original creditors first try to collect their own debts. When you owe money, you'll first receive a series of letters or phone calls from the original creditor's collection department (they may call themselves "customer service representatives"). Although most creditors make first contact a few weeks after you miss a payment, some more aggressive companies begin hard core collection efforts within 24 to 36 hours after your payment is due. If you don't respond to the letters or calls within about six months, most original creditors will either send your account to a collection agency or write it off as a bad debt.

Some original creditors concerned about their reputations hire "mild" collection agencies. They realize that you may be a customer again in the future and they don't want to alienate you. Some original creditors, however, couldn't care less about what you think of them. They are fed up with you for not paying and will find the most aggressive agency around to be sure you do.

---

[1] See *Masuda v. Thomas Richards & Co.*, 759 F. Supp. 1456 (1991); *Clomon v. Jackson*, 988 F.2d 1314 (2d Cir. 1993).

Original Creditors "Pretending" to Be Collection Agencies

Some creditors buy fill-in-the-blanks collection letters. The letters list a collection agency's name at the top to give the false impression that the letters come from the agency. These creditors, especially those with small bills—such as magazine publishers and doctors—simply want to scare you into paying. They have found that some debtors will be more apt to pay if they think they are being pursued by a collection agency and not the original creditor.

The practice isn't illegal. If you're wondering who sent you the "collection agency" letter—and thus how aggressive you can expect the bill collector to get—call the collection agency and ask to speak to the person handling your account. If the agency has no record of your account, you know the original creditor sent you the letter.

B. Original Creditors' Collection Efforts

HOW AN ORIGINAL CREDITOR goes about collecting an outstanding bill will depend on the type of creditor it is. Small local creditors, like a corner store or accountant's office, may have a person on staff who handles delinquent accounts. More often than not, however, the responsibility of collecting overdue money rests with the business owner or manager. Department stores, banks and other creditors with several branches begin their collection efforts with the store or office that handled your transaction. National creditors—for example, banks that issue credit cards—have centrally located, in-house collection departments.

If you've moved since you incurred the debt, many original creditors will still try to find you. Several have access to computer databases compiled to help creditors find debtors. You may supply information about your new location to these databases when you rent a new place, send your

credit card company a change of address or apply for a credit card at your new address.

If the original creditor can't find you, it will probably just send your account to a collection agency.

1. Collection Letters

Original creditors usually begin their collection efforts with collection ("dunning") letters.

One day, several weeks after a bill is past due, you open your mail box and find a polite letter from a creditor reminding you that you seemed to have overlooked the company's most recent bill. "Perhaps it is already in the mail. If so, please accept our thanks. If not, we would appreciate prompt payment," the letter states.

This "past due" form letter is the kind that almost every creditor sends to a customer with an overdue account. If you ignore it, you'll get a second one, also automatically sent. In this letter, most creditors remain friendly, but want to know what the problem is. "If you have some special reason for withholding payment, please let us know. We are here to help." Some creditors also suspend your credit at this point; the only way to get it back is to send a payment.

If you don't answer the second letter, you'll probably receive three to five more form letters. Each will get slightly firmer. The next to last letter will likely contain a veiled threat: "Paying now will protect your credit rating." By the last letter, however, the threat won't be so subtle: "If we do not receive payment within ten days, your credit privileges will be canceled (if they haven't already been), your account sent to a collection agency and your delinquency reported to a credit reporting agency. You could face a lawsuit, wage attachment or lien on your property."

Original creditors hate it when collection efforts reach this stage. They want you to pay your bill, but they also want to be nice so that you'll remain a customer. In fact, one collector wrote a book entitled

Make Them Happy/Make Them Pay. If the original creditor's letter-writing campaign fails—or the person assigned to your account concludes, after you ignore the first letter or two, that writing to you is useless—you'll probably receive a phone call.

> **Examples:** "We are not here to beat you up or yell at you. Tell us your problems so we can help you and your family. We want you to remain our customer."
>
> "Oh-no; don't tell me you're considering bankruptcy! It's a big mistake. I'll bet you didn't know that a bankruptcy will stay on your credit record for *ten years.*"
>
> "Is the payment schedule convenient for you? Would it help if we moved your due date up a few days so that your payment is due just a day or two after you get paid?"
>
> "Do you need help planning a budget or deciding which creditors to pay? Let me suggest that you contact your local Consumer Credit Counseling Service office." Consumer Credit Counseling Service (CCCS) is a national, nonprofit organization, sponsored and paid for by major creditors. CCCS helps debtors plan budgets and pay their bills. CCCS can be very helpful, but you, not the creditor, should make that decision. See Chapter 13 for a full discussion on CCCS.
>
> "How would you, if you were a creditor, handle overdue accounts?"
>
> "Do you have $100 a month to pay your debts? I'm sure you realize that our debt is your most important one. We would have to insist that you pay us $75 a month and distribute the rest to your other creditors."
>
> "Did you know that our store's 75th anniversary sale is next month? Everything will be on sale at 50% off. We'll be happy to let you have your $1,000 line of credit back as soon as you clear up this debt."
>
> "Please, why don't you just send the minimum—$20—to prove to me that you are a sincere person."

If the letters and telephone calls fail, the original creditor will report your delinquency to a credit bureau—which means that it goes on your credit record. Some creditors won't wait until they have exhausted their phone calls and letters to report your account to a credit bureau. These creditors report your default as soon as it becomes obvious (to them) that you aren't planning to pay—that is, after you ignore one letter or call. And if they really want the money, they'll turn your account over to a collection agency.

An increasing number of collectors working for original creditors are abandoning the standard letter/phone call tactic if it is obvious early on that it won't work. Instead, these collectors contact debtors and encourage them to call an 800 number to set up a repayment plan.

2 How to Respond

When the first overdue notice arrives, your first response may be to throw it away. And if the letter is from a creditor whose debt is on your "nonessential" debt list (Chapter 3), throwing it away may be your best alternative. Remember, however, that the original creditor won't end its collection efforts with that first letter. Assuming the debt is one you want to pay, but you need a little more time, you're better off writing or calling the creditor and asking for an extension. And if you got a message to call an 800 number and work out a repayment, by all means call back if you can squeeze out a steady amount each month.

⚠ Beware of "Urgency-Payment" Suggestions

If your bill is seriously past-due (90 days or more) and you've just agreed to a send a bill collector some money, don't be surprised if he urges you to waste no time. Here are some suggestions the collector may make.

- Send the check by express or overnight mail. This will add another $10 or more to how much you have to lay out. A first class stamp is just fine.

- Wire the money, using Western Union's Quick Collect or American Express' Moneygram. As with using overnight mail, wiring money will cost you another $10 or more.

- Put the payment on a (or another) credit or charge card. If you're having debt problems, the last thing you need to do is incur more debt.

- Have a bank wire the money.

- Visit the creditor directly and bring the payment.

- The collector will come out to your home to pick up the check.

You will need to explain your problem and say when you expect to be able to make full payments. Don't give a work phone number unless the creditor already knows where you work and you don't mind calls at your job.

Sending a partial, even token, payment will show that you are earnestly trying to pay. It is not essential, however, especially if it will keep you from paying priority debts. A sample letter asking for more time is set out below.

Sample Letter Asking for More Time

```
                          Collections Department
                          Rease's Department Store
                          5151 South Keetchum Place
                          Chicago, IL 60600

                          April 18, 19__

Re:    Amy Jones
       Account No. 1294-444-38XX


To Whom It May Concern:

I've received your notice indicating that my
account is overdue.

I would like to pay, however, a family
emergency has prevented me from doing so. My
daughter was in a severe automobile accident.
She is unable to go to school and I have had
to take time off to care for her.

My financial situation will improve in the
near future. I will be returning to work in a
few weeks and I expect to be able to pay you
on June 1, 19__.

Thank you for your consideration in this
matter. If you wish to speak to me, please
feel free to call me at my home at (312) 555-
9333.

Sincerely,


Amy Jones
```

If the creditor rejects your proposal or wants more evidence that you are genuinely unable to pay, consider asking a counselor with Consumer Credit Counseling Service to intervene on your behalf. (See Chapter 13, Section C.) Or, if the debt is quite large, or one of many, consider hiring a lawyer to write a second letter asking for additional time (also Chapter 13). The lawyer won't say anything different than you would, but a lawyer's stationery carries clout. Yes, this will cost a few dollars, but it may be worth it. When a creditor learns that a lawyer is in the picture, the creditor often suspects that you'll file for bankruptcy if he isn't accommodating. So you can often save more in payments than the lawyer costs.

 Don't Be Shamed or Guilt-Riddened into Paying an Unessential Bill

After reading Chapter 1, and Chapter 3, Section A, you should have a clear understanding of your debts and which to pay. If your first priority is your house payment, second priority is buying food and third priority is a car payment, don't let a department store talk you into sending $50 unless the other priorities have been met.

C. When Your Debt Is Sent to a Collection Agency

IF YOU IGNORE THE ORIGINAL creditor's letters and phone calls, or you set up a repayment schedule but fail to make the payments, your bill will most likely be turned over to a collection agency and your delinquency reported to a credit bureau. By taking some time to understand how collection agencies operate, you'll know how to respond when they contact you so that you can best negotiate a payment plan or you can get the agency off your back.

First, if a collection agency has been hired by an original creditor, it must take its cues from the creditor. It can't hire an attorney—or use one on staff—to sue you without the original creditor's authorization. If the original creditor insists that the agency collect 100% of the debt, the agency cannot accept less from you, although it can agree to accept installment payments. To reduce the actual amount you pay, the collection agency must get the original creditor's okay, or you'll have to contact the original creditor yourself. More and more original creditors are giving the collection agencies more discretion, however. Some agencies are authorized to settle a

debt for only 75%. Others can decide to drop collection efforts altogether, if it's unlikely the debtor will pay.

Second, you can expect to hear from a collection agency immediately. Professional debt collectors know that the earlier they strike, the higher their chance of collecting. For example, if an account is three months overdue, bill collectors typically have a 75% chance of collecting it. If it's six months late, the chances of collecting drop to 50%. And if the bill has been owed for more than a year, collectors have only a one in four chance of recovering the debt.

Third, bill collecting is a serious—and lucrative—business. Collection agents are good at what they do. Many agents are screened before they are hired. One owner of an agency bragged that before offering a job to someone, he observed the person's body language, had the person make mock collection calls, administered an IQ and a polygraph test, and checked employment agency and credit bureau reports. What was the agency owner looking for? A tenacious troll that would hang on a debtor like a bloodthirsty tick.

Tips for Collection Agents

People employed by collection agencies aren't necessarily the smartest folks around. To help its collectors more effectively collect debts, one of the largest collection agencies in California provides this list of "tips" to its employees.

- *50% of the residents of Northern California have unlisted telephone numbers.* Therefore debtors in Northern California may be contacted at work or by letter more often than other debtors.

- *A "temporary disconnect" phone message usually means the person did not pay her phone bill.* If your phone has been disconnected, expect an increase in calls at work or dunning letters.

- *Use an answering machine to motivate, not castigate.* Answering machine messages from employees of collection agencies will be vague, asking you to return a call to an unknown person. You'll often be encouraged to call back collect.

- *You can never have enough phone numbers for a debtor.* And so collection agents will try to get phone numbers for your home, work, relatives, neighbors and anyone else the agent thinks knows you.

- *Money is the number one received Christmas gift.* Expect to hear from a collection agency on December 26.

- *Tax refunds arrive in the first quarter of the year.* Any time between January 1 and April 1, a collection agent will suggest that you pay its bill with your tax refund.

Fourth, a collection agency usually keeps between 10% and 60% of what it collects. The older the account, the higher the agency's fee. Sometimes, the agency charges per letter it writes or phone call it places—usually about 50¢ per letter or $1 per call. Thus, some collection agencies are more aggressive at collecting some debts than others.

Fifth, before a collection agency tries to collect, it evaluates its likelihood of success. It may carry thousands—or even tens of thousands—of delinquent accounts and must prioritize which ones to go after. If success looks likely, the agency will move full speed ahead. If the chances of finding you are low, the odds of collecting money from you are somewhere between slim and nil or your credit file shows that you've defaulted on 20 other accounts, the agency may give your debt low priority.

As a part of prioritizing, the agency may do a zip code analysis. Collection agencies know that debtors in certain zip code areas—usually more affluent ones—are more apt to pay. Debtors living in those areas may receive up to 12 collection letters, while debtors in poorer areas might find that only two or three collection letters make it to their mailboxes.

1. How Collection Agencies Find Debtors

 If You Don't Want to Know How Collection Agencies Find Debtors

Before a collection agency can contact you, it must find you. If you've already been found, you can skip this section. If the agency hasn't found you, however, and you want some tips on minimizing the chances of being found, keep reading.

Collection agencies hunt people down using several possible resources. Some collection agencies only use one or two of the resources described below. Others use more, maybe even all of them. But even agencies that search diligently make mistakes. Some hire fairly low-paid clerks to collect and sift through mountains of data. These clerks can put information about other people into your file and information about you into other files, effectively losing you. Thus, some collection agencies are good at finding people while other agencies are not.

Just because a collection agency calls or writes to you, don't assume that it knows where you live, especially if you've moved since you transacted business with the original creditor. All the bill collector knows is that it mailed a letter that wasn't returned.

Example: Your name is Richard Gregg. After moving, you received a letter from a collection agency. The agency doesn't know you received it unless it pays the post office for an address forwarding verification. Even then, the collection agency doesn't know that you are the Richard Gregg it is looking for. Using many sources for names, the agency sent out several hundred letters to every Gregg it found.

Here are the primary resources a collection agency uses to find people.

Information on your credit application. The original creditor provides the collection agency with the information on your credit application—address, phone number, employer, bank, credit references, nearest living relative and the like. If you've moved, someone listed on a credit application may know where you are.

Relatives, friends, employers and neighbors. Collection agents often call relatives, friends, employers or neighbors, posing as a friend or relative. The collector typically cries out that he's in some kind of bind and needs to speak to you. Before you move, make sure you tell only the most trusted people where you are going. To find neighbors, the agent can check a criss-cross or street address directory published by the phone company. (Unlisted phone numbers don't appear in the criss-cross directory.) These give the names and phone numbers of people living near you.

Post office. The agency may check the post office for a forwarding address and is likely to examine several regional phone books. Also, one major credit bureau which has its own collection agency—TRW—receives change-of-address information for two million people each month from the U.S. Postal Service. And some bill collectors are successful at getting a post office employee to give out the street address associated with a P.O. box.

State motor vehicle department. The collector may contact your state's motor vehicle department in the event you re-registered your car. In most states, collectors can get this information for a few dollars, though a few states now restrict motor vehicle records to only people with a legitimate reason for requesting the information. Often an original creditor collecting a court judgment is entitled to this information, but a collection agency isn't.

Voter registration records. Some collection agents check voter registration records in the county of your last residence. If you've re-registered in the same county, the registrar will have your new address. If you've moved out of county and re-registered, your new county would have forwarded cancellation information onto your old county, and the registrar may make that information available. So if you move, re-register only if you don't have to provide a former address.

Your former landlord. A collection agent may call the county property tax office and find your old landlord. The collector then calls the landlord, and often using a pretext (your long lost cousin), tries to get your forwarding address.

Utility companies. Although this process is difficult, an agency collector may be able to find you through the electric or phone company, especially if you are still in the same service area. Even if you move farther, the company may have your new address as a place to send your final bill.

Banks. If you move but leave your old bank account open—even if you don't still do business with the bank—the bank will probably have your new address and may provide it to a collection agency.

Credit bureaus. If a collection agency is associated with a credit bureau (see Chapter 12), the collection agency will have access to all kinds of information, such as your address, phone number, employer and credit history. Even if the collection agency isn't part of a credit bureau, for a small fee the collector can place your name on a credit bureau locate list. In theory at least, if you apply for credit—even if you've moved hundreds or thousands of miles from where you previously lived—your name will be forwarded to the collection agency.

Home delivery services. Some local merchants who deliver, such as pizza places, keep customers' addresses on file. When the customer places an order, the clerk may simply confirm an address ("Are you still at 433 Gilroy Lane?"). Some collection agents pose as debtors and order merchandise, hoping that the debtor has done business with the merchant and the merchant will simply confirm the debtor's address. After getting the address, the agent waits ten minutes, calls back and cancels the order.

Can a Collection Agency Get Government Records?

Social Security, unemployment, disability, census and other government records are not public documents, so bill collectors can't get them. A few government employees with access to these records, however, have been paid off by bill collectors for providing this information. But the risk involved is extremely high and bill collectors rarely push for this kind of data.

If the collection agency is not connected to any credit bureau—which is more likely if the original creditor is a small business—it may have a hard time collecting an out-of-state debt, even if it has found you. The agency can call a collection agency located in the place where you've moved and assign the debt to the second agency, but forwarded debts have low priority. The second agency must split its commission with the referring agency and can't count on any repeat business.

Some Steps to Avoid Being Found by Collection Agencies

- Don't reveal your new address, city or state to anyone except a few trusted people who won't tell anyone else.

- Don't send the post office a change-of-address form; instead, directly write to the people who need your new address.

- Keep your new phone number unlisted.

- Don't re-register to vote if you are required to provide a previous address.

- Close your old bank accounts; open new ones at different banks—not at the banks closest to where you work or live. It's best to pick a bank clear across the other side of town.

- Don't, under any circumstance, apply for new credit.

If you're contacted by a collection agency located far from the original creditor, you can delay the collection efforts by raising legitimate questions about the debt. If you question the accuracy of the balance owed or the quality of the goods you allegedly received, the agency will have to verify the information with the forwarding collection agency. That agency will in turn have to check with the original creditor. This often slows the process down by several months and sometimes stops it altogether.

2 Your First Contact With the Collection Agency

Normally, the collection agent's first letter or phone call gives you the following information. If it doesn't, by law she has five days of initially writing or calling to tell you:

- the amount of the debt

- the name of the original creditor

- that you have 30 days to dispute the validity of the debt, and

- that if you dispute the debt's validity, the collector will send you verification of it.

a. Requesting Verification

It's wise to request verification of the debt. Then you may want to dispute it. A collection agent cannot resume collection efforts until she double-checks the information on the debt with the original creditor. Collection agencies and original creditors are busy. While verification may seem like it should take only a simple phone call, it often takes several weeks or months.

b. Asking That the Creditor Take Back the Debt

If you are ready to negotiate on a debt, you will probably be better off if the debt is with the creditor, not a collection agency. This is because the creditor has more discretion and flexibility in negotiating with you, and the creditor sees you as a former and possibly future customer. So ask the collection agency collector for the phone number of the collections department of the original creditor. Then call the creditor and ask if you can negotiate on the debt.

Here are the possible responses:

- The creditor immediately begins negotiations with you, takes the debt back from the collection agency, and keeps it as long as you make the agreed-upon payments. Only a few creditors will do this.

- The creditor rejects your proposal, but lets you know that if you negotiate with the collection agency, establish a repayment plan and make two or three payments under the plan, the creditor will take your debt back and eventually give you a new line of credit. This helps you take care of your debt problems and begin to rebuild your credit. Many creditors will do this.

- The creditor rejects your proposal, but negotiates a payment plan with you and requires that its

collection agency abide by the plan. A few creditors, including American Express, will do this.

- The creditor rejects your proposal and tells you that your only option is to negotiate with the collection agency. Some creditors will do this.

If You Cosigned for a Loan

When you cosign for a loan, you assume full responsibility for paying back the loan in the event the primary borrower defaults. In all states but Maine, the creditor can go after a cosigner without first trying to collect from the primary borrower. But most creditors try to collect first from the primary borrower, and if you've been contacted by a collection agency, you can assume that the primary debtor defaulted.

Your best bet is to pay the debt (and save your credit rating) and then try to collect yourself from the primary debtor. For more information on cosigned debts, see Chapter 6, Section C3e.

3. Negotiating an Unsecured Debt With a Collection Agency

Although collection agencies must follow original creditors' instructions, few original creditors put significant restrictions on collection agencies. The original creditor has all but given up on you and will be thrilled if the collection agency can use legal means to collect anything. The collection agency knows you're having debt problems and have been evading your creditors. If the original creditor is flexible, it may be happy to accept a settlement below the full amount to avoid spending months futilely trying to collect the whole thing.

Remember two key points:

- The collection agency didn't lay out the money initially. It doesn't care if you owe $250 or $2,500.

It just wants to maximize its return, which is usually a percentage of what it collects.

- Time is money. Every time the collection agency writes or calls you, it spends money. The agency has a strong interest in getting you to pay as much as you can as fast as possible. It has less interest in collecting 100% over five years.

Before you contact a collection agency, review your debt priority plan. If you don't have the cash to make a realistic lump sum offer, or to propose a payment plan, don't call—you may give the agency more information than it already has.

a. Offering a Lump-Sum Settlement

If you decide to offer a lump sum, understand that no two collection agencies will take from you the same amount to settle a debt. Some want 75-80%. Others will take $.50 on the dollar. Those that have all but given up on you may settle for one-third of what you owe. No matter how much you offer originally, however, decide what your top amount is and stick to it. Once the agency sees you are willing to pay something, it will assume it can talk you into paying more. Be sure you don't go any higher than what you can afford.

A collection agency will have more incentive to settle with you if you can pay all at once. If you owe $500 and offer $300 on the spot to settle the matter, the agency can take its fee, pass the rest on to the original creditor (who writes off on its tax returns as a business loss the amount you *don't* pay) and close its books.

If the collection agency agrees to settle a debt with you, try to get the agency—as a condition of your paying—to get any negative information about the debt removed from credit bureau files. This decision ultimately rests with the original creditor, but the original creditor may be happy to do it if it means getting paid.

b. Offering to Make Payments

If you offer to make monthly payments, the agency has little incentive to compromise for less than the full amount. It still must chase you for payment, and there's a good chance that after a month or two, you'll stop paying.

Before a collection agency considers accepting monthly payments, it will probably have you fill out asset, income and expense statements. These forms must be completed under penalty of perjury—meaning if you lie, you could be prosecuted for perjury. Filling out these forms will give the collection agency much more information on you than it previously had, something you may want to keep to a minimum.

Negotiating Tips

- Be honest but paint the bleakest possible picture of your finances. Explain illnesses and accidents, job layoffs, car repossessions, major back taxes that you owe and the like.

- If you are seriously considering bankruptcy, say so.

- Never disclose where you work or bank. If you are asked, simply say "no comment"—this isn't the time to worry about being polite. If the collection agency or original creditor later sues you and gets a judgment, knowing where you bank or work will make it easy to collect the judgment.

- If you do make a payment, don't send a check from your bank—buy a money order from a different bank or the post office.

Before Hiring a Lawyer, Weigh the Pros and Cons

If you're thinking of hiring a lawyer, remember that while a lawyer can carry clout, is probably experienced at negotiating and can convincingly mention bankruptcy, a lawyer costs money.

Don't hire one unless you owe a lot and the lawyer has a realistic chance of negotiating a favorable settlement, such as getting a debt reduced to $5,000 from $10,000. After all, if the amount you pay the collection agency and the lawyer combined totals what you originally owed, you should have just sent the full amount to the collection agency. Also, make sure the lawyer states his fee and doesn't charge more, or you could have one more creditor at your door.

Can a Collection Agency Add Interest?

The Fair Debt Collection Practices Act prohibits a collection agency from collecting interest on a debt unless interest was called for in the written agreement between you and the original creditor or interest is permitted under your state's law. Many states do authorize the collection of such interest. For example, collection agencies in California can add interest because Civil Code § 3289(b) permits a creditor to charge interest after default, even if the contract doesn't say so.

4. Negotiating a Secured Debt With a Collection Agency

As explained in Chapter 2, a secured debt is linked to a specific item of property, such as a car or item of furniture. The property guarantees payment of the debt. If you don't pay, the creditor can repossess the property, called the collateral. In general, your negotiations with the collection agency won't differ with secured and unsecured debts. But there are some special considerations.

Can you just give back the collateral and call it even? If you don't need or want the collateral, you can offer to give it back to the collection agency. The agency, however, doesn't have to take it. If the item's value has substantially decreased, for example, it's a car a few years old or an item hard to sell, the agency probably won't take it back.

Even if the collection agency takes the property back, in most states, for most items of property for which you originally paid over $2,000, you'll still be liable for the difference between what you owe and what the collection agency is able to sell the repossessed property for. This difference is called a deficiency judgment and, as explained in Chapter 4, is reason enough, often, for you to avoid having your property repossessed.

Your best strategy with secured property is to offer to give it back to the collection agency in exchange for a written agreement not to sue you for any deficiency judgment. If the bill collector refuses, you may be better off trying to sell the item yourself and using the proceeds to pay your debts.

Exemptions won't help you. In Chapter 11, I discuss exempt property—the property your creditors, including collection agencies, can't take even if you file for bankruptcy or the creditor sues you. There's one major exception to exempt property—collateral for a secured debt. You can't keep a creditor from repossessing the collateral just because it's exempt.

5. When the Collection Agency Gives Up

If all collection efforts by the collection agency fail, the agency is likely to send the bill back to the original creditor. Many original creditors will hire a second or even third collection agency to try and collect the debt, and many of the tactics described in this section will be used by the secondary and tertiary agencies.

Negotiating with a Secondary or Tertiary Collection Agency

By the time your debt reaches a secondary or tertiary collection agency, you've done an excellent job of avoiding paying your bill. The original creditor and at least one collection agency have given up on you.

A collection agency that agrees to take your debt at this time will insist that the original creditor pay a generous fee (usually 50–60% of what's recovered) and give the agency substantial freedom in negotiating with you.

It's at this point that you can probably settle the bill for far less than you owe. Many secondary and tertiary agencies will take 50¢ on the dollar. If the agency hasn't been able to reach you by phone but knows that you are receiving its letters, it may even settle for less.

When all collection efforts fail, the original creditor and the collection agency currently holding the debts will put their heads together and decide whether or not to pass your debt on to an attorney for collection. No matter what the amount of the debt, before filing a lawsuit the creditor will consider the following:

- the likelihood of winning

- the likelihood of collecting—are you currently employed or apt to become employed?

- the lawyer's fees

- whether or not you recently filed for bankruptcy (you have to wait seven years to file again), and

- the relationship of the lawyer and the creditor. Sometimes, a lawyer will take small debts along with several large ones to stay in good with the creditor.

If you are sued, the court papers will name as the plaintiff (the company suing you) the original creditor, the collection agency or both. If only the collection agency is named, you may have difficulty figuring out who the original creditor is. For this reason, most collection lawsuits are filed in the name of the original creditor or both the original creditor

and the collection agency. This may not be the case in Missouri, however, where collection agencies are specifically permitted to sue in only their name.[2]

If you are sued, turn to Chapter 9.

D. Debt Collection Practices— Legal and Illegal

THE FAIR DEBT COLLECTIONS Practices Act (FDCPA) prohibits a collection agency from engaging in all kinds of behavior.[3] Most important, it gives you the right to tell a collection agency— including an original creditor collecting its own debt under a separately named collections business and attorneys collecting debts on behalf of their clients— to cease communicating with you. Unfortunately, virtually no original creditors fall into this category. And so as you read Sections 1 through 3, bear in mind that the information pertains only to collection agencies.

1. Actions You Can Take Under the Fair Debt Collections Practices Act

Your most powerful weapon against a collection agency is your right to tell it to leave you alone. Simply tell a bill collector from a collection agency in writing to cease all communications with you. She must do this, except to tell you that:

- collection efforts against you have ended, or

- she or the original creditor may or will invoke a specific remedy against you, such as suing you.

Furthermore, if the collection agency employee does contact you to tell you that she intends to invoke a specific remedy, she must intend to do so. She cannot simply write to you four times saying "we're going to sue you."

---

[2] Annotated Missouri Statutes § 425.300.

[3] 15 U.S.C. § 1692 et seq.

New York City Residents—You've Got Some Additional Protection

Residents of the City of New York can rely on local law to cease communications with *any* bill collector—one working for a collection agency or one working for an original creditor. New York City's Debt Collection Rule, part of the Consumer Protection Law, allows debtors to write to any bill collector and say "Stop!"[4]

Below is a sample letter to send to a collection agency to get it off your back.

Sample Letter to Collection Agency to Tell It to Cease Contacting You

```
                    Sasnak Collection Service
                    49 Pirate Place
                    Topeka, Kansas 69000
                    November 11, 19__
Attn:  Marc Mist

Re:    Lee Anne Ito
       Account No. 88-90-92

Dear Mr. Mist:

For the past three months, I have received
several phone calls and letters from you
concerning my overdue Rich's Department Store
account. As I have informed you, I cannot pay
this bill.

Accordingly, under 15 U.S.C. § 1692c, this is
my formal notice to you to cease all further
communications with me except for the reasons
specifically set forth in the federal law.

Very truly yours,


Lee Anne Ito
```

[4]Rules of the City of New York § 5-77(b)(4).

In addition to telling the bill collector to go away, you have the right to obtain written verification of the debt. (See Section C2a, above.)

2. Prohibited Collection Agency Actions

Under the FDCPA, a collection agency cannot legally engage in any of the following:

Communications with third parties. A collection agent cannot contact third parties, with the exception of your attorney or a credit bureau, except to locate you. In fact, if you have an attorney, the agent must not contact you unless you give the agent permission to, or your attorney doesn't respond to the agent's communications. If the agent contacts any other third person, she must state her name and can state only that she's confirming or correcting location information about you. Specifically, she cannot:

- give her collection agency's name, unless she is specifically asked

- state that you owe a debt

- contact a third party more than once unless requested to do so by the third party, or unless she believes the third party's earlier response was wrong or incomplete and that the third party has correct or complete information

- communicate by postcard, or

- put any words or symbols on the outside of an envelope that indicate she's trying to collect a debt. This includes the business logo or letterhead, if either would give away the purpose of the letter.

Communications with a debtor. In *all* communications, the bill collector from a collection agency must state that he is trying to collect a debt and that any information he collects will be used for that purpose.

Also, a bill collector from a collection agency cannot contact you:

- at an unusual or inconvenient time or place—calls before 8 a.m. and after 9 p.m. are not allowed

- directly, if she knows you have an attorney, or

- at work if she knows that your employer prohibits you from receiving collections calls at work. If you are contacted at work, tell her your boss prohibits such calls.

Harassment or abuse. A bill collector from a collection agency cannot engage in conduct meant to harass, oppress or abuse you including:

- using or threatening to use violence

- harming or threatening to harm you, another person, or your or another person's reputation or property

- using obscene or profane language

- publishing your name, such as in a "deadbeats" list, as a person who doesn't pay bills (state-sponsored child support collection agencies appear to be exempt from this—see Chapter 8, Section D5)

- listing your debt for sale to the public

- calling you repeatedly, or

- placing telephone calls to you or any other person without identifying himself as a bill collector.

False or misleading representations. A debt collector from a collection agency can't lie by:

- claiming to be a law enforcement officer or suggesting that she is connected with the federal, state or local government (anyone making this kind of claim is probably lying, unless she is trying to collect child support)

- falsely representing the amount you owe or the amount of compensation she will receive

- claiming to be an attorney

- claiming that you'll be imprisoned or your property will be seized, unless the bill collector or original creditor intends to take action that could result in your going to jail or your property being taken (you can go to jail only for extremely limited reasons—see Chapter 4, Section G)

- threatening to take action that isn't intended or can't be taken (such as stating that your welfare will be cut off)

- falsely claiming that you've committed a crime

- communicating false credit information, including failing to tell someone you dispute a debt, if you in fact do

- sending you a document that looks like it's from a court, government agency or attorney

- using a false business name

- claiming to be employed by a credit bureau, unless the collection agency and the credit bureau are the same company, or

- claiming to be taking a survey, to be casting a movie or television show, that she has a prepaid package for you or that money or a valuable gift will be sent to you if you disclose certain information.[5]

Unfair practices. A bill collector from a collection agency cannot engage in any unfair or outrageous method to collect a debt. Specifically, he can't:

- add interest, fees or charges not authorized in the original agreement or by state law (but most states allow a collection agency to add interest)

- accept a check post-dated by more than five days unless he notifies you between three and ten days in advance of when he will deposit it; deposit a post-dated check prior to the date on the check

- solicit a post-dated check by threatening you with criminal prosecution

- call you collect or otherwise cause you to incur communications charges

- threaten to seize or repossess your property if he has no right to do so or no intention of doing so

- communicate with you by postcard, or

---

[5]These are prohibited by 16 C.F.R. § 237.1, a Federal Trade Commission regulation interpreting the Fair Debt Collection Practices Act.

- put any words or symbols on the outside of an envelope sent to you that indicates he's trying to collect a debt.

3. If a Collection Agent Violates the Law

That collection agencies aren't supposed to engage in any of the above practices doesn't mean they don't. More than a few do. In fact, for many years the number one consumer complaint to the Federal Trade Commission had to do with credit bureaus. Since 1992, however, complaints against collection agencies top the list.

Low income and non-English-speaking debtors are especially targeted. So are non-U.S. citizens. Here are some of the more atrocious acts by bill collectors:

- Sending debtors fake legal papers and then pretending to be sheriffs. They tell debtors to pay immediately or threaten that the debtors will lose their personal possessions.

- Using vulgarity and profanity to threaten debtors.

- Harassing a debtor's parents—in particular, impersonating a government prosecutor before the parent and requesting that the parent ask the debtor to contact the collector.

- Soliciting a post-dated check in order to later threaten the debtor with a criminal bad check prosecution.

- Suggesting to a female debtor that she take up prostitution to increase her income.

- Threatening to report Latino and Asian debtors to the Immigration and Naturalization Service and posing as INS officers.

- Engaging in repeated violations of the law—such as verbal harassment, late night calls and calls to neighbors and friends—at the end of each month when collectors are trying to reach their monthly collection quotas.

If a bill collector from a collection agency violates the law—be it a large or small violation—try to get someone to witness the violation and then complain loud and clear. Try to get a witness, "invite" the collector back to your home and pretend to negotiate. Say whatever you said the first time that caused the collector to make whatever illegal statement(s) he made. Make sure you friend hears the entire conversation. Then complain. Complain even if you didn't get a witness. If you're loud enough about the abuse you suffered—and you've got a witness backing you up—you have a chance to get the whole debt canceled in exchange for shutting up.

To complain, contact the Federal Trade Commission (see Chapter 12, Section B7, for the list of addresses). Also complain to the state agency that regulates collection agencies for the state where the agency is located. (See "State Consumer Protection Office" in Chapter 13, Section D2.)

The Federal Trade Commission or the state agency may send you a form to help it process your complaint. Be thorough. Include dates, times and the names of any witnesses to unlawful conversations, and attach copies (keep the originals for yourself) of all offending materials you received.

Also, write to the original creditor and send a copy of this letter to the collection agency, the Federal Trade Commission and the state agency that regulates collection agencies. The original creditor may be disturbed by the collection agency's tactics and concerned about its own reputation. It might prefer to have you come back some day as a customer than have you be abused by a collection agency. A sample letter is provided.

Sample Letter to Original Creditor

Stonecutter Furniture
Factory
4500 Wilson Boulevard
Bloomington, IN 47400

April 19, 19__

Dear Stonecutter:

On May 10, 19__, I purchased a bedroom set from you for $2,000 ($500 down and the rest at $100 per month). I paid $900 and then lost my job and became ill, and was unable to pay you.

In early 19__, I was contacted by the Drone Collection Agency. The collectors called me twice a day for nearly three weeks, used profanity at me, my husband, and my 11-year-old son. In addition, a collector called my father and threatened him with a lawsuit, even though he is a 76-year-old diabetic with a heart condition and has had no connection with this transaction.

I have contacted the Federal Trade Commission and I am considering seeing an attorney. I am fully prepared to take the steps necessary to protect myself and my family from further harassment. I am writing you in the hope that you have not condoned Drone's practices and can do something to help me.

Very truly yours,

Karen Wood

cc: Indiana Secretary of State
        Drone Collection Agency
        Federal Trade Commission

You also have the right to sue a collection agency for harassment. You can represent yourself in small claims court or hire an attorney. (Attorney fees and court costs are recoverable if you win.) You're entitled to any actual damages (including pain and suffering) and up to $1,000 in punitive damages.

To win, you'll probably need to have a witness and to document repeated abusive behavior. If the collector calls five times in one day and then you never hear from him again, you probably don't have a case.

If you sue a collection agency, you should also name the original creditor as a defendant in the lawsuit. Although the FDCPA doesn't say that creditors are liable for the actions of collection agencies they hire, a court might hold otherwise. A court might declare the collection agency the "legal agent" of the creditor if the agency's actions are outrageous enough or the creditor was aware of the agency's actions.

4. State or Local Laws Prohibiting Unfair Debt Collections

Several states have enacted laws prohibiting unfair debt collection practices. So has New York City. A few of those laws are quite similar to the federal legislation and thus add little or nothing. Some, however, prohibit additional collection actions. The most valuable prohibit unethical and abusive collection practices by original creditors—remember, the federal law applies only to collection agencies. And some states add prohibitions to what collection agencies can do that go beyond the federal law.

Laws Covering Original Creditors and Collection Agencies

No bill collector—original creditor who regularly collects on his or her own behalf or collection agency—in the following jurisdictions may engage in any communication, harassment or abuse, false or misleading representation, or unfair practice prohibited by the Fair Debt Collection Practices Act.

Jurisdiction	Code Section
California	CC 1788.2
Connecticut	36-243b
District of Columbia	28-3814
Florida	559.72
Hawaii	480D-3
Iowa	537.7103
Louisiana	9:3562
Maine	9-A-5-116 32-11011 to 32-11016
Maryland	Comm. 14-201
Massachusetts	Ch. 93 ¶ 49
Michigan	19.658(2)
New Hampshire	358-C:3
New York City	6 RCNY §§ 5-76 through 5-80
North Carolina	75-50
Oregon	646.39
South Carolina	37-5-108
Texas	Civ. Stat. 5069-11.01
West Virginia	46A-2-122
Wisconsin	427.103

State	Code Section	Miscellaneous State Debt Collection Laws
Illinois	815 ILCS 505/2I	No bill collector—original creditor or collection agency—can contact your employer unless you are in default 30 days and have been notified at least 5 days in advance that collector intends to contact your employer.
Nebraska	45-173	Bank lender cannot contact any person who does not live in your home except your spouse, your attorney, another creditor or a credit bureau.
New York	GBL 601	Original creditor cannot contact your employer unless creditor has a court judgment, is seeking a wage attachment or you consent.
West Virginia	46A-2-126	No bill collector—original creditor or collection agency—can contact your employer before having a court judgment.

E. Turning the Tables on a Bill Collector

MANY BILL COLLECTORS, whether working for an original creditor or a collection agency, sit at their desks with pre-written scripts of what to say to you. Nine out of ten debtors respond to given questions with the same, predictable answers. Often, these consist of employment excuses, promises to pay and general statements of guilt. None of this will get you anywhere—the collector has heard it all before and is ready to hurl the next question at you. To help the collectors respond to your predictable answers, one collector wrote a color-coded guide. If you respond with answer X, the bill collector flips to the green page. If you respond with answer Y, he turns to the blue page.

The key to your success with a bill collector is to be the one in ten who unpredictably turns the table on the collector. Your goal is to get the bill collector to hang up, tongue tied with frustration. And engaging the collector in conversation may even be to your advantage, especially if you have a witness pick up the extension and listen in on the conversation. (It's illegal for you to tape any conversation without the other party's consent, however.) If the bill collector says something illegal, you can report the violation to the federal government, your state government and the original creditor. The original creditor may be willing to drop the whole thing.

Here is a made up dialogue between a bill collector ("Betty Collins") and a debtor, ("Donald Drake") that shows you how to turn the tables.

BC: Hello, this is Ms. Collins. Is Donald Drake there?

D: This is Donald Drake.

BC: Mr. Drake, I work for Collins Collection Agency and I'm calling about your Apex charge account. Your balance of $1,744 is six months overdue. I know you have money and will send us the full amount today. [At this point, the bill collector will pause. Bill collectors are trained to outlast debtors—they hope that the debtor will break the silence and tell the collector something the collector doesn't know. Many debtors are uncomfortable with the silence and offer to pay.]

D: I can't.

BC: Why not, Mr. Drake? Are you having employment or health problems?

D: Quite frankly, it's none of your business.

BC: Mr. Drake, I am here to help you. Not paying your bill is unacceptable. We need to receive some payment from you. Perhaps you can take out a personal loan to pay us.

D: What are you, crazy?

BC: Now Mr. Drake, like I said, I only want to help. Have you considered refinancing your home, or taking a second job in order to raise some cash?

D: Ms. Collins, you have some nerve. I am doing all I can to support my family—it just so happens that I just can't pay your bill right now. It's awfully insulting of you to tell me how to manage my financial affairs.

BC: Mr. Drake, we'll be happy to take a post-dated check from you.

D: But Ms. Collins, I don't know when I will have the money to pay. If I write you a post-dated check, it may bounce. I hope you aren't suggesting that I get into trouble for bouncing a check. [Many states let creditors sue debtors who bounce checks. See Chapter 3, Section F.]

BC: Mr. Drake, you realize that I will have to report your nonpayment to a credit reporting agency. Good credit should be your most valued asset, but now your credit rating will fall.

D: My credit is already damaged and I don't care. I have no interest in buying more things on credit. In fact, I'd really appreciate it if you report this to a credit bureau—certainly it would help decrease the amount of junk mail I now receive.

BC: I know you want to do the right—the moral—thing and pay your bill.

D: Yes, and I have a moral responsibility to feed and clothe my family before I pay my Apex account. I guess you do too or you wouldn't be spending all this time trying to earn a commission.

BC: You know we can attach your wages and other property.

D: Yes, but not until you get a court judgment and that takes a lot of time. Of course, threatening to do it before you get a court order is illegal.

BC: Mr. Drake, we can send our lawyer to court in 15 minutes.

D: Oh, I doubt that, Ms. Collins. If your lawyer is any good he probably has other priorities. Anyway, before you can do much to me you must first serve me with papers, wait for my response, have a trial and get a court judgment. And that usually takes many months. Even if you get a judgment, you can attach only my nonexempt property. [Much of your property is exempt from your creditor's taking, even if the creditor has a court judgment. This includes most of your wages, public benefits, your clothing and household furniture and some of the equity in your car. See Chapter 11.]

BC: Mr. Drake, I will have to call your employer.

D: Contacting my employer would be illegal. You can only call my employer to try and find me. You have obviously found me.

BC: How did you know that? Oh (mumble, mumble). Well, I'll call you later....

D: Wait, Ms. Collins. Don't hang up. I know you are busy and make most of your money when people send you payments for their bills. Just because I have no money now and know my rights is no reason for you to get huffy and hang up on me.

BC: Listen, Mr. Drake, I'm going to get you.

D: Not legally you can't. Ms. Collins, I've had enough of your threats. May I have your address? I plan to send you a letter telling you to stop communicating with me. I know this is my right under the federal law.

BC: Collins Collection Agency, P.O. Box 19044, Portland, Maine 00011.

D: And your supervisor's name? I'd like to report this conversation to your boss and the Federal Trade Commission.

Click—the bill collector hung up.

The bill collector tried to frighten and shame the debtor by mentioning his credit rating, moral obligation, wages being attached and employer. But none worked. And when the debtor threatened to report the collector to the FTC, the bill collector hung up. ∎

Chapter 6

CREDIT CARDS, CHARGE CARDS AND OTHER LOANS

A bank is a place where they lend you an umbrella in fair weather and ask for it back when it begins to rain.

—Robert Frost, American poet, 1875-1963

IN THE EARLY 1950S, A GROUP of New York restaurants got together and developed a card to let their customers dine now and be billed later. Little did they know that the industry started by their "Diners Club" card would quickly became an indispensable part of our economy. Today, almost every adult has and uses at least one credit or charge card. Your requirement to repay the debts you incur in using these cards is governed both by your agreement with the bank, merchant or other creditor who issued the card, and by a federal law called the Fair Credit Billing Act.

A. Credit and Charge Cards

CREDIT CARDS CAN amount to nothing other than very expensive loans made by banks, credit card companies, gasoline companies and department stores. Your first reaction to this sentence may be "That isn't always true. I don't pay interest on American Express, Diners Club and similar cards." Technically, these cards are charge cards—or travel and entertainment cards—not credit cards.

1. Credit Cards

The credit card issuer gives you a card. You use the card to pay for items and services up to a certain total amount—your credit "limit." The store merchant or service provider collects what you owe from the card issuer, who you repay. You're allowed to pay off what you owe over monthly periods, as long as you pay a minimum amount each period. You're charged interest on the balance you owe (as high as 22% a year) at the end of each period unless you pay the full balance when your bill arrives.

Credit cards yield high profits to their issuers for several reasons. The most important is the high rate of interest—interest alone accounts for 75% of the profits earned by banks that issue credit cards. Also, many companies charge an annual fee for issuing a credit card, and most companies charge late fees, over-the-limit fees and other miscellaneous charges. Finally, the companies profit by charging merchants and service providers a fee each time a customer uses the company's credit card in the merchant's establishment.

Evaluating Credit Card Costs When You Plan to Close Some of Your Accounts

Which accounts should you close? If you have more than one credit card and, as part of dealing with your debts, you plan to close all of your accounts but one, you may be wondering which card to keep. If you're delinquent on any account, close it—otherwise, the credit card issuer may close it for you. If you're delinquent on all your accounts, keep open the account you are least behind on.

How to close accounts. To close your account, send a letter—and the card cut up—to the customer service department of the card issuer. You can do this even if you haven't paid off the balance—the card issuer will close your account, cancel your privileges and send you monthly statements until you pay off your balance. Don't write to the company at the address where you send payments.

Evaluating the cost of a credit card. If you still don't know which card to keep, consider how much it will cost you to have the card. If you don't carry a monthly balance (or only occasionally do), keep a card with no annual fee, but make sure it has a grace period. If the card issuer later charges an annual fee, call and say you'll cancel your card if they don't waive the fee. Virtually all will.

If you carry a balance each month or most of the time, consider getting rid of the cards that come with the worst of the following features:

High interest rates. If possible, keep the card with a lowest rate. If the only card you plan to hang on to has a high interest rate and you're up to date on your payments, call and ask for an interest rate reduction. Many banks will do this over the phone, but you must be current on your account. Also, understand that when banks state their annual percentage rate (APR), the rate is computed as simple interest—the interest on purchases not paid in full each month. In fact, interest is compounded because you pay on purchases and interest charges carried forward each month. That means on a card with an 18.5% APR, you're probably paying 20.15% or more.

Early interest posting dates. Banks used to charge interest from the date a charge was posted. Now, most charge from the date of the purchase.

Unfair interest calculations. Most banks charge interest on the balance owed. A growing number, however, charge interest based on the average daily balance. For example, say you charge $1,500 on your credit card and pay $1,200 on the due date. When your next bill arrives, a bank using the average daily balance will charge interest on the $1,500 average daily balance from the previous month, not on the $300 you still owe.

No grace periods. A few card issuers have done away with grace periods. Even if your bank offers a grace period, understand that its usually forfeited on all new purchases. This means that not only does interest accrue on the balance carried from the previous month, but it also accrues on new charges from the date of purchase.

Nuisance fees. Banks are more frequently assessing late fees (averaging more than $8) and over-the-limit fees (averaging more than $11) than in years past. A few banks also now charge a fee when you ask them to close your account.

To request a list of banks issuing cards with low interest rates, send $5 to Ram Research's Cardtrack, Box 1700, Frederick, MD 21702, or $4 to Bankcard Holders of America, 524 Branch Drive, Salem, VA 24153. BHA's list also includes banks issuing cards with no or low annual fees. For BHA's list of gold cards with low interest rates and annual fees, send $5 and request the gold card list.

2. Charge Cards

Charge cards, also called travel and entertainment cards, are a little different from credit cards. With charge cards, such as American Express and Diners Club, you have no credit limit. You can usually charge as much as you'd like, but you are required to pay off your entire balance when your bill arrives, with one exception. If you charge air fare, cruise fees or hotel fees on a hotel booked through a travel agent on an American Express card, you can pay off

your balance over 36 months. You'll be charged between 19% and 21% interest and will have to make minimum monthly payments of $20 or 1/36 of your balance, whichever is greater.

If you don't pay your charge card bill in full (and haven't charged travel expenses on an American Express card), you'll get one month's grace, when no interest is charged. After that, you'll be charged interest in the neighborhood of 20%. If you don't pay after about three months, your account will be closed and your bill sent to the collections department. And American Express collectors are notoriously difficult to negotiate with.

The charge card company makes its profit by charging very high annual fees—up to $75—and by charging merchants fairly high fees—higher than when the customer uses a credit card—each time a customer pays using the company's charge card.

3. Unrequested Credit and Charge Cards

A company that issues credit or charge cards cannot legally send you one except in response to your request or application. If a card issuer sends you an unrequested card (except to replace an expiring one), the company assumes full responsibility for its use.[1] Unfortunately, however, few states impose any penalties on companies for sending an unrequested card. In fact, in many states if you "accept" the card, that is, if you use it, sign it or notify the card issuer in writing that you plan to keep it, you become liable for all charges made after your acceptance.

If a company wants to issue you a credit card without a detailed application, it can legally send you a letter of congratulations (or something similar) telling you that you have pre-qualified for a certain amount of credit, accompanied by a very simple application form, which usually requires little more than your signature. This is called a pre-approved solicitation.

---

[1]15 U.S.C. § 1642.

In the past, credit and charge card issuers asked credit bureaus to compile lists of people with certain credit traits, such as earning over $40,000 and having a mortgage. The card issuer then sent out pre-approval letters to all names given by the credit bureau. Before granting any applicant credit, the card issuer would do one last credit check. Today, however, a pre-approval letter must be an actual offer of credit—that is, once a pre-approved customer sends back a completed application, the applicant must be granted credit.[2] The card issuer can't check a credit file one last time and reject an applicant it no longer likes. Card issuers are getting around this law by pre-approving very low credit limits—like $500—and then doing a second credit check before offering any increase.

What to Do With Unwanted Credit and Charge Cards

If you receive an unrequested card that you don't want—either for a new account or to replace an expiring card—don't just throw the card away. That doesn't tell the card issuer that you don't want the account or that you want to close it. Your credit file will show that you have an account with an open line of credit for whatever amount you were granted by the card issuer. Today, many creditors refuse credit to people they believe already have too much credit. Having an unused account could be grounds for denying you future accounts you do want or limiting increases on existing accounts. Instead, cut up the card and return it to the card issuer with a letter stating that you don't want the card or the account.

4. Required Disclosures by Credit and Charge Card Issuers

 If You Aren't Concerned About Disclosures

If you aren't concerned that a credit or charge card company failed to disclose the interest rate, grace period, annual fee or other terms, you can skip this section. If you are concerned, however, it is sometimes possible to sue the company and get the debt wiped out.

When a credit or charge card company sends you an application form or pre-approved solicitation letter, it must, under the federal Truth in Lending Act, fully disclose the terms of your agreement.[3]

For credit cards, such as Visa, MasterCard, Sears and Chevron, where the card issuer charges you interest and lets you pay off the entire balance by taking as long as you'd like—as long as you pay the minimum required each billing period—the application or solicitation must state:

- the monthly finance charge—this is the total of all interest costs and fees such as service charges

- the yearly interest rate (called the annual percentage rate or APR)—this is the monthly finance charge multiplied by 12

- whether the interest rate is fixed or variable, and if variable, how it's determined

- where more than one interest rate applies, the range of balances to which each rate applies

- the period of days you have to pay off the entire balance without incurring any interest charge (called the grace period)—or that no period is available

- any minimum amount of interest imposed

---

[2]16 C.F.R. § 604(3)(A)(6).

[3]15 U.S.C. § 1637.

- how the balance on which the interest is imposed is calculated

- any annual, periodic or membership fee, and

- any per transaction, cash advance, late or over-the-limit fee.

For charge cards such as American Express and Diners Club, where you are not charged interest but must pay off the entire balance when you get the bill, the application or solicitation must include all the items listed above that apply, and any fee imposed or interest charged for granting an extension to pay.

Unfortunately, if a card issuer fails to disclose information or discloses wrong information, you have little recourse. The law states that you can sue to recover your actual damages, attorneys' fees, court costs and twice the amount of any interest you were wrongfully charged—not less than $100 nor more than $1,000. But the law has two huge loopholes. [4]

First, if the card issuer, within 60 days of discovering its error, notifies you of the error, makes the necessary corrections and does not charge you any interest in excess of the amount it actually disclosed, it has no liability. Second, if the card issuer's mistake was unintentional and resulted from a clerical, calculation, computer, printing or similar error, the card issuer will not be liable.

Nevertheless, if you were never told the terms of a credit or charge card, you can argue that the credit card issuer obtained an account from you fraudulently and that you don't owe a penny. This is not apt to be a defense to charges made on a card issued by Citibank, Bank of America or another major lender. But an unsophisticated lender who recently started issuing secured credit cards may not be complying with the rules. See Section D, below.

5. Lost or Stolen Credit and Charge Cards

Federal law limits your liability for unauthorized charges made on your credit or charge card after it has been lost or stolen. [5] If you notify the card issuer within a reasonable time—usually 30 days—after you discover the loss or theft, you're not responsible for any charges made after the notification, and are liable only for the first $50 for charges made before you notified the card issuer. If you don't notify the card issuer within a reasonable time, you could be liable for all charges made on your card before the time of your notification.

When you discover that a credit or charge card is lost or stolen, call the customer service department of the card issuer at once. By calling, you provide quick notice. You should be able to call most bank card issuers at any time (many have 24-hour customer service departments), while department stores and gasoline companies probably answer their phones only during regular business hours. When you call a card issuer, find out who you are speaking to, get an address and send a confirming letter. Do not send the letter to the address where you send your monthly payments. Be sure to keep a copy for yourself.

You will find the address and phone number of where to report a lost or stolen card on your monthly billing statements or on the disclosures you've received from the card issuer. If you can't find either of those, look in the phone book for local merchants or call toll-free information (800-555-1212). Many credit and charge card issuers, especially large banks, have toll-free phone numbers.

Given that the credit or charge card company is liable for any unauthorized charge over $50, it will act fast. Most likely the company will cancel your existing account, open a new one for you, issue you a new card and remove all charges above $50 from your statement. If the company doesn't respond adequately, refuse to pay the bill and have a lawyer

---

[4]15 U.S.C. § 1640.

[5]15 U.S.C. § 1643.

write a letter on your behalf. If that doesn't work, you may have to sue.

A rare company may decide that losing a credit card makes you a poor credit risk—especially if you have a history of late payments—and will cancel your account. Nevertheless, still call and report your card missing if it's lost or stolen. The chance of the issuer closing your account is slim. The chance of someone using your lost or stolen card is high.

Below is a sample letter to use to notify a credit or charge card issuer of a lost or stolen card. Be sure to keep a copy for your file.

Letter Confirming Telephone Notice of Lost or Stolen Card

> Large Oil Company
> Customer Service
> Department
> 1 Main Street
> Enid, OK 77777
>
> March 2, 19__
>
> Attn: Natalie Revere
>
> Dear Ms. Revere:
>
> This is to confirm my telephone call of March 1, 19__ notifying you that I lost my Large Oil Company credit card on February 26, 19__ while I was on vacation at the Grand Canyon.
>
> I understand that under the law, my telephone call serves as reasonably timely notice to your company. I further understand that I am not liable for any unauthorized use of this card from the time of my telephone call, and the maximum I am liable for on charges made before my notification is $50.
>
> Sincerely,
>
> Wendy Piter

Credit Card "Protection"

Many banks or national credit or charge card companies send letters to their cardholders urging them to buy—for about $35 per year—credit card "protection" to guard against unauthorized use of credit and charge cards. Given that your liability for unauthorized charges is $50 maximum, and then only for charges that are made prior to your notifying the card issuer, this "protection" is a waste of money.

6. Unauthorized Charges

Are you liable when your credit or charge card is used by a friend or relative? That depends. In general, you are not liable if you didn't know the person was using your card.

But if you gave your card to your 25-year-old son, anything he charges—until you take the card away from him—is authorized by you and you owe the bill. On the other hand, if your adult daughter took your card without your knowledge and charged a trip to Hawaii, you don't have to pay.

Your biggest obstacle will be convincing your card issuer that you did not authorize your son or daughter—or any other person—to use your card. Your best bet is to send a letter explaining the situation to the card issuer. With your daughter, emphasize that you were not at home and your daughter went to your bedroom, took your card and charged the trip without your ever knowing it.

If the credit or charge card company still claims you owe the bill—that is, that you authorized the charges—you can choose not to pay. The company will no doubt close your account and if the amount is high enough, sue you. If you want to fight it, you'll probably need a lawyer to help you prepare your defense of "unauthorized charges." See Chapter 13 for tips on finding a lawyer.

7. Disputes Over Credit or Charge Card Purchases

If you buy a defective item or service and pay for it with your credit or charge card, you can often withhold payment if the seller refuses to replace, repair or otherwise correct the problem. All you must do is explain to the credit or charge card company in writing why you are withholding payment.[6]

This is not an unlimited right. Before refusing to pay, you must attempt in good faith to resolve the dispute with the merchant. In addition, if your credit or charge card was not issued by the seller (for example, you used a Visa, MasterCard, Discover, American Express or Diners' Club card), you can refuse to pay only if the purchase was for more than $50 and was made within the state you live in or within 100 miles of your home.

If the credit or charge card was issued by the seller, such as a department store or gas company card, or the seller obtained your order by mailing you an ad where the card issuer participated and urged you to use the credit card in question, the purchase need not have been for more than $50, nor made within your state or 100 miles of your home.

> **Example:** Nan charged a raincoat from Cliff's Department Store on her Cliff's account. When she got it home, she discovered that the lining was torn. Cliff's refused to replace the coat or refund her money. Nan has the right to refuse to pay her bill. Had Nan charged the coat on her Visa card, she could refuse to pay only if Cliff's was located in the state where she lived or within 100 miles of her home.

For interstate transactions, the 100-mile limitation is easy to calculate when purchases are made in person. If you live in northern New Jersey and buy a suit in New York City (about 25 miles away) with your Visa card, you can refuse to pay if the suit falls apart and the seller won't make good. But what if a Georgian orders that same suit from the New York store through the mail or over the telephone? Is the purchase made in Georgia (the state in which the buyer lives) or New York (more than 100 miles away)?

The law is unclear. You can claim that the purchase was made in Georgia, not New York, and assert your right to not pay. The credit card company will ask the seller for its version of the dispute. Often, the seller won't push the issue, as it would rather keep you as a customer, even if it means writing off the bill. If the seller refuses to compromise, the credit card company will include the charge on your monthly bill, and add interest each month. After several months, the company may threaten to cancel your credit card account if you don't pay. Some companies will let you keep the account, as long as you make payments on the undisputed balance.

Blocked Credit Cards

Have you ever tried using a credit card shortly after checking out of a hotel and been told by the merchant that your card was rejected? It happens because many hotels, when you check in and give the clerk your card for an imprint, put a "hold" on your credit card for the estimated amount you will spend. Hotels claim that they are merely protecting themselves in the event you go on a spending spree during your trip and don't have enough credit left on your account to cover the hotel costs. Unfortunately, they've been known to hold much more than the estimated amount you'll spend and keep the hold on for up to 45 days after you check out.

Hotels have gotten a bad rap for doing this, so the amount they hold is less than in the past. When you check in ask if the hotel will place a hold and if so, for how much. When you check out, insist that the hotel order the hold lifted.

Rental car companies, too, often put a hold on credit cards, fearing that you'll total the car and run off leaving them to pay the bill. These holds are illegal in a few states. If you rent a car, ask the company if it is placing a hold, and if so for how much, before you leave the agency with your rental car. The Federal Trade Commission has information on credit card blocking. See Chapter 12, Section B7, for FTC addresses and phone numbers.

---

[6] 15 U.S.C. § 1666i.

8. Billing Errors

Credit and charge card billing errors are governed by the Fair Credit Billing Act (FCBA).[7] If you find an error in your credit or charge card statement, immediately write a letter to the company that issued the card; don't just scribble a note on your bill. Send your letter to the customer service department—the address should be on the back of the billing statement—not to where you send your payment. Give your name, account number, an explanation of the error and the amount involved. Also enclose copies of supporting documents, such as receipts showing the correct amount of the charge.

The credit or charge card company must receive your letter within 60 days after it mailed the bill to you. A sample letter is below.

Sample Letter to Notify of Billing Error

> Eighteenth Bank of
> Cincinnati
> 1 EBC Plaza
> Cincinnati, OH 44444
>
> May 20, 19__

Attn: Customer Service

Re: Bradley Green

Account Number: 123 456 789 0000

To Whom It May Concern:

I have found an error on my MasterCard statement dated May 15, 19__.

On March 25, 19__, I purchased with my MasterCard two roundtrip tickets on Skyway Airlines from New York to San Diego, for $1150. My bill, however, is for $1510. Obviously, the digits were reversed.

I understand that the law requires you to acknowledge receipt of this letter within 30 days unless you correct this billing error before then. Furthermore, I understand that within two billing cycles (but in no event more than 90 days), you must correct the error or explain why you believe the amount to be correct.

I have enclosed a copy of the receipt my travel agent sent me.

Sincerely,

Bradley Green

Remember to keep a copy of your letter as well as any original receipts or documentation. The credit or charge card company must acknowledge receipt of your letter within 30 days, unless it corrects the bill within that time. Furthermore, the card issuer must, within two billing cycles (but in no event more than 90 days), correct the error or explain why it believes the amount to be correct. If the card company does not comply with these time limits, you don't have to

---

[7] 15 U.S.C. § 1666 et seq.

pay $50 of the disputed balance. In California, if the card company doesn't comply with the 90-day time limit, you don't have to pay *any portion* of the disputed balance.[8]

During the two-billing-cycle/90-day period, the credit or charge card company cannot report the amount to a credit bureau or to other creditors as delinquent. Likewise, the card issuer cannot threaten or actually take any collection action against you for the disputed amount. But it can send you periodic statements. In addition, it can apply the amount in dispute to your credit limit, thereby lowering the amount available for you to charge.[9]

Also, during the two-billing-cycle/90-day period, the credit or charge card company can charge you interest on the amount you dispute, but if the company later agrees that you were correct, it must drop the interest accrued.

If the card company sends you an explanation but doesn't correct the error and you are not satisfied with its reason, send a second letter explaining that you still refuse to pay. You must send this letter to the company within ten days of receiving the explanation. If the card company then reports your account as delinquent to a credit bureau or anyone else, the company must also state that you believe you don't owe the money and tell you to whom the reports were made.

If the credit or charge card company violates any provision of the FCBA, you can sue to recover the damages you incurred. You're entitled to your actual damages, such as costs you incur in trying to remove erroneous information from a credit bureau file, twice the amount of any interest (but not less than $100 nor more than $1,000), attorneys' fees and court costs.[10]

---

[8]California Civil Code § 1747.50.

[9]15 U.S.C. § 1666a.

[10]15 U.S.C. § 1640.

9. Credit Cards, Charge Cards and Merchants

Frequently, when you use a credit card in a store, the merchant takes the card, runs it through a computer and punches in a few numbers, or places a phone call. Either way, these merchants are contacting a credit card guarantee company that has a record of your credit status. That information comes directly from your card issuer. If you don't want to be denied use of your credit card, be sure you know how much you've charged and paid for. The guarantee company checks for:

- *Your overall credit limit.* If you've exceeded your line of credit and attempt to make further purchases, the guarantee company will tell the merchant to reject your card.

- *Your daily limit.* Many credit card companies do not let cardholders use their card more than a certain number of times a day or spend more than a certain amount per day. This is meant to protect against the use of stolen cards. If you've exceeded the daily limit, the merchant will be told to reject the card.

- *The amount of the particular purchase.* Merchants must check with the guarantee company for approval on purchases larger than a certain dollar amount (called a "floor limit"), which varies among guarantee companies and merchants.

- *Whether you are late on a payment.* If you are often late, the guarantee company may tell the merchant to reject your card.

- *Whether the card should be taken away from you.* In some cases, the merchant receives a code on the machine to call the guarantee company directly on the telephone. If the merchant still has the card, the guarantee company will tell her to keep it. This can happen if the card was reported stolen or if you are excessively delinquent in your payments and the credit card company has revoked your card. Some merchants receive rewards for turning in revoked cards. Most merchants, however, refuse to confiscate cards and instead simply tell you your card was not accepted.

Must You Put Personal Information on a Credit Card Slip?

If merchants call up guarantee companies for purchases made with credit cards, can they still ask for other identification—such as a phone number? Many do, but growing numbers of customers are resisting and now the District of Columbia and over a dozen states—California, Delaware, Georgia, Kansas, Maryland, Massachusetts, Minnesota, Nevada, New Jersey, New York, Oregon, Pennsylvania, Rhode Island and Wisconsin—ban the practice. In addition, Virginia allows the merchant to collect the information but prohibits the merchant from selling that information to anyone else.[11]

If a merchant correctly processes a credit card transaction, he'll be paid even if the charge exceeds the card's credit limit, so he has no reason to contact the customer. In fact, merchants' agreements with Visa and MasterCard prohibit them from requiring a customer to furnish a phone number when paying with Visa or MasterCard. Many merchants who request telephone numbers use that information in direct marketing.

---

[11]District of Columbia Code Annotated § 47-3153; California Civil Code § 1747.8; Delaware Code Annotated § 11-914; Revised Georgia Code Annotated § 10-1-393.3; Kansas Statutes Annotated § 50-691; Annotated Code of Maryland § 13-317; Annotated Laws of Massachusetts § 93-105; Minnesota Statutes Annotated § 325F.982; Nevada Revised Statutes § 598.088; New Jersey Statutes Annotated § 56:11-17; New York General Business Law § 520-a; Oregon Revised Statutes § 646.894; Pennsylvania Statutes § 69-2602; General Laws of Rhode Island § 6-13-16; Wisconsin Statutes Annotated § 423.401; Code of Virginia 59.1-442.

Can a Merchant Require that You Charge a Minimum Amount?

Many merchants have a minimum amount a customer must charge before being allowed to pay by credit card. Is this legal? No, according to MasterCard and Visa. They claim that their agreements with merchants prohibit merchants from requiring a minimum purchase.

If a merchant refuses to accept your card for a small purchase, send a letter of complaint to the bank that issued the card. If that doesn't resolve the matter, contact Visa or MasterCard directly.

10. When You Can't Pay Your Credit or Charge Card Bill

If you owe a credit or charge card bill you can't afford, you have a couple of options.

Ignore the bill. You'll get a series of monthly statements and bills. After about six months, your account will be closed and your bill sent to a collection agency. Some companies act sooner, especially if you exceeded your credit limit with your charges. Some companies wait a little longer, especially if you have a good payment history. If you still don't pay after being contacted by a collection agency, you may be sued.

Ask to make lower monthly payments. You can write to the credit or charge card company and ask to make lower monthly payments. As explained in Chapter 3, most companies insist that you make the minimum payment. But if you can convince the company that your immediate financial situation is truly difficult, your payments may be further reduced to 2% to 3% of the outstanding balance. Or, the company might accept a half-payment, but it will freeze your credit line in doing so—that is, not let you incur any more charges.

Your delinquent payments—or arrangement to make reduced payments—will probably be reported to a credit bureau. Most credit card companies send customer information to bureaus once a month. Usually, all accounts more than 60 days past due with a balance over $50 are reported. See Chapter 12, Section B, to understand what it means when negative information is reported to a credit bureau.

B. Automated Teller Machine (ATM) and Debit Cards

ATM CARDS ARE ISSUED by banks, essentially to give bank customers flexibility in their banking hours. In most areas, with an ATM card you can withdraw money, make deposits, transfer money between accounts, find out your balance, get a cash advance and even make loan payments at all hours of the day or night.

Debit cards combine the functions of ATM cards and checks. Debit cards are issued by banks, but are used at stores, not at the banks themselves. When you pay with a debit card, the money is automatically deducted from your checking account. Many merchants accept ATM cards as debit cards.

Until recently, technological disagreements between merchants and banks meant that the use of debit cards was very limited. More and more merchants, however, especially grocery stores, convenient stores and gasoline stations, now accept debit cards. Many consumers prefer them over checks for two reasons:

- They don't have to carry around their checkbook and present identification, but are still able to make purchases direct from their checking account.

- They are paying their bills immediately, unlike when they use credit cards and get the bill later.

Still, there is consumer resistance to using debit cards. In general, consumers prefer having 20–25 days to pay their credit card bills.

1. Statement or Receipt Errors

Although ATM statement or debit receipts are not known for containing errors, mistakes do happen— perhaps more often on bank statements than on receipts. So always check your receipt and bank statement carefully. If you find an error, you have 60 days from the date of the statement or receipt to notify the bank.[12] Always call first and follow up with a letter, keeping a copy for your records. If you don't notify the bank within 60 days, it has no obligation to investigate the error and you're out of luck.

The financial institution has ten business days from the date of your notification to investigate the problem and tell you the result. If the bank needs more time, it can take up to 45 days, but only if it deposits the amount of money in dispute into your account. If the bank later determines that there was no error, it can take the money back, but it first must send you a written explanation.

---

[12]15 U.S.C. § 1693f.

2. Lost or Stolen ATM or Debit Cards

If your ATM or debit card is lost or stolen (never, never, never keep your personal identification number—PIN—near your card), call your bank *immediately*, and follow it up with a confirming letter. Under the Electronic Fund Transfer Act, your liability is:

- $0—after you report the card missing
- up to $50—if you notify the bank within two business days (unless you were on extended travel or in the hospital) after you realize the card is missing
- up to $500—if you fail to notify the bank within two business days (unless you were on extended travel or in the hospital) after you realize the card is missing, but do notify the bank within 60 days after your bank statement is mailed to you listing the unauthorized withdrawals
- unlimited—if you fail to notify the bank within 60 days after your bank statement is mailed to you listing the unauthorized withdrawals.[13]

If a financial institution violates any provision of the Electronic Fund Transfer Act, you can sue to recover the damages you incurred. You're entitled to your actual damages, twice the amount of any finance charge (but not less than $100 nor more than $1,000), attorneys' fees and court costs.[14]

C. Handling Delinquent Loans

 Terminology Shift

The rest of this chapter deals with personal, bank, auto and other similar loans, not credit card, ATM or debit transactions.

IF YOU HAVE A LOAN that you are having trouble paying back, contact your creditor and try to work out an arrangement. If you explain that your situation is temporary, the lender will probably grant you an extension, meaning the delinquent payments are put at the end of your loan and your account is brought up-to-date. Or, the lender may waive interest—that is, have you pay just principal—for a month or two. Some lenders will even rewrite loans to reduce the monthly payments. You'll probably pay longer and more interest, however.

Before contacting your lender, carefully re-read your loan agreement to try to understand all of its terms. This will help you intelligently negotiate with the lender. Below is a discussion of the law that covers loans—disclosures, applications and fine-print terms. If, after reading these sections, you think that the lender may have violated the law, use the violation as leverage in negotiating with the lender.

Negotiating With a Lender

If you're having trouble paying a loan and need to negotiate with a lender, be sure to read the appropriate sections in Chapter 3. As indicated there, the lender may waive interest, reduce your payments or let you skip a payment but tack it on at the end. But the lender won't do something for nothing. In exchange, you might have to get a cosigner, waive the statute of limitations (see Chapter 9), pay higher interest or for a longer period, or let the lender take a security interest in your house or car.

You are most vulnerable at this time. Be sure you truly understand any new loan terms and can afford to make the payments under any new agreement.

---

[13]15 U.S.C. § 1693g.

[14]15 U.S.C. § 1640.

1. Loan Disclosures

 If You Aren't Concerned About the Terms of Your Agreement

If you aren't concerned that a lender failed to disclose the interest rate, grace period, annual fee or other terms, you can skip this section.

The Truth in Lending Act, the law that requires credit and charge card companies to disclose interest rates and other information, also requires other lenders to disclose the terms of a loan.[15] When you applied for a mortgage, personal loan, car loan or almost any other loan, the lender before offering you credit—or, with a mortgage, within three days of receiving your loan application—must have disclosed the following in writing:

- your right to a written itemization of the amount borrowed

- the total amount of the loan—the amount you borrow, plus interest and noninterest charges, minus any down payment, trade-in amount and pre-paid interest

- the monthly finance charge—the amount of interest you'll pay

- the annual interest rate—this is not required if the total loan did not exceed $75 and the total interest does not exceed $5 or if the loan did exceed $75 but the total interest does not exceed $7.50

- the number, amount and due dates of all payments necessary to repay the loan

- if the creditor is also the seller, the total sale price—cash price of the item or service plus all other charges

- any late payment that may be imposed

- a statement of whether you're entitled to a rebate, or will be assessed a penalty, if you prepay the loan, and

- for mortgages, whether or not the loan is assumable—that is, whether a subsequent buyer of your house can take over your loan.

2. Credit Scoring

When you submit your loan application, the lender has to decide if you qualify. The standard used for making this decision depends on the lender and the type of loan. To simplify the process—and to protect themselves from charges of discrimination—lenders often "score" applicants.

Scoring means that they award points based on credit factors. Most lenders consider between ten and 25 factors, which vary tremendously.

Lenders essentially use two different scoring systems. The following is an example of a credit scoring system used by lenders who do not analyze information in a credit file. (See Chapter 12, Section B, for information on credit files.)

Example: Martha, a recently graduated nurse, applied to Omaha Bank for a $12,000 personal loan. The lender required a minimum credit score of 75 for her to qualify for the loan. He compared the information on Martha's application to his credit factor chart. Martha's scores are marked with an asterisk (*). Martha scored an 85, which means she easily qualified for the loan.

Credit Factors	Points Awarded	
Age		
Under 28	11	
28-34	5	*
35-48	3	
48-60	11	
61 and over	15	
Monthly income		
Less than $500	0	
$501 to $1000	2	
$1001 to $1500	5	
$1501 to $2000	9	*
$2001 to $3000	12	
$3001 and over	15	
Length at job		
under 6 months	2	
6 months to 18 months	4	*
18 months to 30 months	7	
30 months to 66 months	11	
66 months to 12 years	20	
Over 12 years	30	
Occupation		
Professional or manager	15	
Clerical or service	12	*
Skilled labor	11	
Unskilled labor	6	
Agriculture	9	
Own or rent home		
Own	15	
Rent	5	*
Length at address		
0 to 3 years	4	
Over 3 years	12	*
Telephone in borrower's name		
Yes	8	*
No	0	

Credit Factors	Points Awarded	
Number of bank credit cards		
0	0	
1-3	10	*
4 or more	3	
Monthly payment on non-mortgage debts		
$0 to $200	12	
$201 to $500	9	*
$501 to $1200	7	
$1201 or more	3	
Payment history		
30 days	15	
60 days	11	*
90 days	5	
Collection or bankruptcy	0	

When a lender obtains a credit file on a consumer, the credit scoring factors change somewhat. Now, most lenders concentrate on the following:

- prediction of default based on comparison with similar accounts

- negative information in the file, including outstanding judgments and tax liens

- the number of inquiries in a credit file—inquiries are notations in a file that a creditor has requested a copy of your file; many inquiries often means shopping around for credit after being rejected, and

- how often you use the credit you have.

3. Other Terms of a Loan

In looking over your loan agreement, these are the terms you may come across.

a. Acceleration Clause

This clause lets the lender declare the entire balance due ("accelerate" the loan) if you default—that is, miss a payment or otherwise violate a term of your loan agreement. If you miss one or two payments, the lender will probably agree to hold off accelerating the loan if you pay up what you owe and pay the remaining balance on time. If you miss additional payments, however, you can be sure you'll fall from the lender's good graces.

Once a loan is accelerated, it's almost impossible to get the lender to "unaccelerate" and reinstate your old loan. More than likely, you will have to enter into a new loan with the lender, and often the lender will require that you give it several additional years to sue you if you default on the new loan. This is called extending the statute of limitations.

Acceleration Clauses and Failed Financial Institutions

If you have a consumer (such as a car) loan through a bank, savings and loan or credit union that has failed, and you're behind on your payments, beware. Many institutions taken over by federal regulators are accelerating such loans and demanding payment in full. So if a financial institution you make loan payments to seems headed for trouble, be sure to keep (or get) current on that debt.

b. Attorneys' Fee Provision

Many creditors include a provision in a loan contract awarding them attorneys' fees if you default and they have to sue you to get paid. If your contract contains this provision, but says nothing about your right to attorneys' fees, in most states you nevertheless have the right to attorneys' fees in the event you are sued—or you sue—and *you* win. Several states, however, prohibit any consumer contract from including a provision where the creditor's attorneys' fee may exceed 15% of the balance owed.

c. Balloon Payment

Many borrowers can't afford the monthly payments when they apply for a fixed amount of money to be repaid in equal monthly payments for a set period. To help them qualify, lenders lower the monthly payments and collect the difference at the end of the loan in one large payment called a balloon payment. If you now have a balloon payment due, you may have trouble affording it. If you don't pay, the lender may have the right to repossess or foreclose on the property pledged as collateral for the loan—often a house.

To minimize the risk to borrowers, many states prohibit balloon payments in loans for goods or services primarily for personal, family or household use. Or, they give borrowers the right to refinance these loans at the lender's prevailing rate when the balloon payment comes due. In practice, many lenders let borrowers refinance balloon payments as long as the borrowers have decent credit at the time of the refinancing. Unfortunately, many borrowers don't have good credit and instead lose their property. But before you panic, see if you have the right—or at least the possibility—of refinancing the loan.

Balloon payment is prohibited		You have the right to refinance a final balloon payment	
State	**Code Section**	**State**	**Code Section**
District of Columbia	28-3803	Alabama	5-19-7
Maine	9-A-3-308	California	CC 1807.3
Maryland	12-1003	Colorado	5-3-405
North Carolina	25A-34	Delaware	6-4326
North Dakota	13-03.1-15	Hawaii	481C-3
Wisconsin	422.402	Idaho	28-43-307
		Indiana	24-4.5-2-405
		Iowa	537.3308
		Kansas	16a-3-308
		Kentucky	367.390
		Massachusetts	255D-10
		Ohio	1317.06
		Oklahoma	14A-2-405
			14A-3-402
		Pennsylvania	69-1703
		South Carolina	37-2-405
			37-3-402
		Utah	70C-3-102
		Virginia	6.1-330.90
		Washington	63.14.159
		West Virginia	46A-2-105
		Wyoming	40-14-239
			40-14-333

d. Confession of Judgment

A "confession of judgment" is a provision that lets a lender automatically take a judgment against you, if you default, without having to sue you in court. Federal law prohibits any non-real-estate consumer contract from including a confession of judgment.[16] This type of provision is very anti-consumer and few lenders try to include it in their loans.

---

[16]Federal Trade Commission's Credit Practices Rule, 16 C.F.R. § 444.

e. Cosigner or Guarantor

If you didn't qualify for a loan, a lender may have loaned you money because you presented a cosigner or guarantor. This person assumed full responsibility for paying back the loan if you don't. The cosigner or guarantor need not benefit from the loan to be liable for it.

If you file for bankruptcy and the cosigner or guarantor is a relative or personal friend, it is possible that the person could be stuck with more than just what you haven't paid on the debt. If you did make payments on the bill during the year before you filed for bankruptcy, the cosigner or guarantor may be required to pay to the bankruptcy court the total amount of what you paid during the year. This is because your payments may be considered an "illegal preference" in bankruptcy.[17]

Many young adults with no credit history have their parents cosign or guarantee loans. Other borrowers, who may have had a serious financial setback (repossession, foreclosure or bankruptcy), or simply don't earn enough to get a loan, ask a friend or relative to cosign or guarantee. Cosigners and guarantors should fully understand their obligations before they sign on.

Federal Trade Commission Cosigner Notification

The Federal Trade Commission's Credit Practices Rule requires that cosigners be given the following notice:

NOTICE TO COSIGNER

You are being asked to guarantee this debt. Think carefully before you do so. If the borrower doesn't pay the debt, you will have to. Be sure you can afford to pay if you have to, and that you want to accept this responsibility.

You may have to pay up to the full amount of the debt if the borrower does not pay. You may also have to pay late fees or collection costs, which increase this amount.

The creditor can collect this debt from you without first trying to collect from the borrower. The creditor can use the same collection methods against you that can be used against the borrower, such as suing you, garnishing your wages, etc. If this debt is ever in default, that fact may become a part of your credit record.

Three states offer additional protection to cosigners. In California, the cosigner notification must be in English and Spanish. In addition, if a debtor defaults, the creditor must give notice to a cosigner before or at the same time the creditor reports the delinquency to a credit bureau. In Illinois, before a lender can try to collect from a cosigner or report negative information about a cosigner to a credit bureau, the cosigner must be told that the primary debtor has defaulted and be given the opportunity to arrange for payments. In Maine, a cosigner is not obligated on a loan unless the lender has tried to collect from the primary debtor and has told the cosigner of his right to make payments and the consequences of not doing so.[18]

f. Credit Insurance

Credit insurance is required by many lenders to protect themselves in case you die or become disabled before you repay the loan. As a condition of making the loan, you must buy a credit life or credit disability policy that repays the lender in the event you can't make your loan payments. In most states, the lender can't require insurance in excess of the amount of the loan. In a few states, such as Alaska and Maryland, lenders cannot require credit insurance except for loans for real property. In New Jersey, credit insurance on second mortgages is prohibited.[19]

Credit insurance, for the most part, is a consumer rip-off. Insurance companies collect over $2 billion a year in premiums, yet pay out only $900 million a year. But that doesn't mean you should ignore your required credit insurance payments. If you let them slide, your lender may cancel your loan, or make the payments herself and charge you for them. Your best bet is to talk to your lender about letting you drop the insurance. Many will drop the requirement if you've repaid more than 50% of the loan.

---

[17]One court ruled this way in *In re Finn*, 909 F.2d 903 (6th Cir. 1990). If this is a concern for you, speak to a bankruptcy lawyer. (See Chapter 13.)

[18]California Civil Code §§ 1799.91 and 1799.101; Illinois Annotated Statutes Chapter 121 1/2 ¶ 262S; Maine Revised Statutes Annotated § 9-A-3-206.

[19]Alaska Statutes § 21.36.165; Annotated Code of Maryland Commercial Law § 12-1007; New Jersey Statutes Annotated § 17:11A-49.

g. Prepayment Penalties

Lenders make money on the interest they charge for lending money. If you pay your loan back early, they don't make as much as they had anticipated. To make up some of the loss, some lenders impose "prepayment penalties"—if you pay the loan off before it is due, you have to pay a penalty, usually a percentage of the balance paid off early.

A number of states believe that you ought to be able to pay back your loan early without being penalized. In Colorado, Idaho, Indiana, Iowa, Kansas, Louisiana, Maine, Maryland, Massachusetts, Oklahoma, South Carolina, Utah, Virginia, West Virginia, Wisconsin and Wyoming, you can prepay non-real-estate consumer loans in full without incurring any penalty.[20] In Maine, prepayment penalties are prohibited on non-real-estate consumer loans under $25,000 and in New Mexico on consumer loans for $2,500 or less; in West Virginia, they aren't allowed on non-real-estate consumer loans of 36 months or less.[21]

If you are having trouble paying your loan, you are probably not too concerned about a prepayment penalty. But if you have a choice of loans, consider any loan without a prepayment penalty, if possible.

h. Security Interest

As described in Chapter 1, when you take out a secured loan you give the creditor the right to take your property or a portion of it if you don't pay. This is called a security interest. The two most common security interests are mortgages, where you give the lender the right to foreclose on your home if you miss payments, and car loans, where the lender can take the car if you default.

Some consumer loans, especially for large appliances and furniture, include a security interest in the item being purchased. Also, some personal loans that are not used to purchase a specific item—and in fact, are often used to pay off other loans—include a security interest in your home, car or important items around your house. These personal loans can be hazardous to borrowers. The interest is usually very high, and if you default, the lender can take the item identified in the contract.

To protect borrowers, federal law prohibits lenders from taking a security interest in the following, unless you are actually buying the item: your clothing, furniture, appliances, linens, china, crockery, kitchenware, one radio and one television, wedding ring and personal effects.[22]

In Kansas, New York, North Carolina, Virginia, West Virginia and Wisconsin, borrowers have additional protections.[23] In Kansas, a lender cannot take a security interest in real estate for a consumer loan in which the interest exceeds 12% and the amount financed is $1,000 or less.

In Virginia, a lender cannot take a security interest in real estate for a consumer loan. In New York, retailers are prohibited from taking a security interest in goods purchased and charged on a store credit card or any other revolving credit card.

In North Carolina, West Virginia and Wisconsin, creditors may take a security interest in only the following:

---

[20]Colorado Revised Statutes § 5-2-209; Idaho Code § 28-42-306; Indiana Statutes Annotated § 24-4.5-3-209; Iowa Annotated Code § 537.2509; Kansas Statutes Annotated § 16a-2-509; Louisiana Statutes Annotated § 9:3531; Maine Revised Statutes Annotated § 9-308; Code of Maryland Commercial Law § 12-308; Annotated Laws of Massachusetts § 255-13L; Oklahoma Statutes Annotated § 14A-2-209; Code of Laws of South Carolina § 37-3-209; Utah Code § 70C-3-101; Code of Virginia § 6.1-282; West Virginia Code § 46A-3-110; Wisconsin Statutes Annotated § 422.208; Wyoming Statutes Annotated § 40-14-220.

[21]Maine Revised Statutes Annotated § 9-A-2-509; New Mexico Statutes Annotated § 58-15-15.1; West Virginia Code § 47-6-5d.

---

[22]Federal Trade Commission's Credit Practices Rule, 16 C.F.R. § 444.

[23]Kansas Statutes Annotated § 16a-2-307; New York Personal Property Law § 413(12); General Statutes of North Carolina § 25A-23; Code of Virginia § 6.1-281; West Virginia Code § 46A-2-107; Wisconsin Statutes Annotated § 422.417.

- the item being sold

- an item previously sold by that creditor if the creditor has an existing security interest

- personal property in which the item sold is installed or annexed (amount financed must exceed $300 in North Carolina, $500 in Wisconsin)

- real property to which the item sold is affixed (amount financed must exceed $1,000 in North Carolina and Wisconsin, $1,500 in West Virginia), or

- a motor vehicle (North Carolina only and the amount financed must exceed $100).

i. Wage Assignment

Some lenders, especially credit unions, try to ensure your repaying the loan by suggesting that you voluntarily agree to a wage assignment. This means that each time you are paid, a sum of money is deducted from your pay check by your employer to pay the lender before you ever see that money. Most people feel that this method of payment is overly intrusive and prefer to pay on their own.

With the exception of real estate loans, a voluntary wage assignment is allowed only if you have the power to revoke it.[24] If you are considering agreeing to one, keep in mind that it can help you discipline yourself if you think you won't pay on your own—and you can revoke it if you don't like it.

In many states, your spouse must consent (if you're married) before the lender can take a voluntary wage assignment.[25] In Oklahoma,

consumer loan wage assignments are barred for loans under $45,000, while in South Carolina, they are not allowed on loans under $25,000.[26] In Arizona, Kentucky, Montana, Rhode Island, South Dakota, Vermont and Virginia, the assignment can't exceed 10% of your salary; in Illinois, the limit is 15%. And in Oregon, wage assignments are not allowed on retail installment contracts.[27]

j. Waivers of Exemptions

As explained in Chapter 11, if a creditor sues you and gets a court judgment, or you file for bankruptcy, some of your property is protected from your creditors—that is, it can't be taken to pay what you owe. This property is called your exempt property. It usually includes your clothing and personal effects, household goods and some of the equity in your home and car.

Some creditors try to get around the laws that let you keep exempt property by including a provision in a loan agreement whereby you waive your right to keep your exempt property. These provisions are prohibited under federal law in any non-real-estate consumer contract.[28]

D. Where to Report Credit Violations

IF A CREDITOR VIOLATES provisions of the Truth In Lending, Fair Credit Billing or Electronic Fund Transfer Act, report the creditor to the appropriate

---

[24]Federal Trade Commission's Credit Practices Rule, 16 C.F.R. § 444.

[25]See, for example, California Labor Code § 300; Colorado Revised Statutes § 8-9-102; Hawaii Revised Statutes § 373-11; Indiana Statutes Annotated § 22-2-7-2; Iowa Code Annotated § 598.23; Annotated Code of Maryland Commercial Law § 15-302; Massachusetts General Laws Annotated Ch. 154 ¶ 3; Montana Code Annotated §§ 31-1-306 and 32-5-310; Code of Virginia § 6.1-289; Wyoming Statutes Annotated § 27-4-111.

[26]Oklahoma Revised Statutes § 14A-3-403; Code of Laws of South Carolina § 37-5-104.

[27]Arizona Revised Statutes § 6-631; Kentucky Revised Statutes § 288.570; Montana Code Annotated §§ 31-1-306 and 32-5-310; General Laws of Rhode Island § 19-25-34; South Dakota Codified Laws § 54-6-20; Vermont Statutes Annotated § 8-2229; Code of Virginia § 6.1-290; Illinois Annotated Statutes Ch. 48 ¶ 39.4; Oregon Revised Statues § 83.150.

[28]Federal Trade Commission's Credit Practices Rule, 16 C.F.R. § 444.

federal agency.[29] Write a letter giving the identity of the creditor and the name of the particular person who violated the law. Describe the violation in detail. Be sure to keep a copy of your letter for your records.

National banks. Consumer Examinations, Office of the Comptroller of the Currency, 250 E Street, SW, Washington, DC 20219, (202) 874-5000. Or contact a regional office.

Regional Offices of the Comptroller of the Currency

Marquis Tower I, Suite 600
245 Peachtree Center Avenue, NE
Atlanta, GA 30303
(404) 659-8855

1 Financial Place
440 South LaSalle Street, Suite 2700
Chicago, IL 60605
(312) 663-8000

1600 Lincoln Plaza
500 North Akard
Dallas, TX 75201-3394
(214) 720-0656

2345 Grand Avenue, Suite 700
Kansas City, MO 64108
(816) 556-1800

1114 Avenue of the Americas, Suite 3900
New York, NY 10036
(212) 819-9860

50 Fremont Street, Suite 3900
San Francisco, CA 94105
(415) 545-5900

Federal savings and loans. Office of Consumer Affairs, Office of Thrift Supervision, 1700 G Street, NW, 5th Floor, Washington, DC 20552, (202) 906-6000. Or contact a regional office.

---

[29]To report violations of the Fair Credit Reporting Act, see Chapter 12, Section B7, for addresses.

Regional Offices of Thrift Supervision

P.O. Box 105217
Atlanta, GA 30348-5217
(404) 888-0771

111 East Wacker Drive, Suite 800
Chicago, IL 60601-4360
(312) 540-5900

P.O. Box 619027
Dallas, TX 75261-9027
(214) 281-2000

10 Exchange Pl., 18th Floor
Jersey City, NJ 07302
(201) 413-1000

P.O. Box 7165
San Francisco, CA 94120
(415) 616-1500

National credit unions. Public Affairs Division, National Credit Union Administration, 1775 Duke Street, Alexandria, VA 22314-3428, (703) 518-6300. Or contact a regional office.

National Credit Union Administration Offices

9 Washington Square
Washington Avenue Extension
Albany, NY 12205
(518) 464-4180

1775 Duke Street, Suite 4206
Alexandria, VA 22314-3427
(703) 838-0401

7000 Central Parkway, Suite 1600
Atlanta, GA 30328
(404) 396-4042

4807 Spicewood Springs Road, Suite 5200
Austin, TX 78759-8490
(512) 482-4500

2300 Clayton Road, Suite 1350
Concord, CA 94520
(510) 825-6125

4225 Naperville Rd., Suite 125
Lisle, IL 60532
(708) 245-1000

State banks (members of the Federal Reserve System). Division of Consumer and Community Affairs, Board of Governors Federal Reserve System, 20th & Constitution Avenues, NW, Washington, DC 20551; (202) 452-3000. Or contact a regional federal reserve office by writing to Federal Reserve Bank of [*name of city*], Office of Consumer Affairs, [rest of address as listed below].

Regional Federal Reserve Offices

104 Marietta Street, NW
Atlanta, GA 30303-2713
(404) 521-8500

600 Atlantic Avenue
Boston, MA 02106
(617) 973-3000

230 South LaSalle Street
Chicago, IL 60604
(312) 322-5322

1455 E. Sixth Street
Cleveland, OH 44114
(216) 579-2000

2200 N. Pearl St.
Dallas, TX 75201
(214) 922-6000

925 Grand Avenue
Kansas City, MO 64198
(816) 881-2000
(800) 333-1010

250 Marquette Avenue
Minneapolis, MN 55401-2171
(612) 340-2345

33 Liberty Street
New York, NY 10045
(212) 720-5000

10 Independence Mall
Philadelphia, PA 19106
(215) 574-6000

701 East Byrd Street
Richmond, VA 23219
(804) 697-8000

411 Locust Street
St. Louis, MO 63102
(314) 444-8444

101 Market St.
San Francisco, CA 94105
(415) 974-2000

State banks (not members of the Federal Reserve System). Office of Consumer Affairs, Federal Deposit Insurance Corp., 550 17th Street, NW, Washington, DC 20429, (202) 393-8400. Or contact a regional office.

Department store, gasoline company or any other creditor. Federal Trade Commission (addresses and phone numbers are in Chapter 12, Section B7). ■

Regional Federal Deposit Insurance Corporation Offices

Marquis Tower I, Suite 1200
245 Peachtree Center Avenue, NE
Atlanta, GA 30303
(404) 525-0308

30 South Wacker Drive, Suite 3100
Chicago, IL 60606
(312) 382-7500

1910 Pacific Avenue, Suite 1900
Dallas, TX 75201
(214) 220-3342

2345 Grand Avenue, Suite 1500
Kansas City, MO 64108
(816) 234-8000

5100 Poplar Avenue, Suite 1900
Memphis, TN 38137
(901) 685-1603

452 Fifth Avenue, 19th Floor
New York, NY 10018
(212) 704-1200

25 Ecker Street, Suite 2300
San Francisco, CA 94105
(415) 546-0160

Westwood Executive Center
200 Lowderbrook Drive
Westwood, MA 02090
(617) 320-1600

Chapter 7

STUDENT LOANS

If a man empties his purse into his head, no man can take it away from him. An investment in knowledge always pays the best interest.

—Benjamin Franklin, American statesman, philosopher & inventor, 1706-1790

THE FEDERAL GOVERNMENT has been helping students with higher education costs for nearly 50 years. After War World II, veterans were rewarded with grants and loans for serving their country. In the 1960s, anti-poverty programs helped many low-income people go to college, again, through grants and loans.

Then, during the 1970s and 1980s, the government expanded eligibility to help millions of people. Today, nearly $14 billion in student loans are guaranteed each year by the federal government, an increase of more than 75% from the early 1980s. A student who borrows the maximum for undergraduate and graduate studies will come out of school owing $65,000, plus interest.

But the 1970s, 1980s and early 1990s also saw an escalation in the number of former students who did not repay their loans. During those years, the default rate peaked at 22%. In terms of actual dollars owed, the worst year for the government was 1991, when the default on student loans was $3.6 billion.

These defaults horrified Congress. During the early 1990s, Congress enacted several pieces of legislation to control student defaults. Much of the legislation limited the amount of loan money available to students who attend proprietary or trade schools, where the default rate at some schools is as high as 68% and averages 35%. But new collections laws apply to all ex-students in default—the ones who attended trade schools, as well as those who went to two-year colleges (average default rate of about 15%) and those who went to four-year schools (average default rate of about 6%).

The efforts appear to be working. The latest statistics put the default rate at 15% and the annual outstanding amount at $2 billion, significantly lower than $3.6 billion.

In 1980, if an ex-student didn't repay a student loan, he might hear from the government in seven or eight years, if at all. Today, he'll probably hear from the government much sooner, have his federal (and possibly state) income tax refund intercepted, 10% of his wages garnished (taken from his paycheck) before being sued, and eventually sued. If he still doesn't pay the debt, the government will probably put a lien on his property and garnish up to 25% of his wages.

And the responses a former student can make to the government's collection efforts are more limited than they were ten years ago. Specifically:

- The government (Department of Education and any agency collecting on behalf of the Department of Education) has decreased its willingness to negotiate on student loans.

- Congress has eliminated the main defense asserted by former students—that the statute of limitations has run; that is, that the government waited too long—when sued on a student loan.

- Collection agencies collecting on behalf of the Department of Education are allowed to tack on a 42% collections fee. That is added to the principal, interest and other collection fees you owe.

This introduction isn't meant to lead you to throw this book across the room if your biggest debt problem is a student loan. It is, however, meant to let you know that stopping the government's collection efforts will be a difficult task. Over $15 billion is outstanding in total uncollected student loans. At the same time, the national debt hit record highs during the 1980s. Former students have become an easy target of an angry and frustrated Congress that knows it must take steps to reduce the deficit.

Help! I've Already Paid Off My Loan

In what is becoming a nightmare for some former students, the Department of Education has been demanding payment from people who repaid their loans years ago. The Department claims to have never been paid—often the bank that originally loaned or collected the money is out of business—and is requiring former students to prove they paid. This is obviously very difficult, as few people keep ten-to-15-year-old bank records.

If you face this problem and the bank where you borrowed or repaid the money is still in business, solicit the bank's help in getting copies of your canceled checks. If you're told that the bank doesn't keep such old records, have them check their microfiche and other electronic records.

If the bank is out of business or doesn't have your records, contact the appropriate federal agency—depending on the type of bank—to see if it has old loan records or canceled checks. (If you don't know what kind of institution you borrowed from, contact any agency. It will direct you to the correct one.) See Chapter 6, Section D, for the addresses and phone numbers of the various federal agencies that oversee financial institutions.

You will also need to contact the Department of Education and provide whatever evidence of your paying you have (Department of Education, Office of Postsecondary Education, 400 Maryland Avenue, SW, Washington, DC 20202; (800) 433-3243). Here are some examples:

- If your ex-spouse or former roommate remembers you diligently writing checks every month, have that person sign a sworn statement and send it to the agency.

- Dig up records from lenders for years past for copies of old credit reports listing payments made on the loan.

- Get copies of old tax returns (from the IRS if necessary) showing that you itemized the interest deduction on student loan payments.

- Contact the school attended for a report from the Department of Education showing the loan's status.

- Request a copy of the signed promissory note from the last holder of the loan with a summary of the account.

You might also consider bankruptcy. Be aware, however, that bankruptcy judges look with disfavor at debtors who file for bankruptcy just to get rid of a student loan.

A. What Kind of Loan Do You Have?

 Before Taking Action on Your Loan, You Must Understand What Kind of Loan It Is

Your ability to negotiate with your lender, defer your payments or possibly cancel your loan may depend on what type of loan you have. If yours is a Guaranteed Student Loan (GSL) or Stafford Loan, read Section 1. If it's a National Direct Student Loan (NDSL) or Perkins, read Section 2. If it's any other type of loan, read Sections 3 and 4. If, like many people, you've got more than one type of loan, you'll need to read all applicable sections.

1. Guaranteed Student Loans or Stafford Loans

The largest number of student loans made are Guaranteed Student Loans, which have been called Federal Stafford Loans since the fall of 1987. For convenience, I refer to them as Stafford Loans throughout this chapter. A Stafford Loan is a loan made by a bank to finance your college or graduate school education. The bank takes a 5% loan origination fee out of the amount of the loan. Nevertheless, you must pay back the full amount of the loan (including the 5% you never received). The bank also deducts an insurance premium fee of up to 3% of the amount of the loan.

Repayment of the loan is guaranteed by the federal government.[1] With most Stafford Loans, you have no obligation to start paying the loan back until six months (nine months under an old law) after you graduate or withdraw from school. With a few (non-need-based loans made after October 10, 1992), you may have to make interest payments while you are in school.

Within 120 days after you leave school, the bank or other agency holding your loan must notify you of the date that repayment begins. Even if you never

---

[1] 20 U.S.C. § 1071.

receive this notice, you are obligated to begin repaying the loan within six months of when you leave school (nine months under an old law). If the six-month period is near the end and you haven't heard from the holder of your loan, be sure to contact the agency you borrowed from to find out when your payments are due. And, if you move, be sure to send the holder of your loan a change of address. *If it is at all possible, you do not want to be in default on a Stafford Loan.* (See Section D1, below, on obtaining a deferment.)

2. National Direct Student Loans or Perkins Loans (Need-based College Loans)

National Direct Student Loans (NDSL Loans) have been called Federal Perkins Loans since the fall of 1987. For convenience, I refer to them as Perkins Loans throughout this chapter.

Like Stafford Loans, repayment of Perkins Loans is guaranteed by the federal government. But Perkins Loans are available only to students with financial need. Your school lends you money for your college or graduate school education. For most students, obligation to repay begins approximately nine months after you graduate or withdraw from school.

3. Non-need-based College Loans

Two other common loans made directly by colleges are created and funded by the federal government. These loans are:

- Federal Parental Loans for Students (PLUS)— made to parents to help pay for their dependent children's education, and

- Federal Supplemental Loans for Students (SLS)— made directly to financially independent students.

Like Stafford and Perkins Loans, repayment of these loans is guaranteed by the federal government. Your school lends you money for your college or

graduate school education. And, as with Stafford Loans, the bank takes a 5% loan origination fee out of the amount of the loan that you must pay back when making a PLUS or SLS loan. The bank also deducts an insurance premium fee of up to 3% of the amount of the loan.

Unlike Stafford and Perkins Loans, however, there is no deferment period with a PLUS or SLS for being in school. This means that you must generally make your first payment within 60 days of receiving the money. If you also have a Stafford Loan, however, you can use the Stafford Loan in-school deferment period and the six-month just-out-of-school grace period on both loans.

4. Miscellaneous Loans

There are two other loans created and funded by the federal government. These loans are:

- Health Professions Student Loans (HPSL), and

- Health Education Assistance Loans (HEAL).

The rules regarding repayment, deferment, cancellation and other terms vary from loan to loan. Contact the Department of Education or your school's financial aid office for details.

In addition, some colleges make student loans from private or university sources, and state universities may make loans from state funds. These loans are not guaranteed by the federal government and the rules regarding collection, deferment and cancellation can vary tremendously from school to school and state to state.

B. Canceling a Student Loan Obligation

UNDER THE FOLLOWING CIRCUMSTANCES, you can cancel your obligation to repay a student loan. In some situations, however, you cannot be in default.

You become totally and permanently disabled or die. You can cancel a Stafford, Perkins, PLUS or SLS Loan. PLUS Loans may be canceled if the child for whom you borrowed the money dies and the repayment period began July 23, 1992, or earlier. The standard of "totally and permanently disabled" is defined as "the condition of an individual who is unable to work and earn money or attend school because of an injury or illness that is expected to continue indefinitely or result in death." You will need a statement from your treating physician using a form provided by the Department of Education or a guaranty agency. You can be in default and still cancel a loan because of death or disability.

You serve in the U.S. military. The Defense Department will repay up to 50% of a Perkins Loan, if you are serving in an area of hostility or are in imminent danger.

You're a full-time elementary or secondary teacher in a designated area serving low-income students. You can cancel up to 100% of a Perkins Loan. You can cancel up to 100% of a Stafford Loan made after October 1, 1992, if you have no other outstanding student loans.

You're a full-time teacher of handicapped children. You can cancel up to 100% of a Perkins Loan.

You're a full-time professional provider of early intervention services for the disabled. You can cancel up to 100% of a Perkins Loan made after July 23, 1992, if you have no other outstanding loans.

You're a full-time teacher of math, science, foreign languages, bilingual education or other fields designated as teacher-shortage areas. You can cancel up to 100% of a Perkins Loan made after July 23, 1992. You can cancel up to 100% of a Stafford Loan made after October 1, 1992, if you have no other outstanding loans.

You're a full-time employee of a public or nonprofit agency providing services to low-income, high-risk children and their families. You can cancel up to 100% of a Perkins Loan made after July 23, 1992.

You're a full-time nurse. You can cancel up to 100% of a Perkins Loan made after July 23, 1992. You can cancel up to 100% of a Stafford Loan made after October 1, 1992, if you have no other outstanding student loans.

You're a full-time medical technician. You can cancel up to 100% of a Perkins Loan made after July 23, 1992.

You're a full-time law enforcement or corrections officer. You can cancel up to 100% of a Perkins Loan made after November 29, 1990.

You're a full-time staff member in a Head Start program. You can cancel up to 100% of a Perkins Loan.

You're a Peace Corps or VISTA volunteer. You can cancel up to 70% of a Perkins Loan. You can cancel up to 100% of a Stafford Loan made before October 1, 1992.

You return to school for a teaching certificate. You can cancel up to 100% of a Stafford Loan made before October 1, 1992.

To cancel a student loan—or to determine if you qualify for cancellation—call the holder of your loan or the Department of Education's Debt Collection Services Office at (800) 621-3115. The Department of Education has a free booklet entitled *The Student Guide.* Although it's geared toward students now applying for financial assistance, it contains some important information on canceling student loans and obtaining deferments to repay.

C. Who Collects Student Loans?

UNTIL RECENTLY, BANKS AND COLLEGES, which make most student loans, didn't aggressively try to collect them as long as they were guaranteed by the federal government. Congress has tightened the rules that banks and colleges must follow to remain participants in the federal student loan program, however, so those institutions now diligently try to collect student loans.

1. Stafford Loans

At the end of your six-month grace period after you leave school, toward the end of any deferment period (deferments are discussed in Section D1, below) or if you never paid your loan and are considered "in default," you will hear from one of the following:

- Your **lender**, such as the bank. If the bank decides to collect the loan itself, it will send you a notice to contact it to arrange repayment. If you don't answer, the bank may try other ways to contact you. But the bank doesn't really care whether or not you repay—if you default, the bank will turn the loan back to a guaranty agency and get paid. The only thing the bank loses is future interest, which is somewhere between 6.94% and 10%.

- A company on the **secondary market**, which is a place banks sell nondefaulted loans they decide not to collect themselves. A common secondary market company to which student loans are sold is "Sallie Mae," the Student Loan Marketing Association. Sallie Mae is a private corporation set up by Congress to collect student loans. More and more banks sell Stafford Loans to Sallie Mae, whether or not they have first tried to collect from you.

- A **loan servicer**, which "services" the loan— receives payments—for the lender or secondary market company that bought the loan from the lender, unless you default. (Then the loan is turned over to a guaranty agency.) A frequently used loan servicer for student loans is the Student Loan Servicing Center.

- A **guaranty agency**, which pays the lender or secondary market company that bought the loan from the lender if you default. A guaranty agency attempts to collect defaulted loans for the Department of Education. A frequently used guaranty agency for student loans is a company called USAF. Because a guaranty agency's sole function is to collect student loans, it aggressively goes after defaulters.

- **Department of Education** (DOE), which tries to collect defaulted loans turned over by a guaranty agency.

- A **collection agency**, which may have contracted with a guaranty agency or the Department of Education to try to collect a defaulted loan. The amount you must repay can increase quickly if your loan is with a collection agency. As mentioned at the beginning of the chapter, a collection agency can tack on a 42% collection fee.

Guaranty agencies, DOE and its collection agencies put substantial efforts into collecting delinquent student loans. Hundreds of full-time collectors pursue people in default. You will encounter extreme aggression in the collecting of your loan. DOE will most likely ask the IRS to intercept your federal tax refund, may garnish your wages and may eventually sue you. Also, the Department can request the records of other government departments to find your address, phone number, dependents, employment history and other information in order to find you and get you to pay back your student loan.[2] And you can be sure that notice of your default will be sent to credit bureaus.

2. Other Loans

After your just-out-of-school six-month grace period ends, toward the end of any deferment period (deferments are discussed in Section D1, below) or if you never paid your loan and are considered "in default," your college may or may not keep the loan for collection.

If your college keeps your loan, the college will send you a letter asking you to set up a repayment schedule and start repaying. If you don't respond, or if you start paying and stop sometime down the road, usually the college will try to work with you before taking more severe action. How much patience the college exhibits depends a lot on

---

[2]20 U.S.C. § 1092b.

whether you are in contact with it and how good your excuses are.

If your college decides that you intend to neither pay the loan nor work out any kind of an arrangement, you will hear from any of the following:

- one of the many agencies described in Section C1, above

- the school's legal department, which may sue you

- the IRS or a state tax department, which may intercept your income tax refund

- a collection agency hired by the school to try and collect, or

- the state's collection department, if you attended a public college (some states have set up collection programs).

In addition, the college can—and probably will—do any of the following:

- prohibit you from re-enrolling or using any of the college's alumni services, such as the placement office

- withhold your grades, diploma and transcript, or

- notify local credit bureaus that your student loan is delinquent.

D. When You Intend to Repay

 If You Don't Intend to Pay

If you have no current intention of repaying your loan, skip ahead to Sections E and F, which cover getting sued and filing for bankruptcy. After reading those sections and discovering that you probably will have few defenses to a lawsuit and that your loan may not qualify for elimination in bankruptcy, you might return to this section out of necessity, not desire.

1. Deferring Repayments

In many situations, you can defer (postpone) the repayment of the principal and/or interest on your government-guaranteed student loan.[3] To obtain a deferment, you usually cannot be in default—that is, you must have made your payments since they became due, have received other deferments, or be in the grace period after graduation. Occasionally, you may qualify for retroactive deferment. The rules depend on the kind of loan you have and when you obtained it.

a. Loans Disbursed After July 1, 1993

The grounds for deferment changed radically effective July 1, 1993. As of that date, most loans qualify for deferment in only four situations.

You are enrolled in school at least half-time. You can defer only principal on PLUS and SLS Loans. You can defer interest and principal on a Perkins or Stafford Loan.

You are enrolled in an approved graduate fellowship program or a rehabilitation program for the disabled. You can defer only principal on PLUS and SLS Loans. You can defer interest and principal on a Perkins or Stafford Loan.

You are unable to find full-time employment. You can defer only principal on PLUS and SLS Loans. You can defer interest and principal on a Perkins or Stafford Loan. The deferment is for a maximum of three years.

Your are suffering from economic hardship. You are automatically entitled to the deferment if you receive public assistance—welfare, AFDC, SSI, Food Stamps, and the like. If you don't receive public benefits, qualifying is based on a complex formula which considers your income, the federal minimum wage, the federal poverty level and your monthly loan payments. Essentially, you will qualify if your total income less your monthly federal

---

[3] 20 U.S.C. § 1077.

student loan payments is less than about $800 per month. You can defer only principal on PLUS and SLS Loans. You can defer interest and principal on a Perkins or Stafford Loan. The deferment is for a maximum of three years.

In addition, you can defer a Perkins Loan for any reason listed in Section B, above, except the first and the last.

b. Stafford Loans Disbursed Before July 1, 1993

You may be able to defer your pre-July 1, 1993, Stafford Loan payments under the following conditions. As you read, you will note that many are the same grounds for canceling a loan. Under those conditions, you can defer the loans for a short period—the time mentioned with each deferment ground below. If the condition lasts longer, you may be able to cancel the loan. (See Section B.)

You are in school full-time. You can always obtain a deferment if you're in school full-time. In addition, some banks will let you defer your repayment if you are in school half-time; check with your bank. The deferment lasts until six months after your schooling ends.

You are disabled and enrolled in full-time rehabilitation training. The deferment lasts until six months after your training ends.

You are temporarily totally disabled. The deferment is for a maximum of three years.

You are in the military. The deferment is for a maximum of three years.

You are a full-time volunteer in a tax-exempt organization, the Peace Corps or an ACTION program. The deferment is for a maximum of three years.

You are on active duty with the National Oceanic and Atmospheric Administration Corps. The deferment is for a maximum of three years.

You are a full-time teacher in a government-identified teacher shortage area. The deferment is for a maximum of three years.

You are completing a professional internship. The deferment is for a maximum of two years.

You are unemployed, but are looking for work. The deferment is for a maximum of two years.

You are the mother of preschool children, are entering or reentering the work force and are earning no more than $1 per hour above the federal minimum wage. The deferment is for a maximum of one year.

You are on parental leave. The deferment is for a maximum of six months.

c. Perkins, PLUS and SLS Loans Disbursed Before July 1, 1993

You may be able to defer your pre-July 1, 1993, Perkins, PLUS and SLS Loan payments if:

You are in school full-time. You can defer only principal on PLUS and SLS Loans; you cannot defer a Perkins Loan.

You are disabled and enrolled in full-time rehabilitation training. You may defer only principal on PLUS and SLS Loans; you cannot defer a Perkins Loan.

You are temporarily totally disabled. You may defer only principal on PLUS and SLS. You may defer principal and interest on a Perkins Loan. The deferment is for a maximum of three years. If you have a Perkins Loan from before the fall of 1987 (called an NDSL), you cannot defer any of it.

You are in the military. You may defer only principal on an SLS. You may defer principal and interest on a Perkins Loan. You may defer principal and interest on a PLUS Loan made before August 15, 1983. The deferment is for a maximum of three years.

You are a full-time volunteer in a tax-exempt organization, the Peace Corps or an ACTION

program. You may defer only principal on an SLS. You may defer principal and interest on a Perkins Loan. You may defer principal and interest on a PLUS Loan made before August 15, 1983. The deferment is for a maximum of three years.

You are on active duty with the National Oceanic and Atmospheric Administration Corps. You may defer only principal on an SLS. You may defer principal and interest on a Perkins Loan. The deferment is for a maximum of three years. If you have a Perkins Loan from before the fall of 1987 (called an NDSL), you cannot defer any of it. Nor can you defer a PLUS Loan.

You are a full-time teacher in a government-identified teacher shortage area. You may defer only principal on an SLS. The deferment is for a maximum of three years. You cannot defer a Perkins or PLUS Loan.

You are completing a professional internship. You may defer only principal on an SLS. You may defer principal and interest on a Perkins Loan. The deferment is for a maximum of two years. You cannot defer a PLUS Loan.

You are unemployed, but are looking for work. You may defer only principal on an SLS, PLUS or Perkins Loan. The deferment is for a maximum of two years.

You are the mother of prsschool children, are entering or reentering the work force and are earning no more than $1 per hour above the federal minimum wage. You may defer only principal on an SLS. You may defer principal and interest on a Perkins Loan. The deferment is for a maximum of one year. If you have a Perkins Loan from before the fall of 1987 (called an NDSL), you cannot defer any of it. Nor can you defer a PLUS Loan.

You are on parental leave. You may defer only principal on an SLS. You may defer principal and interest on a Perkins Loan. The deferment is for a maximum of six months. If you have a Perkins Loan from before the fall of 1987 (called an NDSL), you cannot defer any of it. Nor can you defer a PLUS Loan.

d. How to Obtain a Deferment

To obtain a deferment of a government-backed loan, contact the current holder of your loan—see the list in Section C1, above. If you don't know who currently holds your loan, contact the bank or college you initially borrowed from. If that institution has sold your loan or turned it elsewhere, it will tell you.

Ask the holder of your loan to send you a deferment application form. Fill it out thoroughly. Don't lie, but be sure to use language that fits the language of the deferments described above. For example, if you are out of work, be sure to state that you are "unemployed but looking for work." For this deferment, the holder of your loan may require that you submit periodic verifications of your job search (similar to what an unemployment office requires). Be sure to comply or you will no doubt lose your deferment.

Whether or not you will be granted more than one deferment is up to the holder of your loan. Your best approach is to explain your needs and to be cooperative with the holder. If you are asked to fill out a seemingly meaningless 16-page application, don't complain within earshot of the holder of your loan. Smile politely, complete the form and complain to your friends when you get home.

> **Example:** Lisa owes $12,000 in Stafford Loans. When her six-month grace period expired, she had just returned from a trip to Asia. She was unemployed but starting to look for work. She contacted her bank and was given a deferment. She eventually found a job and dutifully made her monthly payments. Several years later she had a child, took a year off from work and her bank gave her an "economic hardship" deferment.

2. Negotiating With the Holder of the Loan

If you don't qualify for a deferment, and either can't afford what you are supposed to pay or stopped paying (defaulted) in the past, try negotiating with a person from whoever holds your loan. That person can grant you a forbearance—let you temporarily not make payments—extend your overall time to make payments or make smaller payments.

a. Banks

A bank will probably be the least receptive to your negotiating overtures. A bank rarely accepts less than what it is owed. Normally, it would rather turn the loan over to a company on the secondary market, a loan servicer or the government, collect its money and forget about you. If a bank does agree to lower your payments, you'll be required to pay back at least $600 per year—$50 per month—on a Stafford Loan.[4]

b. Colleges

Colleges often extend a lot of flexibility, on both their own loans and government-backed loans, especially if you graduated from the school. You should have little trouble contacting someone from the college and explaining your situation. If the college sees that you are earnestly trying but unable to pay, it will often suspend or lower your payments until your financial situation improves. If you lose touch with the college, however, it will likely begin collection efforts.

If the college suggests a minimum monthly amount you can't afford, offer one you can live with. Below is a sample letter to your college to work out a repayment schedule.

---

[4]20 U.S.C. § 1077(c).

Sample Letter to College

1818 Jane Street
New York, NY 10000

December 1, 19__

Donald Havana
Student Loan Department
The Randolph Institute
Alexandria and Peanut Streets
Oxnard, MS 34567

Dear Mr. Havana:

I graduated from The Randolph Institute last June. While there, I borrowed $15,000 in Perkins Loans. I know that my nine-month grace period is nearly over and that I must begin making payments soon.

In your letter of November 11, you stated that I must repay a minimum of $159 per month. Recently, however, I took a job as a dancer for Equinox (a small avant garde improvisational dance troupe) and my income barely covers my expenses. Nevertheless, I do not want to avoid my obligation to repay.

Consequently, I am able and wish to make payments of $50 a month at this time. Should my income increase, I will try to raise my payments.

Very truly yours,

Miki Campbell

---

c. When Your School or Bank No Longer Holds Your Loan

If the bank or college has sold your loan to a company on the secondary market, such as Sallie Mae, you may be able to work out a convenient payment schedule. These companies try to set up schedules that student borrowers can live with. But they aren't pushovers—they will insist on your making regular monthly payments.

If a guaranty agency, the Department of Education or a collection agency holds your loan, it means the holder of your loan probably will play hardball in negotiating with you. In addition, as we've mentioned, regulations allow a collection agency to charge former students collection fees—including employee salaries, telephone and mailing costs, computer costs, court costs and attorney fees up to 42% of the amount of the loan—even if the loan papers don't authorize it. Also, a collection agency keeps 28% of every dollar it collects—and this money isn't counted toward your loan repayment. Thus, you will have to pay about $140 on every $100 outstanding to pay off your loan. And the final bit of bad news: except in rare situations, the Department of Education will not take your loan back from the collection agency so you can avoid the fee.

If you want to find out who holds your loan, call the Debt Collection Services for Student Loans at (800) 621-3115. If the Department of Education holds your loan, you must negotiate with the regional office that holds your file—which won't necessarily be the office closest to you. Start by calling one of the following numbers to find out which office has your loan: (202) 708-4766 (Washington, D.C.); (404) 331-2501 (Atlanta); (312) 353-6874 (Chicago); (415) 556-7918 (San Francisco); or (800) 241-4710.

You can beg to be put on a repayment schedule, but don't be alarmed if your pleas go unanswered. After the holder of your loan adds all the fees, your balance will be enormous. The holder has little incentive to take $75 a month from you on a balance now $30,000. If you don't get anywhere negotiating with the holder of your loan, consider contacting a local Consumer Credit Counseling Service office. (See Chapter 13, Section C.) Many CCCS offices try hard to negotiate for former students who can't afford their loan payments.

3. Repaying an Old Loan to Obtain a New One

The Higher Education Amendments of 1992 authorize three ways in which a student in default—even a student with a court judgment against her—can nevertheless obtain a new student loan:

- **Make six consecutive reasonable and affordable monthly payments on your old loan.**[5] The guaranty agency holding your loan decides what is reasonable and affordable based on your financial picture. If the agency lets you pay less than $50 per month, it must add documentation to your file.

- **Make 12 consecutive reasonable and affordable monthly payments on your old loan.** At that time, the guaranty agency holding your loan can sell it back to a company on the secondary market and remove the default from your credit record. Once your loan is sold back, you can be given a full ten years to repay it.

- **Repay a loan discharged in bankruptcy.** As discussed in Section F, below, some loans may be erased (discharged) in bankruptcy. According to the new regulations, you will have to repay any loans discharged in bankruptcy in order to obtain a new loan.

This provision probably violates the Bankruptcy Code. But you may nonetheless get rejected if you apply for a loan after discharging one in bankruptcy and not repaying it. If so, you will probably need the help of a lawyer to obtain the new loan after bankruptcy.

4. Requesting an Extended or Flexible Payment Option

Former students who want to repay their loans but cannot currently afford the payments and don't qualify for any deferral may be able to consolidate their loans or enter into a flexible repayment schedule.

---

[5]20 U.S.C. § 1078-6(b).

a. Consolidating Your Loans

Sallie Mae and a few other companies, including USAF, let you consolidate any Stafford or GSL, Perkins or NDSL loans. Health Professions Student Loans (HPSL), SLS (or the former ALAS) and PLUS loan payments can be included only if you consolidate through Sallie Mae.

To consolidate, you must be in the repayment period or grace period preceding repayment (meaning you can't be in school full-time). If you consolidate loans or reduce the interest without extending the payment period, you can make lower monthly payments. If you can't afford high payments, you can request a graduated or income-sensitive repayment option to keep your payments down.

A HEAL loan cannot be consolidated with reduced interest, but it can be combined with the other loans so that you only have to make one payment per month. If a HEAL payment is combined with other payments, you pay different rates of interest on the HEAL and non-HEAL portions of the loan.

If you are in default, consolidating loans will bring you out of default and help you qualify for deferment or new loans. Even if you're not in default but your loans were disbursed before July of 1993, consolidating will let you take advantage of the economic hardship deferment.

For more information on consolidating your loans, call Sallie Mae at (800) 524-9100. If your loans are still with someone other than Sallie Mae, Sallie Mae will pick them up in the consolidation process.

b. Requesting a Flexible Payment Option

In the mid-1990s, the Department of Education began a small program of direct lending. Under the program, certain selected students receive their loans directly from the government—there is no bank or college financial aid office to apply to. Students in the direct lending program are entitled to pay back their student loans through any of these four ways:

- the standard ten-year repayment schedule
- an extended repayment schedule—the length of your payback period depends on the amount of your loan—ranges from 12 years for loans under $10,000 to 30 years for loans over $60,000
- a graduated repayment schedule—you can pay off your loan in as many as 30 years by making lower payments in the early years of the loan and higher payments later, and
- an income-contingent repayment plan—your payments change each year based on the amount of your income and student loan.

While these payment options can offer much relief, opting for one could cost you a lot. For example, if you stretch your payments out for 20 or 30 years, you will wind up paying thousands— possibly tens of thousands—of dollars more in interest than you would have if you paid your loans off in ten years. The graduated repayment schedule can work the best, especially if you are able to make large payments when your income goes up.

While banks are not obligated to offer extended, graduated or income-contingent repayment plans, many do. So even if you aren't participating in the direct lending program, ask your lender about a flexible payment schedule.

E. When the Holder of Your Loan Gets Tough

IF YOU HAVEN'T MADE ANY PAYMENTS on your student loan for quite some time and haven't arranged for a deferment, or you've ignored efforts by the holder of your loan to collect, the holder will probably step up its collection efforts. You may have any income tax refund to which you are entitled intercepted or your wages garnished, or you may be sued.

1. Losing Your Income Tax Refund

The Internal Revenue Service can intercept your income tax refund until your loan is paid off in full.[6] The IRS can intercept a refund only if the holder of the loan is a guaranty agency, the Department of Education or a collection agency hired by the Department. If your school, the bank, a loan servicer or a company on the secondary market has your loan, your tax refund is safe.

Here is how the intercept program works:

1. The guaranty agency or Department of Education notifies the IRS that your loan is delinquent. The agency or Department can notify the IRS every year until your loan is paid up.

2. The IRS determines if you're entitled to a tax refund.

3. If you are entitled to a refund, you are notified by the agency collecting the loan that the IRS proposes to keep it. This notice often comes out of the blue, years after you've ever thought about your student loan.

4. You are given 60 days to raise questions about the debt, inspect the holder of the loan's file on the debt, enter into a repayment schedule or request an administrative review. In requesting a review, you must present written evidence to the holder of your loan showing any of the following:

- You've repaid the loan.

- You are making payments under a repayment agreement you reached with the holder of your loan.

- You have filed for bankruptcy and your case is still open.

- The loan was discharged in a bankruptcy case.

- The debtor has died.

- You are totally and permanently disabled.

- The school closed down while you were enrolled, school officials falsely certified you as eligible to

benefit from the program or the school owed you a refund but never paid you. (School closings, false certifications and unpaid refunds will apply only if you attended a trade or proprietary school.)

- It is not your loan.

- The loan is not legally enforceable for any other reason.

5. The guaranty agency or the Department of Education considers your evidence.

6. If the agency or Department decides you owe the debt, it notifies the IRS, which must decide whether or not the agency or Department has made reasonable efforts to collect. If the IRS feels that the agency or Department has made reasonable efforts (which the Secretary usually does), the IRS intercepts your tax refund. The IRS can also deduct the costs, such as a collection agency's fee, incurred in trying to collect from you.

A few states assist the federal government by intercepting your state tax refund and turning it over to the Department of Education. And if your loan is from a public college, which has turned it over to the state for collection, the state may try to collect your student loan by intercepting your state income tax refund.

You can avoid having your income tax refund intercepted by figuring out how much in taxes you'll owe and making sure your employer withholds the minimum amount necessary to cover your taxes. If you're going to try this strategy, be careful not to underpay your income taxes, or you could be hit with a "failure to pay" penalty from the IRS of 0.25% per month.

2. Having Your Wages Garnished

Since 1991, a guaranty agency or the Department of Education has been authorized to garnish 10% of a former student's take-home wages if the former student is in default on his loan. For virtually all debts (income taxes are the one notable exception), a creditor must first sue you, obtain a court judgment

---

[6]31 U.S.C. 3720A; 26 C.F.R. § 301.6402-6T(b)(1).

and then enlist the help of the local sheriff in order to garnish wages. But now, the Department of Education joins the IRS as the only creditors entitled to grab a portion of your pay before suing you.

At least 30 days before the garnishment is set to begin, you must be notified in writing, of the following:

- the amount the agency or Department believes you owe

- how you can obtain a copy of records relating to the debt

- how to enter into a repayment schedule, and

- how to request a hearing on the proposed garnishment.

The law gives only one specific ground upon which you can object to the garnishment—that you returned to work within the past 12 months after having been "involuntarily separated from employment" (fired or laid off). If you don't qualify on that basis, try raising one of the objections permitted when the IRS seeks to intercept your tax refund listed in Section E1, above. Most former students who avoid the wage garnishments are being put on repayment plans.

3. Getting Sued

Until April 9, 1991, this section was much longer because if you were sued on any government-backed student loan, you might have had the defense that the statute of limitations had elapsed. The statute of limitations was the time that the holder of your loan had to sue you after you defaulted. In April of 1991, however, the Higher Education Technical Amendments took effect, retroactively doing away with the statute of limitations as a defense on any student loan lawsuit.[7] The retroactivity goes as far back as when the first student loans were disbursed.

More thorough coverage of lawsuits for any debt—and what to expect if the creditor gets a judgment—is covered in Chapter 9. Just below, I cover two other possible defenses you may be able to raise if you are sued for a delinquent student loan—laches and misrepresentation.

a. Laches

Laches is a legal concept that essentially means "although a lawsuit is not barred by a statute of limitations, the plaintiff (person suing) unreasonably delayed in bringing the lawsuit and it would be prejudicial to the defendant (person being sued) to have to defend this case." In general, a defendant cannot assert the defense of laches against the government.

In one student loan case, however, the former student (Bennie Rhodes)—who borrowed money in 1972 and was sued in 1991—successfully claimed laches against the United States.[8] The court allowed Rhodes to raise the laches defense against the government because he could have raised it against the former holder of the loan, and the court stated that he didn't lose his defenses just because the lender returned the loan to the Department of Education.

---

[7]20 U.S.C. § 1091a(a).

[8]*U.S. v. Rhodes*, 788 F. Supp. 339 (E.D. Mich. 1992).

Don't assume that all laches claims against the government will succeed. The facts in the *Rhodes* case were very much in his favor. He claimed he had paid the loan in full; the Department of Education claimed otherwise. Neither Rhodes nor the Department could come up with supporting documentation. In addition, when the government sued Rhodes, it claimed that he owed just $295 in principal. With interest and collection costs, the total amount sought was a mere $730.

b. Misrepresentation

Many former students who attended trade or proprietary schools (to learn, for example, word processing, dental technology, how to earn a high school equivalency degree, beauty care, computer skills, auto mechanics, business, truck driving and the like) were seriously misled by the school. In some cases, the student took out the loan, turned it over to the school and then the school went out of business before the student could complete (or even start) the course. In other situations, the schools had none of the equipment, teachers or curriculum advertised and the student received no effective education. In other instances, students were promised employment at a certain pay that never materialized. And in yet other situations, students lacked the minimum skills necessary to successfully benefit from the course—that is, they were falsely certified as eligible.

If this or any other similar situation involving a trade or proprietary school sounds familiar, you may have a legal way out of paying your loan. Several new laws regulate the trade and proprietary schools (many of which are no longer eligible to participate in the government-backed student loan program) and will extinguish loans taken out by students who were defrauded. Essentially, retroactive to 1986, if the school closed before you completed the program or you left within 90 days of when a school closed, the school falsely certified you as eligible for its program, or you were entitled to refund from the school but never received it, the Department of Education must fully cancel your

loan. By Department of Education estimates, close to 350,000 currently outstanding loans are eligible for cancellation.

Be sure to notify the Department of Education or guaranty agency holding your loan if you qualify. Provide whatever documentation you can (such as your loan application or promissory note). Also ask for a copy of the "list of closed schools." If your school is on that list, you are automatically entitled to cancellation of your loan.

If this doesn't work and the Department or agency goes ahead with the lawsuit, you may have to defend. A local Legal Aid or Legal Services office may help if you are poor enough to qualify for their help. Suggest that they (or you) get a copy of *Getting Student Loans Discharged on the Basis of School Closing or False Certification,* by Elizabeth Imholz. It's available from the National Clearinghouse for Legal Services, 205 West Monroe Street, 2nd Floor, Chicago, IL 60606. Request Clearinghouse No. 49966 and enclose a $5 check.

You will also want to contact your state's Attorney General's office, as most trade and proprietary schools are state-registered. Often, state officials know of lawsuits already pending against fraudulent schools.

F. Bankruptcy and Student Loans

BANKRUPTCY IS COVERED MORE THOROUGHLY in Chapter 10. I cover bankruptcy and student loans here, however, because many debtors consider filing for bankruptcy to get rid of (discharge) their student loans. Understand that student loans are seldom discharged in bankruptcy. But bankruptcy may be useful in some circumstances.

There are essentially two types of bankruptcies— Chapter 7 and Chapter 13. In a Chapter 7 bankruptcy, you get your debts erased (discharged); in exchange, you may have to give the court some of your property. In a Chapter 13 bankruptcy, you agree to make monthly payments to pay off a portion of your debts for three to five years. You must have a steady source of income—wages, pension payments, benefits, investment income or receipts as an independent contractor—but you normally don't give up any property. At the end of the three to five year period, the balance of what you owe on most types of debts is wiped out.

In general, student loans cannot be discharged in Chapter 7 or Chapter 13 bankruptcy. If you owe a lot of debts, however, including a student loan in a Chapter 13 bankruptcy can help. You can include the loan as part of your repayment plan. During that period, all collection efforts for the loan must end. You will have to pay off the entire student loan during your plan, or still owe any balance remaining at the end of your plan, but the reprieve from collection efforts for those years may be a great relief.

The rest of this chapter focuses on when a student loan may be discharged in a Chapter 7 or Chapter 13 bankruptcy. These times are essentially when:

- payments on the loan first became due more than seven years before you filed for bankruptcy, or

- it would cause you undue hardship to repay the loan.

1. Payments First Became Due Over Seven Years Ago

Under the bankruptcy law, you can discharge a student loan if your first installment payment became due over seven years before you filed for bankruptcy.

> **Example:** Pam borrowed $15,000 in student loans between 1984 and 1988; her first installment payment was due in March 1989. If Pam files for bankruptcy any time before March 1996, she won't be able to discharge the loan.

If your repayment obligation was deferred any time during the seven years before you file for bankruptcy, the seven-year period is extended for the length of the deferral. Thus, if Pam returned to graduate school from September 1992 to August

1993 (12 months) and the lending institution allowed her to suspend paying back her loan during that time, the loan can't be discharged until March 1997, not March 1996.

2. Undue Hardship

On rare occasions, courts allow student loans to be discharged in bankruptcy in advance of the seven year waiting period if you can show that repaying the loan would cause you undue hardship. In determining undue hardship, the bankruptcy courts look to several factors, discussed below. If you can show that all or most factors are present, the court will grant an undue hardship discharge of your student loan. If you show only some of the factors, however, the court may grant you a partial discharge.

- **Poverty.** Based on your current income and expenses, you cannot maintain a minimal living standard and repay the loan. The court must consider your current and future employment and income (or employment and income potential), education, skills and the marketability of your skills, health, and family support obligations.

  In one case, a couple who earned $23,500 annually and had four children were not permitted to discharge their student loans because they earned $4,230 a year above the federal poverty level for a family of six.[9]

- **Persistence.** It is not enough that you can't currently pay your loan. You must also demonstrate to the court that your current financial condition is likely to continue for a significant portion of the repayment period of the loan.

- **Good Faith.** The court must conclude that you've made a good faith effort to repay your debt. Someone who files for bankruptcy immediately after getting out of school or after the payback

---

[9]*In re Reyes*, 154 B.R. 320 (E.D. Okla. 1993).

period begins will not fall into good favor with the court. Nor will someone who hasn't looked extensively for employment.

- **Policy.** Some courts also require that you show that you filed for bankruptcy for more reasons than just to discharge your student loan. Other courts will want to make sure you haven't financially benefited from the education made possible by the loan.

Special Rules for HEAL, PLUS and Consolidated Loans

HEAL. The dischargeability of Health Education Assistance Loans (HEAL) is governed by the federal HEAL Act, not the bankruptcy law. Under the HEAL Act, to discharge the loan, you must show that the loan became due more than five years past, and that repaying it would not merely be a hardship, but would impose an unconscionable burden on your life. [10]

PLUS. Parental Loans for Students (PLUS) are granted to a parent to finance a child's education. Even though the parent does not receive the education, if the parent files for bankruptcy, the loan is treated like any other student loan. The parent must meet the seven year or undue hardship test to discharge the loan. [11]

Consolidated. Consolidated loans result when the lender combines multiple student loans into one, with one interest rate and payment schedule. (See Section D2c, above.) If the first payment on your consolidated loan became due fewer than seven years ago, the bankruptcy court probably will not let you discharge any of the consolidated loan even if some of the original loans are older than seven years. [12]

Getting Your Transcript Out of Hock

If you don't pay back loans obtained directly from your college, the school can withhold your transcript. [13] But if you file for bankruptcy and receive a discharge of the loan, the school can no longer withhold your records.

In addition, while your bankruptcy case is pending, the school cannot withhold your transcript even if the court eventually rules your school loan nondischargeable. [14]

■

[10]42 U.S.C. § 294f (g).

[11]*Hudak v. Union National Bank of Pittsburgh*, 113 B.R. 923 (W.D. Penn. 1990); *In re Wilcon*, 143 B.R. 4 (D. Mass. 1992).

[12]*U.S. v. McGrath*, 143 B.R. 820 (D. Md. 1992); *In re Menendez*, 151 B.R. 972 (M.D. Fla. 1993).

[13]*Juras v. Aman Collection Service, Inc.*, 829 F.2d 739 (9th Cir. 1987).

[14]*In re Gustafson*, 111 B.R. 282 (9th Cir. BAP 1990).

Chapter 8

CHILD SUPPORT AND ALIMONY

The fundamental evil of the world arose from the fact that the good Lord has not created money enough.

—Heinrich Heine,
German poet and critic, 1797-1856

BENJAMIN FRANKLIN ONCE SAID that only two things in life are certain: death and taxes. Of course, Franklin's remark was made in the 18th century. If he were alive today and a parent with a child support obligation, he would undoubtedly add child support to the list.

If You Are Owed Child Support or Alimony

This chapter addresses the concerns of debtors who pay child support or alimony, not those entitled to receive it. I recognize, however, that many people have debt problems because they aren't receiving support to which they are entitled. In fact, in 1990, an estimated 49% of all mothers entitled to child support were not receiving it. While this chapter doesn't cover that concern directly, reading it will nevertheless help you to understand your rights and the strategies available to you.

You might increase the likelihood of getting that support by contacting a national organization or a for-profit collection agency that helps custodial parents collect child support. One group to call is ACES—Association for Children for Enforcement of Support, (800) 537-7072. One collection agency increasing its presence around the country is Children's Support Services—this agency charges a $35 application fee and keeps 25% of what it collects. If you're interested in pursuing it, call your local operator to find an office near you.

Whether parents live together or apart, they are legally obligated to support their children. But when they live together, a court rarely involves itself with how the parents raise or support their children—unless someone claims that the children are being abused or neglected.

As soon as the parents split up, however, or one of the parents applies for welfare, the law gives the state the right to involve—perhaps over-involve—itself in how the children are supported. Sweeping laws enacted by Congress during the 1980s have resulted in greatly stepped-up state child support collection efforts. These laws have changed the way child support is established, paid and collected when past due.

Below I outline child support enforcement techniques used in most states, and give you some strategies for dealing with your child support debt when you can't pay. Before I do, however, a few personal words: pay your child support obligation unless you will starve or go homeless. No children—not yours, not anybody's—should grow up poor. Obviously, you can do little about the poverty endured by millions of children in this country. But you can do everything humanly possible to see that your own kids are adequately supported.

Okay, enough of my personal views. It's true that many parents who don't pay child support believe they have a good reason for not doing so:

- they have a new family to support
- their ex won't let them see their kids
- their ex moved their kids far away
- their ex misuses the support
- their ex plays all day while they have to work, or
- the court ordered them to pay too much.

But your reason makes no difference to a judge. If you owe child support and have the ability to pay, a judge will use a variety of harsh legal techniques to see that you do, and may lock you up if all else fails.

Child Support and Visitation Rights

If your ex is interfering with your custody or visitation rights, you don't have the right to withhold support. But you can schedule a court hearing (see Section D6, below) to show substantial interference with your visitation or custody right and ask the judge to rectify the situation. You'll need to document a persistent pattern of your being denied your right. Missing a weekend or two won't fly. If you've seen the kids once in eight months, however, a court may well hold your ex in contempt of court for violating the court order allowing you visitation. In addition, some judges will order your child's other parent to reimburse you for expenses you incur trying to exercise your visitation rights.

A. How Child Support Is Determined

The federal Family Support Act of 1988 requires all states to have a formula or guidelines for calculating child support.[1] As your state adopts its mandatory guidelines, either you or your child's other parent may request that a court review an existing order to see if it is in accordance with the guideline. Don't request a review unless you know you are paying above your state's guideline. If you're not, you might wind up being ordered to pay more. Section C, below, describes how you go to court to have the judge review the support order.

Expedited Child Support (California)

California has a simple method of setting child support called the Expedited Child Support Program.[2] The custodial parent fills out four forms, files them with the court and serves them on the other parent. If he doesn't object within 30 days, child support is set for the guideline minimum without a court hearing.

The noncustodial parent can object and request a hearing if:

- he's not the child's parent

- his ex listed his income or the ex's income incorrectly

- he is entitled to a hardship deduction, such as medical bills or back taxes

- his ex isn't entitled to a hardship deduction listed, or

- the support amount requested is computed incorrectly.

If your ex serves you with a request for expedited support and you want to challenge it, schedule a hearing. At the hearing, bring your income tax returns, pay stubs, bills—especially for any new children you have an obligation to support—and the like. If you're about to be laid off or are having other employment problems, bring a statement from your employer. After hearing from both sides, the judge will make a decision about how much child support to order.

---

[1] Public Law No. 100-485; 102 U.S. Statutes at Large § 2343.

[2] California Family Code § 3600 et seq.

Other Child Support Obligations

In addition to your obligation to make monthly child support payments, a court may require you to pay some of the following expenses as a part of child support:

- Health and dental insurance for your children, or your child's health and dental costs if neither parent has insurance covering the children. In fact, many states mandate that a parent pay for medical insurance if the costs are "reasonable."

- Life insurance naming your child's custodial parent as the beneficiary.

- Child care so that the custodial parent can work or go to school.

- Education costs for your children.

B. Enforcement of Child Support Obligations

THIS SECTION DESCRIBES the methods used to collect child support as it becomes due. Section D, below, discusses the methods used to collect past due child support, called arrears.

If your child support order was issued by a judge five or ten years ago, it probably just requires you to send a certain amount of money each month to your child's other parent. If your order was issued within the past five years, however, it may be very different. Today, you may have money withheld from your paycheck, or may be required to send money to a court clerk or state agency which in turn sends a check on to the custodial parent.

1. Automatic Wage Withholding

The automatic wage withholding program is mandated by the federal Family Support Act of 1988. It requires that all new or modified child support orders include an automatic wage withholding order. If child support is combined with alimony and paid as family support, the wage withholding provision of the law must be followed. It does not apply, however, for orders for alimony only.

An automatic wage withholding order works quite simply. After a court orders you to pay child support, the court—or your child's other parent—sends a copy of the court order, along with the custodial parent's name and address, to your employer. At each pay period, your employer withholds a portion of your pay and sends it on to the custodial parent. If you and your child's other parent agree—and the court allows it—you can avoid the wage withholding and make payments directly to her or through a third party.

If you don't receive regular wages, but do have a regular source of income, such as income from a pension, retirement fund, annuity, Social Security, unemployment compensation or other public benefits, the court can order the child support withheld. Instead of forwarding a copy of the order and the custodial parent's name and address to an employer, the court sends the information to the retirement plan administrator or public agency from whom you receive your benefits.

If your income is from Social Security or a private pension governed by either ERISA (Employee Retirement Income Security Act) or REA (Retirement Equity Act)—federal laws that limit access to pension plans—the administrator might not honor the court order. This is because Social Security and many private pensions have "anti-alienation" clauses which prohibit the administrator from turning over the funds to anyone other than the plan beneficiary (you).

States have implemented mandatory wage withholding orders with some variations. In Texas and Vermont, for example, all current orders include automatic wage withholding, regardless of the parent's payment history. The rationale is that by not distinguishing between parents with poor payment histories and parents who have paid regularly, no parent is stigmatized.

In California, wage withholding orders are automatic as well. But parents who show a reliable history of paying child support may be exempt. In all states, employers must withhold wages if the payer is one month delinquent in support.

2. Required Job Training

While requiring wage withholding orders, Congress has tried to address a major reason why some noncustodial parents don't pay child support—low wages, underemployment and unemployment. The Family Support Act created a Joint Opportunities and Basic Skills (JOBS) training program. A state may require a parent who owes—but is not paying —support to undergo job training and placement. If you're required to participate, you may be exempted only if you are:

- ill, incapacitated or of advanced age

- needed in the home because of the illness or incapacity of another member of your household

- the parent or care-taking relative of a child under age three (the state may lower this to age one)

- employed 30 hours or more per week

- under age 16 or attending elementary, secondary or vocational school full-time, or

- in your third trimester of pregnancy.

If you are able to participate in the program but refuse, the state can force you to attend mediation sessions in an effort to resolve the matter. And if you still refuse—and your child's custodial parent receives welfare—she may have her benefits reduced. Thus, if you can participate but you refuse, the only person you'll really be hurting is your child.

3. Establish Paternity

As an additional effort to find fathers and make them pay child support, the Family Support Act requires states to meet certain standards for establishing paternity. To help states foot the bill, the Act authorizes the federal government to reimburse states up to 90% of the costs spent on paternity lab tests.

If you've got a kid you're not paying child support for and you never married the child's mother, you may find yourself hauled into court on a paternity and child support action—up to 18 years after the child was born. If the court declares that you are the father, you are likely to be ordered to pay support until the child turns 18, and, in many states, will probably be required to pay back support covering up to three years.

Ways to Fight Paternity

To establish paternity, the mother of the child, or the district attorney if the mother receives welfare, will sue the alleged father. To successfully fight it, you will have to refute the following kinds of evidence:

- *access*—that you and the mother had an opportunity to engage in sexual intercourse during the period of conception.

- *potency and fertility*—that you are neither impotent nor sterile.

- *blood tests*—blood tests are used to rule out the possibility of paternity. Initially, your blood will be compared for types (A, B, AB, O) and Rh factor. If you are not excluded by those two tests, your blood will be HLA tested. HLA tests can disprove paternity with nearly 98% accuracy.

- *genetic typing*—DNA "fingerprinting" tests your cells against the child's and can prove or disprove paternity with 99.99% accuracy, when the tests are administered correctly. One problem with genetic testing is the frequency of errors in the testing procedure.

- *acknowledgment of paternity*—if you paid for the mother's hospital costs, had your name put on the birth certificate, ever acknowledged that the child is yours, voluntarily sent support or took other steps that would make you seem like the father, you'll have to overcome this evidence.

- *resemblance*—if you look like the child, the mother or district attorney will probably march the kid past you while you are sitting in the court for the judge to see.

4. Other Efforts to Collect Support as It Becomes Due

Below are a few other efforts being undertaken to help collect child support payments as they become due. What these efforts point out is how much the states are getting into the act of collecting child support.

- Computers are used to track parents and make sure they pay.

- States are theoretically required to collect the Social Security numbers of both parents when a child is born, and must pass those numbers on to the state agency that enforces child support. (None of my friends with kids said they've ever been required to do this.)

- Judges may order noncustodial parents to pay child support to the state's child support enforcement agency, which in turn pays the custodial parent. These programs are often used when the noncustodial parent is without regular income (because, for instance, he is self-employed) or when parents agree to waive the automatic wage withholding.

- Some states let judges order noncustodial parents to make payments to court clerks or court trustees who in turn pay the custodial parents.

C. Modifying the Amount of Child Support

IF YOU OWE CHILD SUPPORT you can't afford, you must take the offensive to change your child support order. This requires that you go to court, request a modification and show the judge that you have inadequate income and cannot afford the ordered support. If you don't get the order modified, and child support you cannot pay builds up, a court won't retroactively decrease it, even if you were too sick to get out of bed during the affected period. To repeat—once child support is owed and unpaid, it remains a debt until it is paid.

In most states, filing a motion to modify child support requires you to fill out and file court papers, schedule a hearing and present evidence to a judge. To do this, you'll probably need the help of a lawyer or legal typing service. (See Chapter 13.) The kind of evidence to show the court includes:

- a sworn statement from your most recent employer, if you were recently let go

- records of your job search, if you've been looking unsuccessfully

- sworn statements from all medical and healing professionals, if you are sick, injured, depressed or whatever.

Simplified Modification Procedures

A few states, including Vermont, New York and California, try to make it easy for parents to request a modification (increase or decrease) of child support.

The procedure is meant to be handled by a parent without an attorney. Court clerks and personnel are required to assist you in filling out the papers. The hearings often take place before a court magistrate or hearing examiner, not a judge. And decisions must be rendered within about 30 days.

To find out if your state has a simplified modification procedure, call the court clerk or the district attorney's office. In California, parents can use Nolo's *How to Raise or Lower Child Support*, by Duncan and Siegel.

1. Legal Reasons to Justify a Support Change

To get a judge to reduce a child support order, you must show a "significant change of circumstance" since the last order. What constitutes a "significant change of circumstance" depends on your situation. Generally, the condition must not have been considered when the original order was made and must affect your—or your child or the custodial parent's—current standard of living. Changes that qualify as significant are:

- Your income has substantially decreased. The decrease must be involuntary or for the ultimate benefit of your child. If you quit your job to become a basket weaver, the court probably won't modify your support obligation. If you quit your job to attend business school, however, the court may temporarily decrease the amount, expecting to increase it significantly when you graduate.

- The custodial parent's income has substantially increased. Not all increases in the custodial parent's income will qualify. For example, if your child's needs have increased as the custodial parent's income has risen, you probably won't get a reduction. Or, if the custodial parent's income increase is from her new spouse's earnings, few courts will consider that money because her new spouse has no obligation to support your child. In community property states (Arizona, California, Idaho, Louisiana, Nevada, New Mexico, Texas, Washington or Wisconsin), however, although the new spouse has no obligation to support the child, one half of the spouse's income is property of the parent.

- Your expenses have increased. You may be entitled to a reduction, for instance , if you have a new child.

- Your child's needs have decreased. You may be entitled to a reduction, for example, if your child is no longer attending private school.

- The children spend more time in your custody than when the court initially ordered the support. In this situation, you're entitled to a reduction because the other parent needs less money for the children.

In sum, a judge won't be inclined to modify your support order if your financial condition—or the financial condition of your child or your child's other parent—hasn't changed substantially since the order was initially issued. If you just feel the court was wrong the first time, you're probably out of luck.

If your state has a simplified modification procedure, you may also seek to change the amount of the support under the state's annual percentage change. If you miss a year, you can usually request two times the annual change.

Changing the Support Amount to Fit Your State's New Guidelines

If your child support obligation exceeds what you would now owe under your state's new mandatory child support guidelines, you may be able to get a modification on that basis. The Family Support Act specifically requires that a child support order be reviewed to determine its accordance with the guidelines. Be aware, however, that the effect of the Family Support Act has been to raise child support amounts nationwide. If your current payment isn't what is required by the Act, it's probably too low, not too high.

2 Negotiate With Your Child's Other Parent

Your request to modify the amount of child support you have to pay will be either contested or uncontested. Contested means your child's other parent opposes it, files formal papers with the court in opposition and shows up at the hearing with evidence refuting what you say. Uncontested means that your child's other parent does not file a response in court.

Child support modification hearings can be time-consuming, costly and unpleasant. If at all possible, avoid a contested hearing. Thus, before you file the court papers to modify your child support, call your child's other parent and let her know of your changed circumstance. She may voluntarily agree to reduce the amount. If you were laid off or in an accident, she knows the court will probably order some change in the amount and may agree ahead of time.

Get Your Agreement Signed by a Judge

If your child's other parent agrees to reduce the amount of child support you owe, make sure you get your new agreement in writing. Then bring it to the court for its approval. You may need the help of a lawyer or legal typing service to do this. (See Chapter 13.) Keep in mind that once a court sets support, only a court can change it. If you make an informal modification and your ex changes her mind, you won't have any recourse.

3. File Modification Papers If Negotiations Fail

If your child's other parent won't agree to a reduction in child support, you will have to go to court. If the judge denies your request, you will have to reassess your position. This may mean filing for bankruptcy to get rid of your other debts. But whatever you do, remember the point stressed at the beginning of this chapter: ignoring child support can land you in jail.

4. When You Can Stop Paying Child Support

You must pay child support for as long as your child support court order says you must pay, unless the court changes the order. If the order does not contain an ending date, depending on the state, you must:

- support your children until they reach 18

- support your children until they are 19 or finished with high school, whichever occurs first

- support your children until they reach 21

- support your adult disabled children as long as they are dependent, or

- support your children until they complete college.

To find out exactly what your state law requires, you'll need to do a little legal research or talk to a lawyer. (See Chapter 13.)

In addition, your child support obligation will probably end early if your child joins the military, gets married or moves out of the house to live independently, or a court declares your child emancipated—a few states, however, do not require a court order of emancipation.

Just because your child turns 18 (or whatever age you are no longer liable for support) doesn't mean the back child support you owed is erased. If the custodial parent went to court and had the back support made into a judgment (see Section D, below), that judgment can be collected for as long as your state lets a creditor enforce a judgment. This is 20 years in many states. (See Chapter 9.) Even if a custodial parent doesn't get a judgment, many states give the parent ten or 20 years to collect back support. And the custodial parent can usually collect interest on the amount owed.

D. How Back Child Support Is Collected

TO YOU, BACK CHILD SUPPORT is back child support. You owed it but you didn't pay it. But back child support can take two forms, and the difference is important in how that support can be collected.

The first type of back child support is the money that accumulates when you don't pay what you owe under a court order to pay child support. This back child support is generally called arrears. If you owe a lot in arrears, your child's other parent may go to court and ask a judge to issue a judgment for the amount of the arrears. This, the second type of back child support, is generally called a judgment for child support.

Under both the Family Support Act and various state laws, states' child support enforcement agencies, custodial parents, judges and district attorneys use nearly ten different methods to collect arrears. To use a few of the methods, the custodial parent must have a court judgment.

> **Example:** Al was ordered to pay his ex-wife Cindy $550 per month in child support. He lost his job and hasn't made the last three payments. He is in arrears under the order a total of $1,650. Cindy can try to collect on Al's violation (nonpayment) under the order, or can go to court and ask the judge to grant her a judgment for the amount he owes. Then she can use some additional techniques for collecting.

You Can Run but You Cannot Hide

You may think that by moving frequently, you can avoid paying child support. It's possible for a while, but unlikely if your ex is persistent. Each state and the federal government maintains a parent locator service that searches federal, state and local records to find missing parents. The federal parent locator service has access to Social Security, IRS and all other federal information records except census records. The state locator services check welfare, unemployment, motor vehicle and other state records.

1. Intercept Income Tax Refunds

One of the most powerful collection methods available is an interception of your federal income tax refund. If you owe more than $150 and the custodial parent receives welfare, the District Attorney (D.A.) where the custodial parent lives—who collects child support for welfare families (see Section 8, below)—will notify the U.S. Department of the Treasury. Similarly, if the custodial parent doesn't receive welfare but asks the D.A. for help in collecting what's owed, the D.A. can call on the Treasury Department.

Before your refund is taken, you'll receive a written "intercept notice" which will tell you what's going on and give you the chance to request a

hearing. But the claims you can make at a hearing are limited. Judges only want to hear that the back support has been paid or that the notice requests more than you owe. If the intercept notice incorrectly states an amount you owe, and is based on information given by the custodial parent, you need to ask her to attend the hearing, or ask the court to order her to attend if she won't on her own.

Only in rare cases will a judge listen to a hard-luck story and a claim of a desperate need for the funds. To most judges, adult hard-luck stories are not as heart-breaking as kids not being supported.

If you are now married (to someone other than the custodial parent to whom you owe support), your spouse should attend the hearing and file a claim for her share of the refund. The IRS cannot send her portion to your child's other parent to satisfy a child support debt of yours, even in community property states.[3]

If all or a part of your refund is intercepted wrongly—for example, you were never told of your right to schedule a hearing, the IRS took too much, or your spouse's share was not exempted from the withholding—you can request a reimbursement. You do this by filing an amended tax return (Form 1040X). If you're requesting the refund because your spouse's share was not exempted, you must also complete Form 8379, Injured Spouse Allocation. You can obtain copies of both forms—and directions for filling them out—by calling (800) 829-3676.

States (with income taxes) also intercept tax refunds to satisfy child support debts. In Nebraska, for example, court clerks report all child support arrears to the state for an interception of the tax refund. As with federal intercepts, you must be sent a notice and given the chance to schedule a hearing. And your spouse can file a claim to have her share withheld from what is sent to your child's other parent. Also, many states with lotteries let custodial

---

[3]See *Marcello v. Regan*, 574 F. Supp. 586 (D. R.I. 1983); *Coughlin v. Regan*, 584 F. Supp. 697 (D. Me. 1984), *aff'd*, 768 F.2d 468 (1st Cir. 1985); *Sorenson v. Secretary of the Treasury*, 557 F. Supp. 729 (W.D. Wash. 1982), *aff'd*, 752 F.2d 1433 (9th Cir. 1985), *rev'd on other grounds*, 475 U.S. 851 (1986).

parents apply to the state for an interception of the other parent's winnings.

2. Place Liens on Property

In some states, a custodial parent can place a lien—a notice that tells the world that the custodial parent claims you owe her some money—on your real or personal property. The liens stay in effect until your child is no longer entitled to support and you've paid all the arrears, or until you and the other parent agree to remove the liens. The custodial parent can force the sale of your property to be paid, or can wait until the property is sold. Some states require that the custodial parent obtain a judgment before putting a lien on property; other states allow liens to be imposed on property when you miss payments under the court order for support.

Your best defense is to schedule a hearing before a judge and claim that the lien on your property impairs your ability to pay your current support. If the lien, for example, is on your bank account and prior to the lien you were using money from that account to pay your current support, the lien may make it impossible for you to pay your current support if you have no other source of funds. If so, make that clear to the judge.

3. Post Bonds or Assets to Guarantee Payment

Some states allow judges to require parents with child support arrears to post bonds or assets, such as stock certificates, to guarantee payment. In some states, for example, if a self-employed parent misses a child support payment and the custodial parent requests a court hearing, the court can order the noncustodial parent to post assets (such as putting money into an escrow account).

Michigan, Mississippi, New York, Oklahoma, Rhode Island, Tennessee, Vermont and other states also sometimes require parents to post bonds or assets. In practice, few bond companies will write bonds for child support debts. Most parents will find

that they must put property into an escrow account, or, as is done in Montana and Wyoming, into a trust account that is managed and invested for the child's benefit.

You must be given notice of the possible action and an opportunity to contest. Again, your best defense is that having to post the assets or bond impairs your ability to pay your current support.

4. Report Arrears to Credit Bureaus

If you owe more than $1,000 in child support, that information may find its way into a credit file maintained by a credit bureau. See Chapter 12, Section B, for information on credit bureaus.

Before reporting information to a credit bureau, the child support enforcement agency must send you a notice of its intention to report the information and must give you an opportunity to contest the information's accuracy.

Many child support enforcement agencies automatically send information about owed child support to credit bureaus, regardless of the amount owed. Creditors and lenders see the information and often deny credit to parents in arrears. Creditors and lenders also sometimes report the whereabouts of missing parents to child support enforcement agencies.

If you are notified that your arrears are about to be reported to a credit bureau, try to negotiate—agree to pay what you owe in exchange for keeping the information out of your credit file. But few child support enforcement agents will agree to eliminate all information. Most will report you as having been delinquent but now owing $0.

If you've moved, especially if you've moved out of state and haven't told anyone of your new address, the enforcement agency's notice will probably never reach you. You'll learn that the information is in your file when you apply for a loan and are denied, based on information in your credit file.

5. Humiliate Debtors Publicly

Congress is encouraging states to come up with creative ways to embarrass parents into paying the child support they owe. One method used nationwide by an association of state child support enforcement agencies is the publishing of "most wanted" lists of parents who owe child support.

In Delaware County, Pennsylvania, for example, the family court lists the names of parents not paying child support on cable television 300 times a week and in a full-page newspaper advertisement once a month. The county claims to have located over 50% of the parents owing support. The Iowa attorney general reports that 90% of missing fathers who owe child support have been located through the state's "most wanted" poster program.

If your name is included on a most wanted list, about your only recourse to get your name off the list (unless you don't mind being a local "celebrity") is to turn yourself in. You'll be ordered to make monthly payments henceforth—and possibly your wages will be attached—and the court will take steps to see that you pay your back child support. But that may be better than having your Andy Warhol 15-minutes of fame 43 times a day or all over town.

Another way of embarrassing parents who owe support has been adopted in California. No parent in arrears will be granted an original or the renewal of a driver's or a professional license (doctor, lawyer, contractor, and the like).

6. Hold Debtors in Contempt of Court

Failing to follow a court order is called "contempt of court." A parent owed child support can schedule a hearing before a judge and ask that you be held in contempt of court. You must be served with a document ordering you to attend the hearing, and then must attend and explain why you haven't paid the support you owe. If you don't attend, the court can issue a warrant for your arrest. Many courts do issue warrants, so county jails have become resting stops for fathers who don't pay child support and fail to show up in court.

If you attend the hearing, the judge can still throw you in jail for violating the order to pay the support. And the judge may very well do so, depending on how convincing your story is as to why you haven't paid. If the judge isn't inclined to throw you into the slammer, the judge will instead order you to make future payments and will set up a payment schedule for you to pay any back support still owed.

At the hearing, you can tell the judge that you couldn't afford the payments, but it may fall on deaf ears. The judge will want to know why you didn't file a motion to modify the ordered amount. (See Section C, above.) The judge won't reduce the amount of your back support—arrears cannot be modified retroactively—but may decrease your future payments. The judge may also order your wages withheld or a lien placed on your property, or may order you to post a bond or other assets.

Convincing a Judge to Keep You Out of Jail

To stay out of jail, you may have to convince the judge that you're not as irresponsible as the judge probably thinks you are. Preparing evidence is a must. Your first step is to show why you didn't pay. If you've been out of work, get a sworn statement from your most recent employer stating why you were let go. If you went job searching but to no avail, provide records of when you interviewed or filled out an application, and with whom you spoke. Remember—disputes with your ex about custody or visitation are never an acceptable excuse for not paying child support.

Next, you want to explain why you didn't request a modification hearing. If you've been in bed or otherwise out of it—depressed, sick, or whatever—get sworn statements from all medical and healing professionals who treated you. Also, get statements from friends or relatives who cared for you. Emphasize that you couldn't get out of bed.

If you spoke to lawyers about helping you file a modification request, but you couldn't afford their fees, be sure to come to court ready to show the judge a list of names and lawyers you spoke to, the date you spoke to each one, and the fee the lawyer wanted to charge. If you tried to hire a legal aid lawyer to help you but you made too much money to qualify for such assistance, the office had too many cases and couldn't take yours or the office doesn't handle child support modifications, make sure you note the name of the lawyer and the date you spoke to her.

The burden of proving to the judge that you had legitimate reasons for not paying and not coming to court to request a modification is on you. The difference between carrying your burden and not carrying your burden may be the difference between going to jail and having the court order a repayment plan you can live with.[4]

Holding a parent in contempt of court and throwing him in jail used to be the primary method of enforcing child support orders. Today, the technique is still used, but usually only if a wage withholding order (see Section B1, above) and a wage garnishment (see Section D7, below) won't work.

7. Garnish Wages and Other Assets

Child support arrears that have been made into a court judgment can be collected by all the normal methods of collecting judgments. (See Chapter 9.) Even if the judgment was obtained in one state and you have since moved to another state, the Revised Uniform Reciprocal Enforcement of Support Act will allow the custodial parent to register the judgment in the second state and enforce it there.

The most common method of collecting a judgment for support is a wage garnishment. A wage garnishment is similar to a wage withholding—a portion of your wages is removed from your paycheck and delivered to the custodial parent before you ever see any of it. (In many states, the arrears need not be made into a judgment to be collected by way of a wage garnishment.)

To garnish your wages, the custodial parent obtains authorization from the court in a document usually called a writ of execution. Under this authorization, the custodial parent directs the sheriff to seize a portion of your wages. The sheriff in turn notifies you and your employer of the garnishment.

Wage withholdings and wage garnishments differ in one way: The amount of a wage withholding is *the amount of child support you have been ordered to pay each month*. The amount of a wage garnishment, however, *is a percentage of your paycheck*. What you were once ordered to pay is irrelevant. The court simply wants to take money out of each of your paychecks—and leave you with a minimum to live on—until the back owed support is made up.

If a court orders that your wages be garnished to satisfy any debt *except* child support (or, in most states, alimony), only 25% of your wages can be taken. With back owed child support, however, courts in most states can order that up to 50% of

---

[4] A U.S. Supreme Court case upholding the right of a state to jail a parent for failing to pay child support is *Hicks on behalf of Feiock v. Feiock*, 485 U.S. 624 (1988).

your wages be taken. If your check is already subject to a wage withholding for your future payments, the total amount of the wage withholding and garnishment cannot exceed 50% of your paycheck.

To put a wage garnishment into effect, the court, custodial parent or district attorney (depending on the state) must notify your employer. Once your employer is told to garnish your wages, your employer tells you of the garnishment. You can request a court hearing, which will take place shortly after the garnishment has begun. At the hearing, you can make only a few objections:

- the amount claimed that you owe is wrong

- the amount to be taken will leave you with too little to live on

- the custodial parent actively concealed your child, as opposed to merely frustrating or denying your visitation (not all states will allow this objection), or

- the child was living with you at the time the support arrears accrued.

If the wage garnishment does not cover the amount you owe, or you don't have wages or other income to be garnished, the custodial parent may try to get the debt for the back support paid out of other of your property. See Section D2, above.

Other Property a Custodial Parent May Target

Keith M. Clemens, a lawyer who spent many years with the Center for Enforcement of Family Support in Los Angeles (the only private law office in the country devoted solely to the enforcement of child support and alimony), described what property he and his colleagues went after for their clients:

"Bank accounts are an easy target if you know where the debtor banks. We also take cars, motorcycles, boats and airplanes, houses and other real property, stock in corporations, horses, rents payable to the debtor and accounts receivable. It's harder to do, but we also successfully attack trusts, even spendthrift trusts, and the debtor's interest in partnerships. [A spendthrift trust contains a clause prohibiting the trust funds from being paid out to anyone other than the trust beneficiary—the debtor.] We were even able to take the debtor's community property share of the television game show winnings of his new wife."

---

8. District Attorney Collections

If the custodial parent receives welfare, the local D.A. is required to help collect unpaid child support. In addition, in most states a local D.A. will help— and in some states is required to help—a custodial parent who doesn't receive welfare. If you've moved out of state, the Revised Uniform Reciprocal Enforcement of Support Act requires that when the custodial parent contacts a D.A. in her state, that D.A. calls a D.A. in your state. The D.A. in your state contacts you, and orders you to pay a sum of money. If you pay that money to the D.A. in your state, he sends it to the D.A. in the custodial parent's state.

When the D.A. is involved, you'll receive a notice requesting that you attend a conference. If you don't show up, the D.A. may initiate criminal charges against you for failure to appear. The purpose of the conference is to establish your income, expenses— including support for other children—and how much you should pay. The D.A. is likely to propose that you pay a lot. You must emphasize your other necessary expenses—food, shelter, clothing, other kids, and the like—to get that amount reduced. Bring receipts, bills and all other evidence of your monthly costs.

9. Criminal Prosecutions

In many states, it's a misdemeanor to fail to provide support for your child. While criminal prosecution isn't all that likely, the involvement of a D.A. increases the possibility. Also, if you have violated a judge's order enough times, the judge may contact her buddies in the police department and D.A.'s office and let your crimes be known.

E. Alimony

ALIMONY, SOMETIMES CALLED SPOUSAL support or maintenance, is money paid by one spouse to the other for support, after a marriage is over. No federal law requires states to have guidelines for setting the amount of alimony. In some courts, however, judges have adopted informal written schedules to help them determine the appropriate level of support. Mostly, judges consider:

- the age, health, earnings and obligations of each spouse

- whether a spouse contributed to the education, training or career advancement of the other

- the length and standard of living of the marriage

- who will have custody

- the time needed for a supported spouse to become self-sufficient, and

- the tax consequences to each person.

If you cannot pay the amount of alimony you've been ordered to pay, you must file a motion for modification. You must show a material change in circumstances since the last court order. Your ex-spouse's cohabitation with someone of the opposite sex may qualify, especially in Alabama, California, Connecticut, Georgia, Illinois, Louisiana, New York,

Oklahoma, Pennsylvania, Tennessee and Utah, where such cohabitation raises a presumption of a decreased need for alimony.

Your ex-spouse's remarriage is also a good change of circumstance. Your divorce decree probably states that alimony terminates on your ex-spouse's remarriage. Even if it doesn't, in most states a recipient spouse's remarriage ends an obligation to pay alimony.

Other common reasons for changes in alimony include your decreased income or your ex-spouse's substantially increased income. Where you have voluntarily decreased your income, however, the judge may instead consider your ability to earn, not just your actual earnings.

If child support and alimony are lumped together in one payment, often called family support, the collection techniques discussed in Sections B and D, above may be used against you. If they are kept separate, however, only the following techniques can be used to collect alimony:

- interception of income tax refunds (for ex-spouses receiving welfare)

- court hearings, and

- wage garnishments and other judgment collection methods, such as property liens.

F. Bankruptcy

BANKRUPTCY IS COVERED MORE thoroughly in Chapter 10. I discuss bankruptcy here, however, because many debtors consider filing for bankruptcy to get rid of back child support or alimony obligations. Be aware that bankruptcy won't cancel arrears or a support judgment. But it may help in some limited situations.

There are essentially two types of bankruptcies—Chapter 7 and Chapter 13. In a Chapter 7 bankruptcy, you can get most of your debts erased; in exchange, you may have to give the court some of your property. In a Chapter 13 bankruptcy, you agree to make monthly payments to pay off a portion of your debts for three to five years. You must have a steady source of income—wages, pension payments, benefits, investment income or receipts as an independent contractor—but you don't usually give up any property. At the end of the three to five year period, the balance of what you owe on most types of debts is wiped out.

If you owe your alimony and child support debts under a separation agreement, divorce decree, court order or marital settlement agreement (virtually all obligations to pay child support or alimony come under one of these), you generally cannot eliminate them in Chapter 7 or Chapter 13 bankruptcy. If you owe a lot of debts, including back support, however, Chapter 13 bankruptcy can help. You can include the back support as part of your repayment plan. During that period, most courts halt collection efforts for the back support. At the end you'll have to pay the balance, but the reprieve from collection efforts for those years may be a great relief.

Your back child support or alimony may be eliminated in only the following situations:

Support owed someone other than a spouse, ex-spouse or child. If an ex-spouse or child gave (assigned, in legal terms) the right to receive the support to someone else—such as a university to pay a child's tuition or the welfare department—the debt can be eliminated.

Support owed under a state's general support law, not a court order. If your support debt arose under a general state law to support a child or spouse and no court actually ordered the support, the debt can be eliminated. Support obligations rarely fall into this category.

Support paid under an agreement between unmarried persons. If an unmarried couple enters into an agreement that includes support, the obligation can be eliminated in bankruptcy unless one person won a lawsuit against the other and obtained a court judgment for the support.

Eliminating Marital Debts in Bankruptcy

If you filed for bankruptcy before 1995, you probably could have eliminated any debts you assumed as a part of your divorce—including your obligation to make payments to your ex-spouse to even up a property settlement—unless a bankruptcy court ruled that your obligation was in lieu of paying alimony. In that case, the court probably would not have let you eliminate the debts.

Under the Bankruptcy Reform Act of 1994, Congress created a new category of debts that cannot be wiped out in bankruptcy if the creditor objects in the bankruptcy court: debts incurred in the course of a divorce or separation or in connection with a separation agreement, divorce decree or other court order. So if you agreed to pay the Visa bill and the Sears charges in your divorce agreement, or owe your ex-spouse $15,000 to even up the property division, you cannot eliminate those debts in bankruptcy if the creditor or your ex-spouse objects.

There are two exceptions, however, and you will be allowed to wipe out the debts if the bankruptcy court determines either of the following:

- After you pay all necessary expenses to support yourself and your dependents and to run any business you own, you do not have enough money to pay the marital debts.

- The benefit you would receive by discharging your obligation outweighs any detriment to your ex-spouse or children.

Chapter 9

IF YOU ARE SUED

Lawsuits consume time and money, and rest and friends.
    —George Herbert, English poet, 1593-1633

IF YOU DON'T PAY YOUR DEBTS, you'll probably be sued unless:

- you file for bankruptcy
- the creditor can't find you, or
- the creditor believes he can't collect on the judgment and probably won't be able to collect in the foreseeable future.

Being sued is not the end of the world. It doesn't make you a bad person—millions of people are sued each year. Yes, it can be scary and may cause sleepless nights, but in large part that's because few people actually know what goes on in a lawsuit. Our perceptions, which typically have been shaped by *L.A. Law* and *Perry Mason*, are usually off the mark.

As this chapter explains, if you are sued on a debt you do owe and have no real defense to not paying, the lawsuit usually takes very little time and money. And if you have a good defense, you may be able to assert it without hiring a lawyer.

The premise of this chapter is that you owe someone money and haven't paid. Usually this is a breach of a contract. Thus, this chapter explains negotiating and the types of defenses you can raise in response to being sued for breaching a contract.

You may, however, be sued for any number of other reasons—for example, you allegedly caused a car accident, defamed someone or infringed on a copyright. Before you are sued, you do not owe those people money. If you are sued and you have a defense to the allegations made against you, you will have to consult a source beyond this book for help. (See Chapter 13.) If the lawsuit is successful you will owe a debt (in the form of a money judgment), and this chapter will highlight what you can expect.

Being Sued in Small Claims Court

Virtually every state has a small claims court to hear disputes involving modest amounts of money. Small claims courts handle matters without long delays and formal rules of evidence, and are intended for people to represent themselves. If you owe the creditor a few thousand dollars or less, you may be sued in your state's small claims court, which has a maximum dollar limit. The range is from $1,000 to $10,000, with most states falling between $2,000 and $3,500. Even if the amount you owe is above your state's limit, the creditor may opt to sue you in small claims court and give up (waive) the excess.

Small claims court has one substantial limitation. If the creditor has turned the debt over to a collection agency and it's the agency, not the original creditor suing you, the agency can't sue you in small claims court in 17 states—it must sue you in your state's regular civil court.[1]

In most states, you don't need to file a written response to a lawsuit in small claims court. You simply show up on the date of the hearing. If, however, you plan to file your own claim against the creditor for money—for example, if the creditor breached a warranty—you have to file a Claim of Defendant before the hearing so that both the creditor's claim and your claim are heard together.

Be sure you show up at the hearing. If you don't, most of the time you will lose the case. At the hearing, just be yourself and tell your side of the dispute. You don't normally need to hire a lawyer, even if your state allows them in small claims court and the creditor has one. Small claims court is designed to operate without lawyers and most small claims judges feel that people do as well or better without them. If you lose the case, the judge may let you set up a schedule to pay off the judgment in monthly payments—but don't count on it.

If you're sued in small claims court, an excellent resource is *Everybody's Guide to Small Claims Court*, by Ralph Warner (Nolo Press). Use that book as a guide to representing yourself. The rest of this chapter assumes that you are sued in your state's regular civil court, not small claims court.

---

[1] Arizona, Arkansas, California, Colorado, Idaho, Kansas, Kentucky, Michigan, Missouri, Montana, Nebraska, New Jersey, New York, Ohio, Oklahoma, Texas and Utah don't allow collection agencies to sue in small claims court.

Filing for Bankruptcy When You've Been Sued

One way to immediately stop a lawsuit is to file for bankruptcy. (See Chapter 10.) Filing for bankruptcy stops all collection efforts, including lawsuits, dead in their tracks and most debts can be erased (discharged) in the bankruptcy case. If your total debt burden isn't so much that you consider bankruptcy a real option, you'll want to deal with the suit in another way. But if bankruptcy is inevitable, now may be the time to file.

A. How a Lawsuit Begins

A LAWSUIT STARTS when a creditor's lawyer or the creditor herself prepares a document called a complaint or petition, claiming that you owe money. The lawyer or creditor files the document with a court clerk and pays a filing fee. She then has a copy of the complaint, along with a Summons, served on you. The Summons is a document issued by the court, notifying you that you are being sued.

The complaint identifies:

- the plaintiff—that's the creditor or possibly a collection agency or other third party the creditor sold the debt to

- the defendant—that's you and possibly your spouse, or a cosigner or guarantor

- the date the complaint was filed (this is important if you have a statute of limitations defense—see Section D1, below)

- the court you are being sued in

- why the creditor is suing you, and

- what the creditor wants out of the lawsuit.

1. Where the Lawsuit Is Filed

The creditor must normally sue you in the state either where you live or where the transaction took place. The creditor usually selects the state where you live if it's different from where the transaction took place because the court must see a substantial connection between you and the state in which you are sued in order for it to decide the case. For example, if you send a check from your home in South Carolina to a mail-order business in Wisconsin, and your check bounces, the creditor can sue you in South Carolina, but probably not in Wisconsin. Your connections with Wisconsin—even assuming the transaction took place there—are too insubstantial to sue you there.

After selecting the state, the creditor must select a county within the state. (This is called the venue for the case.) In most states, the creditor can choose the county where you live, the county where the transaction took place or the county where the creditor is located. If your home, the location of the transaction and the location of the creditor's business aren't all in one county, most creditors will choose the county where they are located simply because that is more convenient for them. If the creditor has chosen a county that is terribly inconvenient for you, you can file a motion to have the case transferred to somewhere else. You'll almost certainly need the help of a lawyer.

Once the creditor has selected the state and county, the creditor must choose the court—small claims court or regular civil court. You'll probably be sued in your state's regular civil court if:

- the amount of money you owe exceeds your state's small claims limit

- a collection agency has your debt and is prohibited from suing in small claims court, or

- the creditor simply chooses not to use small claims court—no plaintiff is obligated to use small claims court, even on a $10 debt.

The exact name of the regular civil court depends on your state, and possibly the amount of money involved. It may be a Circuit Court, City Court, County Court, District Court, Justice Court, Justice of the Peace Court, Magistrate's Court, Municipal Court or Superior Court. Although the names differ, what goes on in each court is pretty much the same.

You might also be sued in a federal district court if you owe money to the federal government—for example, on a federally-guaranteed student loan.

In regular civil court, a lawsuit can be time-consuming and expensive, although routine debt collection cases rarely are. In theory, you are required to strictly follow formal (and often absurd) procedural and evidentiary rules, but many judges are flexible when dealing with a person representing herself. While it can be extremely difficult to represent yourself in regular civil court, more and more people are doing it.

Californians sued in Municipal Court will want to obtain a copy of *Everybody's Guide to Municipal Court,* by Judge Roderic Duncan (Nolo Press). People who decide to handle their own case—in any state—will find indispensable *Represent Yourself in Court*, by Bergman and Berman-Barrett (Nolo Press).

2. Service of Court Papers

After the creditor files papers with the court, she must serve them on you. In most regular civil courts, to be served you must be handed the papers personally. If you can't be found, the papers can be left with someone over 18 at your home or business, as long as another copy is mailed to you. The creditor himself cannot serve the papers on you because a party to a lawsuit can't do the actual serving. Most creditors hire professionals called process servers or have a local sheriff or marshal do the job.

Sometimes, a creditor will mail you a copy of the summons and complaint with a form for you to sign and date, acknowledging that you have received the papers. If you sign and date the form, you are deemed to have been served on that date.

It's often a good idea to sign the form and send it back promptly because you can save money. If you refuse to sign and the creditor can later prove that you declined the opportunity to do so, you may have to pay whatever costs—frequently between $35 and $150—the creditor incurred in hiring a process server or sheriff to serve the papers on you personally.

If Service Was Done Wrong

Suppose the creditor has a friend serve you, and the friend simply slides the papers under your door. Sure, you got the papers, but service was technically "improper" because they were not handed to you or left with a responsible person at your home or office, followed by a mailed copy. You now have two choices. You can either ignore the impropriety or complain in court. Unless you complain, the court won't know that service was improper, and it will proceed as if service was fine. If you don't formally respond, a default judgment will probably be entered against you.

Should you complain? In most cases, no. Fighting an improper service will probably require your hiring a lawyer. That gets expensive. The creditor's friend (or other process server) will simply serve you again—most likely on the day you show up in court to fight the initial improper service.

All you will have bought is a little time. And you might have paid a lot for that time.

3. Understanding the Complaint

Complaints are usually written in hyped-up legalese. You may be referred to as the "party of the second part," not simply "the defendant," and almost never just by your name. The document will probably include "heretofores," "thereafters," "saids," and much more.

To find out what exactly the plaintiff wants from you, turn to the final pages. Find the word "WHEREFORE" and start reading. You'll not only learn how much the creditor says you owe, but most of the time you'll also find out that the creditor is claiming you must pay interest, court costs incurred, possibly attorneys' fees, and "whatever other relief the court deems appropriate."

4. When Is Your Response Due?

In regular civil court you will probably have between 20 and 30 days to respond in writing (in a document usually called an answer) to the creditor's complaint. The Summons tells you precisely how much time you have. If you don't respond in time, the creditor can come into court and ask that a default judgment be entered against you. Usually the default judgment is granted for the amount the creditor requested. Some judges, however, will scrutinize the papers. If the judge feels that the creditor's claim for interest or attorneys' fees is excessive, the judge may not allow it. Other judges will require the creditor to present evidence of actual damages before awarding any money.

 If There's Already a Judgment Against You

In most (80%–90%) routine debt cases, a default judgment is taken against the defendant. Often the defendant has no real defense or the money to hire a lawyer to put up a fight. If you owe money and decide to let a default be taken against you, skip ahead to Section F on what to do if the creditor has a judgment.

B. Negotiate

Even if you've avoided your creditor up to this point, it's never too late to try to negotiate. If you call a creditor and offer to settle the matter, the creditor may agree to suspend (though not withdraw) the lawsuit while you are negotiating. For tips on negotiating, see Chapter 3. If your efforts to negotiate with your creditor are unsuccessful, consider contacting Consumer Credit Counseling Service, a nonprofit organization that will work with you to set up a repayment plan by contacting your individual creditors. (See Chapter 13.)

1. Lump Sum Settlement

You will be in the best position vis-a-vis your creditor if you can offer a lump sum of cash to settle the case. Usually, the creditor will insist that you pay between one-half and three-fourths of what you owe. The creditor, not wanting to have to start all over if you miss the payments, is unlikely to stop a lawsuit in exchange for a promise to pay in installments.

If the creditor agrees to take your lump sum offer, make sure he also agrees to do so in complete settlement of what you owe and further agrees to dismiss (withdraw)—and in fact *does* dismiss—the lawsuit filed against you. You can check to see that the lawsuit has been dismissed by visiting the courthouse filing office and asking to see the case file. Bring the papers the creditor served on you with you to the filing office; these papers include the case number, which you will need to request the file. The file should contain a paper filed by the creditor called a Request for Dismissal, or something similar.

If the creditor hasn't filed the Request for Dismissal, you may have to take some action yourself. Ask the court clerk if your state has a form used for requesting dismissals. If it does, get a copy and fill it out, but don't sign it. If it doesn't, you may have to visit a law library, find a form book, and prepare a Request for Dismissal yourself. Once your request is completed, make a copy and send the original to the creditor. Ask the creditor to sign it and send it back to you. Once it comes back, file it with the court clerk yourself.

2. Settlement Involving Installment Payments

Assuming a creditor does agree to settle the case on the basis of your promise to make installment payments, chances are she will probably insist that you agree ("stipulate") to having a court judgment entered at the courthouse against you if you fail to make payments. If you agree to this, sign the stipulation, but make sure the creditor commits in writing not to file it with the court unless you fail to make the installment payments. This way, your credit file won't show that there's a judgment against you.

3. If the Negotiations Hit a Sour Note

If your negotiations are going nowhere, or you're uncomfortable handling them yourself, consider hiring an attorney to negotiate for you. An attorney carries clout—he can raise oppositions to the lawsuit, threaten to have you file for bankruptcy or generally be litigious. Any of these actions might lead the creditor to settle for a good deal less than what you owe. But don't hire an attorney unless it's cost-effective. If an attorney charges $250 to negotiate a $700 debt down to $500, you've actually lost $50. (See Chapter 13 for information on finding an attorney.)

Sample Settlement Agreement or Release

This Agreement is entered into on the date below between __Christopher's Contracting Company__, Creditor, and __Donna Markell__, Debtor.

Whereas Creditor has alleged that __Debtor owes him $7,745 for construction work he did on Debtor's home__;

Whereas Debtor agrees that __she has not paid Creditor any money for the work done but alleges that Creditor damaged her home while doing the construction work__;

Whereas Creditor has filed __Civil Action No. C49903 in the Superior Court for the County of Fairfield, State of Connecticut, seeking a money judgment__; and

Whereas Creditor and Debtor desire to settle their differences and end the above-identified litigation.

Therefore, in consideration of the undertakings set forth below, Creditor and Debtor hereby agree as follows:

1. Within 20 days of the date this agreement is entered into, Creditor shall file in the __Superior Court for the County of Fairfield, State of Connecticut__, a Dismissal With Prejudice in the above-identified litigation.

2. Creditor further agrees not to make any future claim or bring any future action against Debtor for the acts alleged, or which could have been alleged, in __Civil Action No. C49903__, occurring up to the time of the entry of the Dismissal With Prejudice identified in Paragraph 1 of this Agreement.

3. Debtor agrees not to make any future claim or bring any future action against Creditor for acts alleged, or which could have been alleged as a counterclaim, in __Civil Action No. C49903__.

4. Debtor shall, at the time of executing this Agreement, pay to Creditor the sum of ___$5,000___ as full settlement of any claim of Creditor against Debtor.

5. [California only] The releases recited in this Agreement shall cover all claims under California Civil Code Section 1542 and Creditor and Debtor hereby waive the provisions of Section 1542 which read as follows:

"A general release does not extend to claims which the creditor does not know or suspect to exist in his favor at the time of executing the release, which if known by him must have materially affected his settlement with the debtor."

6. Creditor and Debtor shall bear their own costs, expenses and attorneys' fees.

7. This Agreement embodies the entire understanding between Creditor and Debtor relating to the subject matter of this Agreement and merges all prior discussions between them.

Dated: _____

Creditor's signature, address and phone number:

_____

_____

_____

Debtor's signature, address, and phone number:

_____

_____

_____

C. Alternative Dispute Resolution

IF YOU CLEARLY OWE A DEBT and are looking for some way to avoid going to court, most creditors won't agree to using mediation, arbitration or some other alternative dispute resolution (ADR). If you really don't think you owe the money or have some other credible defense to the creditor's lawsuit, however, the creditor may agree to resolve the lawsuit through ADR.

ADR is usually informal, fast and inexpensive. Because of the informality of ADR, you are often not constrained by formal procedural and evidentiary rules. You just tell your story. These are the main ADR options:

Arbitration. This is the most formal and widely used form of ADR. You and the plaintiff agree to submit your dispute to at least one neutral third person—often a lawyer or judge—and to be bound by the arbitrator's decision. Where a lot of money is at stake, arbitrators usually let the parties use attorneys at arbitration hearings, and impose formal rules of evidence. In other disputes, arbitration is less formal and can take place without lawyers. You often have to pay the arbitrator's fees in advance, and they can be high. If you win, however, you're frequently refunded the amount.

Mediation or conciliation. This is the second most common type of ADR. You and the plaintiff work with a neutral third party to come up with a solution to your dispute. Mediation is informal, and the mediator does not have the power to impose a decision on you.

Mini-trial. You and the plaintiff present your positions to a neutral third person who listens as a judge would and then issues an advisory opinion. You and the plaintiff can agree to be bound by that opinion. A growing number of states have "rent-a-judge" programs to encourage the use of mini-trials to settle disputes.

Several states encourage mediation or arbitration and encourage the court to make ADR available. In Colorado and Oregon, for example, each judicial district or county must set up a voluntary, simple, nonadversarial, informal, neutral mediation program to which a judge may refer any case.

If your state doesn't encourage ADR, you can call on a private organization. Many are listed in the phone book. Before hiring one, ask the company for the names of some clients. Call and find out if they were satisfied with the company's service. Also, the National Council of Better Business Bureaus operates a nationwide system for settling consumer disputes through arbitration and mediation. Local BBB offices handle over two million consumer disputes each year. One advantage to BBB arbitration over more formal arbitration is that it is free to consumers and is geared toward operating without lawyers.

The creditor doesn't have to agree to ADR just because you suggest it, unless your original contract (such as a loan agreement) with the plaintiff called for ADR in the event of a disagreement, or your state requires ADR for the type of dispute you are having.

State	Mandatory Arbitration or Mediation
Alaska	Client may choose arbitration to resolve fee disputes with lawyer; lawyer must participate if client chooses.
California	Client may choose arbitration to resolve fee disputes with lawyer; if lawyer refuses to be bound by the decision, arbitrator's opinion is advisory only.
	In all cases filed in Superior Court in which the presiding judge does not believe the plaintiff will recover more than $50,000, arbitration is required. In any case filed in Municipal Court, the court can order arbitration.
District of Columbia	Arbitration is required for all civil actions under $50,000, except those in small claims court.
Illinois	In counties with over 2 million people, judges must send disputes to the county dispute resolution center.
Maine	Client may choose arbitration to resolve fee disputes with lawyer; lawyer must participate if client chooses.
Maryland	If a consumer chooses to arbitrate a consumer dispute, the merchant must participate.
Minnesota	Judge may require any two parties to a civil action to arbitrate. Party unhappy with outcome may request trial.
New Jersey	Client may choose arbitration to resolve fee disputes with lawyer; lawyer must participate if client chooses.
North Carolina	Arbitration is required for all civil actions under $15,000. Party unhappy with outcome may request trial.
Pennsylvania	Arbitration is required for all civil actions $10,000 or less, that don't affect title to real property. Party unhappy with outcome may request trial.
South Carolina	Client may choose arbitration to resolve fee disputes with lawyer; lawyer must participate if client chooses.

If you'd prefer ADR over going to court, but it's not required in your situation, you will have to convince the creditor why it is to her advantage to use ADR. You want to emphasize the advantages of ADR in a letter such as the one below.

⚠ Even if You Send a Letter Requesting ADR, File a Response to the Complaint

The creditor may say no, may say yes and then decide not to participate, or may say yes but sometime after the time limit has passed for you to file an answer. As explained in Section A4, above, if the deadline passes and you haven't filed a response, the creditor can ask the court to have a default judgment entered against you. If that happens, you will automatically lose.

If you suggest ADR and the creditor agrees, and you fail to file a response and the creditor gets a judgment against you, a court may set it aside. But this will take a lot of effort and probably the help of a lawyer.

Sample Letter to Creditor Requesting ADR

Merrily Andrews, Esq.
Legal Department
Presley Hospital
900 Hollis Boulevard
Carson City, NV 88888

March 15, 19__

Re: Shawn Smith
        Account # 7777-SMI
        Civil Case # 93-0056

Dear Ms. Andrews:

I have just been served with the Summons and Complaint for the lawsuit filed by Presley Hospital against me for $7,400. I would very much like to resolve this matter and suggest that we mediate the dispute with the help of a mediator from the Nevada Consumer Council. I know that the Consumer Council has helped many people resolve their differences quickly, informally and inexpensively.

Although I did not respond to your earlier collection efforts, it was not because I did not want to settle the matter. My wife and I were both very ill and hospitalized at Presley. My wife died, and taking care of my debts was not my highest priority. I admit that I owe you some money, but nowhere near $7,400.

I hope you'll agree to mediate this dispute. If so, please contact me by April 10, 19__.

Thank you,

Shawn Smith

D. Respond in Court

IF YOU WANT TO RESPOND to the creditor's lawsuit, you must do so in writing, within the time allowed. (See Section A4, above.) This means you must file

formal legal papers, usually in what is called an answer, and the task can be difficult. Regular civil court is designed and operated by lawyers. Arcane rules dominate and the language is often indecipherable. Clerks may be rude and hostile, and many don't answer simple questions, such as "Where do I file the forms?" Instead, they often stonewall even the most routine request for information with the claim that they "can't give legal advice."

This doesn't mean you can't or shouldn't represent yourself in court. You can, but you will have to educate yourself and do some legal research.

Again, I suggest that Californians sued in Municipal Court obtain a copy of *Everybody's Guide to Municipal Court*, by Judge Roderic Duncan (Nolo Press), and that others obtain a copy of *Represent Yourself in Court*, by Bergman and Berman-Barrett (Nolo Press).

You'll also need patience to play the game according to the lawyers' and judges' rules. For example, if you raise an argument or a defense completely unsupported by the facts of your case or by the law, the judge could fine you for filing frivolous papers. It's an extreme measure and rarely invoked, but judges who get angry and frustrated by people who represent themselves have been known to do it.

You can also hire a lawyer to represent you in court. (See Chapter 13.) As you know, lawyers are expensive. But you may be able to hire a lawyer to represent you in court while you keep your expenses down by doing some other work yourself. Also, if you have a pretty strong claim against the creditor (see Section D2, below) that could generate substantial money for you if you win, the lawyer may take your case on a contingent fee basis—you don't pay the lawyer unless you win.

In going to court, you want to raise any possible defenses you have, such as the statute of limitations has expired or the goods you received were defective.

1. Statute of Limitations

The creditor has a limited number of years to sue you after you fail to pay your debt. This is called the statute of limitations. The time allowed varies greatly from state to state and for different kinds of debts—written contracts, oral contracts, promissory notes and open-ended accounts, such as credit card payments. The statute of limitations begins to run from the day the debt—or payment on an open-ended account—was due.

If the creditor has waited too long to sue you, you must raise this as a defense in the papers you file in response to the creditor's complaint.

> **Example:** Bart lives in Delaware, where the statute of limitations on open-ended accounts is three years. Bart had a large balance on his Visa card, made a small payment in July 1993, and then paid no more. His August Visa statement included a payment due date of August 15, 1993. Bart was sued in September of 1996, three years and a few days after he missed his payment. Bart has a statute of limitations defense. Bart must raise this defense in the papers he files opposing Visa's lawsuit. If Bart doesn't, he loses the defense.

Statutes of Limitations

State	Written Contracts	Oral Contracts	Promissory Notes	Open-Ended Accounts
Alabama	6 years	6 years	6 years	3 years
Alaska	6 years	6 years	6 years	6 years
Arizona	6 years	3 years	6 years	3 years
Arkansas	5 years	3 years	5 years	3 years
California	4 years	2 years	4 years	4 years
Colorado	6 years	6 years	6 years	6 years
Connecticut	6 years	3 years	6 years	6 years
Delaware	3 years	3 years	6 years	3 years
District of Columbia	3 years	3 years	3 years	3 years
Florida	5 years	4 years	5 years	4 years
Georgia	6 years	4 years	6 years	4 years
Hawaii	6 years	6 years	6 years	6 years
Idaho	5 years	4 years	5 years	4 years
Illinois	10 years	5 years	10 years	5 years
Indiana	6 years	6 years	6 years	6 years
Iowa	10 years	5 years	10 years	5 years
Kansas	5 years	3 years	5 years	3 years
Kentucky	15 years	5 years	15 years	5 years
Louisiana	10 years	10 years	5 years	3 years
Maine	6 years	6 years	6 years	6 years
Maryland	3 years	3 years	3 years	3 years
Massachusetts	6 years	6 years	6 years	6 years
Michigan	6 years	6 years	6 years	6 years
Minnesota	6 years	6 years	6 years	6 years
Mississippi	3 years	3 years	3 years	3 years
Missouri	10 years	10 years	10 years	5 years
Montana	8 years	5 years	8 years	3 years
Nebraska	5 years	4 years	5 years	4 years
Nevada	6 years	4 years	6 years	4 years

State	Written Contracts	Oral Contracts	Promissory Notes	Open-Ended Accounts
New Hampshire	6 years	6 years	6 years	6 years
New Jersey	6 years	6 years	6 years	6 years
New Mexico	6 years	4 years	6 years	4 years
New York	6 years	6 years	6 years	6 years
North Carolina	3 years	3 years	3 years	3 years
North Dakota	6 years	6 years	6 years	6 years
Ohio	15 years	6 years	15 years	6 years
Oklahoma	5 years	3 years	5 years	3 years
Oregon	6 years	6 years	6 years	6 years
Pennsylvania	4 years	4 years	4 years	4 years
Rhode Island	10 years	10 years	10 years	10 years
South Carolina	3 years	3 years	3 years	3 years
South Dakota	6 years	6 years	6 years	6 years
Tennessee	6 years	6 years	6 years	6 years
Texas	4 years	2 years	4 years	4 years
Utah	6 years	4 years	6 years	4 years
Vermont	6 years	6 years	6 years	6 years
Virginia	5 years	3 years	5 years	3 years
Washington	6 years	3 years	6 years	3 years [2]
West Virginia	10 years	5 years	10 years	5 years
Wisconsin	6 years	6 years	6 years	6 years
Wyoming	10 years	8 years	10 years	8 years

[2]Washington's statute of limitations for open-ended accounts is not crystal clear. No written statute expressly states that it is three years. Courts interpreting the Revised Code of Washington § 46.16.150 have concluded it is three years.

In response to your claim that the statute of limitations prevents the creditor from going forward with the lawsuit, the creditor might claim that you waived, extended or revived the statute of limitations in your earlier dealings.

a. Waiving a Statute of Limitations

Waiving the statute of limitations means giving up your right to assert it as a defense. You may have waived the statute of limitations in writing when a creditor extended your time to pay or lowered the monthly payments on an installment debt. If you did, you probably did not waive the statute of limitations forever. Instead, you probably gave the creditor the right to sue you for the same number of years—from the time you miss any payment under your new agreement—that the creditor originally had under your state's statute of limitations.

b. Extending or Reviving a Statute of Limitations

Extending or reviving the statute of limitations happens differently than waiving the statute of limitations. A statute of limitations is automatically extended for the length of time you are in prison, you are out of the state or it takes for you to reach the age of 18.

To otherwise extend or revive the statute of limitations you don't have to sign anything. In general, if you either make a partial payment or notify the creditor promising to pay—even if you never get around to paying—the statute of limitations starts all over from the time the payment or promise is made. But a few states have modified this rule. In those states, making a partial payment alone or orally agreeing to pay is not enough to revive or extend the statute of limitations. You must have made a new written promise to pay.

Example (written promise to pay unnecessary): Emily lives in Alabama and owes the Farmer's Market $345. Alabama's statute of limitations is six years. Several months after the statute of limitations ran, Emily sends Farmer's $50 to stall its collection efforts. Emily's partial payment revives the statute of limitations and Farmer's now has an additional six years to sue her.

Example (written promise to pay necessary): Ethan borrowed $812 from Marilyn and agreed to pay her back. They live in Florida, which has a five-year statute of limitations for oral contracts. After the statute of limitations runs, Marilyn begins demanding her money. Ethan sends her $75, hoping to send more later. Sending the payment alone does not revive the statute of limitations and if Ethan doesn't pay more, Marilyn must extract a written promise to pay from him to revive the statute of limitations.

Statute of Limitations Revived or Extended Only by Written New Promise to Pay; Sending Payment Does Not Revive or Extend Statute of Limitations

State	Code Section	State	Code Section
Arizona	12-508	Minnesota	541.17
California	CCP 360	Mississippi	15-1-73
Colorado	13-80-113	Missouri	516.320
Florida	95.04	Nevada	11.390
Iowa	614.11	New York	GOL 17-101
Kansas	60-520	Texas	16.065
Maine	14-860	Virginia	8.01-229
Massachusetts	260-13	West Virginia	55-2-8
Michigan	27A.5866	Wisconsin	893.45

2. Other Defenses and Claims

If you file a response in court, you'll want to state any reason why the plaintiff should not recover all or part of what he asked for in the complaint. You bring up each reason either as an affirmative defense in your answer or as a separate claim, called a counterclaim, in a complaint that you file against the plaintiff.

An affirmative defense goes beyond simply denying the facts and arguments in the plaintiff's complaint. It sets out new facts and arguments. If you prove your affirmative defense, even if what is in the plaintiff's complaint is true, you will win, or at least reduce the amount the plaintiff is entitled to recover against you.

A counterclaim is the basis of a lawsuit you have against the plaintiff. It may be based on different issues than are in the plaintiff's complaint. You may even be asking for more money than the plaintiff wants from you. The counterclaim, however, must arise out of the same transaction for which the plaintiff is suing you.

Listed below are some affirmative defenses you might be able to list in your answer:

- You never received the goods or services the creditor claims to have provided.

- The goods or services provided were defective. (See Chapter 2.)

- The creditor damaged your property when delivering the goods or services.

- The creditor lied to you to get you to enter into the agreement. (See Chapter 2.)

- You canceled the contract as you were entitled to and therefore owe nothing. (See Chapter 2.)

- You cosigned for the loan and were not told of your rights as a cosigner. (See Chapter 6.)

- The creditor was not permitted to accelerate the loan. (See Chapter 6.)

- The contract was too ambiguous to be enforced. (See Chapter 2.)

- After repossessing your property, the creditor did not sell it in a "commercially reasonable manner." (See Chapter 4.)

Here are some counterclaims you might want to make against the creditor. As mentioned, you will usually have to serve and file your own complaint (and pay a filing fee) within the time you have to respond to the plaintiff's complaint. (See Sections A2 and A4, above.) If you succeed on a counterclaim, you may be entitled to monetary damages from the creditor, or at least to rescind (cancel) the contract with the creditor.

- The creditor breached a warranty (Chapter 2).

- The creditor violated the Fair Credit Reporting Act (Chapter 12), Truth in Lending Act (Chapter 6), Electronic Fund Transfer Act (Chapter 6) or Equal Credit Opportunity Act (Chapter 12).

- A collection agency (if hired by the creditor) illegally harassed you (Chapter 5).

3. How to Respond Formally

To avoid having the creditor ask the court to enter a default judgment against you, you are best off filing formal papers in response. If you don't have access to a law library and can't afford a lawyer, however, and you don't want a default entered against you, file a paper with the court saying why you oppose the lawsuit. In many states, as long as you file any paper resembling an answer, the plaintiff cannot take a default.

If you can get into the courtroom, a judge sympathetic to someone representing himself will listen. If all you want is the right to pay in installments, the judge may have a harder time saying no to you when you are standing in the courtroom than if you let the creditor get a default.

Here's how to respond; a sample is below:

- Get yourself a stack of plain white, 8-1/2" x 11" unlined paper.

- Make sure you have the complaint in front of you.

- Take a sheet of your paper. In the top left corner type your name, address, phone number and the words "Defendant in Pro Per" single spaced. Look at the way this is done on the complaint.

- Type the name of the court and the caption—the caption contains the name(s) of the plaintiff(s), the word "Plaintiff(s)," "v," your name and any other defendants, and the word "Defendant(s)"—and the case number. Copy all of this information off of the complaint. Place this information at approximately the same place on the page that it is on the complaint.

Okay—stop typing. Now go back to the complaint and read through it. Write the word "admit" near the paragraphs where you agree with absolutely everything said in it, such as "Plaintiff's sporting goods store is located at 74 Hollis Road, Cranston, Rhode Island."

Next, write the word "deny" near each paragraph in which you deny all or a part of what was said. For instance, if the paragraph says "Defendant bought a gym set and has refused to pay for it for no good reason" and you agree that you bought a gym set but haven't paid because it doesn't do what you want and the store won't refund your money, deny the whole paragraph.

For each paragraph where you are not sure what the truth is, but you believe the plaintiff's statement is probably more false than true write "deny on information and belief." An example is if the plaintiff wrote that you bought the gym set at night, but you think—and aren't completely sure—it was in the afternoon.

Finally, if you have no idea whether or not the allegation in a paragraph is true, for example, a paragraph saying that plaintiff is a corporation, write "deny because no information."

- Now start typing again, this time double-spaced. Type as follows; following each colon, type the corresponding paragraph numbers for the paragraphs in the complaint you just marked up:

"1. Defendant admits the allegations in the following paragraphs:"

"2. Defendant denies the allegations in the following paragraphs:"

"3. Defendant denies on information and belief the allegations in the following paragraphs:"

"4. Defendant denies because no information the allegations in the following paragraphs:"

- Now, type your statute of limitations defense (if applicable) and any affirmative defenses. Use Sections 1 and 2, above, for the appropriate language, but feel free to add a sentence or two if you feel further explaining is needed. List each defense and affirmative defense separately, and be sure you are still typing double-spaced. Don't worry about how many pieces of paper you need.

- Type your name, sign your name and date it at the bottom.

Sample Answer

```
Judith Morrison
355 Bryce Avenue
Hackensack, NJ 07123
(201) 555-7890
Defendant in Pro Per


              Municipal Court for the County of Bergen

              In and For the State of New Jersey




Bergen Bank, Inc.,                      )
                                        )
Plaintiff,                              )
                                        )    Case No. BC—455522
    v.                                  )
                                        )
Judith Morrison,                        )
                                        )
Defendant.                              )
_____)

                              ANSWER

    1. Defendant admits the allegations in the following paragraphs: 1, 2, 3,

4, 7, 9, 16, 22 and 23.

    2. Defendant denies the allegations in the following paragraphs: 5, 6, 8,

12, 13, 14, 15, 17, 24 and 26.
```

3. Defendant denies on information and belief the allegations in the following paragraphs: 10, 11, 19, 20, 21, and 25.

4. Defendant denies because no information the allegations in the following paragraphs: 18, 27 and 28.

5. Defense: Plaintiff is not entitled to the money it claims because the applicable statute of limitations has run.

6. First Affirmative Defense: I canceled the contract as I was entitled to and therefore I owe nothing.

7. Second Affirmative Defense: Clause 14 of my loan agreement prohibits the creditor from accelerating the loan. In violation of Clause 14, the creditor has accelerated the loan and now claims the entire balance is due.

_____   June 17, 1995
                                             _____

Judith Morrison   Date

E. What to Expect While the Case Is in Court

ONCE YOU TYPE UP YOUR ANSWER and any counterclaim, you'll have to serve it on the plaintiff. You can usually have the plaintiff served by having a friend over the age of 18 send the plaintiff your papers through the mail. Details on serving your answer and counterclaim vary considerably from state to state, but you can ask a court clerk or check a local law library for the rules. (See Chapter 13.)

After your papers are served, you must file the papers at the court. You must also file a "proof of service," a document that shows that the plaintiff was served in the proper manner. After your papers are filed, you will receive written notification of all further proceedings in your case. If yours is a routine debt collection case, the next paper you will probably receive is a notice of the plaintiff's request for a trial and date. The paper after that will probably be a notice of the trial date. In some courts, however, you will be sent a notice of a settlement conference before the trial date. Be sure to attend the settlement conference or trial. If you move, make sure you notify the plaintiff and court of your address change.

Sample Proof of Service

Judith Morrison
355 Bryce Avenue
Hackensack, NJ 07123
(201) 555-7890
Defendant in Pro Per

Municipal Court for the County of Bergen

In and For the State of New Jersey

Bergen Bank, Inc.,   )
)
Plaintiff,   )
) Case No. BC—455522
  v.   )
)
Judith Morrison,   )
)
Defendant.   )
_____)

PROOF OF SERVICE

I, Gordon Freed, declare that:

I am over the age of 18 years and not a party to the within action. I reside [or am employed] in the County of Bergen, New Jersey. My residence [or business] address is 56 Trainor Court, Englewood, New Jersey.

On June 22, 1995, I served the within ANSWER on the plaintiff by placing a true and correct copy of it in a sealed envelope with first-class postage fully prepaid in the United States mail at Englewood, New Jersey, addressed as follows:

Deb Miles, Esq.
Bergen Bank, Inc.
1400 Fort Lee Circle
Fort Lee, New Jersey 07333

I declare under penalty of perjury that the foregoing is true and correct. Executed on June 23, 1995, at Englewood, New Jersey.

_____

Gordon Freed

If yours isn't a routine debt collection case, or the creditor's lawyer wants to play the litigation game, a whole lot can go on between when you file your answer and any counterclaim and when you get a notice of the trial. You may want to take the offensive with some of this, especially if you filed a counterclaim. Below is a brief description of the most common of these proceedings. It's difficult for someone without a lawyer to undertake them, but it's not impossible. These descriptions are not meant to be a detailed account of how to cope with court procedures. For that, you'll want to look at *Represent Yourself in Court*.

1. Discovery

Discovery refers to the formal procedures used by parties to obtain information from each other and from witnesses. The information is meant to help the party prepare for trial or settle the case. In routine debt collection cases where you don't have any defense, don't expect the plaintiff to engage in discovery. Discovery can be expensive, and quite frankly, there is nothing for the plaintiff to "discover." You owe the money. You haven't paid.

If you raise a strong affirmative defense or file your own counterclaim, however, the plaintiff may want to engage in discovery. These are the primary discovery methods.

Deposition. A proceeding in which a witness or party is asked to answer questions orally under oath. A court reporter is present and takes down the entire proceeding.

Interrogatories. Written questions sent by one party to the other to be answered in writing under oath.

Request for production of documents. A request from one party to the other to hand over certain defined documents. If you are adamant in your defense of a lawsuit that you paid the debt, the other side will most likely request that you produce a check, money order receipt or other document supporting your assertion.

Request for admissions. A request from one party to the other to admit or deny certain allegations in the lawsuit.

Request for inspection. A request by one party to look at tangible items (other than writings) in the possession of the other party. For instance, if you raise as an affirmative defense that the painter who sued you spilled paint on your rug and it cannot be removed, the painter may request to inspect the rug.

Request for physical examination. A request by one party that the other party be examined by a doctor if his health is at issue.

Subpoena. An order telling a witness to appear at a deposition.

Subpoena duces tecum. An order telling a witness to turn over certain documents to a specific party.

In some states, the trend is toward limiting discovery. For example, parties to a lawsuit can ask only a limited number of questions in their interrogatories. Also, a party or witness can be deposed only once. If the creditor sends you volumes of interrogatory questions or schedules your deposition after it's already been taken, you can ask the court to issue a "protective order" to stop the harassment.

If you don't respond to a discovery request, the creditor will probably schedule a court hearing and ask the judge to order you to comply. The creditor will also ask the court to fine you whatever amount it cost the creditor—including the attorney's fees the creditor had to pay—to get the hearing. If you still don't comply, the judge will probably order that judgment be entered for the plaintiff and that you lose the case.

2. Summary Judgment

The creditor may try to convince the judge that none of the facts of the case are in dispute—for example, that you signed a legal loan agreement, made no payments and have no defense as to why you're not paying. The creditor does this by filing a summary judgment motion. If the judge agrees with the creditor, the judge can enter a judgment against you without any trial taking place. You're entitled to file papers opposing the creditor's summary judgment motion. If you don't oppose it, you'll probably lose.

3. Settlement Conference

Several states require that the parties come together at least one time before the trial and try to settle the case. To assist you in settling, you'll be scheduled to meet with a judge or attorney who has some familiarity with the area of law your case involves. You don't have to settle, but the judge or attorney will give you an honest indication of your chance of winning in a trial.

4. Trial

If you are not overwhelmed by discovery and any summary judgment motion, and you don't settle your case, you will eventually find yourself at a trial. In a trial, a judge makes all the legal decisions, such as whether or not a particular item of evidence can be used. At the same time, either a judge or a jury makes the factual decisions, such as whether or not the item sold to you was defective.

At the trial, you will be required to present your case according to very specific rules of procedure and evidence. The book that can help you in any trial is *Represent Yourself in Court*, by Bergman and Berman-Barrett (Nolo Press). Or, you may want to consult with a lawyer before the trial to get some help.

Some Guidelines on Presenting Evidence

- You can testify only as to facts in your knowledge. You can't testify that "someone told you" something.

- Bring all relevant documents—receipts, bills, letters, warranties, advertisements and the like. Try to bring originals (and make a few copies of each before the trial), but if you only have copies, bring them.

- Your witnesses can testify only to facts in their knowledge—that is, something they saw or heard. For example, if a bill collector threatened to have you jailed, your witness can only testify that she heard the threat, not that you called and told her about the threat.

F. If the Creditor Gets a Judgment Against You

IF YOU DON'T RESPOND TO THE COMPLAINT, don't comply with a judge's order that you respond to a discovery request or lose a summary judgment motion or a trial, the creditor will get a judgment against you. This judgment is a piece of paper issued by the court stating that the plaintiff wins the lawsuit and is entitled to a certain sum of money. The judgment must be "entered"—that is, filed with the court clerk, and this usually happens a day or two after the judge issues it. After it is filed, the court or the creditor's attorney sends you a copy.

1. What Is in a Money Judgment

When you get a copy of the judgment, your first step is to understand the amount the plaintiff is entitled to, and what each portion represents. Keep in mind that the judge may have knocked some money off in response to a defense or counterclaim you asserted.

A judgment usually consists of the following components.

The debt itself. This is the amount of money you borrowed from the creditor, charged on a credit card or owe on a repossession deficiency judgment.

Interest. Part of the judgment will be the interest the creditor is entitled to collect under the loan agreement or contract. If you defaulted on a $1,000 loan at 9% on February 1, 1995, and the creditor obtains a judgment on February 1, 1996, the court will award the creditor $90 in "pre-judgment" interest ($1,000 x .09 = $90).

Interest on the judgment can be added from the time the judgment is entered into the court clerk's record until you pay the judgment in full. The post-judgment interest rate is set by your state's law. (See below.)

Court costs. Almost every state awards the winner of a lawsuit the costs incurred in bringing the suit. These include filing fees, service costs, discovery costs, jury fees and the like.

Attorney's fees. If your original contract with the creditor includes the creditor's right to collect attorney's fees in the event the creditor sues you and wins, these fees will be added on to the judgment. They can add up to thousands of dollars. Even without an attorney's fees provision in a contract, the creditor can be entitled to attorney's fees if a state law allows it—but few states provide for attorney's fees. One state that does—Washington—grants the winning party reasonable attorney's fees if the amount of the debt requested in the complaint is $10,000 or less.[3]

---

[3]Revised Code of Washington Annotated § 422.403.

State	Code Section	Post-Judgment Interest Rates
Alabama	8-8-10	12% unless contract calls for different post-judgment rate
Alaska	09.30.070	10.5% unless contract calls for lower post-judgment rate
Arizona	44-1201, 12-347	10% unless contract calls for different post-judgment rate
Arkansas	16-65-114	10% unless contract calls for greater post-judgment rate
California	CCP 685.010	10%
Colorado	5-12-102	8% unless contract calls for different post-judgment rate
Connecticut	37-1	8%
Delaware	6-3-122, 6-2301	0.5% above the Federal Reserve discount rate, unless contract calls for different post-judgment rate
District of Columbia	28-3302	70% of the interest rate set by the IRS for underpayment of federal income taxes; that rate is currently 25% making the DC judgment rate 17.5%
Florida	55.03	12% unless contract calls for lower post-judgment rate
Georgia	57-108	12% unless contract calls for different post-judgment rate
Hawaii	478-3	10%
Idaho	28-22-104	5% above the weekly average yield on U.S. Treasury bills
Illinois	Ch. 100 ¶ 2-1303	9%
Indiana	24-4.6-1-101	10% unless contract calls for lower post-judgment rate
Iowa	535.3	10% unless contract calls for lower post-judgment rate
Kansas	16-204, 16-205	10% unless contract calls for lower post-judgment rate
Kentucky	360.040	12% unless contract calls for different post-judgment rate
Louisiana	CC 2924	Average prime rate given by five major banks to their most favored corporate clients on October 1 of each year, unless contract calls for lower post-judgment rate
Maine	14-1602-A	15% for judgments under $30,000; if judgment in excess, rate set by formula
Maryland	CJP 11-106, 11-107	10% unless contract calls for different post-judgment rate
Massachusetts	235-9, 107-3	6% unless contract calls for different post-judgment rate
Michigan	438.7, 600.6013	12% unless contract calls for different post-judgment rate, but not to exceed 13%
Minnesota	549.09	Tied to one-year U.S. Treasury bills, not to be lower than 8%
Mississippi	11-7-171, 75-17-7	Rate stated in contract; if contract is silent, rate set by judge

State	Code Section	Post-Judgment Interest Rates
Missouri	408.040	9%
Montana	25-9-205	10%
Nebraska	45-103	Tied to one-year U.S. Treasury bills unless contract calls for different post-judgment rate
Nevada	17.130	2% over the prime rate in the largest bank in Nevada on the January 1 or July 1 preceding the judgment
New Hampshire	336:1	10%
New Jersey	12A:3-122, 31:1-1.1	8% unless contract calls for different post-judgment rate
New Mexico	56-8-3	15% unless contract calls for different post-judgment rate
New York	CPLR 5001, GOL 5-501	9%
North Carolina	24-1	8% unless contract calls for different post-judgment rate
North Dakota	28-20-34	12%
Ohio	1343.03	10%
Oklahoma	12-727	4% over average U.S. Treasury bills for preceding year
Oregon	24.140, 82.010	9%
Pennsylvania	41-3, 42-8101	6%
Rhode Island	9-21-8	12%
South Carolina	34-31-20	14%
South Dakota	54-3-5.1	12%
Tennessee	47-14-121	10%
Texas	CC 5069-1.05	18% unless contract calls for lower post-judgment rate
Utah	15-1-4	12% unless contract calls for different post-judgment rate
Vermont	9-41a	12%
Virginia	8.01-382, 6.1-330.54	Up to judge's discretion; if judge doesn't specify, 8%
Washington	4.56.110, 19.52.020	12% or 4% above 26-week U.S. Treasury bills, whichever is higher; if contract calls for different rate, that rate governs as long as the judgment so states
West Virginia	47-6-5	6% unless contract calls for different post-judgment rate, but not to exceed 8%
Wisconsin	138.05, 806.06	12%
Wyoming	1-16-102	10% unless contract calls for different post-judgment rate

2. How Judgments Are Enforced— An Overview

Once judgment against you is entered, the creditor is now called a judgment creditor and you are called a judgment debtor. Judgment creditors have many more collection techniques available to them than do creditors trying to collect debts before getting a court judgment. For example, in some states a judgment creditor can order you to come to court and answer questions about your property and finances. (See Section 5, below.) Also, a judgment creditor can direct a sheriff to seize some of your property to pay the judgment.

What property the creditor can take varies from state to state. Usually, the creditor can go after a portion of your wages (for most debts up to 25%), bank and other deposit accounts, and your valuable personal property, such as cars and antiques.

Not all of your property can be taken, however. Every state has certain property it declares "exempt." This means it is off limits to your creditors, even your judgment creditors. Exemption laws don't apply to back income taxes, however. Just because you owe money, you shouldn't have to lose everything. You still need to eat, keep a roof over your head, clothe yourself and provide for your family. If you have very few possessions you may find that most of what you own is exempt. (Exempt property is covered in Chapter 11.)

3. Enforcing Judgments in Different States

If the judgment creditor obtains a judgment against you in a state other than where you currently live, or you have assets located outside the state where the judgment was obtained, the creditor can often go into a court in the other state and have the original judgment made into a judgment in the new state. This gives the judgment creditor the right to use all the judgment enforcement remedies available in that state.

If the creditor goes into the second state to make the original judgment into a judgment of that state,

you will be sent a notice and are given the opportunity to object. You can object if you don't have any property in that state, but it's usually not worth the bother. And one court has held that a creditor cannot try to enforce against a debtor a judgment from one state in another state unless the debtor resides, signed the contract that's the basis of the lawsuit or owns real estate in the second state.[4]

4. How Long Do Judgments Last?

Judgment creditors usually have many years—often as many as 20—to collect a court judgment, be it in the original state or a second state. In addition, in most states a judgment creditor may renew the judgment indefinitely if he didn't collect it during the original period, thus giving him an unlimited amount of time to collect a judgment.

---

[4]*Fox v. Citicorp Credit Services, Inc.* 15 F.3d 1507 (9th Cir. 1994).

Time Limit to Collect Court Judgment
(These periods can be renewed in most states)

State	In-State Judgments	Out-of-State Judgments
Alabama	20 years	20 years
Alaska	10 years	10 years
Arizona	5 years	4 years, or whatever time is allowed in state where judgment was entered, whichever is less
Arkansas	10 years	10 years
California	10 years	10 years
Colorado	20 years	6 years
Connecticut	20 years (10 years for small claims court judgments)	20 years
Delaware	10 years	10 years
District of Columbia	3 years	whatever time is allowed in state where judgment was entered
Florida	20 years	7 years
Georgia	7 years	5 years
Hawaii	10 years	6 years
Idaho	6 years	6 years
Illinois	20 years	5 years
Indiana	20 years	20 years
Iowa	20 years	20 years
Kansas	5 years	5 years
Kentucky	15 years	15 years
Louisiana	10 years	10 years
Maine	20 years	20 years
Maryland	12 years	12 years
Massachusetts	20 years	20 years
Michigan	10 years	10 years
Minnesota	10 years	10 years
Mississippi	7 years	7 years
Missouri	10 years	10 years
Montana	10 years	10 years

State	In-State Judgments	Out-of-State Judgments
Nebraska	5 years	5 years
Nevada	6 years	6 years
New Hampshire	20 years	20 years
New Jersey	20 years	20 years
New Mexico	14 years	14 years
New York	20 years	20 years
North Carolina	10 years	10 years
North Dakota	10 years	10 years
Ohio	21 years	15 years
Oklahoma	5 years	3 years
Oregon	10 years	10 years
Pennsylvania	6 years	6 years
Rhode Island	20 years	20 years
South Carolina	10 years	10 years
South Dakota	20 years	10 years
Tennessee	10 years	10 years
Texas	10 years	10 years
Utah	8 years	8 years
Vermont	8 years	8 years
Virginia	20 years	10 years
Washington	10 years	10 years
West Virginia	10 years	10 years
Wisconsin	20 years	20 years
Wyoming	5 years	5 years

5. Debtor's Examination

A number of states—including Alabama, California, Connecticut, Hawaii, Idaho, Louisiana, Maryland, Mississippi, North Dakota, Ohio, Oregon, South Dakota, Washington and West Virginia—let a judgment creditor question you about your property and finances. Basically, the judgment creditor is looking for money or property that can be legally taken to pay the debt. High on the list of property the creditor looks for are deposit accounts (savings, checking, certificate of deposit, money market and the like), income tax refunds due and other easy cash. The procedure is usually called a debtor's examination or an order of examination.

a. Written Questions

In some states, a judgment creditor sends you a form and asks you to fill it out, listing your employer's name and address, your assets and other financial information. You must do this under penalty of perjury. If you don't comply or the judgment creditor believes you're lying or not disclosing all relevant information, the judgment creditor can ask the court to issue an order requiring you to come to court and answer the questions.

b. Court Appearance

In other states, the creditor serves you with a paper ordering you to show up in court and bring certain financial documents, such as bank statements or pay stubs. You don't have to be sent the questions and given a chance to answer them in writing first. Whether you're sent the questions first or simply ordered to appear in court, if you receive an order to appear in court and you don't show up, the court can declare you in contempt and issue a warrant for your arrest.

In a few states, if the judge issues an order for you to come to court, serving that order on you creates a lien on your personal property. The lien may make it difficult for you to sell the property without first paying the judgment. Also, if the judgment creditor believes you are about to leave the state or conceal your property to avoid paying, the creditor can ask the judge to issue a warrant for your immediate arrest. This is quite drastic, but it's been known to happen when a lot of money is owed.

If you receive an order to appear but can't take the time off from work or otherwise can't make it, call the judgment creditor or her lawyer and explain your situation. Tell her you're willing to answer questions over the phone or even in person but at another time. If you haven't already been sent a form about your finances and property, and she thinks you're telling the truth, she may be happy to get the information over the telephone.

If the judgment creditor agrees to change the date or to let you answer the questions over the phone, ask her to send you—and the court—a letter verifying that you need not appear at the hearing. If the creditor refuses, write your own letter to the creditor verifying your conversation.

If you can attend the hearing, or you reschedule it to a convenient time, heed this piece of advice: Do not take any money or expensive personal items such as a college ring or leather jacket with you. The judgment creditor can ask you to empty your pockets or purse and can ask the court to order you to turn over any money or valuable personal property in your possession.

6. Wage Attachments

The first item of your property most judgment creditors will go after is your paycheck through a wage attachment (or wage garnishment). A wage attachment is an easy technique for a creditor to use to get paid, assuming you receive a regular paycheck. Your employer takes a portion of your wages out of your check each pay period and sends that money to your creditor before you ever see it.

In most states, the judgment creditor can't take more than 25% of your net earnings, or the amount by which your weekly net earnings exceed 30 times the federal minimum wage—currently $4.25 an hour, whichever is less. Net earnings are your gross earning less all mandatory deductions such as withheld income taxes and unemployment insurance.

A few states offer greater protections for judgment debtors about to lose their wages. In Delaware, for example, a judgment creditor cannot take more than 15% of your wages.[5] These wage attachment limitations do *not* apply when the creditor is collecting child support, where up to 50% of your wages can be taken, or when the creditor is the IRS, who can leave you with about $100 per week.

To attach your wages, the judgment creditor obtains authorization from the court in a document usually called a Writ of Execution. Under this authorization, the judgment creditor directs the sheriff to seize a portion of your wages. The sheriff in turn notifies you and your employer of the attachment. Unless you object, your employer sends the amount withheld at each pay period to the sheriff, who deducts his expenses and sends the balance to the judgment creditor.

You can object to the wage attachment by requesting a court hearing. (See Section G, below.) In some states, the attachment can't begin until after the hearing, unless you give up your right to a hearing. In most states, however, as long as you have the opportunity to have your objection promptly considered, the attachment can take effect immediately. Beginning January of 1994, federal employees' wages can be attached, just like anyone else's.[6] Until then, a federal employee could keep his income away from his judgment creditors.

Can You Be Fired for a Wage Attachment?

Your employer may consider a wage attachment a hassle and may threaten to fire you if you don't settle the debt right away. Under the law, however, an employer cannot fire you because your wages are attached to satisfy a single debt.[7] If two judgment creditors attach your wages or one judgment creditor attaches your wages to pay two different judgments, however, you can normally be fired. Although in Washington, an employer can't fire someone unless his wages are attached by three different creditors or to satisfy three different judgments within a year. And in Connecticut, you can't be fired unless your employer has to deal with more than seven creditors or judgments in a single year.

Most employers will work with employees who are honestly trying to clear up their debt problems. If your wages are attached, talk with your employer and explain that you are working hard to settle the matter as soon as possible. If, however, you are fired because your employer was not aware of the law or because your employer was "suddenly" unhappy with your work, consider filing a complaint or lawsuit. (See Chapter 13 for tips on finding a lawyer.)

---

7. Property Liens

One collection device commonly used by judgment creditors is the property lien. In a little under half of the states, a judgment entered against you auto-matically creates a lien on the real property you own in the county where the judgment was obtained. In the rest of the states, the creditor must record the judgment with the county, and then the recorded judgment creates a lien on your real property. In Alabama, Georgia, Massachusetts and Mississippi, the lien is on your real and personal property.

In some states, if a judgment creditor does not get a lien on personal property after the judgment is entered or recorded, the judgment creditor may be able to get a lien on your personal property by

---

[5] Delaware Code Annotated § 10-4913.

[6] Hatch Act Reform Amendments, Public Law 103-94.

[7] The Consumer Credit Protection Act, 15 U.S.C. § 1674(a).

recording the judgment with the Secretary of State. If, for example, you then tried to sell your car, the lien would appear and you'd have to pay off the judgment creditor before selling.

Once the judgment creditor has a lien on your property, especially your real property, he can safely assume he'll eventually be paid. When you sell or refinance your property, the buyer's lender, or your lender in the case of a refinance, will see the judgment creditor's lien on your property. The judgment creditor will be notified of the sale and paid out of the proceeds.

Instead of waiting for you to sell your property, the creditor can "execute" on the lien, that is, have the sheriff seize your property—typically a house—and arrange for a public sale from which the creditor is paid out of the proceeds. This is unusual, however, because arranging a public sale is time-consuming and expensive. Furthermore, the judgment creditor may not get very much money by selling your property at this kind of sale, called a distress sale. Any mortgage holder, government taxing authority or other creditor who has placed a lien on your property before the judgment creditor will be paid first. Then you get any homestead exemption to which you are entitled. (See Chapter 11.) Only then does the judgment creditor get her share.

Liens on Your Property After Judgment

State	Code Section	Property	How Obtained	How Long?
Alabama	6-9-211	Real & personal	Creditor registers judgment with county clerk in any county where debtor has property now or may have property in future	10 years
Alaska	09.30.010	Real	Creditor files judgment with county recorder in any county where debtor has property now or may have property in future	10 years
Arizona	33-964	Real, except any declared homestead	Creditor files and records judgment with county recorder in any county where debtor has property now or may have property in future	5 years
Arkansas	16-65-117	Real	Automatic on property in county where judgment is entered; creditor must file judgment with county clerk for property outside county where judgment entered	10 years
California	CCP 697.310	Real	Creditor records judgment with county recorder in any county where debtor has property now or may have property in future	10 years
Colorado	13-52-102	Real	Creditor files judgment with county recorder in any county where debtor has property now or may have property in future	6 years
Connecticut	49-88, 52-327, 52-389, 52-598	Real	Creditor must have attached debtor's property during the lawsuit; then record judgment with town clerk where property is located	20 years
Delaware	10-4711	Real	Automatic on property in county where judgment is filed with Superior Court; creditor must file judgment with Superior Court for property outside county where judgment entered	10 years
District of Columbia	15-101	Real	Creditor files and records judgment with office of recorder in any county where debtor has property now or may have property in future	12 years
Florida	55.08	Real	Creditor records judgment with county recorder in any county where debtor has property now or may have property in future	20 years
Georgia	8-906, 24-608	Real & personal	Creditor enters judgment on general execution docket in any county where debtor has property now or may have property in future	7 years
Hawaii	636-3	Real	Creditor records judgment with Bureau of Conveyances where property is located	10 years

State	Code Section	Property	How Obtained	How Long?
Idaho	10-1110	Real	Creditor records judgment with county clerk in any county where debtor has property now or may have property in future	5 years
Illinois	Ch. 10 ¶ 12-101	Real	Creditor files judgment with registrar of titles in any county where debtor has property now or may have property in future	7 years; may be renewed additional 7
Indiana	34-1-45-2	Real	Automatic on property in county where judgment is entered; creditor must file judgment with county clerk for property outside county where judgment entered	10 years
Iowa	624.23	Real	Automatic on property in county where judgment is entered; creditor must file judgment with district court clerk for property outside county where judgment entered	10 years
Kansas	60-2202	Real	Automatic on property in county where judgment is entered; creditor must file judgment with district court clerk for property outside county where judgment entered	15 years
Kentucky	426.720, 413.090	Real	Creditor records judgment with county clerk in any county where debtor has property now or may have property in future	15 years
Louisiana	CCP 2291, Civil 3501	Real	Creditor records judgment with recorder of parishes in any county where debtor has property now or may have property in future	10 years
Maine	14-3132	Real	Creditor must have attached debtor's property during the lawsuit; then automatic when judgment entered	20 years
Maryland	CJP 11-402	Real	Automatic on property in county where judgment is entered; creditor must file judgment with county clerk for property outside county where judgment entered	12 years
Massachusetts	223-42, 223-59	Real & personal	Creditor records judgment with registrar of deeds in any county where debtor has property now or may have property in future	20 years
Michigan	600.6017	Real	Creditor records judgment with registrar of deeds in any county where debtor has property now or may have property in future	10 years
Minnesota	548.09	Real	Automatic on property in county where judgment is entered	10 years
Mississippi	11-7-191	Real & personal	Creditor records judgment with clerk of Circuit Court in any county where debtor has property now or may have property in future	7 years

State	Code Section	Property	How Obtained	How Long?
Missouri	511.250	Real	Automatic on property in county where judgment is entered; creditor must file judgment with county circuit clerk for property outside county where judgment entered	10 years
Montana	25-9-301	Real	Automatic on property in county where judgment is entered	6 years
Nebraska	25-1303, 25-1542	Real	Automatic on property in county where judgment is entered; creditor must file judgment with district court clerk for property outside county where judgment entered	5 years
Nevada	17.150	Real	Creditor files judgment with county recorder in any county where debtor has property now or may have property in future	6 years
New Hampshire	511:55	Real & personal	Creditor must have attached debtor's property during the lawsuit; then automatic when judgment entered	6 years–real 60 days–personal
New Jersey	2A:14-5, 2A:26-11	Real	Automatic on property in county in any county where debtor has property now or may have property in future	20 years
New Mexico	39-1-6	Real	Creditor files judgment with county clerk in any county where debtor has property now or may have property in future	14 years
New York	Lien 208, CPLR 211, 5019	Real	Automatic on property in county where judgment is entered; creditor must file notice of levy pursuant to an execution for property outside county where judgment entered	20 years
North Carolina	1-234	Real	Automatic on property in county where judgment is entered; creditor must file judgment with county clerk for property outside county where judgment entered	10 years
North Dakota	28-20-13	Real, except debtor's home	Automatic on property in county where judgment is entered; creditor must file judgment with county clerk for property outside county where judgment entered	10 years
Ohio	2305.25, 2329.02	Real	Creditor files judgment with Common Pleas Court clerk in any county where debtor has property now or may have property in future	6 years
Oklahoma	12-706	Real	Creditor files judgment with county clerk in any county where debtor has property now or may have property in future	5 years
Oregon	18.350	Real	Creditor files judgment with county clerk in any county where debtor has property now or may have property in future	10 years
Pennsylvania	42-4303, 42-5526	Real	Automatic on property in county where judgment is entered	5 years

State	Code Section	Property	How Obtained	How Long?
South Carolina	15-35-810	Real	Automatic on property in county where judgment is entered	10 years
South Dakota	15-16-7	Real, except debtor's home	Automatic on property in county where judgment is entered	10 years
Tennessee	25-5-101	Real	Automatic on property in county where judgment is entered	3 years
Texas	52.001	Real	Creditor files judgment with county clerk in any county where debtor has property now or may have property in future	10 years
Utah	78-5-119	Real	Automatic on property in county where judgment is entered	8 years
Vermont	12-2901	Real	Creditor records judgment with county recorder in any county where debtor has property now or may have property in future	8 years
Virginia	8.01-251, 8.01-458	Real	Creditor records judgment on county recorder's lien docket in any county where debtor has property now or may have property in future	20 years
Washington	4.56.190	Real	Automatic on property in county where judgment is entered; creditor must file judgment with county clerk for property outside county where judgment entered	10 years
West Virginia	38-3-6	Real	Automatic on property in county where judgment is entered	10 years
Wisconsin	806.15	Real	Automatic on property in county where judgment is entered	10 years
Wyoming	1-17-302	Real	Automatic on property in county where judgment is entered	5 years

Example: Lin lives in Wisconsin and owns a house worth $200,000. Child-Aid Medical Clinic obtained a judgment against Lin for emergency treatment of his daughter for $2,500 and, consequently, got a lien on Lin's house. Child-Aid considers seizing his house to sell it and be paid, but realizes that it won't get any money because:

- Lin owes $125,000 on his first mortgage
- Lin owes $23,000 on a home equity loan
- Lin owes the IRS $17,000
- Lin's homestead exemption is $40,000.

These items total $205,000, more than the value of Lin's house.

8. Property Levies

A judgment creditor can go after your personal property by "levying" on it. If you have money in a bank account or safe-deposit box, the sheriff can usually take it. Or, if you own valuable personal property such as a car or antique, the judgment creditor might send a sheriff or marshal to take it, sell it at a public auction and apply the proceeds toward the debt. You do not have to let the sheriff into your home, however, unless she has a special court order allowing entry. The judgment creditor won't be interested in any other property, as it usually has little value.

Here's is how the levying process generally works.

- The judgment creditor gets a court order letting him levy on your property. This order is usually called a writ of execution.

- The judgment creditor directs the sheriff to seize a particular asset, such as your car.

- The sheriff comes to your home. If you are present, he explains that he has an order to take a particular item of your property to sell to pay off your debt.

- If you aren't home or don't cooperate, the sheriff can use a duplicate car key or hotwire a car, as long as it is not in a locked garage. Stay calm; in most states you can be arrested for interfering with the sheriff. The sheriff can't enter your house without your authorization to take other property, unless he has a special court order allowing entry. But again, if the sheriff insists on entering anyway, don't interfere.

- The sheriff puts the item into storage.

- If you don't file an objection (see Section G, below) within the time allowed by your state, the sheriff will place the item up for sale.

- After the sale, the proceeds are used to pay whatever you still owe the original lender, then to pay the sheriff's costs (seizing, storage and sale), and then to pay the judgment creditor's debt. If the sale doesn't cover all of what you owe, the judgment creditor may come after more property or use other post-judgment collection techniques.

9. Assignment Orders

An assignment order lets creditors go after property you own that cannot be levied on, such as a due tax refund, the loan value of an unmatured life insurance or annuity policy. Independent contractors and other self-employed people who have no regular wages to be garnished are particularly susceptible to an assignment order against their account receivables.

An assignment order works simply. The judgment creditor applies to the court for an order prohibiting you from disposing of money you have a right to receive—such as a tax refund, insurance loan, royalties, dividend payments or commissions. You are given notice of the hearing and an opportunity to contest the assignment. If the creditor gets the order, the creditor serves it on whomever holds your money. When payment to you comes due, the money is sent to the judgment creditor instead.

G. Stopping Judgment Collection Efforts

Having your property taken or your wages attached can be devastating. It's miserable enough to owe lots of money; it's worse to have your creditors take what little property you may have left. You don't need to be a victim. Although you may doubt it, you still can fight. The process of trying to grab property to pay a judgment can be quite time-consuming and burdensome for a judgment creditor. Also, the creditor might fear that your employer will fire you if the creditor sets up a wage attachment or that you'll quit your job or file for bankruptcy.

Thus, it's never too late to negotiate. A judgment creditor who receives a reasonable offer to pay will often stop a lien, levy, wage attachment, garnishment suit or assignment order. (For tips on negotiating, see Chapter 3.) Or consider contacting Consumer Credit Counseling Service (CCCS), a nonprofit organization that will negotiate for you and help you set up a repayment plan. (See Chapter 13.)

Negotiating, filing for bankruptcy or visiting a CCCS office are not the only ways you have to stop post-judgment collection efforts. Just because a judgment creditor levies on your property or attaches your wages, it doesn't mean that the creditor is entitled to take that property. As mentioned, above, every state exempts certain property from creditors. This means that creditors simply cannot have that property, even if you owe $100,000 and have no other resources. In addition, you may be able to keep property that isn't exempt if you can prove to the court that you need it to support yourself or your family.

Exempt property is described in detail in Chapter 11. In most states, your clothing, furniture, personal effects and public benefits can't be taken to pay a debt. Nor can some of the equity in your car, most of your wages and most retirement pensions. Charts for each state are in Appendix 2. What follows is a discussion on how to claim that your property is exempt (or that you need nonexempt property) when the judgment creditor pursues a lien, levy, wage attachment or assignment order.

Any time the judgment creditor seeks to take your property you must be notified. You can request a hearing called a claim of exemption (or something similar) to argue that it will be a financial hardship on you if the property is taken, or that your property is exempt under state law. If you lose that hearing and your wages are attached, you can request a second hearing if you suffer a hardship and your circumstances have changed—for example, you have sudden medical expenses or must make increased support payments.

Exemptions and Debts for Necessities

In most states, property such as clothing is exempt—that is, that property cannot be taken by your creditors to pay for your debts. At the same time, however, you cannot request a claim of exemption hearing to protect your wages from being attached to pay for a debt for basic necessities, such as rent or mortgage, food, utilities or clothing.

The logic behind these laws is that you should not have your basic necessities taken away from you, but you should pay for those necessities, even if you suffer a hardship in doing so.

This doesn't mean you shouldn't request a claim of exemption hearing for a debt for a basic necessity. The judgment creditor may not challenge your claim and you might win automatically. In addition, the judge might not care whether the debt is for a basic necessity and may only look at whether or not you need the money to support your family.

Here is an overview of how a claim of exemption hearing normally works.

- When your employer notifies you of a wage attachment request, or you are notified of a property levy or assignment order, you will be told in writing how to file a claim of exemption—that is, how to tell the judgment creditor that you consider the property unavailable to her.

- Complete and send a copy of your claim of exemption to the judgment creditor. The judgment creditor will probably file a challenge to your claim. She may abandon her attachment, levy or assignment order, however, if it's too expensive or time-consuming to challenge you. If she does abandon it, your withheld wages or taken property will be returned to you.

- If she doesn't abandon her attachment, levy or assignment order, she'll schedule a hearing before a judge. If you don't attend, you'll probably lose. On the day of the hearing, come early and watch the way the judge handles other cases. If you're nervous, visit the court a day earlier to get accustomed to the surroundings.

- At the hearing, you'll have to convince the judge that your property is exempt or that you need a nonexempt item to support yourself or your family. This is your key opportunity to defend yourself from having your wages or other property taken. You must do all that you can to prepare for this hearing if you want to keep your property.

For example, if the creditor tries to take your "tools of trade," which are exempt to a certain value in most states, bring along someone who works in your occupation. A supervisor, union boss or shop leader can say that you use the items in your job. You'll need to add the fact that the items' value does not exceed the exemption amount. If you have high income one month, bring in pay stubs to show that you usually make less. Or if your bills are higher than average, bring copies. Be creative.

- The judge will listen to both you and the judgment creditor, if the judgment creditor shows up. Sometimes the judgment creditor relies on the papers he filed with the court. The judge may make a ruling, or may set up an arrangement for you to pay the judgment in installments. ■

Chapter 10

BANKRUPTCY—THE ULTIMATE WEAPON AND LAST RESORT

Thou whom avenging powers obey.
Cancel my debt (too great to pay).
Before the sad accounting day.

— Wentworth Dillon, English poet and translator,
1633-1685

BANKRUPTCY MIGHT BE THE ULTIMATE SOLUTION
to your debt problems. For a court fee of $160 (which
may be waived in a few states under certain
circumstances) and the cost of a self-help law book,
most people can wipe out all—or a good portion—of
their outstanding debts. Your creditors know this,
and try hard to keep you from filing for bankruptcy.
But deciding whether or not to file for bankruptcy
isn't easy. You need to understand the different
types of bankruptcies and what bankruptcy can and
cannot do for you.

Many people consider filing for bankruptcy to
wipe out (discharge) student loans, child support or
alimony. Those debts, however, can be discharged in
bankruptcy only under very limited circumstances.
See Chapters 7 and 8 for explanations of when
student loans, child support or alimony can be
discharged in bankruptcy. This chapter addresses
those debts only briefly.

Nolo's Bankruptcy Resources

Nolo Press publishes several bankruptcy aids; this
chapter contains only an overview of the bankruptcy
process. *How to File for Bankruptcy*, by Elias, Renauer
and Leonard, contains all the information necessary for
you to decide whether or not to file for Chapter 7
bankruptcy, and instructions on how to do it yourself.

Nolo's Law Form Kit: Personal Bankruptcy, by Elias,
Renauer, Leonard and Goldoftas, is a streamlined
bankruptcy guide for people who are certain they want to
file for Chapter 7 bankruptcy and simply need the forms
and instructions.

Chapter 13 Bankruptcy: Repay Your Debts, by Robin
Leonard, contains all the information needed for you to
decide whether or not to file for Chapter 13 bankruptcy
and instructions on how to do it yourself.

How to File for Bankruptcy, *Nolo's Law Form Kit: Personal
Bankruptcy*, and *Chapter 13 Bankruptcy: Repay Your
Debts* are available in most bookstores. Or, to order either
directly from Nolo Press with a credit card, call 1-800-992-
6656. To order by check, see the catalog at the back of
this book.

Congress has devised two different kinds of
bankruptcies, Chapter 7 bankruptcy and Chapter 13
bankruptcy, to help most individual debtors. Two
other bankruptcies—Chapter 11 (business
reorganizations and consumer repayment plans for
debtors with very high debts) and Chapter 12
(family farmer reorganizations)—are not covered
here.

In a Chapter 7 bankruptcy, you ask the court to
discharge your debts. In exchange, you must give up
all of your nonexempt property, or its equivalent in
cash or other property. (See Section F2, below, for a
discussion on exempt property.)

In a Chapter 13 bankruptcy, you set up a court-
approved plan to repay your debts. Under the plan,
you make monthly payments to the bankruptcy
court—usually for three years. The court in turn
pays your creditors a percentage of the money they
are owed. Under the plan, you must pledge all of

your disposable income to pay off your debts. In addition, your creditors must receive at least as much as they would have had you filed for Chapter 7 bankruptcy—that is, the value of your nonexempt property. Some creditors, however—such as a former spouse to whom you owe alimony—must receive 100% of what you owe. In Chapter 13 bankruptcy, you don't have to give up any property, and if you can't finish your payment plan, a court may let you convert your case to a Chapter 7 bankruptcy.

If you're deeply in debt, bankruptcy may seem like a magic wand. It often is. But it has its drawbacks too. First, it's intrusive. A court-appointed person, the bankruptcy trustee, must approve almost all financial transactions you make while your bankruptcy case is open. For a Chapter 7 bankruptcy, this is several months. For a Chapter 13 bankruptcy, it can be as many as five years. Second, it can cause practical problems, especially if you must surrender property you desperately want to keep. Finally, it can be depressing—some people would rather struggle along under mountains of debt than acquire the label of bankrupt.

You may also be concerned about your credit rating. If you are considering bankruptcy, however, your credit rating is probably already shot and bankruptcy isn't likely to do much more damage. And although a bankruptcy filing can stay on your credit file for ten years, you can take steps to start rebuilding your credit almost immediately. After two or three years of a record of paying on time, many creditors will ignore the bankruptcy and extend you credit. (See Chapter 12.)

A. Don't Feel Guilty

PRACTICAL PROS AND CONS ASIDE, some people feel badly at the prospect of filing for bankruptcy. If this describes you, pause for a moment and consider bankruptcy in the context of the American consumer economy. "No down payment!" "Easy credit!" sing the salespeople. You're bombarded with special deals—and several credit card solicitations each

day—to wear down your resistance and get you to buy and buy some more. When you buy, sales clerks are friendly and kind. But when you miss a payment the smiles disappear. They want to be paid—now. Letters and phone calls, not special deals and offers, soon bombard you, trying to make you feel guilty.

In one form or another, aggressive creditors demanding to be paid have been around for a long time. Not surprisingly, so has bankruptcy, which originates in the Old Testament and has been entrenched in this country since 1800.[1] Over 900,000 people a year file for bankruptcy. Hundreds of companies—often the same ones that offered you loans "at no money down" and then screamed about the "horrors of bankruptcy"—themselves file bankruptcy each year. Bankruptcy is here to stay, and creditors know it. You have no reason to feel guilty.

B. Filing for Bankruptcy Stops Your Creditors

WHEN YOU FILE FOR BANKRUPTCY, a protection called the "automatic stay" immediately stops any lawsuit filed against you and any other action against your property by a creditor, collection agency or government entity—including the IRS. Especially if you are at risk of being evicted or foreclosed on, or losing your utility service, the temporary protection of the automatic stay may seem like a powerful reason for filing for bankruptcy.

---

[1]Bankruptcy can be traced to Deuteronomy 15:1-2—"Every seventh year you shall practice remission of debts. This shall be the nature of the remission: Every creditor shall remit the due that he claims from his neighbor; he shall not dun his neighbor or kinsman."

Bankruptcy Isn't Needed to Stop Bill Collector Harassment

Usually, it isn't necessary to file for bankruptcy just to get annoying collection agencies off your back. As discussed in Chapter 5, they cannot threaten you, lie about what they can do to you or invade your privacy. Also, you can legally stop collection agencies from phoning or writing you simply by demanding that they stop, even if you owe them a bundle and can't pay a cent.

Creditors collecting their own debts (except those that create their own collection agencies and operate them under a different name) are not governed by this law. While they cannot harass you, they don't have to stop contacting you because you write them a letter saying so. Still, if you have little or no property that the creditor can take, it is less drastic to toss their letters in the trash than it is to file for bankruptcy.

The automatic stay may be "lifted" by the bankruptcy court as it applies to a particular creditor if that creditor convinces the court that the stay isn't serving its intended purpose: to freeze your assets and debts so that the court can deal with them. The stay can be lifted within a week or two, though a few months is more common.

Here is how the automatic stay affects some common emergencies.

Utility disconnects. If you're behind on a utility bill and the company is threatening to disconnect your water, electric, gas or telephone service, the automatic stay will prevent the disconnection for at least 20 days. Bankruptcy will probably discharge past due debts for utility service.

Foreclosure. If your home mortgage is being foreclosed on, the automatic stay temporarily stops the proceedings. If you face foreclosure, Chapter 13 bankruptcy is always better than Chapter 7 bankruptcy if you want to keep your house. You can make up past due payments as part of your Chapter 13 repayment plan, and get back on track with your regular payments. In Chapter 7 bankruptcy, the creditor will get the stay lifted and continue the foreclosure.

Eviction. If you're being evicted, the automatic stay can buy you a few days or a few weeks. But if the landlord asks the court to lift the stay—which landlords almost always do—the court will probably agree, figuring that eviction won't affect the bankruptcy. Despite the attractiveness of even a temporary delay, filing for bankruptcy solely because of an eviction is seldom a good idea. You're probably better off looking for a new place to live or fighting the eviction if you have a defense.

Enforcement of child support or alimony. If you owe child support or alimony, bankruptcy will not interrupt your obligation to make current payments. And the automatic stay will not stop proceedings to establish, modify or collect back support you owe.

Public benefit overpayments. If you receive public benefits and were overpaid, normally the agency is entitled to collect the overpayment out of your future checks. The automatic stay prevents this collection. Furthermore, the overpayment you owe can be wiped out in bankruptcy unless the agency convinces the court it resulted from fraud on your part. Whether or not the threatened collection of an overpayment justifies bankruptcy depends on how severely you'll be affected by the proposed reduction in benefits.

Loss of driver's license because of damages you owe. In some states, your driver's license may be suspended until you pay a court judgment for damages resulting from an automobile accident. The automatic stay can prevent this suspension if it hasn't already occurred. If you are absolutely dependent on your ability to drive for your livelihood and family support, keeping your driver's license can be a powerful reason to file for bankruptcy, assuming your debt burden justifies it.

If your driver's license has already been suspended, you'll probably be able to get it back after bankruptcy. This is because after bankruptcy, a federal, state or local government agency cannot deny, revoke, suspend or refuse to renew a license, permit, charter, franchise or other similar grant solely because you filed for bankruptcy.

Multiple wage attachments. Although no more than 25% of your wages may be taken to satisfy a court judgment (up to 50% for child support or alimony and virtually all your money to the IRS), many people file for bankruptcy especially if creditors threaten to attach their wages for more than one debt. For some, *any* loss of income is devastating; also, some employers get angry at the expense and hassle of taking money out of an employee's wages for a succession of attachments and may take it out on their employees. (Legally, an employer cannot fire you because your wages are attached to satisfy a single debt. If two judgment creditors attach your wages or one judgment creditor attaches your wages to two different judgments, however, you can be fired.)

Filing for bankruptcy stops attachments dead in their tracks. Not only will you take home a full salary, but chances are you can discharge the debt in bankruptcy.

 You Can File for Chapter 7 Bankruptcy Only Once Every Six Years

Before filing for bankruptcy just to stop a wage attachment, eviction, foreclosure, utility disconnect or whatever, keep that limitation in mind. If the creditor gets the stay lifted and you dismiss your case, your only bankruptcy choice for the next several years will be a Chapter 13 bankruptcy, assuming you have the income to make payments under a repayment plan.

C. Bankruptcy Might Not Help You

BANKRUPTCY IS A POWERFUL LEGAL PROCEEDING meant to give debtors a fresh start in facing the world. Most people with overwhelming debt problems find that bankruptcy helps, because the majority of debts can be discharged. Even if you owe recent taxes, child support, a student loan or other debts normally not dischargeable, getting rid of many or most other debts will no doubt leave you better able to pay the debts you can't discharge.

But you must understand that bankruptcy won't always help or isn't always available. Most of the rest of this chapter focuses on these situations. But keep the negatives in perspective—assume that bankruptcy will help you unless you read something to the contrary.

1. If You Previously Received a Bankruptcy Discharge

You cannot file for Chapter 7 bankruptcy if you obtained a discharge of your debts under Chapter 7 or Chapter 13 in a case begun within the past six years. The six-year period runs from the date you filed the earlier bankruptcy case, not the date of your discharge. Chapter 13 bankruptcy has no such restriction; you can file for it at any time, assuming you have the income to fund a repayment plan.

Also, you cannot file for bankruptcy if a previous bankruptcy case was dismissed within the past 180 days because you violated a court order, the court ruled that your filing was fraudulent or an abuse of the bankruptcy system, or you requested the dismissal after a creditor asked the court to lift the automatic stay.

2. If You Don't Want to Stick a Codebtor with a Debt

A friend, relative or anyone else who guarantees or cosigns a loan or otherwise takes on a joint obligation with you can be held wholly responsible for the debt if you can't pay it. So, if you don't want your guarantor or cosigner to be stuck, you should either not file for bankruptcy or file to discharge your debts but agree to repay the guaranteed or cosigned debt anyway.

If you discharge the debt in Chapter 7 bankruptcy, you will no longer be liable for the debt, but the guarantor or cosigner will be left on the hook. And if the cosigner or guarantor is a relative, it's possible that she could be stuck owing more than just the amount that you discharge. If you made payments on the cosigned or guaranteed debt during the year before filing for bankruptcy, the cosigner or guarantor may owe the bankruptcy court the total amount of what you paid during that year. This is because your payments may be considered an "illegal preference" in bankruptcy.

When you file for bankruptcy, the bankruptcy trustee will look to see if you made any payments to creditors within the 90 days before filing—within one year of filing if those payments were to, or for the benefit of, a relative or close business associate. These payments are called "preferences" and not allowed, because you are not allowed to single out certain creditors for special treatment. The bankruptcy trustee can demand that the creditor give the money back. If this is a concern for you, speak to a bankruptcy lawyer before filing.

If you file for Chapter 13 bankruptcy, you include the cosigned or guaranteed debt as part of your repayment plan, and your cosigner or guarantor will not be pursued during your bankruptcy case. You can pay the debt in full during your case. Or, at the end of the repayment period you can discharge whatever balance remains. At that time, the creditor will go after the guarantor or cosigner for the balance.

3. If You Could Pay Your Debts Over Three to Five Years

A bankruptcy judge can dismiss a Chapter 7 bankruptcy petition if he decides that you have enough assets or income to repay most of your debts either in a Chapter 13 bankruptcy or outside of bankruptcy altogether. While a dismissal for this reason is unusual, the judge may consider it if all of the following are true:

- a substantial majority of your debts are consumer (not business) debts

- you have an adequate and steady income, and

- with a modification of lifestyle, you could pay off all or most of your debts over three to five years.

Even if a bankruptcy judge wouldn't throw out your Chapter 7 bankruptcy case, if you can repay your debts over time you may be better off negotiating with your creditors than filing for bankruptcy. (See Chapter 3.)

4. If You Want to Prevent Seizure of Wages or Property

You may not need to file for bankruptcy to keep creditors from seizing your property and wages. Normally, a creditor's only legal means of collecting an unsecured debt is to sue you, win a court judgment and then try to collect the amount of the judgment out of your property and income. If a debt is secured by collateral, however, the creditor can usually repossess it.

Much of your property, including food, clothing, personal effects and furnishings, is exempt from being taken to pay a court judgment. And, quite likely your nonexempt personal property is not worth enough to tempt a creditor to go after it, as the costs of seizure and sale can be quite high.

Creditors usually first go after your wages and other income. But only 25% of your net wages can be taken to satisfy a court judgment, except if the judgment is for back alimony or child support. And in some states, you can keep more than 75% of your wages if you show that you need the extra amount to support yourself and your family. Income from a pension or other retirement benefit is usually treated like wages. Usually, creditors cannot touch public benefits such as AFDC, unemployment insurance, disability insurance or Social Security.

5. If You Defrauded Your Creditors

Bankruptcy is geared toward the honest debtor who got in too deep and needs the help of the bankruptcy court to get a fresh start. A bankruptcy court does not want to help someone who has played fast and loose with creditors or tries to do so with the bankruptcy court. Certain activities are red flags to bankruptcy courts and trustees, and if you have engaged in any of them during the past year, do not file for bankruptcy unless you first consult a bankruptcy lawyer. These red flag no-no's are:

- Unloading assets or cash to your friends or relatives to hide the assets or cash from creditors or from the bankruptcy court—for example, if you own a house and you simply transfer title (ownership) from yourself to your child.

- Incurring non-necessity debts when you were clearly broke—for instance, if you have a high credit card limit and charge a month-long trip to Tahiti when you were earning nothing and couldn't even pay your rent.

- Concealing property or money from your spouse during a divorce proceeding.

- Lying about your income or debts on a credit application—such as stating your income as $28,000 when you earn only $18,000. If the creditor, however, encouraged your misrepresentation—for example, suggesting that you list only your "major" debts, the creditor will have a hard time crying fraud.

6. If You Recently Incurred Debts for Luxuries

If you've recently run up large debts for a vacation, hobby or entertainment, filing for Chapter 7 bankruptcy probably won't help you, at least with regard to those debts. Most luxury debts incurred just before filing are not dischargeable if the creditor objects. And running up unnecessary debts shortly before filing casts a suspicion of fraud over your entire bankruptcy case. Luxury debts can, however, be included in a Chapter 13 bankruptcy case.

Last-minute debts presumed to be nondischargeable in Chapter 7 bankruptcy include debts to any one creditor of $1,000 or more for luxury goods or services purchased within 60 days

before filing and debts for cash advances in excess of $1,000 obtained within 60 days of filing for bankruptcy.

This means that to discharge these debts in Chapter 7 bankruptcy—assuming a creditor objects to the discharge—you'll have to prove that extraordinary circumstances required you to make the charges and that you really weren't trying to put one over on your creditors. It's an uphill job. Judges often assume that people who incur last minute charges for luxuries were on a final buying binge and had no intention of paying.

Creditors, too, are getting aggressive about crying "fraud." Visa USA claims that 30% to 40% of its bankruptcy losses come from fraudulent debts. In an effort to minimize the number of last-minute debts that may be discharged, Visa challenges nearly one-half of all bankruptcy cases filed by people who made large luxury charges or cash advances shortly before filing for bankruptcy.

If You Expect to Incur Debts Soon

If you expect to incur more debts for necessities, you should consider delaying filing for bankruptcy. Most debts you incur before you file will be discharged, but debts incurred after you file won't be. Waiting until after you incur these debts to file will let you include them in your bankruptcy papers. A go-slow approach works best in the case of debts for necessities, such as additional medical costs you anticipate because of an existing illness, the cost of buying your children new school clothes or substantial heating costs during the upcoming winter.

D. An Overview of Chapter 7 Bankruptcy

THE CHAPTER 7 BANKRUPTCY PROCESS takes about three to six months, currently costs $160 in filing and administrative fees (which may be waived in certain circumstances) and commonly requires only one or two trips to the courthouse. To begin a Chapter 7 bankruptcy case, you fill out several forms and file them with the bankruptcy court in your area. (In an emergency, you can file only a couple of forms, obtain the benefits of the automatic stay, and file the rest of the forms within 15 days.) The forms ask you to describe:

- your property and income
- your debts and monthly living expenses
- the property you claim to be exempt, and
- your property transactions of the prior two years.

As stated earlier, filing for bankruptcy immediately stops all creditors and collection agencies from trying to collect what you owe. At least temporarily, creditors cannot attach your wages, empty your bank account, repossess your car, foreclose on your house or cut off your utility service.

Until your bankruptcy case ends, the trustee assumes legal control of the nonexempt property you own as of the date you file, and the debts you owe as of that date. Nothing can be sold or paid without the trustee's consent. You have control only over your exempt property and the property and income you acquire ownership of after you file for bankruptcy.

If you are entitled to receive property when you file for bankruptcy (and in some instances within 180 days after you file for bankruptcy), but haven't yet received it, you must turn the property over to the trustee when you eventually get it (assuming it's nonexempt)—even if it's after your case has closed. Examples include tax refunds, inheritances and life insurance from someone who has died, and personal injury recoveries.

The trustee's primary duty is to see that your unsecured creditors are paid as much as possible on what you owe them. As incentive, the trustee is paid a percentage of the assets he recovers for your creditors. Thus, the trustee is mostly interested in what property you claim as exempt.

The trustee goes through the papers you file and asks you questions at a short hearing, called the

creditors' meeting, held 20–40 days after you file. For example, if your list of property is sparse, the trustee might ask you if you've forgotten anything. You must attend the creditors' meeting, though few of your creditors will.

After this hearing, the trustee collects your nonexempt property to sell to pay your creditors. You don't have to surrender the nonexempt property if you pay the trustee the property's value in cash, or the trustee is willing to accept exempt property of roughly equal value instead. But the value of your nonexempt property belongs to your creditors, not to you.

If you file for bankruptcy and then change your mind, you can ask the court to dismiss your case. As a general rule, a court will dismiss a Chapter 7 bankruptcy as long as the dismissal won't harm your creditors. Usually, you can file again if you want to.

At the end of your bankruptcy case, most of your debts are discharged by the court. You no longer legally owe your creditors. The court schedules a final discharge hearing, but you rarely have to attend. Instead, you are sent a court paper stating that your debts have been discharged. You can't file for Chapter 7 bankruptcy again for another six years from the date of your first filing.

Are Secured Debts Dischargeable in Bankruptcy?

As explained in Chapter 1, secured debts are linked to specific items of property, called collateral. The property guarantees payment of the debt. Common secured debts include personal loans from banks, car loans, department store charges for major items and home loans.

Bankruptcy eliminates your personal liability for your secured debts—the creditor can't sue you for the debt itself. But bankruptcy doesn't eliminate the creditor's lien on the secured property. To eliminate the lien, you'll have to give the secured property to the creditor, or pay the creditor its current value or the debt amount, whichever is less. You can keep certain exempt secured property, however, without paying anything, but you'll need approval of the bankruptcy court. And if you wish, you can agree to have the debt survive bankruptcy, keep the collateral and make payments under the original loan agreement.

E. An Overview of Chapter 13 Bankruptcy

CHAPTER 13 BANKRUPTCY is similar in many ways to Chapter 7, but there are substantial differences. Chapter 13, like Chapter 7, currently costs $160 in filing and administrative fees and immediately stops your creditors from taking further action against you. But in a Chapter 13 bankruptcy, you keep your property. In exchange, you pay off your creditors (sometimes in part, sometimes fully) over three years. (Some repayment plans can last as long as five years.) Also, you cannot file for Chapter 13 bankruptcy if your unsecured debts exceed $250,000 or your secured debts are over $750,000.

Chapter 13 Bankruptcy and Consumer Credit Counseling Service

Filing for Chapter 13 bankruptcy and using Consumer Credit Counseling Service (CCCS) to help repay your debts have a few things in common. First, you devise a repayment plan, under which you make one monthly payment to a third person who in turn pays your creditors. And both cost money. Chapter 13 bankruptcy is $160 plus any fee you must pay if you hire a lawyer or typing service to help you. CCCS will charge you a monthly fee of about $20 for helping with your repayment plan, but will waive the fee if you can't afford it.

But there are two major differences. If you miss a payment, Chapter 13 protects you from creditors who would start collection actions. A CCCS plan has no such protection. Also, a CCCS plan usually requires that your debts be repaid in full; in Chapter 13 bankruptcy, you usually pay less than the full amount. If you feel a moral obligation to pay *all* of your debts, devising a CCCS repayment plan may be the better option.

To begin a Chapter 13 bankruptcy, you fill out a packet of forms—much like the forms in a Chapter 7 bankruptcy—listing your income, property, expenses and debts, and file them with the bankruptcy court. In addition, you must file a workable plan to repay your debts, given your income and expenses. The plan is designed so that most of your creditors are paid at least the value of your nonexempt property within three years. (A few creditors may be entitled to be repaid in full.) You are also required to pay your "disposable income" (what's left over after paying reasonable monthly expenses) each month.

The income you use to repay creditors need not be wages. You can use benefits, pension payments, investment income or receipts as an independent contractor. At the end of the three or five year period, the remaining unpaid balance on your dischargeable debts is wiped out.

As in Chapter 7 bankruptcy, you are required to attend a creditors' meeting. You must also attend a confirmation hearing where the judge reviews your plan and then confirms or denies it. Once your plan is confirmed, you make payments directly to the bankruptcy trustee, who in turn distributes the money to your creditors. If your plan is denied, you can modify it, refile it, and try again.

As mentioned, you can file for a Chapter 13 bankruptcy at any time, even if you wound up a Chapter 7 bankruptcy the day before or just completed another Chapter 13 repayment plan.

If for some reason you cannot finish a Chapter 13 plan—for example, you lose your job—the trustee can modify your plan. He can give you a grace period if the problem looks temporary, reduce your total monthly payments or extend the repayment period. As long as you're acting in good faith, the trustee will try to help you through rocky periods. If it's clear that you won't be able to complete the plan because of circumstances beyond your control, the court might let you discharge the remainder of your debts on the basis of hardship.

If the bankruptcy court won't let you modify your plan or give you a hardship discharge, you have the right to:

- convert to a Chapter 7 bankruptcy (unless you are prohibited from filing for Chapter 7 bankruptcy because of an earlier Chapter 7 bankruptcy filing), or

- dismiss your Chapter 13 petition, which means you'll owe what you owed before filing for Chapter 13, less the payments you made.

F. Does Bankruptcy Make Economic Sense?

IN EVALUATING WHETHER OR NOT bankruptcy makes economic sense, answer these questions:

- Will bankruptcy discharge enough of your debts to make it worth your while?

- Will you have to give up property you desperately want to keep?

1. Will Bankruptcy Discharge Enough of Your Debts?

Most Debts Are Dischargeable

This section highlights the debts you may not be able to discharge in bankruptcy. If the majority of your debts are the ones listed below, you have little to worry about—these debts are normally wiped out in bankruptcy:

- back rent
- utility bills
- deficiency balances (see Chapter 4, Sections B and C)
- court judgments
- credit card charges
- charge card charges
- department store charges
- gasoline charges
- loans from friends and relatives
- newspaper and magazine subscriptions
- legal, medical and accounting bills, and
- other unsecured loans.

If you file for Chapter 7 bankruptcy, you may not be allowed to discharge several types of debts. These debts, however, can be included in your Chapter 13 repayment plan. Some are not completely dischargeable in Chapter 13 bankruptcy—which means at the end of your repayment period, you'll have to pay whatever balance remains on these debts. But that shouldn't necessarily deter you from filing for Chapter 13 bankruptcy. Including these debts as part of your repayment plan may give you room to breathe.

For example, one type of debt usually not dischargeable in Chapter 13 bankruptcy is recent federal income taxes. But if the IRS wants the $12,500 bill you owe *now*, having three to five years to pay it—or to pay some of it and then owe the balance after your case is over—may be just the relief you need.

The debts that are nondischargeable in both Chapter 7 and Chapter 13 bankruptcy are:

- debts you forget to list in your bankruptcy papers and where the creditor hasn't otherwise learned of the bankruptcy

- child support and alimony (see Chapter 8)

- debts for personal injury or death caused by your intoxicated driving

- recent student loans (see Chapter 7)

- fines and penalties imposed for violating the law, such as traffic tickets, criminal court penalties, criminal fines and restitution, and

- recent taxes.

Bankruptcy and Income Taxes

The only time income taxes—and the penalties and interest assessed for failing to pay income taxes—can be discharged in bankruptcy is if the taxes were first owed at least three years before you file for bankruptcy and you properly filed a tax return for the year in question. In practice, however, back taxes rarely fall into this category and therefore are not dischargeable.

Even if your back taxes do qualify, the taxes aren't dischargeable if you've recently negotiated with the IRS or been involved in a tax court case. This is because bankruptcy law says that any income tax assessed within 240 days of filing for bankruptcy can't be discharged. This means that when you end your negotiations or case, and your tax liability is set, you must wait at least 240 days before filing for bankruptcy if you want a chance at having your taxes discharged.

And even that discharge may be of little relief. Although the bankruptcy court may erase your obligation to pay your back taxes, if the IRS placed any liens on your property before you file for bankruptcy, those liens will remain after bankruptcy and the IRS can take steps—such as seizing your bank account or selling your house—to be paid.

Don't despair completely if you have a recent large tax debt and want to file for bankruptcy. Chapter 13 bankruptcy might help. Although you may have to pay your entire bill, you can include your tax debt as part of your repayment plan. During that period, the IRS will have to cease all collection efforts, including adding penalties and interest, enforcing liens and taking your wages. The reprieve from IRS collection efforts may be a great relief.

Only a debt you couldn't discharge in a previous bankruptcy is dischargeable in Chapter 13 bankruptcy but not in Chapter 7 bankruptcy.

In addition, the bankruptcy judge may rule any of the below debts nondischargeable in a Chapter 7 bankruptcy if the creditor challenges your request to discharge them. These debts are dischargeable in Chapter 13 bankruptcy.

- debts the creditor proves you incurred on the basis of fraud, such as writing a bad check or lying on a credit application

- credit purchases of $1,000 or more for luxury goods or services within 60 days of the bankruptcy filing

- loans or cash advances of $1,000 or more within 60 days of the bankruptcy filing

- debts from willful or malicious injury to another or another's property, including assault, battery, false imprisonment, libel and slander

- debts from embezzlement, larceny or breach of trust, and

- debts you owe under a marital settlement agreement or divorce decree—such as marital credit card debts or a property settlement owed to your ex-spouse—unless you convince the court either that you won't be able to pay the debts after bankruptcy or that the benefit you'd receive from the discharge outweighs any detriment to your ex-spouse or children.

As a general rule, if more than 50% of your debts are nondischargeable, bankruptcy's disadvantages probably outweigh the advantages. But this is an individual choice, and if your biggest debt is nondischargeable, getting rid of the rest to let you pay the nondischargeable one may make sense.

If the bulk of your indebtedness is from debts that are nondischargeable only if the creditor files an objection with the court, it may still make sense to file for Chapter 7 bankruptcy and hope your creditors don't object. And you'd certainly be able to include those debts as part of a Chapter 13 bankruptcy.

2 How Much Property Will You Have to Give Up?

You'll Get to Keep A Lot of Your Property

This section highlights the property you can keep if you file for Chapter 7 bankruptcy. Only if you have the kind of property listed below—and you don't want to lose it—should you be concerned.

- a lot of equity in a house or motor vehicle
- a second house or motor vehicle
- expensive musical instruments
- stamp, coin and other collections
- cash, deposit accounts, stocks, bonds and other investments
- expensive clothing and jewelry, and
- family heirlooms.

Exempt property—or a portion of a partially exempt item—is the property you can keep during a Chapter 7 bankruptcy. (Remember, in a Chapter 13 bankruptcy you keep all your property whether or not it is exempt.) Nonexempt property (or its equivalent in value) is the property you must surrender to the bankruptcy trustee, who will use it to pay your unsecured creditors. The more you can claim as exempt, the better off you are.

Each state has laws that determine which items of property are exempt in bankruptcy, and in what amounts. A list of each state's exemptions is in Appendix 2; also, Chapter 11 covers the subject of exempt property in detail.

If you are inclined to file for bankruptcy but have mostly nonexempt property, consider Chapter 13 bankruptcy or negotiating with your creditors. If you prefer Chapter 7 bankruptcy, you need to evaluate exactly how much of your property is not exempt and take steps to preserve its value by selling some of it and buying exempt property before you file. Converting your nonexempt property into exempt property is introduced in Chapter 11 and covered extensively in *How to File for Bankruptcy*, by Elias, Renauer and Leonard (Nolo Press). ■

Chapter 11

PROPERTY YOU GET TO KEEP

The reason why men enter into society is the preservation of their property; and in the end, they choose and authorize a legislature so that there may be laws made, and rules set, as guards and fences to the properties of all the society.

—John Locke, English philosopher, 1632-1704

AS MENTIONED THROUGHOUT THIS book, and specifically in Chapters 9 and 10, if a creditor gets a judgment against you or you file for bankruptcy, much of your property cannot be taken to pay your debts. The items you are allowed to keep are called your exempt property or exemptions.

A. What Property Is Exempt?

THE WORKSHEET , BELOW, helps you determine what property you own, which property is exempt and the value of that exempt property. Instructions for completing the Worksheet are set out immediately following it. This information is important for two reasons.

First, being judgment proof means that if your creditors sue you and get a court judgment, little, if any, of your property can be taken to pay that judgment. To be judgment proof, you can't receive regular income from a job or pension (or any source other than public benefits). If you are judgment proof, writing a letter to a creditor explaining your judgment-proof status may convince the creditor not to sue you.

Second, it will help you to decide if bankruptcy is appropriate. If much of your property is exempt from being taken by creditors and your debts are large, bankruptcy may be the best solution.

How Exemptions Relate to Secured Debts

As explained in Chapter 1, secured debts are linked to specific items of property, called collateral. The property guarantees payment of the debt. Common secured debts include personal loans from finance companies, car loans, department store charges for major items and home loans. Common items of collateral are houses, cars, large furniture and major appliances.

In general, the fact that an item of property otherwise qualifies as exempt doesn't mean you can keep it if it has been pledged as collateral on a secured debt and are behind on your payments. Rather, you stand to lose the property unless you file for bankruptcy, which provides several ways to hang on to the property.

Property Worksheet

1 Your Property	2 Value of property (actual dollar value or garage sale value)	3 Ownership share (%, $)	4 Value of liens	5 Amount of your equity	6 Exempt? (If no, enter nonexempt amount)
REAL ESTATE					
PERSONAL PROPERTY 1. Cash on hand (indicate sources of money)					
2. Money deposits (indicate sources of money)					
3. Security deposits					

1 Your Property	2 Value of property (actual dollar value or garage sale value)	3 Ownership share (%, $)	4 Value of liens	5 Amount of your equity	6 Exempt? (If no, enter nonexempt amount)
4. Household goods, supplies and furnishings					
5. Books, pictures, art objects; stamp, coin & other collections					
6. Apparel					

1 Your Property	2 Value of property (actual dollar value or garage sale value)	3 Ownership share (%, $)	4 Value of liens	5 Amount of your equity	6 Exempt? (If no, enter nonexempt amount)
7. Jewelry					
8. Firearms, sports equipment & other hobby equipment					
9. Interests in insurance policies					
10. Annuities					
11. Pension or profit-sharing plans					
12. Stock and interests in incorporated and unincorporated companies					
13. Interests in partnerships					

1 Your Property	2 Value of property (actual dollar value or garage sale value)	3 Ownership share (%, $)	4 Value of liens	5 Amount of your equity	6 Exempt? (If no, enter nonexempt amount)
14. Government and corporate bonds and other investment instruments					
15. Accounts receivable					
16. Family support					
17. Other debts owed to you, where the amount is known and definite					

1 **Your Property**	2 **Value of property (actual dollar value or garage sale value)**	3 **Ownership share (%, $)**	4 **Value of liens**	5 **Amount of your equity**	6 **Exempt? (If no, enter nonexempt amount)**
18. Powers excercisable for your benefit other than those listed under real estate					
19. Interests due to another person's death					
20. All other contingent claims and claims where the amount owed you is unknown					
21. Patents, copyrights and other intellectual property					
22. Licenses, franchises and other general intangibles					

1 Your Property	2 Value of property (actual dollar value or garage sale value)	3 Ownership share (%, $)	4 Value of liens	5 Amount of your equity	6 Exempt? (If no, enter nonexempt amount)
23. Automobiles and other vehicles					
24. Boats and accessories					
25. Aircraft and accessories					
26. Office equipment, furnishings and supplies					
27. Machinery, fixtures, equipment and supplies					

1 Your Property	2 Value of property (actual dollar value or garage sale value)	3 Ownership share (%, $)	4 Value of liens	5 Amount of your equity	6 Exempt? (If no, enter nonexempt amount)
28. Business inventory					
29. Livestock, poultry and other animals					
30. Crops					
31. Farming equipment and implements					
32. Farm supplies, chemicals and feed					

1 Your Property	2 Value of property (actual dollar value or garage sale value)	3 Ownership share (%, $)	4 Value of liens	5 Amount of your equity	6 Exempt? (If no, enter nonexempt amount)
33. Other personal property					
TOTALS:					

Instructions for Completing Worksheet

1. Your Property (Column 1)

In Column 1 of the worksheet you list all property you own that could bring in more than $50 at a garage sale. The categories on the worksheet may seem illogical; however, these are roughly the categories you would use if you file for bankruptcy. Even if you are not considering filing for bankruptcy, these categories will help you think of everything you own.

In listing all property that could bring in more than $50, keep in mind that many items you originally paid hundreds of dollars for are now worth much, much less. If you're married, enter all property owned by you or your spouse, and indicate whether the property is owned by husband (H), wife (W) or jointly (J).

For cash on hand and deposits of money, indicate the source of each, such as wages or salary, insurance policy proceeds, or proceeds from sale of an item of property.

Real Estate

☐ Residence

☐ Condominium or co-op apartment

☐ Mobile home

☐ Mobile home park space

☐ Rental property

☐ Vacation home or cabin

☐ Business property

☐ Undeveloped land

☐ Farm land

☐ Boat/marina dock space

☐ Burial site

Personal Property

1.   Cash on hand (include source)

☐ In your home

☐ In your wallet

☐ Under your mattress

2   Deposits of money (include source)

☐ Bank deposit

☐ Brokerage account (with stockbroker)

☐ Certificates of deposit (CD)

☐ Credit union deposit

☐ Escrow account

☐ Money market account

☐ Money in a safe deposit box

☐ Savings and loan deposit

3.   Security deposits

☐ Electric

☐ Gas

☐ Heating oil

☐ Prepaid rent

☐ Security deposit on a rental unit

☐ Rented furniture or equipment

☐ Telephone

☐ Water

4.   Household goods, supplies and furnishings

☐ Antiques

☐ Appliances

☐ Carpentry tools

☐ China and crystal

☐ Clocks

☐ Dishes

☐ Food (total value)

☐ Furniture

☐ Gardening tools

☐ Home computer (for personal use)

☐ Iron and ironing board

☐ Lamps

☐ Lawn mower or tractor

☐ Microwave oven

☐ Radios

☐ Rugs

☐ Sewing machine

☐ Silverware and utensils

☐ Small appliances

☐ Snow blower

☐ Stereo system

☐ Telephones and answering machines

☐ Televisions

☐ Vacuum cleaner

☐ Video equipment (VCR, camcorder)

5.   Books, pictures and other art objects, stamp, coin and other collections

☐ Art prints

☐ Bibles

☐ Books

☐ Coins

☐ Collectibles (such as political buttons, baseball cards)

☐ Compact disks, records and tapes

☐ Family portraits

☐ Figurines

☐ Original artworks

☐ Photographs

☐ Stamps

☐ Video tapes

6.   Apparel

☐ Clothing

☐ Furs

7.   Jewelry

☐ Engagement and wedding ring

☐ Gems

☐ Precious metals

☐ Watches

8.   Firearms, sports equipment and other hobby equipment

☐ Board games

☐ Bicycles

☐ Camera equipment

☐ Electronic musical equipment

☐ Exercise machine

☐ Fishing gear

☐ Guns (rifles, pistols, shotguns, muskets)

☐ Model or remote cars or planes

☐ Musical instruments

☐ Scuba diving equipment

☐ Ski equipment

☐ Other sports equipment

☐ Other weapons (swords and knives)

9.   Interests in insurance policies

☐ Credit insurance

☐ Disability insurance

☐ Health insurance

☐ Homeowner's or renter's insurance

☐ Term life insurance

☐ Whole life insurance

10.   Annuities

11.   Pension or profit sharing plans

☐ IRA

☐ Keogh

☐ Pension or retirement plan

☐ 401(k) plan

12.   Stock and interests in incorporated and unincorporated companies

13.   Interests in partnerships

☐ General partnership interest

☐ Limited partnership interest

14.   Government and corporate bonds and other investment instruments

☐ Corporate bonds

☐ Deeds of trust

☐ Mortgages you own

☐ Municipal bonds

☐ Promissory notes

☐ U.S. savings bond

15.   Accounts receivable

☐ Accounts receivable from business

☐ Commissions already earned

16.   Family support

☐ Alimony (spousal support, maintenance) due under court order

☐ Child support payments due under court order

☐ Payments due under divorce property settlement

17.   Other debts owed you where the amount owed is known and definite

☐ Disability benefits due

☐ Disability insurance due

☐ Judgments obtained against third parties you haven't yet collected

☐ Sick pay earned

☐ Social Security benefits due

☐ Tax refund due under returns already filed

☐ Vacation pay earned

☐ Wages due

☐ Worker's compensation due

18. Powers exercisable for your benefit other than those listed under real estate

☐ Right to receive, at some future time, cash, stock or other personal property placed in an irrevocable trust

☐ Current payments of interest or principal from a trust

☐ General power of appointment over personal property

19. Interests due to another person's death

☐ Beneficiary of a living trust, if the trustor has died

☐ Expected proceeds from a life insurance policy, if the insured has died

☐ Inheritance from an existing estate in probate (the owner has died and the court is overseeing the distribution of the property) even if the final amount is not yet known

☐ Inheritance under a will that is contingent upon one or more events occurring, but only if the owner has died

20. All other contingent claims and claims where the amount owed you is not known, including tax refunds, counterclaims and rights to setoff claims (claims you think you have against a person, government or corporation but haven't yet sued on)

☐ Claims against a corporation, government entity or individual

☐ Potential tax refund but return not yet filed

21. Patents, copyrights and other intellectual property

☐ Copyrights

☐ Patents

☐ Trade secrets

☐ Trademarks

☐ Trade names

22. Licenses, franchises and other general intangibles

☐ Building permits

☐ Cooperative association holdings

☐ Exclusive licenses

☐ Liquor licenses

☐ Nonexclusive licenses

☐ Patent licenses

☐ Professional licenses

23. Automobiles and other vehicles

☐ Car

☐ Minibike or motorscooter

☐ Mobile or motor home if on wheels

☐ Motorcycle

☐ Recreational vehicle (RV)

☐ Trailer

☐ Truck

☐ Van

24. Boats and their accessories

☐ Boat (canoe, kayak, rowboat, shell, sailboat, pontoon, yacht, etc.)

☐ Boat radar, radio or telephone

☐ Outboard motor

25. Aircraft and accessories

☐ Aircraft radar, radio and other accessories

☐ Aircraft

26. Office equipment, furnishings and supplies

☐ Artwork in your office

☐ Computers, software, modems, printers

☐ Copier

☐ Fax machine

☐ Furniture

☐ Rugs

☐ Supplies

☐ Telephones

☐ Typewriters

27. Machinery, fixtures, equipment and supplies used in business

☐ Military uniforms and accoutrements

☐ Tools of your trade

28. Business inventory

29. Livestock, poultry and other animals

☐ Birds

☐ Cats

☐ Dogs

☐ Fish and aquarium equipment

☐ Horses

☐ Other pets

☐ Livestock and poultry

30. Crops—growing or harvested

31. Farming equipment and implements

32. Farm supplies, chemicals and feed

33. Other personal property of any kind not already listed

☐ Church pew

☐ Health aids (for example, wheelchair, crutches)

☐ Portable spa or hot tub

☐ Season tickets

2 Value of Your Property (Column 2)

In Column 2, enter a value for each item of property listed in Column 1. For your cash, deposits, publicly traded stock holdings, bonds, mutual funds and annuities, enter the cash amount. For shares of stock in small business corporations, any ownership share in a partnership, business equipment, copyrights, patents or other assets that may seem hard to sell, do your best to assign a reasonable dollar amount.

If you own an item jointly, put its entire value here. In Column 3 you'll enter your share.

Here are some suggestions for valuing specific items:

Cars. Start with the low *Kelly Blue Book* price. (You can find this book at the public library.) If the car needs substantial repairs, reduce the value by the amount it would cost you to fix the car.

Older goods. Want ads in a local flea market or penny-saver newspaper are a good place to look for prices. If an item isn't listed, use the garage sale value—that is, begin with the price you paid and then deduct about 20% for each year you've owned the item. For instance, if you bought a camera for $400 three years ago, subtract 20% ($80) for the first year (down to $320), $64 for the second year (down to $256), and $51 for the third year (down to $205). If you paid top dollar for the item, begin with the price you could have paid had you bought it at a discount outlet, not the actual price you paid.

Life insurance. Put the current cash surrender value; call your insurance agent to find out. Term life insurance has a cash surrender value of zero. Don't put the amount of benefits the policy will pay, unless you're the beneficiary of an insurance policy and the insured person has died.

Real estate. If your interest is ownership of a house, get an estimate of its market value from a local real estate agent or appraiser. If you own another type of real estate—such as land used to grow crops—put the amount it would bring in at a forced sale.

Stocks, bonds, etc. You can check the stock's current value by looking it up in a newspaper business section. If you can't find the listing, or the stock isn't traded publicly, call your broker and ask. If you have a brokerage account, use the value from your latest statement.

Jewelry, antiques, and other collectibles. Any valuable jewelry or collection should be appraised.

If you don't know how to arrive at a value, or if you have an unusual asset such as a life estate, a current right to live in a house until you die, but no right to own it, or a lease, leave this column blank.

Total Column 2 and enter the figure in the space provided.

3. Your Ownership Share (Column 3)

In Column 3, enter two amounts: the percentage of your separate ownership interest in the property and the dollar value of your ownership interest in the property.

If you own an item alone, your percentage is 100%. If you are married and own an item together, and either have a judgment against you both or are both considering filing for bankruptcy, enter an ownership percentage of 100%. If you are married and own an item together, but only one of you owes a judgment or is considering filing for bankruptcy, enter your actual ownership share. If you own an item with someone other than a spouse, enter your separate ownership share.

> **Example:** Audrey and her brother jointly bought a music synthesizer currently worth $10,000. They still owe the music store $3,000; but that is not subtracted in this column. Audrey's ownership share is one half, or $5,000.

4. Value of Liens (Column 4)

In Column 4, put the value of any legal claim (lien) against the property. For example, if you owe money on your house, car or couch, the creditor has a security interest in that item of property. The property is collateral for the debt. If you didn't sign a security agreement or the creditor has not put a lien on your property, there is no lien, even if you still owe money. Even if you own only part of the property (for example, your spouse or partner owns a share), enter the full value of the lien.

> **Example:** Marian owns a house, and owes her mortgage lender $135,000. Last winter Marian had a new roof put on her house. She was not satisfied with the roofer's work and therefore didn't pay him all of his bill. He filed a mechanic's lien on her house for $5,000. Marian also owes the IRS $25,000, and so the IRS put a lien on her house. In Column 4, Marian enters $165,000.

Liens must be paid off before property can be transferred to a new owner—such as a creditor with a judgment against you or the bankruptcy trustee. If the value of the lien exceeds the property's value, you're in luck. The creditor or trustee won't want the property; once the lien holders are paid, there won't be anything for the creditor or trustee.

Include all of the following:

- mortgages and home equity loans

- personal loans where you pledge items of property that you already own as security for your repayment

- security agreements when you make significant furniture purchases or buy major appliances

- motor vehicle—car, truck, boat, RV—loans

- liens held by contractors who worked on a house without getting paid what they claim you owe (mechanic's lien)

- liens placed by the IRS after you fail to pay a bill for past taxes, and

- judgment liens recorded against property by someone who won a lawsuit.

5. Amount of Your Equity (Column 5)

Your equity is the amount you would get to keep if you sold the property. If you own the property alone, calculate your equity by subtracting the amount in Column 4 from the property's total value. Put the amount in Column 5. If you get a negative number, enter "0."

Co-ownership note. If you own the property with your spouse and the two of you are considering filing for bankruptcy or you together owe a creditor, you don't need to do the co-ownership calculation. If, however, you co-own the property with someone other than a spouse, the calculation for Column 5 is a little more complex:

1. If the liens in Column 4 are from debts jointly incurred by you and the other owner of the property, figure the total equity (Column 2 less Column 4). Then multiply that number by your ownership share (the percentage you figured in Column 3). Enter this figure in Column 5.

Example: Bill and Lee, brother and sister, inherited their parents' $150,000 house in equal proportions. Bill and Lee owe $100,000 on the house's mortgage. Bill owes money to several creditors and wants to figure out his equity in the house. It's $25,000—the total value of the house ($150,000) less what he and Lee owe on the mortgage ($100,000), multiplied by Bill's percentage share (50%).

2. If the liens in Column 4 are from debts incurred solely by you, then deduct the total amount of the lien from the figure in Column 2. Only your assets—not a co-owner's—are calculated to pay your secured creditors.

Example: Now assume that Bill and Lee inherited the $150,000 house free and clear of any mortgage. Bill owes the IRS $30,000, however, and the IRS placed a lien for that amount on the property. Now Bill's equity is $45,000—the total value of the house ($150,000), multiplied by Bill's percentage share (50%), less the lien ($30,000).

6. Is the Property Exempt? (Column 6)

By this time, you may be ready to put down the book and quit thinking about all these technicalities. Don't. Figuring out exactly what property you're legally entitled to keep if a creditor has a judgment against you or you file for bankruptcy takes work, but it is not inherently difficult.

a. An Overview of Exemptions

Each state has laws that determine which items of property are exempt from being taken away from people with debt problems, and in what amounts. The lists for each state are in Appendix 2. For instance, many states exempt health aids, "personal effects" (things such as electric shavers, hair dryers and toothbrushes), ordinary household furniture and clothing without regard to their value.

Other kinds of property are exempt up to a limit. For example, in Massachusetts, furniture is exempt to $3,000. Cars, too, are exempt up to a certain amount—$2,500 in Washington. These exemption limits mean that any equity you have in the property above the limit isn't exempt. The judgment creditor or bankruptcy trustee can take the property and sell it, pay off any lien holders, give you the exemption amount and keep the rest.

Many states also provide a general-purpose exemption, called a "wild card" exemption, which can be applied to any type of nonexempt property. For example, Washington has a $1,000 wild card exemption, so you could add it to the $2,500 vehicle exemption and exempt up to $3,500 equity in a car, or use it to exempt up to $1,000 of any other property.

State and Federal Exemptions in Bankruptcy

If you file for bankruptcy in Connecticut, Hawaii, Massachusetts, Michigan, Minnesota, New Jersey, New Mexico, Pennsylvania, Rhode Island, Texas, Vermont, Washington, Wisconsin or the District of Columbia, you can choose either your state exemptions or the federal bankruptcy exemptions. In California, you must choose between two state lists, one of which is very similar to the federal list. California's two lists, and the federal exemptions are in Appendix 2. An analysis of how to choose the better system for your needs is in Section 6b, below. In all other states, you must use your state exemptions—the ones that apply to your judgment creditors.

Appendix 2 also includes a list of federal non-bankruptcy exemptions, mostly federal retirement benefits. If you file for bankruptcy and select your state exemptions or you're pursued by a judgment creditor, you may also select from this list.

Special Rules for Married Couples

If you are married and you and your spouse are jointly planning to file for bankruptcy, or jointly owe judgment creditors, you are entitled to double your exemptions, except in a few states, for a few exemption types. (The exceptions are noted in Appendix 2.) For example, if you live in New Hampshire, which has a $1,000 automobile exemption, you and your spouse can exempt up to $2,000 in your car.

Also, if you are married but only one of you owes a judgment creditor or is considering filing for bankruptcy, your spouse's separate property cannot be taken by the judgment creditor or bankruptcy trustee to pay your debts. For a complete list of what property of your spouse's is protected, see the chart at the end of Chapter 1.

b. Determining Which of Your Property is Exempt

Step 1: Choose an exemption system. If you only care about your exemptions with respect to your judgment creditors, turn to your state exemption list. If you want to figure out what property you can keep if you file for bankruptcy, you may have to choose between two exemption lists. In Arkansas, Connecticut, Hawaii, Massachusetts, Michigan, Minnesota, New Jersey, New Mexico, Pennsylvania, Rhode Island, South Carolina, Texas, Vermont, Washington, Wisconsin or the District of Columbia, you must choose either your state exemptions or the federal bankruptcy exemptions. In California, you must choose between two state exemption lists.

 If You Don't Have a Choice

If your state isn't listed above (and you want to know what property you might lose in bankruptcy) or you're only concerned about your judgment creditors, skip to Step 3.

If you must choose between two exemption systems in bankruptcy, locate these exemption lists from Appendix 1:

- the federal bankruptcy exemptions list (it appears after all the state lists), and

- your state's exemptions list plus the federal *nonbankruptcy* exemptions list.

If you live in California, take out the System 1 exemptions list, the System 2 exemptions list and the federal *nonbankruptcy* exemptions list.

Compare the federal bankruptcy exemptions list to your state's list (or compare the two California lists) for large items, such as your home and car.

- **Your home.** If the equity in your home is your major asset, your choice may be dictated by the homestead exemption alone. Compare your state's homestead exemption to the federal $15,000 exemption. In Arkansas, California (System 1), Hawaii, Massachusetts, Minnesota, New Mexico, Texas, Vermont, Washington and Wisconsin, the homestead exemption is $20,000 or more, so you'll get greater protection by using your state exemption. In California (System 2), Connecticut, the District of Columbia, Michigan, New Jersey, Pennsylvania, Rhode Island and South Carolina, the state homestead exemption is $7,500 or less and so the federal exemptions offer more.

- **Your valuable property.** If the equity amount in your home isn't a factor in your decision, identify the most valuable items you own. Look at the federal bankruptcy exemptions and your state and the federal *nonbankruptcy* exemptions. Which lets you keep the most?

- **Small items.** If you're still having trouble choosing, look for small differences. For example, federal bankruptcy exemptions limit most personal property exemptions to $400 per item, $8,000 total. Some states have no such limit. On the other hand, if you don't have a house, the federal bankruptcy system has an $8,300 wild card exemption, allowing you to claim anything you want.

Step 2: Decide which items you listed on Worksheet 2 might be exempt under the exemption system you're using. Use the notes and glossary in Appendix 1 if you need more information or an explanation of terms.

> **Example:** The exemption system you're using exempts "furnishings and household goods." You could argue that all of your household furniture, fixtures, appliances, kitchenware and electronic equipment are exempt.

In evaluating whether or not your cash on hand and deposits of money are exempt, look to the source of the money, such as welfare benefits, disability benefits, insurance proceeds or wages.

Step 3: Decide which items you listed on Worksheet 2 might be exempt under the federal *nonbankruptcy* exemptions, if available. If you use your state exemptions—this includes all Californians—you may also select from a list of federal *nonbankruptcy* exemptions, mostly military and other federal benefits, as well as 75% of wages you have earned but have not yet been paid. You cannot, however, stack your exemptions if the federal *nonbankruptcy* exemptions duplicate your state's exemptions. For example, if you're using your state's exemptions and your state exempts 75% of unpaid wages, that's all you can claim.

Step 4: Double your exemptions if you're married and state law allows it. If you are married and filing jointly, you can double all exemptions unless your state expressly prohibits it. Look in your state's listing in Appendix 2 to see whether or not doubling is allowed. If you're using the federal bankruptcy exemptions, you may double all exemptions. If your state's chart doesn't say doubling is prohibited, go ahead and double.

Step 5: Use any wild card exemption to which you are entitled. If the exemption system you are using has a wild card exemption, apply it to property you couldn't otherwise exempt, such as property whose value exceeds the exemption limit or an item that isn't exempt at all.

Step 6: Determine the value of all nonexempt items. If an item (or group of items) is exempt to an unlimited amount, put "0" in Column 6.

If an item (or group of items) is exempt to a certain amount (for example, household goods to $4,000), total up the value of all items that fall into the category using the values in Column 5. Subtract from the total the amount of the exemption. What is left is the nonexempt value. Enter that in Column 6.

If an item (or group of items) is not exempt at all, copy the amount from Column 5 to Column 6.

Step 7: Total up Column 6. This is the value of your nonexempt property.

Special Exemption Rules for Pensions When You File for Bankruptcy

If your pension is covered by the federal law called ERISA, pay special attention to these rules.

Rule 1: Your ERISA pension is exempt if you use the federal bankruptcy exemption system.

Rule 2: Your ERISA pension is yours to keep if you use a state exemption system, even if your state exemption list doesn't refer to ERISA pensions. The reason is somewhat complex, involving both ERISA law and bankruptcy law. But the upshot for you is that you don't even need to list your ERISA pension on Worksheet 2 because it's not considered to be part of your bankruptcy estate. [1]

If your pension is not covered by ERISA, it is exempt only if:

- you use your state's exemptions, and

- the pension is listed in either your state exemption list or the federal *nonbankruptcy* exemption list.

If it looks like you might lose your pension in bankruptcy, see a lawyer before filing.

Exempting "Tenancy by the Entirety" Property

"Tenancy by the entirety" is a property ownership form available only to married couples in 15 states and the District of Columbia. Property held as tenancy by the entirety is exempt, but only for debts incurred by one spouse. States that exempt tenancy by the entirety property are identified in Appendix 2.

B. Turning Nonexempt Property Into Exempt Property

IF YOU HAVE AN ASSET THAT IS NOT EXEMPT, you may want to sell it before you file for bankruptcy or before a judgment creditor has a chance to grab it. Converting property is not only sensible, it's legal in most circumstances, but it requires careful planning.

1. If a Creditor Has a Judgment Against You

Unless you file for bankruptcy, you remain indebted to your judgment creditors. This doesn't mean, however, that you must willingly turn over your property to your creditors, unless a court orders you to. Thus, you can convert your nonexempt property into exempt property, even if the judgment creditor is on your tail.

> **Example:** Charlie, a carpenter, lives in Alaska. He has a savings account of $1,500. He also owes a judgment creditor $1,300. Charlie's bank account isn't exempt. But Alaska's tools of trade exemption is $2,800. Charlie closes his account and buys new carpenter's tools, fully protecting his $1,500 from his judgment creditor.

There is one caveat to converting property. If you give away nonexempt property, or sell it for less than it is worth, a creditor may claim that you were fraudulently trying to hide assets. Selling property to close friends and relatives is especially suspicious. The creditor can sue the recipient of the property, and ask the court to order the recipient to turn the property over to her. If this happens, the recipient, especially if she bought the item from you (even for a ridiculously low amount), could sue you for compensation. And if the judge is anti-debtor, you could be fined severely.

If you plan on unloading—or have already unloaded—some nonexempt property, you may want to see a lawyer. (See Chapter 13.)

---

[1] *Patterson v. Shumate*, 112 S.Ct. 2242 (1992).

2. If You Plan to File for Bankruptcy

Converting nonexempt property into exempt property in contemplation of bankruptcy is more difficult because bankruptcy rules prohibit some types of conversions as constituting fraud on your creditors. (See Section 3, below.) Still, if you understand the rules and follow our advice, it can be done.

There are two ways to reduce your nonexempt property. You can replace nonexempt property with exempt property or use your nonexempt property to pay debts.

a. Replace Nonexempt Property With Exempt Property

There are several ways to replace your nonexempt property holdings with exempt property. You can:

- Sell a nonexempt asset and use the proceeds to buy an asset that is completely exempt. For example, you can sell a nonexempt coin collection and purchase clothing, which in most states is exempt without regard to its value.

- Sell a nonexempt asset and use the proceeds to buy an asset that is exempt up to the amount received in the sale. For example, you can sell a nonexempt coin collection worth $1,200 and purchase a car that is exempt up to $1,200 in value.

- Sell an asset that is only partially exempt and use the proceeds to replace it with a similar asset of lesser value. For example, if typewriters are only exempt up to a value of $200, you could sell your $500 typewriter and buy a workable second-hand one for $200, putting the remaining cash into other exempt assets such as clothing or appliances.

- Use cash (which isn't exempt in most states) to buy an exempt item, such as furniture or tools.

b. Pay Debts

If you choose to reduce your nonexempt property by using the money from the sale of your nonexempt property to pay debts, keep the following points in mind.

Don't pay off a debt that could be discharged in bankruptcy. Dischargeable debts such as credit card bills can be completely discharged in bankruptcy. The only reason to pay a dischargeable debt would be if you want to:

- keep good relations with a valued creditor, such as a department store that you rely on for necessities, or

- pay a debt for which a relative or friend is a co-signer, because the friend or relative will be stuck with paying the whole debt if you get it discharged.

In either case, if the payment is more than $600 you must wait at least 90 days—one year if the creditor is a friend, relative or close business associate—after you pay that creditor before filing for bankruptcy. Otherwise, the payment is considered a "preference," and the trustee can set it aside and take back the money for your other creditors.

You can, however, pay regular monthly bills right up until bankruptcy. So keep paying monthly phone bills, utilities, rent and mortgage payments.

3. Fraudulent Transactions in Anticipation of Bankruptcy

There's one major limitation on selling nonexempt property and using it to purchase exempt property before filing for bankruptcy. You can't do it to defraud your creditors. The two main factors a judge looks at are:

Your motive. The bankruptcy court will probably approve your conversion if your primary motive is to buy property that will help you make a fresh start after bankruptcy. You probably can sell a second car and buy some tools needed in your business or clothing for your kids. But if you sell your second car and buy a diamond ring or new stereo system, a court might consider it a greedy attempt to cheat your creditors, even if the item is legally exempt.

The amount of property involved. If the amount of nonexempt property you get rid of before you file is enough to pay off a healthy portion of your debts, the court may dismiss your bankruptcy case.

If you make pre-bankruptcy conversions that the bankruptcy court questions, the burden will be on you to justify your actions. Here are important guidelines to keep in mind in making pre-bankruptcy conversions and then dealing with the court.

- *Be honest.* If the subject comes up, freely admit that you arranged your property holdings to exempt the maximum property and get a better fresh start. If you attempt to cover up your actions, the court may consider it evidence of fraudulent intent.

- *Sell and buy for equivalent value.* If you sell a $500 nonexempt item and purchase an exempt item worth $100, the court will want to know where the other $400 went.

- *Sell property at reasonable prices.* When you sell nonexempt property to purchase exempt property, make the price as close to the item's market value as possible.

- *Don't make last-minute transfers or purchases.* The longer you can wait to file for bankruptcy after making these kinds of property transfers, the less likely the court will disapprove.

- *Don't merely change the way you hold title to property.* Merely changing the way property is held from a nonexempt form to an exempt form usually arouses suspicion. For example, if tenancy by the entirety property is exempt in your state, but you and your spouse hold your house in joint tenancy (not exempt), don't just change the title from joint tenancy to tenancy by the entirety.

C. Claiming Your Exemptions

IN ABOUT HALF OF THE STATES, to take advantage of the personal property or homestead exemption you must file an exemption declaration with the court clerk, county recorder, county clerk or similar official. The declaration is a simple form in which you describe (or list) your property and give its location. If a creditor has already sued you or you've filed for bankruptcy, don't despair. In the states where you must file a declaration, you can file it after you've been sued or after you file for bankruptcy.

In most states, any real estate or personal property (such as a mobile home or boat) in which you reside will qualify for the homestead exemption. And, to take advantage of the homestead protection, you usually must be living in the homestead when you claim it exempt.

When you file a homestead or personal property exemption declaration, you put your creditors on notice that they shouldn't bother to go after that particular property. If they do, you need only point out your filed declaration for protection.

If you don't have to file an exemption declaration, it doesn't mean that you need not do anything to take advantage of your state's exemptions. If you file for bankruptcy, you must list all of the exemptions you claim on your bankruptcy forms. And, as pointed out in Chapter 9, if a judgment creditor goes after your exempt property, you must file a claim of exemption. ∎

REBUILDING YOUR CREDIT

Credit is like a looking-glass, which, once sullied by a breath, may be wiped clear again.

—Sir Walter Scott, Scottish poet and novelist, 1771-1832

IF YOU'VE GONE THROUGH a financial crisis—a bankruptcy, repossession, foreclosure, history of late payments or something similar—you may think that you'll never get credit again. Not true. Although, in general, a bankruptcy filing can be reported on your credit record for ten years, and all other negative information can be reported for seven, in about two years you can probably rebuild your credit to the point that you won't be turned down for a major credit card or loan. Even in the limited situations in which negative information can be reported indefinitely (see Section B2, below), if you successfully rebuild your credit, creditors will ignore old, negative information.

When reviewing a credit application by someone with poor credit, most creditors look for steady employment, a history of making and paying for purchases on credit and maintaining a checking and savings account since the financial setback. And many creditors disregard a bankruptcy discharge, often thought of as the most devastating of all financial setbacks, after about five years.

A. Keep from Overspending

AN ESSENTIAL STEP IN rebuilding your credit is to understand where your money goes. With that information in hand, you can make intelligent choices about how to spend your money. If you'd rather not create a budget yourself, you can contact a local Consumer Credit Counseling Service (CCCS) office. This nonprofit organization, which primarily helps debtors negotiate with creditors, can also help you set up a budget for free or a nominal fee. (See Chapter 13, Section C, for more information.)

1. Figure Out Where Your Money Goes

Before you put yourself on a budget that limits how much you spend, take time to figure out exactly how much money you spend now. To do this, make several copies of the Daily Expenses Form, below, and fill them out for 30 days. Write down every cent you spend—50¢ for the paper, $2 for your morning coffee and muffin, $7 for lunch, $2 for the bridge or tunnel toll, and so on. Be sure to include the money you lay out maybe only once a month, such as $20 for your child's swim class, $5 for an office party gift or a $10 donation to a local AIDS charity.

If you charge an item, list it now, not later when you pay the bill. But don't include credit card payments when you make them. Be sure to also include large monthly payments such as your rent or mortgage, educational loans, car payments, insurance payments and other similar expenses.

Be tough-minded—if you omit any money, your picture of how much you spend, and your budget, will be inaccurate.

At the end of the 30 days, review your Daily Expense Forms. Are you surprised at the total or the number of items you purchased? Are you impulsively spending your money or do you tend to consistently spend it on the same types of things?

Daily Expenses Form

Daily Expenses	Date:
Item	**Cost**
	Total:

Daily Expenses	Date:
Item	**Cost**
	Total:

Daily Expenses	Date:
Item	**Cost**
	Total:

Daily Expenses	Date:
Item	**Cost**
	Total:

2. Make a Spending Plan

After you've kept track of your expenses for a month, you're ready to create a spending plan, or budget. Your twin goals in making a spending plan are to control your impulses to overspend and to help you start saving money—an essential part of rebuilding your credit.

Begin with a blank piece of paper. At the top, write down your monthly income from all sources—such as wages, receipts if you're an independent contractor, child support or alimony and interest or dividends on investments. For your income, list the net—the amount after taxes and other mandatory deductions have been taken out.

At the left, create broad categories of expenses based on the items you listed in your Daily Expenses Forms. For example, if you spend money on coffee at work, lunch out and groceries, you can combine that into "food." Or you can separate groceries from the rest, and use two categories—"food at home" and "food out." Here are some suggested categories:

- rent/mortgage (including taxes and insurance)
- telephone and utilities (water, gas, electric, cable, garbage)
- household supplies
- furnishings and furniture
- food/groceries
- clothing
- personal care (haircut, cosmetics, toiletries)
- health care (insurance, medications, doctors, therapist)
- transportation (car payment, car insurance, gasoline, tolls)
- entertainment
- dependent care
- vacation and travel
- educational expenses
- insurance (other than homeowner's car and health)

- business expenses (out of your own pocket).

Be sure to include a category for any bank or other deposit accounts you do, or plan to, deposit money into, and any loans you make payments on.

To the right of each category, write down the amount of money you spend, deposit or pay each month—using the figures you entered on your Daily Expenses Forms.

Finally, total up the amount you spend each month. If it exceeds your monthly income, you will need to make some changes—eliminate or reduce expenditures for non-necessities—and start over.

Once you are able to break even, go one step further. Think about the changes you need to make to put away a few dollars at the end of every week. If you think there's nothing to spare, try to set a small goal—even $5 a week. It will help. If you spend $2 per day on coffee and a muffin, that adds up to $10 per week and at least $40 per month. Eating breakfast at home might save you most of that amount.

If you buy the newspaper at the corner store every day, consider subscribing. A subscription doesn't involve extending credit; if you don't pay, the newspaper company simply stops delivering. And you can usually get clothes for your kids at a thrift shop.

3. Avoid Future Financial Problems

There are no magic rules that will solve everyone's financial troubles. But nine suggestions should help you stay out of financial hot water. If you have a family, everyone will have to participate—no one person can do all the work alone. So make sure your spouse or significant other, and the kids, understand that the family is having financial difficulties and agree together to take the steps that will lead to recovery.

- *Create a realistic budget and stick to it.* This means periodically checking it and readjusting your figures and spending habits.

- *Don't impulse buy.* When you see something you hadn't planned to buy, don't purchase it on the spot. Go home and think it over. It's unlikely you'll return to the store and buy it.

- *Avoid sales.* Buying a $500 item on sale for $400 isn't a $100 savings if you didn't need the item to begin with. It's spending $400 unnecessarily.

- *Get medical insurance if at all possible.* Even a stopgap policy with a large deductible can help if a medical crisis comes up. You can't avoid medical emergencies, but living without medical insurance is an invitation to financial ruin.

- *Charge items only if you can afford to pay for them now.* If you don't currently have the cash, don't charge based on future income—sometimes future income doesn't materialize. An alternative is to toss all of your credit cards in a drawer (or in the garbage) and to commit to living without credit for a while.

- *Avoid large rent or house payments.* Obligate yourself only for what you can now afford and increase your mortgage payments only as your income increases. Consider refinancing your house if your payments are unwieldy.

- *Avoid cosigning or guaranteeing a loan for someone.* Your signature obligates you as if you were the primary borrower. You can't be sure that the other person will pay.

- *Similarly, avoid joint obligations with people who have questionable spending habits*—even a spouse or significant other. If you incur a joint debt, you're probably liable for it all if the other person defaults.

- *Don't make high-risk investments*, such as investments in speculative real estate, penny stocks and junk bonds. Invest conservatively, opting for certificates of deposit, money market funds and government bonds.

Should You Rebuild Your Credit?

Habitual overspending can be just as hard to overcome as excessive gambling or drinking. If you think you may be a compulsive spender, one of the worst things you can do is rebuild your credit. Instead, you need to get a handle on your spending habits.

Debtors Anonymous, a 12-step support program similar to Alcoholics Anonymous, has programs nationwide. If a Debtors Anonymous group or a therapist recommends that you stay out of the credit system for a while, follow that advice. Even if you don't feel you're a compulsive spender, paying as you spend may still be the way to go—because of finance charges, transaction fees and other charges, buying on credit costs between 15% and 20% more than paying with cash.

Debtors Anonymous groups meet all over the country. If you can't find one in your area, send a self-addressed, stamped envelope to Debtors Anonymous, General Services Board, P.O. Box 400, New York, NY 10163-0400. Or call their message machine at (212) 642-8220 and leave you name, address and a request for information.

B. Clean Up Your Credit File

IF YOU'VE GOT SERIOUS DEBT problems, you are probably concerned about what's in your credit file or your "credit rating." No question your credit rating will suffer if you don't pay your bills. Bankruptcies, repossessions, foreclosures, lawsuits to collect debt, and even missed payments get into credit files. Potential creditors see the negative information and often deny you a loan or credit card.

But what exactly is a credit rating? What about a credit file? Few people know or have ever seen one. Yet, to understand the credit world and how to rebuild your credit—you need to know how credit is established and how credit information is used.

Establishing credit involves taking steps to make sure that when you apply for a loan or credit card, or even for an apartment or job, the lender, landlord or employer will find favorable information on you when she runs a credit check. Credit checks search out information found in a computer file assembled and maintained by a credit bureau. (See Section B, below.) If the information indicates that you are a good risk—you'll probably pay the loan (or your rent) on time or will be a reliable employee—you have "good credit." If it shows that you have a history of paying bills late or not at all, you have "bad credit."

If the prospective lender, landlord or employer finds no credit file, she cannot assess your trust-worthiness one way or the other, and may hesitate to lend you money or let you open up a credit card account. Similarly, without a credit history, a landlord may decide against renting to you. An employer, too, may conclude that a 35-year-old applicant doesn't have a stable life if the employer finds no credit file.

Many of us first establish credit in our late teens or early twenties. We may have said "yes" to the steady stream of gasoline and local department store pre-approved credit card applications we received when we graduated from high school or college, borrowed a few hundred dollars from a local bank or applied for a major credit card.

With many of these credit cards, our parents were guarantors. A guarantor promises the lender that he will pay if the primary debtor does not. The guarantor's name does not appear on the credit account. This is similar to a cosigner, who also promises to repay a loan if the primary debtor defaults.

Others of us may have waited until we bought our first car or were in our first job. And anyone who financed his college education with student loans established a credit history the day he made (or missed) his first loan repayment.

A few of us believe we've never taken steps to establish credit. We have no credit cards and pay cash for everything. But as stated above, we don't establish credit just by taking out a loan or buying items with a credit card. Often, by applying for a job, apartment or insurance policy, we start down the road to having credit. Employers, landlords and insurance companies often request copies of credit files from credit bureaus.

> **Example:** On an apartment application, you list a former landlord to whom you paid $700 monthly rent from January 1, 1992, to December 31, 1994. Your prospective landlord checks with a credit bureau and sees that your former landlord reported that once during your three-year residency you were two weeks late on a payment. Your new landlord figures that one late payment out of 36 is nothing to worry about and happily offers you the apartment.

1. Credit Bureaus and Credit Files

Credit bureaus are private, profit-making companies that gather and sell information about a person's credit history. Credit bureaus sell credit files to banks, mortgage lenders, credit unions, credit card companies, department stores, insurance companies, landlords and even a few employers. They in turn use the credit files to supplement applications for credit, insurance, housing and employment.

If the bureau has no information on you, however, it has nothing to sell. Thus, credit bureaus are always searching for more information.

There are three major credit bureaus—Equifax (headquartered in Atlanta, GA), Trans Union (Chicago, IL) and TRW (Orange, CA). Together they have over 1,000 branches throughout the country. Each company maintains a file on nearly every U.S. adult—about 180 million people—for a total of 540 million files.

Credit bureaus get most of their data from creditors such as department stores, banks and credit card companies. Credit bureaus also search court records, looking for lawsuits, judgments and bankruptcy filings. And they go through county records offices to find recorded tax, judgment, mechanic's or other liens (legal claims).

To create a credit report for a given person, a bureau searches its computer files until it finds entries that match the name, Social Security number and any other available identifying information. All matches are gathered together and constitute a credit report or credit file.

Data gathered in a credit file usually includes your name (and any former names), past and present addresses, Social Security number, employment history, marriages, divorces, lawsuits to which you are a party (even if you didn't lose the case) and liens (legal claims on your property). And if you've gone through bankruptcy, you can be sure it will show up in your credit file.

But the bulk of information in a credit file is your credit history—positive and negative. A file typically contains the name of your creditors, the type and number of each account, when each account was opened, your payment history (whether you pay on time or have been 30, 60, 90 or 120 days past due) for the previous 24–36 months, your credit limit or the original amount of a loan and your current balance. The file will show if any accounts have been turned over to a collection agency or if you are disputing a charge.

> **Example:** Conrad visits Cars for Less and finds a used Porsche for $20,000. Conrad plans to put one-third down, and to use the dealer's financing for the rest. Although Conrad brought $6,000 cash, Cars for Less wants to be sure that he can make payments of about $300 per month on the balance.
>
> The salesclerk at Cars for Less calls up her Equifax computer database. She searches the database for Conrad's file by entering his name, address and Social Security number.
>
> The computer digests the information and pulls up Conrad's file. It shows that he makes his credit card payments within 30 days, is current on his mortgage, but does owe the county property tax office about $250. The salesclerk decides that Conrad's property tax is of no concern—it will be paid when Conrad sells his house, if not before—and lends him the money for the car.

Loan Exchanges

Many lenders, especially banks, savings and loans, and credit unions, belong to loan exchanges. As a member of an exchange, the lender supplies the exchange with the identity, loan type and loan amount for any person to whom it makes a loan. Furthermore, when it receives a loan application, the lender contacts the loan exchange and is given information—the loan type and balance—on all of the applicant's outstanding loans.

The information provided by a loan exchange is often quite detailed and is used by lenders to supplement the information they get from credit bureaus. It's also used to check the accuracy of the information obtained from credit bureaus.

2 Laws Regulating Credit Bureaus

Credit bureaus are regulated by the Federal Trade Commission under the provisions of the 1971 federal Fair Credit Reporting Act (FCRA).[1] The FCRA was passed to address consumers' concerns about the proliferation of credit bureaus and the information in credit files. The law is designed to bar inaccurate or obsolete information from staying in a file, and requires that credit bureaus adopt reasonable procedures for gathering, maintaining and disseminating information. In addition, a few states have enacted their own laws regulating credit bureaus. (See Section B2c, below.)

a The Laws' Weaknesses

The FCRA and most state laws, unfortunately, have a major shortcoming. Credit bureaus need only adhere to the deliberately vague standard of "follow[ing] reasonable procedures to assure maximum possible accuracy." These words are not defined, and mean that credit bureaus may report

---

[1] 15 U.S.C. § 1681 et seq.

flat-out wrong data about you as long as they reasonably believed the information was correct when they originally received it. They can also report data they know to be misleading or damaging, as long as the information is "technically accurate."

> **Example:** Austin's credit file stated that he was involved in a lawsuit. Austin sued the credit bureau, believing that it should explain that the lawsuit was in his official capacity as county deputy marshal. The court ruled against him, stating that the credit bureau only had to correct or amend "clear misstatements or inaccuracies."[2]

b. The Fair Credit Reporting Act

The FCRA was designed to address consumer concerns. Under the FCRA, credit bureaus *may* do any of the following:

- Gather any information bearing on your credit worthiness, credit standing, credit capacity, character, general reputation, personal characteristics or mode of living as it relates to your eligibility for credit or insurance, or for employment purposes.

- Provide the information in your credit file to anyone who intends to use the information in a credit transaction, for employment purposes, to underwrite insurance, to determine your eligibility for government benefits or for any other legitimate business need, such as collecting a debt you owe.

- Report lawsuits, paid tax liens, accounts sent out for collection, criminal records and any other adverse information from the date of the last activity on the account up to seven years.

- Report bankruptcies from the date of the last activity for no more than ten years. Equifax, however, often removes Chapter 13 bankruptcies

after only seven years. Although the date of the last activity for most bankruptcies is the date you receive your discharge (or the date of your dismissal if you never receive a discharge), credit bureaus usually start counting the ten-year period from the earlier date of filing.

- Indefinitely report bankruptcies, lawsuits, paid tax liens, accounts sent out for collection, criminal records and any other adverse information if you apply for $50,000 or more of credit or insurance, or if you apply for a job with an annual income of at least $20,000. (As a matter of practice, however, most credit bureaus permanently delete all negative information after seven or ten years.)

- Interview your neighbors, friends, associates or any other acquaintance who may have knowledge about you to gather character, general reputation, personal characteristics or mode of living information. But the credit bureau must tell you in writing that it will be conducting such an investigation (called an investigative consumer report).

In addition, under the FCRA credit bureaus *must* show you your credit file if you present proper identification.

While the FCRA limits, to some degree, the kind of information credit bureaus can report and the length of time the information may be reported, the law does little to decrease the numbers of mistakes in credit files. And unfortunately, mistakes are common. But you have the right to request a copy of your file as often as you want and thus can monitor your file yourself.

c. State Credit Bureau Laws

Because of the number of mistakes found in credit files, a few state legislatures (California being the most active) have enacted laws that further limit creditor and credit bureau activities and increase consumers' rights.

---

[2]*Austin v. BankAmerica Service Corp.*, 419 F. Supp. 730 (N.D. Ga. 1974).

State	Code Section	State Laws Governing Credit Reporting Agencies (Credit Bureaus)
California	CC 1785.13	Credit bureaus: • cannot report an arrest unless it resulted in conviction • must report specific type of bankruptcy (Chapter 7, Chapter 11, Chapter 13) • cannot report *any* information indefinitely; information allowed to be reported indefinitely under federal law may be reported for maximum ten years • must specify when account closed by consumer • cannot furnish medical information without consumer's consent.
	CC 1785.15	Credit bureaus must provide consumer with: • decoded version of information in file, or coded version and list of code explanation • names of all creditors who received copy of file for previous six months (two years if file given for employment purposes) • copy of credit file within five days of receiving consumer's request • telephone disclosure of credit file if consumer provides proper identification.
	CC 1785.16	If consumer requests reinvestigation of information in credit file, credit bureau must provide consumer with written results of reinvestigation within five days of completion. If credit bureau removes information after consumer requests reinvestigation, credit bureau must maintain reasonable procedure to avoid reinsertion. If credit bureau reinserts information because it later verified information's accuracy, credit bureau must notify consumer in writing within five days of reinserting information.
	CC 1785.25	Creditors must: • notify credit bureaus when account closed by consumer • report specific date of any delinquency reported to credit bureau • complete reinvestigation of consumer dispute within 30 days.
	CC 1785.26	Creditor must notify consumer when initially reporting negative information to credit bureau, before, or within 30 days of, reporting the information.
	CC 1799.101	If debtor defaults, creditor must give notice to cosigner before or at the time the creditor reports the default to credit bureau.
Kentucky	367.310	Credit bureaus cannot report an arrest unless it resulted in conviction.
Maine	1320-2-C	If consumer applies for mortgage and is denied because of information in credit file, mortgage lender must provide consumer with copy of credit file unless credit bureau provides consumer with copy.
Michigan	19.655(272)	If debtor defaults, creditor must give notice to cosigner before creditor reports default to credit bureau. Creditor must give cosigner 30 days to pay amount due or make other satisfactory arrangements before reporting delinquency to credit bureau.
Minnesota	13C.02	Credit bureau must notify consumer when it sends credit report to an employer.
New Mexico	56-3-6	Credit bureaus cannot report an arrest unless it resulted in a conviction.

State	Code Section	State Laws Governing Credit Reporting Agencies (Credit Bureaus)
New York	GBL 380-j	Credit bureaus cannot report criminal records other than convictions and pending charges, cannot report any polygraph information and can report paid judgments or accounts sent out for collection for only five years.
		Negative information authorized to be reported under state law, which the federal FCRA allows to be reported indefinitely, may be reported indefinitely only if a job's annual salary is $25,000 or more.
Oklahoma	24-81	Before credit bureau reports consumer's credit rating to creditor, bureau must give consumer opportunity to state his or her assets and liabilities.
Rhode Island	6-13.1-21	Any creditor planning to request credit file must first notify consumer that it may request credit file.
Utah	70C-7-107	Creditor must notify consumer if it plans to report negative information to credit bureaus.
Vermont	2480e	Credit bureau may not provide creditor with consumer's credit file unless creditor has court order or consent of consumer. This does not apply to a creditor reviewing existing account for purposes of increasing credit line, taking collection activity or other legitimate business need. Also, creditor need not have consent to obtain list of "prescreened" names in order to make offer of credit.

3. Get a Copy of Your Credit File

You are entitled to a get a copy of your own credit file. And it's free in these circumstances:

- You've been denied credit because of information in your credit file. You are entitled to a free copy of your file from the bureau that reported the information; even if you request it from a different bureau, that bureau will probably provide you with a copy. (A creditor that denies you credit in this situation will tell you the name and address of the credit bureau reporting the information that led to the denial.) You must request your copy within 60 days of being denied credit. (The law states 30 days, but all credit bureaus will send a copy if you make your request within 60 days.)

- You haven't requested a copy in the last year. Even if you haven't been denied credit, you can get a free copy of your credit report once a year from any credit bureau if you live in Maryland or Vermont. If you live in any other state, you can get a free copy of your credit report from TRW once a year.

To obtain a report under in any other situation (such as from Equifax or Trans Union, or a second copy in Maryland or Vermont) you'll have to pay a fee of probably no more than $8. In fact, the fee is capped at $8 in five states—California, Louisiana, Rhode Island, Minnesota, and Washington. Three other states cap the fee—Maine ($2), Maryland ($5.25) and Vermont ($7.50).[3]

---

[3]California Civil Code § 1785.17; Louisiana Revised Statutes § 9:3571.1; Rhode Island General Laws § 6-13.1-21; Minnesota Statutes Annotated § 13C.01; Revised Code of Washington Chapter 476 § 12; Maine Revised Statutes Annotated § 10-1316; Maryland Commercial Law Code Annotated § 14-1209; Vermont Statutes Annotated § 9-2480c.

Don't Subscribe to a Credit Reporting "Service"

TRW and other companies offer credit check "services." For example, TRW's $44 per year Credentials program claims to give you unlimited access to your credit file. It sends you a copy of your credit file as often as you want, informs you every time a creditor requests a copy of your credit file and provides you with a quarterly report of negative information reported to your file.

What TRW doesn't tell you is that the Fair Credit Reporting Act already lets you see your file as often as you want. You may have to pay a reasonable fee after the first time, but it won't come close to $44. Few people need to see their file more than once a year.

TRW also keeps a financial profile of you—listing your assets and liabilities including your motor vehicles, real estate and deposit accounts. So what? No creditor accepts this information from a credit bureau without having you fill out their application. Mostly, TRW charges you $44 per year for a service you don't need (or could get for less money).

You can request your file from one, two or all three bureaus. Here's how to decide:

- If you've been denied credit, get a copy of your credit report from the bureau that reported the information leading to the denial. If you find problems in your credit file, it's wise to obtain copies of your file from the other two bureaus.

- If you're just beginning to rebuild your credit, get a copy of your file for free from TRW. Again, if there are mistakes in it, you will probably want to get copies of your file from the other two bureaus.

Once you select a credit bureau, you can call and ask if it has a file on you. Under the FCRA, a credit bureau *must* do a search for a credit file if you offer "proper identification." The credit bureau needs little beyond your name (and former names), address (and former addresses), phone number, Social Security number and year of birth to establish your identification. If the clerk searches while you're on the phone with her, she'll only tell you whether or not the bureau has a file. She won't tell you what is in the file. For that, you'll have to put your request in writing or pay a visit to the credit bureau itself.

If you are in a hurry, you may want to visit. Credit reports contain code numbers and symbols pertaining to your payment history. They also contain printed explanations of the numbers and symbols, but these may be unclear. And calling up for clarification can be a bureaucratic nightmare. If you visit the credit bureau office, you can ask for immediate clarification of anything you don't understand, and under the FCRA, you must be given an explanation.

The credit bureau must show you all information in your file (except medical information), the sources of the information, and the names of people who requested copies of your file within the last six months (two years if the information was given to an employer or potential employer).

Obtaining Medical Information

Getting a copy of your medical file isn't impossible. Most medical files are collected by the Medical Information Bureau, P.O. Box 105, Essex Station, Boston, MA 02112, (617) 426-3660. MIB files contain physical and medical data requested by insurance companies from a person who applies for coverage—this is the same type of medical information that is collected by credit bureaus. To obtain a copy of your file, call or write MIB and ask for a copy of the Request for Disclosure of MIB Record Information form. Then complete it and return it to MIB.

If you visit the credit bureau office, you're allowed to bring someone with you. This isn't a bad idea; if the bureau makes you fill out unnecessary forms, rushes through your file or gives you evasive answers to questions, your friend can act as a witness, which will help if you file a complaint against the bureau.

To request a copy of your credit report by mail, you will need to include the following information in a letter.

Full name. A credit bureau cannot process your request without your name. It's important that you provide your full name, including generations (Jr., Sr., III).

Date of birth. A credit bureau may provide your report without your date (or at least year) of birth. But this information helps distinguish you from anyone else with a similar name.

Social Security number. Many people refuse to give out their Social Security numbers to anyone other than their employers, banks and the IRS. That's fine, but realize you may have trouble getting credit or an accurate credit report. If you obtain your credit report without giving your Social Security number and it doesn't include accounts for other people, then continue to keep your Social Security number to yourself. If, however, your file has accounts for other people, you'll want to add your Social Security number and clear up the inaccuracies.

Spouse's name. It's not absolutely necessary, but again, it helps distinguish you from anyone else with a similar name.

Telephone number. You may not get your report if you don't include your telephone number. You may hesitate to include it, knowing that bill collectors can get it by getting a copy of your credit file. But unless it's unlisted, they can also call Directory Assistance and get it. If you're trying to rebuild your credit, you will want to make sure your phone number is in your file. This is one sign of stability your future creditors look for.

Current address. You won't get a copy of your credit report if you don't include your address.

Previous addresses and dates there. Credit bureaus ask for this if you've been at your current address fewer than two years. Again, it helps distinguish you from other people with similar names. If you don't want the bureau to have this information, you can leave it off, but your request may be rejected.

Credit Bureaus' Addresses and Phone Numbers

TRW Complimentary Report Request
P.O. Box 2350
Chatsworth, CA 91313-2350
(annual free copy)

or

TRW
National Consumer Assistance Center
P.O. Box 949
Allen, TX 75002-0949
(800) 682-7654
(subsequent copies or copy after credit denial)

Trans Union
P.O. Box 390
Springfield, PA 19064
(601) 933-1200

Equifax
P.O. Box 105873
Atlanta, GA 30348
(404) 612-3321
(404) 612-3150 (fax)

One Stop Shopping

Confidential Credit
5930 Priestly Drive, Suite 200
Carlsbad, CA 92008-9656
(800) 443-9342

For $28.95 (includes shipping), Confidential Credit will obtain your credit reports from Trans Union, TRW and Equifax, and send you one compiled report. The report indicates which information was reported by which bureau. To challenge incorrect information, you must contact the credit bureau reporting the information, not Confidential Credit.

4. Review Your File for Accuracy

A credit bureau will provide you with the data in your file, the sources of the data and the names of people who requested copies of your file—called inquiries—within the last six months (two years if the information was given to an employer or potential employer).

Review your report carefully. One of the biggest problems with credit files is that they contain incorrect or out-of-date information. Associated Credit Bureaus, the trade association for the credit reporting industry, admits that the "big three" credit bureaus receive 500,000 disputes *each month* from consumers who have inspected their files and have found errors.

Sometimes credit bureaus confuse names, addresses, Social Security numbers or employers. If you have a common name, say John Brown, your file may contain information on other John Browns, John Brownes or Jon Browns. Or your file may erroneously contain information on family members with similar names.

Because consumers are not told when information is placed in their files, they usually discover errors only when they are denied credit and then request a copy of their credit file. The consequences of such errors can be serious. Each year, people are wrongfully denied mortgages, student loans, car loans, insurance policies, employment or a place to live because of credit bureau mistakes. Then the consumer may encounter a bureaucratic nightmare in trying to clear up the file, delaying by months, and sometimes years, the time it takes to eventually get the loan. A cautious consumer could avoid some problems by requesting a copy of his credit file before applying for credit.

As you read through your credit report, make a list of everything that is incorrect, out-of-date or misleading. In particular, look for the following:

- incorrect or incomplete name, address, phone number or Social Security number

- incorrect, missing or outdated employment information

- bankruptcies older than ten years or not identified by the specific chapter of the bankruptcy code

- any other negative information older than seven years

- credit inquiries older than two years

- credit accounts that are not yours

- lawsuits you were not involved in

- incorrect account histories—look especially for late payments when you've paid on time

- a missing notation when you disputed a charge on a credit card bill

- collection agency listed separate from the original creditor, making it appear that you are delinquent on more than one debt

- closed accounts incorrectly listed as open—it may look as if you have too much open credit, and

- any account you closed that doesn't have a "closed by consumer" notation; if it's not there, you'll want it added, otherwise it looks like the creditor closed the account.

5. Dispute Incorrect, Outdated and Misleading Information in Your Credit File

Once you've compiled a list of all information you want changed or removed, complete the "request for reinvestigation" form which was enclosed with your credit report. If the bureau did not enclose such a form, just send a letter. List each incorrect item and explain exactly what is wrong. Be sure to keep a photocopy of your request for reinvestigation.

Requesting a reinvestigation shouldn't cost you anything. In New Mexico, however, a credit bureau can charge up to $5 for a reinvestigation.[4]

Once the credit bureau receives your letter, it must reinvestigate the matter and get back in touch with you within a "reasonable time," usually interpreted as 30 days. (Maine and Maryland require reinvestigation within ten days; Louisiana permits 45.)[5] By the end of 1995, the credit bureaus and 6,000 creditors should be linked by computer, which should speed up the verification process. And if you let them know that you're trying to obtain a mortgage or car loan, they can do a "rush" verification.

You might be concerned that if information is incorrect with one credit bureau it will be wrong with the others. That may be the case, and it's one reason we suggest that you get copies of your files from all three if you find errors in a credit report. But you may not need to request a reinvestigation of the information with all three. Associated Credit Bureaus, the trade association for the credit reporting industry, has initiated a computer-exchange of consumer disputes among TRW, Equifax and Trans Union, and the major creditors. When a credit bureau receives a dispute letter from a consumer, that credit bureau will now electronically forward that letter to the other credit bureaus and the creditor who reported the information. If the credit bureau to whom you sent your letter makes any corrections in your file, it will forward those changes to the other two bureaus.

If you don't hear from the bureau within the deadline, send a follow-up letter. To get someone's attention, send a copy of your second letter to the Federal Trade Commission (addresses are listed in Section B7, below), the agency that oversees credit bureaus. Again, keep a copy for your records.

If you are right, or if the creditor who provided the information can no longer verify it, the credit bureau must remove the information from your file. Often credit bureaus will remove an item on request without an investigation if rechecking the item is more bother than it's worth.

---

[4]New Mexico Statutes Annotated § 56-3-2.

[5]Maine Revised Statutes Annotated § 9-A-8-403; Maryland Commercial Code § 12-918(a)(3)(ii); Louisiana Revised Statutes § 9:3571.1(3).

Example: Jim's credit file with Credit Gatherers reporting agency shows that he has not paid a $275 bill from Acrelong Drug Store. But Jim has never done business with Acrelong. Credit Gatherers contacts Acrelong for verification. Acrelong has no information showing that Jim owes $275 and cannot verify the debt. Credit Gatherers removes the information from Jim's file.

If the credit bureau responds that the creditor reporting the information verified its accuracy, call the credit bureau at its toll free 800 number as follows:

TRW (800) 392-1122

Trans Union (800) 851-2674

Equifax (800) 685-1111.

Credit bureaus set up these 800 numbers to handle consumer disputes about incorrect items in their credit files that are not removed via the normal reinvestigation process.

If you don't get anywhere with the credit bureau, directly contact the creditor and ask that the information be removed. Write to the customer service department, vice president of marketing, and president or CEO. If the information was reported by a collection agency, send the agency a copy of your letter too. Be sure to keep a copy of your letter.

Example: Ellie's credit file claims that she never paid $350 to Jason's Jackets. Ellie is sure that she never purchased anything from Jason's Jackets. She contact Jason's store manager and asked him to show her "her" credit account. Once he realized that the information he reported to the credit bureau was for another person, he contacted the credit bureau and cleared up the mistake.

6. Consider Adding a 100-Word Statement to Your Credit File

If you feel a credit bureau is wrongfully including information in your file, or you want to explain a particular entry, you have the right to put a 100-word statement in your file. Don't always assume that adding a 100-word statement is the best approach. In fact, often it's wiser to simply explain the negative mark to creditors in person than to try to explain it in 100 words or fewer.

If you do add a 100-word statement, the credit bureau must give only a summary—written by the credit bureau—to anyone who requests your file. To avoid this, be clear and concise; use the fewest words possible. If you request it, the bureau must also give the statement or summary to anyone who received a copy of your file within the past six months—or two years if your file was given out for employment purposes.

Unfortunately, many statements or summaries are ineffective. Few creditors who receive credit files read the statements or summaries. In any David (consumer) vs. Goliath (credit bureau) dispute, creditors tend to believe Goliath. Finally, your statement might stay in your file even longer than the disputed information.

Sample 100-Word Statements

As mentioned, be judicious in your use of 100-word statements. But if the information in your file is clearly wrong and can be simply explained, consider adding a statement. Here are a few samples:

"I am not unemployed. Since 19__, I have worked as a free-lance technical writer, and have earned an average of $35,000 per year. My work has appeared in *Data, ComPuter, Plug In, Delicious, BIM PC,* and many other computer magazines."

"Although I was sued by Randy Roofer, I did not pay her because the roof she put on my house is not sealed and she refuses to fix it. Three times I have come home and found drowned squirrels in my toilet. I refuse to pay Randy until she repairs the roof. I filed a complaint with the state contractor's board, which is pending."

"It is technically accurate that I was sued by Jones and Jones Department Store on June 11, 19__. Jones and Jones dismissed the lawsuit, however, when they realized that they had confused my account with another customer's. My account with Jones and Jones has never been delinquent."

"I was hospitalized following a car accident. I sent the medical bills to my insurance company, but the company took over six months to pay the bills. In the meantime, the hospital began collection efforts against me. Those efforts ended when the insurance company paid the bill."

7. Complaints About a Credit Bureau

If a credit bureau employee violates the law, you can complain to the Federal Trade Commission, the federal agency that regulates credit bureaus. For the best result, complain in writing. Include the name of the credit bureau, its address and phone number, the name of the employee you dealt with, the nature of the problem, the dates of your contact with the credit bureau and copies of documents that pertain to the problem. Be sure to send a copy of this letter to the credit bureau.

If a credit bureau insists on reporting out-of-date or wrong information, complaining to the FTC may put a stop to it. Also, if you paid an unreasonable

fee, for example, $50, or a fee above the limits set in a certain state, complaining could help you get a refund.

Federal Trade Commission

National Office

6th & Pennsylvania Avenue, NW
Washington, DC 20580
(202) 326-2222

Regional Offices

1718 Peachtree Street, NW, Suite 1000
Atlanta, GA 30367
(404) 347-4836

10 Merrimac Street, Suite 810
Boston, MA 02114-4719
(617) 424-5960

55 East Monroe Street, Suite 1437
Chicago, IL 60603
(312) 353-4423

668 Euclid Avenue, Suite 520-A
Cleveland, OH 44114
(216) 522-4207

100 N. Central Expressway, Suite 500
Dallas, TX 75201
(214) 767-5501

1405 Curtis Street, Suite 2900
Denver, CO 80202-2393
(303) 844-2271

11000 Wilshire Boulevard, Suite 13209
Los Angeles, CA 90024
(310) 575-7575

150 William Street, Suite 1300
New York, New York 10038
(212) 264-1207

901 Market Street, Suite 570
San Francisco, CA 94103
(415) 744-7920

2806 Federal Building
915 Second Avenue
Seattle, WA 98174
(206) 220-6363

Sample Complaint Letter

```
                           78 Marshall Street
                           Burlington, VT 00011

April 12, 19__

To Whom It May Concern:

Under 15 U.S.C. § 1681s, I wish to lodge the
following complaint about the following
credit reporting agency:

Collect-O Credit Services
503 Grand Avenue, Montpelier, Vermont,
(802) 555-1234

On March 29, 19__, I visited Collect-O
Credit Services to see my credit file. I
paid $10, after complaining that this
exceeds the state's limit of $7.50. After
waiting almost 30 minutes, Maggie Beach
brought me to a small room. She pulled out
my file and started going through it.

I noticed that Ms. Beach refused to show me
certain pages. I asked her why she was
skipping those pages. She just said she
didn't have to show them to me.

Ms. Beach also refused to let ask me ask
questions about some of the entries she did
show me. And when I asked her to double-
check some inaccurate information, she told
me it had just come into their office and
therefore must be correct.

Please investigate this matter and inform me
of the results.

Thank you,


Alex Stewart

cc: Collect-O Credit Services
```

In many states, you should also complain to the state agency that regulates credit bureaus' illegal or unethical conduct. If the credit bureau is associated with a collection agency, see Chapter 5 on complaining about collection agencies. The addresses of state agencies that regulate credit bureaus are in Chapter 13, Section D2.

If you were seriously harmed by the credit bureau—for example, it continued to give out false information after you requested corrections—you may want to sue. The FCRA lets you sue a credit bureau for negligent or willful noncompliance with the law within two years after the bureau's harmful behavior first occurred. You can sue for actual damages, such as court costs, attorney's fees, lost wages and, if applicable, intentional infliction of emotional distress. In the case of truly outrageous behavior, you can recover punitive damages—damages meant to punish for malicious or willful conduct. Under the FCRA, the court decides the amount of the punitive damages. In Florida, you are entitled to at least $500. In California, you may be awarded punitive damages of not less than $100 and not more than $5,000.[6] Consider representing yourself in court or hiring a lawyer. (See Chapter 13.)

8. What's a Credit Rating?

Virtually every credit bureau uses a point system to indicate payment history. In a typical case, each payment entry contains a rating point between 0 and 9. This is what is meant by a "credit rating." Ratings 0-6 pertain to payment time-frames. That is, rating 0 means you pay within 30 days, rating 1 within 60 days, rating 2 within 90 days, etc., up to rating 6. Rating 7 means the creditor repossessed an item, rating 8 means the account has been sent to collection (including if you were sued) and rating 9 means the debt was discharged in bankruptcy.

---

[6]Florida Statutes Annotated § 559.77; California Civil Code § 1785.31.

Rating systems differ among credit bureaus. Some reverse their systems, that is, give a rating of 9 for accounts paid within 30 days and 0 for a debt discharged in bankruptcy. Others use a 9 to indicate any serious creditor action such as repossessions, foreclosures, collections or bankruptcies.

How the negative items in your file affect your ability to get credit depends on each creditor. Most creditors are relatively conservative—that is, they take few risks. If your credit file shows that you routinely take 120 days to pay your bills, most creditors won't lend you money or will insist on a very large down payment or high interest rate to greatly lower their risk. Some creditors will deny you credit if you have any rating in your file other than all 0s or 1s. A small but growing number of extremely risk-adverse creditors to whom you are all paid up may cancel your account if they see a rating of 2 or higher on an account you have with a different creditor. If this happens, there's very little you can do to get your account back.

It's impossible to say whether taking 180 days to pay (rating 5) is better than defaulting and having your account sent to a collection agency (rating 8). Frankly, neither will raise you to "most favored borrower status." If your file contains a rating of 5 and you plan to pay, ask the creditor to remove the negative rating from your file in exchange for your payment. The creditor may be more inclined to do this if your failure to pay was due to an injury, illness or similar setback, not your mismanagement or forgetfulness.

If you negotiate with a creditor and set up a new payment plan, ask the creditor to re-age your account. Re-aging means that the creditor reports your account to a credit bureau as current as long as you make payments under the new payment plan. Many won't immediately re-age accounts, but will after you make three consecutive payments.

If your file shows that you've taken many steps to improve your credit, many creditors won't put too much weight on the negative entries.

More Mortgages Available to People With Poor Credit

For many years, conventional mortgage lenders wrote only "A" loans. An "A" loan was available to a person with flawless credit—someone who had paid every personal loan, student loan, credit card bill and existing mortgage payment on time. (Occasionally, a person with a minor credit blip, such as a one-time late payment on an otherwise perfectly-paid loan, would still qualify for an "A" loan.) "A" loans typically require as little as 5% to 10% down and charge the most favorable interest rate. Anyone who didn't qualify for an "A" loan had only two choices: forego buying a home for several years (until all the negative marks came off the credit report), or borrow from a lender who required a huge down payment (35% or more) and charged near-credit-card interest rates.

More and more mortgage lenders, however, are writing "B" loans and "C" loans for people with poor credit histories. ("D" loans—which require a very large down payment and charge very high interest rates—are still written for people with the worst credit histories.) The following describes "B," "C" and "D" loans:

- **"B" loans.** Some lenders require clean credit for the previous 12 months but allow a few missed payments before that. Others permit one or two late mortgage payments, one late personal or student loan payment and few late credit card payments during the previous year. (Late payments cannot be more than 60 days late.) "B" loans usually require 20% to 25% down; interest rates are usually one or two percentage points higher than "A" loans.

- **"C" loans.** Some lenders require clean credit for the previous 12 months but allow a serious credit problem, such as a bankruptcy or foreclosure, several years before. Others permit three or four late mortgage payments, five or six late loan or credit card payments or late payments more than 60 days past due during the previous year. "C" loans usually require 20% to 35% down; interest rates are usually one or three percentage points higher than "A" loans.

- **"D" loans.** "D" loans are available to people with the worst credit histories—bankruptcy or foreclosure in the past year, or habitual late payments on loans and bills. "D" loans usually require 35% to 60% down; interest rates are usually at least 100% higher than what they are for "A" loans.

C. Add Positive Account Histories to Your Credit File

OFTEN, CREDIT REPORTS DON'T include accounts that you might expect to find. Some creditors don't report account statuses to credit bureaus. Others report only infrequently. If your credit file is missing credit histories for accounts you pay on time, send the credit bureaus a copy of a recent account statement and copies of canceled checks (never originals) showing your payment history. Ask the credit bureaus to add the information to your file. While the bureaus aren't required to do so, they often will.

D. Add Information Showing Stability to Your Credit File

CREDITORS LIKE TO SEE evidence of stability in your file. If any of the items listed below are missing from your file, you may want to send a letter to the credit bureaus asking that the information be added.

- Your current employment—employer's name, employer's address and your job title. You may wisely decide not to add this if you think a creditor may sue you or a creditor has a judgment against you. Current employment information may be a green light for a wage garnishment.

- Your previous employment, especially if you've had your current job fewer than two years. Include your former employer's name and address and your job title.

- Your current residence; and if you own it, say so. (Not all mortgage lenders report their accounts to credit bureaus.) Again, don't do this if you've been sued or you think a creditor may sue you. Real estate is an excellent collection source.

- Your previous residence, especially if you've lived at your current address fewer than two years.

- Your telephone number, especially if it's unlisted. If you haven't yet given the credit bureaus your phone number, consider doing so now. A creditor who cannot verify a telephone number is often reluctant to grant credit.

- Your date of birth. A creditor will probably not grant you credit if it does not know your age. Especially add your age if you are over 50. People over 50 tend to be low credit risks because their incomes are usually higher than people under age 50, their children are grown (no college costs) and their mortgages are paid off.

- Your Social Security number. (See discussion in Section B3, above.)

- Bank checking or savings account number. It's an excellent sign of stability. Again, however, you won't want to add this information if you've been sued or you think a creditor may sue you. A creditor with a judgment against you will likely use this information to try to collect.

Again, credit bureaus aren't required to add any of this information, but they often do. They will especially add information on jobs and residences, as that information is used by creditors in evaluating applications for credit. They will also add your telephone number, date of birth and Social Security number because those items help identify you and lessen the chances of "mixed" credit files—that is, getting other people's credit histories in your file.

Enclose any photocopies of documentation that verifies information you're providing, such as your driver's license, a canceled check, a bill addressed to you, a pay stub showing your employer's name and address or anything else similar. Remember to keep photocopies of all letters you send.

E. Get Credit in Your Own Name

IF YOU ARE MARRIED, SEPARATED or divorced, you are entitled to obtain credit in your own name. This is an excellent strategy for rebuilding your credit if:

- all or most of your financial problems can be attributed to your spouse, or

- you and your spouse have gone through financial difficulties together, but most credit was in only your spouse's name.

Even if both of you have had financial problems, separating your credit histories can help you both rebuild your credit.

> **Example:** Lisa and Harold use several credit cards in Lisa's name and two cards in both names to run up thousands of dollars in bills. They miss payments, have their cards canceled and are sued. By separating their credit histories, they eliminate all of Lisa's cards from Harold's credit file. They then concentrate on rebuilding each of their credit histories. Because Harold's credit record is better, he qualifies for credit in a short time. Once things improve, they apply as a couple for credit. The positive information generated is added to both Harold and Lisa's files, thereby improving Lisa's credit too.

Contact all three credit bureaus and ask that a credit file in your name only be created. Then insist that the credit bureaus remove all accounts your spouse alone was responsible for. If you want to obtain credit in your own name, complete credit applications in just your name.

F. Consider Combining Your Credit History with Your Spouse's

IF YOU ARE MARRIED, YOU and your spouse are entitled to have the same credit information in each of your credit reports. If you have no credit history or have a few negative marks, and your spouse has A-1 credit, getting her credit histories into your file may be just what you need.

Write to all three credit bureaus and request that they merge your file with your spouse's file. Once your request is complete, your file will contain your negative marks and your spouse's positive ones. Your spouse should then take the steps described in Section E to get credit again in her name only and have your credit accounts removed from her file.

G. Use Existing or New Credit Cards

IF YOU SURVIVED YOUR FINANCIAL disaster and managed to hold onto one of your credit cards or a department store or gasoline card, use it and pay your bills on time. Your credit history will improve quickly. Most credit reports show payment histories for 24–36 months. If you charge something every month, no matter how small, and pay at least the minimum required every month, your credit report will show steady and proper use of revolving credit.

 Don't Overuse Your Credit Cards

Charge only a small amount each month and pay it in full. By paying in full, you will avoid incurring interest. Consumer groups such as Bankcard Holders of America point out that the average consumer who pays the minimum each month ends up paying hundreds of dollars in interest charges alone. Their example: If you charge $1,000 on a 19.8% credit card and pay it off by making the minimum payments each month, you'll take over eight years to pay off the loan and will pay almost $850 in interest. This is crazy. Rebuilding your credit might cost you some money, but you don't have to throw it away in the process.

---

1. Applying for Credit Cards

If you don't currently have a credit card, apply for one. Creditors will evaluate your application based on three factors: your character, capacity and credit. Your character refers to who you are—such as where you work and live. Your capacity means the amount of debt you can realistically pay given your income. Your credit refers to your payment history.

It's often easiest to obtain a card from a department store or gasoline company. They'll usually open your account with a very low credit line. If you start with one credit card, charge items and pay the bill on time, other companies will issue you cards. When you use department store and gasoline cards, try not to carry a balance from one month to the next. The interest rate on these cards is as high as 22%.

Your next step is to apply for a regular credit card from a bank, such as a Visa, MasterCard or Discover card. Interest rates and annual fees on these cards have dropped some over the past few years and you may be able to find a card with relatively low rates. Depending on how bad your credit history is, you may be eligible only for a low credit line or a card with a high interest rate and high annual fee. If you use the card and make your payments, however, after a year or so you can apply for an increase in your line of credit and possibly a reduction in your annual fee.

As outrageous as it sounds, you might even apply for an American Express card. If you have a very high income—even if you have horrible credit—you may very well be approved for an American Express card.

Many people who have had serious financial problems misused or overused their credit cards. The following tips will help you when you apply for credit cards or an increased credit limit:

Be consistent with the name you use. Either use your middle initial always or never. Always use your generation (Jr., Sr., II, III, etc.).

Take advantage of preapproved credit for gasoline, department store and bank credit cards. If your credit is shot, you may not have the luxury of shopping around.

Be honest, but forgiving. On applications, paint a picture of yourself in the best light. Lenders are especially apt to give less weight to past credit problems that were out of your control, such as a job layoff, illness or death in the family, recent divorce or new child support obligation. Don't emphasize how you forgot to write checks because you were too busy or on an extended vacation.

Apply for credit when you are most likely to get it. For example, apply when you are working, when you've lived at the same address for at least a

year and when you haven't had an unusually high number of inquiries on your credit report in the last two years. (A lot of inquiries is a sign that you are either desperate for credit or preparing to commit fraud.) Also, if you're in school, now may be the time to apply for an American Express card. The company has been known to give cards to students who simply take four classes.

Apply for credit from creditors with whom you've done business. For example, if you had a Sears charge card from a store in New Jersey and you moved to Hawaii, apply for a Sears card from a store near your new home.

Don't get swept up by credit card gimmicks. Before applying for a credit card that gives you rebates, credit for future purchases or other "benefits," make sure you will benefit by the offer. (And I admit, some are good deals, especially if you like to travel and can get a card that helps you build up frequent flyer miles.) But in general, a card with no annual fee and/or low interest usually beats the cards with deals.

Look carefully at preapproval solicitations for nonbank cards. A "gold" or "platinum" card with a high credit limit (as much as $10,000) may be nothing more than a card that lets you purchase items through catalogues provided by the company itself. No other merchant accepts these cards and the company won't report your charges and payments to the credit bureaus. You usually have to pay a fee for the card and then another one for the catalogue. And the items in the catalogues are usually high priced and of low quality.

Send your creditors a change of address when you move. The post office provides free change of address postcards.

If you need an increase in your credit limit, ask for it. Many creditors will close accounts or charge late fees on customers who exceed their credit limits. But pay close attention; if you're charging to the limit on your credit card, you may be heading for financial trouble.

2. Cosigners and Guarantors

A cosigner is someone who promises to repay a loan or credit card charges if the primary debtor defaults. Similarly, a guarantor promises the credit grantor that he will pay if the primary debtor does not. Usually, neither the cosigner's nor the guarantor's name appears on the credit account.

Cosigned and guaranteed accounts differ in one way. With a cosigned account, the primary debtor's credit rating does not improve. Only the cosigner's credit is affected. With a guaranteed account, however, both the primary debtor's and the guarantor's credit rating are affected. If a credit grantor insists that you have a cosigner, ask instead if you can use a guarantor. It should make no difference to the credit grantor.

 Cosigners and Guarantors Must Understand Their Obligations Before Signing On

If the primary debtor doesn't pay and erases the debt in bankruptcy, the cosigner or guarantor remains fully liable. The Federal Trade Commission's Credit Practices Rule requires that cosigners be given the following notice:

You are being asked to guarantee this debt. Think carefully before you do so. If the borrower doesn't pay the debt, you will have to. Be sure you can afford to pay if you have to, and that you want to accept this responsibility.

You may have to pay up to the full amount of the debt if the borrower does not pay. You may also have to pay late fees or collection costs, which increase this amount.

The creditor can collect this debt from you without first trying to collect from the borrower. The creditor can use the same collection methods against you that can be used against the borrower, such as suing you, garnishing your wages, etc. If this debt is ever in default, that fact may become a part of your credit record.

Must Your Cosigner Live Nearby?

Many people who apply for credit and provide a cosigner are told that their cosigners don't qualify because "it's against the law to accept an out-of-state cosigner." Hogwash. This may be the lender's policy, but it isn't the law.

The lender is concerned that if the primary borrower defaults, the lender will have to run all over the country to collect from the cosigner. Your best bet is to have the cosigner talk directly to the lender, stating something like the following:

I am fascinated that there's a law requiring that a cosigner be from the same state as the primary borrower. Can you tell me a little more about this law—like the citation? I'd like to get a copy of the law and read it. [At this point, the loan officer will admit it is a policy, not the law.]

I can understand your concern that if the primary borrower (my aunt, my brother, my friend, etc.) defaults, you will have to run all over the country to collect from me. How about if I agree in the contract to inform you of any changes in my address. Furthermore, I'll submit to the jurisdiction of your state—that is, if you have to sue me to collect this debt, I'll agree that you can sue me in your state, not just mine. [By now, the loan officer will see that the cosigner is serious about paying the debt if the primary borrower defaults and should accept the cosigner.]

3. Secured Credit Cards

Many people with poor credit histories are denied regular credit cards. If your application is rejected, consider whether you truly need a credit card. Millions of people get along just fine without them. If you decide that you really need a card—for example, you travel quite a bit and need a card to reserve hotel rooms and rent cars—then you can apply for a secured credit card. With a secured credit card, you deposit a sum of money with a bank and are given a credit card with a credit limit for a percentage of the amount you deposit—as low as 50% and as high as 100%. Depending on the bank, you'll be required to deposit as little as a few hundred dollars or as much as a few thousand.

Unfortunately, secured credit cards can be expensive. Many banks charge application and processing fees in addition to an annual fee. Also the interest rate on secured credit cards is often close to 22%, while you earn only 2% or 3% on the money you deposit. And some banks have eliminated the grace period—that is, interest on your balance begins to accrue on the date you charge, not 25 days later. If you find a card with a grace period and pay your bill in full each month, you can avoid the interest charges.

Many secured credit cards have a conversion option. This lets you convert the card into a regular credit card after several months or a year, if you use the secured card responsibly. Because regular credit cards typically have lower interest rates and annual fees than secured credit cards, it's usually preferable to obtain a card with a conversion option.

To find a bank offering a secured credit card:

- call some local banks

- send $4 to Bankcard Holders of America, 524 Branch Drive, Salem, VA 24153 and request "Building Credit: Banks Across the Nation Offering Secured Credit Cards," or

- contact a local Consumer Credit Counseling Service office. (See Chapter 13, Section C.)

Avoid 900 number advertisements for "instant credit" or other come-ons. Obtaining a secured credit card through one of these programs will probably cost you a lot—in application fees, processing fees and phone charges. Sometimes you call one 900 number and are told you must call a second or third number. These ads also frequently mislead consumers into thinking their line of credit will be higher than will be available. If you have to deposit $5,000 to get a card, your credit line may only be $2,500 to $4,000 (50% to 80%).

How Many Credit Cards Should You Carry?

Once you succeed in getting a credit card, you might be hungry to apply for many more cards. Not so fast. Having too much credit may have contributed your debt problems in the first place. Ideally, you should carry one bank credit card, one department store card and one gasoline card. Your inclination may be to charge everything on your bankcard and not bother using a department store or gasoline card. When creditors look in your credit file, however, they want to see that you can handle more than one credit account at a time. You don't need to build up interest charges on these cards, but use them and pay the bill in full.

Creditors frown on applicants who have a lot of open credit. So keeping many cards may mean that you'll be turned down for other credit—perhaps credit you really need. And if your credit applications are turned down, your file will contain inquiries from the companies that rejected you. Your credit file will look like you were desperately trying to get credit, something creditors never like to see.

H. Open Deposit Accounts

CREDITORS LOOK FOR BANK accounts as a sign of stability. Quite frankly, they also look for bank accounts as a source of how you will pay your bills. The overwhelming majority of financial transactions in our society are done by check. If you fill out a credit application and cannot provide a checking account number, you probably won't be given credit.

A savings or money market account, too, will improve your standing with creditors. Even if you never deposit additional money into the account, creditors assume that people who have savings or money market accounts use them. Having an account reassures creditors of two things: You are making an effort to build up savings, and if you don't pay your bill and the creditor must sue you to collect, it has a source from which to collect its judgment.

Just because you've had poor credit history, you shouldn't be denied an account. Shop around and compare fees, such as check writing fees, ATM fees, monthly service charges, the minimum balance to waive the monthly charge, interest rates on savings and the like.

I. Work with Local Merchants

ANOTHER WAY TO REBUILD YOUR credit is to approach a local merchant (such as a jewelry or furniture store) and arrange to purchase an item on credit. Many local stores will work with you in setting up a payment schedule, but be prepared to put down a deposit of up to 30% or to pay a high rate of interest. If you still don't qualify, the merchant might agree to give you credit if you get someone to cosign or guarantee the loan. Or you may be able to get credit by first buying an item on layaway.

Even if a local merchant won't extend you credit, she may very well let you make a purchase on a layaway plan. When you purchase an item on layaway, the seller keeps the merchandise until you fully pay for it. Only then are you entitled to pick it up. One advantage of layaway is that you don't pay interest. One disadvantage is that it may be months before you actually get the item. This might be fine if you're buying a dress for your cousin's wedding that is eight months away. This isn't so fine if your mattress is so shot that you wake up with a backache every morning.

Layaway purchases are not reported to credit bureaus. If you purchase an item on layaway and make all the payments on time, however, the store may be willing to issue you a store credit card or store credit privileges.

J. Obtain a Bank Loan

ONE WAY TO REBUILD YOUR CREDIT is to take some money you've saved and open a savings account. You ask the bank to give you a loan against the money in your account. In exchange, you have no access to your money—you give your passbook to the bank and the bank won't give you an ATM card for the account—so there's no risk to the bank if you fail to make the payments. If the bank doesn't offer these loans, apply for a personal loan and offer either a cosigner or to secure it against some collateral you own.

No matter what type of loan you get, be sure you know the following:

- *Whether the bank reports your loan payments to credit bureaus*—This is key; the whole reason you take out the loan is to rebuild your credit. If a bank doesn't report your payments to a credit bureau, there's no reason to take out a loan.

- *The minimum deposit amount for passbook loans*—Some banks won't give you a loan unless you have $3,000 in an account; others will lend you money on $50. Find a bank that fits your budget.

- *The interest rate*—The interest rate on the loan is usually much higher than what people with good credit pay. You will probably pay between 8% and 12% interest on the loan. Yes, this means you'll lose a little money on the transaction, but it can be worth it if you're determined to rebuild your credit.

- *The maximum amount you can borrow*—On passbook loans, banks won't lend you 100% of what's in your account; most will lend you between 80% and 90%. On other loans, you will face a maximum on how much you can borrow.

- *The repayment schedule*—Banks usually give you one to three years to repay the loan. Some banks have no minimum monthly repayment amount on passbook loans; you could pay nothing for nearly the entire loan period and then pay the entire balance in the last month. Although you can pay the loan back in only one or two payments, don't. Pay it off over at least 12 months so that monthly installment payments appear on your credit file.

K. Avoid Being the Victim of Credit Discrimination

DISCRIMINATION IN OBTAINING credit is barred by the Equal Credit Opportunity Act (ECOA).[7] The ECOA prohibits a creditor from refusing to grant credit because of your:

- sex (see Section K1)

- marital status (see Section K2)

- race or color (see Section K3)

- religion

- national origin, although a nonpermanent resident may be denied credit (discrimination against aliens in and of itself is not forbidden by the ECOA), or

- age, which is meant to protect the elderly; in fact, age can be used in credit scoring (see Chapter 6, Section C2) as long as old age is not assigned a negative value.

The ECOA prohibits a creditor from refusing to grant you credit because you receive public assistance. A creditor can ask about age or public assistance, but only to determine your credit history and the likelihood of your continued income.

If a creditor denies you credit, changes the terms of your credit arrangement or revokes your credit, you are entitled to a written explanation. Some creditors provide this statement automatically, but most don't. If you are denied credit but are not told why, you nevertheless must be told that you can request a written explanation. If you want the written explanation, you must request it in writing (a simple letter will do) within 60 days of being denied credit. The creditor then has 30 days to respond to your request.

1. Sex Discrimination

While a creditor may ask you on an application form to designate a title (Ms., Miss, Mrs. or Mr.), the

application form must make it clear that selecting a title is optional. A creditor may also ask your sex when you apply for a real estate loan; this information is collected by the federal government for statistical purposes. But a creditor cannot deny credit to a woman or offer less favorable terms if a man with the same income and property would be given credit.

Specific examples of prohibited sex discrimination include:

- rating female-specific jobs (such as waitress) lower than male-specific jobs (such as waiter) for the purpose of obtaining credit

- denying credit because an applicant's income comes from sources historically associated with women—for example, part-time jobs, alimony or child support

- requiring married women who apply for credit alone to provide information about their husbands while not requiring married men to provide information about their wives, and

- denying credit to a pregnant woman who anticipates taking a maternity leave.

2. Marital Status Discrimination

A married person must be allowed to apply for credit in only her name—a creditor cannot require an applicant's spouse to cosign an application. A creditor may, however, ask questions that would disclose marital status, such as:

- whether you pay alimony or child support

- your income sources—alimony or child support may be an answer, and

- whether any other person—such as a spouse—is jointly liable for any debts you list on a credit application.

If you live in a community property state (Arizona, California, Idaho, Louisiana, Nevada, New Mexico, Texas, Washington or Wisconsin) or you rely on property located in a community property state to establish your credit worthiness, the creditor

---

[7]15 U.S.C. § 1691.

may ask for your marital status. The creditor cannot, however, deny you credit based on marital status.

The prohibition against marital status discrimination also means that a creditor must consider the combined incomes of an unmarried couple applying for a joint obligation.[8]

If you feel that a creditor has discriminated against you, complain to the Federal Trade Commission. (See Section B7, above.) You also have the right to sue for actual damages, punitive damages up to $10,000, court costs and attorney fees.

3. Race Discrimination

In general, lenders are prohibited from asking a person's race on a credit application or to ascertain it from any other means (such as a credit file) other than the personal observation of a loan officer. There is one important exception to this law: A mortgage lender *must* request a person's race for the sole purpose of monitoring home mortgage applications.

That race discrimination is prohibited in credit of course doesn't mean that race discrimination has disappeared. In fact, lenders are accused of getting around race discrimination prohibitions by "redlining"—that is, denying credit to residents of certain—predominantly black—neighborhoods.

Congress attempted to stop redlining by enacting the Home Mortgage Disclosure Act.[9] Under that law, mortgage lenders must maintain and disclose their lending practices for certain areas. Critics complain, however, that the data lenders must disclose is inadequate to analyze discrimination. In addition, under the HMDA, Congress stopped short of requiring lenders to extend credit to everyone who applied because Congress did not want to encourage unsound lending practices.

A second law, the Community Reinvestment Act, was enacted also to address redlining.[10] The CRA requires that bank mortgage lenders demonstrate that they serve the needs of the communities in which they are chartered to serve. If the bank fails to do so, bank regulators can deny the bank the right to establish branches or other activity requiring regulatory approval.

Redlining is also barred by the Fair Housing Act of the Federal Civil Rights Act.[11] In addition, several states have laws prohibiting redlining.

If you feel that a creditor has discriminated against you because of your race or is redlining your credit application, complain to the Federal Trade Commission. (See Section B7, above.) Under the ECOA, you have the right to sue for actual damages, punitive damages up to $10,000, court costs and attorney fees. There are additional remedies under the HMDA and FHA.

4. Post-Bankruptcy Discrimination

If you're considering filing for bankruptcy or you've been through bankruptcy, you may be worried that you'll suffer discrimination. There are a number of laws that prohibit discrimination by the government. (See "Bankruptcy and Government Discrimination" below.) In addition, private employers may not fire you or otherwise discriminate against you solely because you filed for bankruptcy.[12] It is unclear, however, whether or not the act prohibits employers from not hiring you because you went through bankruptcy.

Other forms of discrimination in the private sector aren't illegal. If you seek to rent an apartment and the landlord does a credit check and refuses to rent to you because you filed for bankruptcy, there's not much you can do other than try to show that you'll pay your rent and be a responsible tenant. If a

---

[8]*Markham v. Colonial Mortgage Service Co.*, 605 F.2d 566 (D.C. Cir. 1979).

[9]12 U.S.C. § 2801 et seq.

---

[10]12 U.S.C. § 2901 et seq.

[11]42 U.S.C. § 3601 et seq.

[12]11 U.S.C. § 525(b).

bank refuses to give you a loan because it perceives you as a poor credit risk, you may have little recourse.

If you suffer illegal discrimination because of your bankruptcy, you can sue in state court or in the bankruptcy court. You'll probably need the assistance of an attorney.

Bankruptcy and Government Discrimination

All federal, state and local governmental entities are prohibited from denying, revoking, suspending or refusing to renew a license, permit, charter, franchise or other similar grant solely because you filed for bankruptcy. [13] Under this law, the government cannot:

- deny you a job or fire you

- deny or terminate your public benefits

- deny or evict you from public housing

- deny or refuse to renew your state liquor license

- exclude you from participating in a state home mortgage finance program

- exclude you from participating in a student loan program

- withhold your college transcript

- deny you a driver's license, or

- deny you a contract, such as a contract for a construction project.

In general, once any government-related debt has been canceled in bankruptcy, all acts against you that arise out of that debt also must end. For example, if a state university has withheld your transcript because you haven't paid back your student loan, once the loan is discharged, you must be given your transcript. If, however, the loan isn't discharged in bankruptcy, you can still be denied your transcript until you pay up.

Keep in mind that only government denials based on your bankruptcy are prohibited. You may be denied a loan, job or apartment for reasons unrelated to the bankruptcy (for example, you earn too much to qualify for public housing), or for reasons related to your future credit worthiness (for instance, the government concludes you won't be able to repay a student loan).

---

[13]11 U.S.C. § 525(a).

L. Should You Use a Credit Repair Clinic?

YOU'VE PROBABLY SEEN ADS for companies that claim they can fix your credit, qualify you for a loan or get you a credit card. Their pitches are tempting, especially if your credit is bad and you desperately want to buy a new car or house.

You will want to avoid these outfits, however. Many of their practices are illegal. Some have been caught stealing the credit files or Social Security numbers of people who are under 18, have died or live in out-of-the-way places like Guam or the U.S. Virgin Islands, and substituting these for the files of people with poor credit histories. Others have been identified as breaking into credit bureau computers and changing or erasing a bad credit file.

But even assuming that the credit repair company is legitimate, don't listen to its come-ons. These companies can't do anything for you that you can't do yourself. What they will do, however, is charge you between $250 and $5,000 for their unnecessary services.

An excellent (and inexpensive) aid in legitimately cleaning up your credit file is *Nolo's Law Form Kit: Rebuild Your Credit*, by Robin Leonard (Nolo Press).

Here's what credit repair clinics claim to be able to do for you:

Remove incorrect information from your credit file. You can do that yourself under the Fair Credit Reporting Act. See Section B5, above.

Remove correct, but negative, information from your credit file. Negative items in your credit file can legally stay there for seven or ten years, as long as they are correct. No one can wave a wand and make them go away. One tactic of credit repair services is to try and take advantage of the law requiring credit bureaus to verify information if the customer disputes it. Credit repair clinics do this by challenging every item in a credit file—negative, positive or neutral—with the hope of overwhelming the credit bureau into removing information without verifying it. Credit bureaus are aware of this tactic and often dismiss these challenges on the ground that they are frivolous, a right credit bureaus have under the Fair Credit Reporting Act. You are better off getting your file and selectively challenging the outdated, incorrect and ambiguous items.

Even if the credit bureau removes information that a credit bureau had the right to include in your file, it's no doubt only a temporary removal. Most correct information reappears after a few months when the creditor that first reported the information to the credit bureaus re-reports it in its next month's report.

Get outstanding debt balances and court judgments removed from your credit file. Credit repair clinics often advise debtors to pay outstanding debts if the creditor agrees to remove the negative information from your credit file. This is certainly a negotiation tactic you want to consider, but you don't need to pay a credit repair clinic for this advice.

Get you a major credit card. Credit repair clinics can give you a list of banks that offer secured credit cards. While this information is helpful in rebuilding credit, it's not worth hundreds or thousands of dollars—you can find it out for little or nothing. (See Section G3, above.)

Many states regulate for-profit credit repair clinics, or even prohibit them from carrying on business. Some dubious credit repair clinics have tried to get around these regulations by setting themselves up as nonprofits, but still take your money and provide poor results. Before using any organization that claims to be a nonprofit, carefully check the company's fees, claims of what it can do and its reputation. Call the Better Business Bureau or ask for the names of satisfied customers.

State	Code Section	State Laws Regulating Credit Repair Clinics
Arizona	44-1705	Credit repair clinics must inform debtors of their rights under the Fair Credit Reporting Act, be bonded and accurately represent what they can and cannot do.
Arkansas	4-91-106 et seq.	Credit repair clinics must inform debtors of their rights under the Fair Credit Reporting Act, be bonded, accurately represent what they can and cannot do and let debtors cancel the contract until midnight of 5th day after signing.
California	1789.15 et seq.	Credit repair clinics must inform debtors of their rights under the Fair Credit Reporting Act, be bonded, accurately represent what they can and cannot do, perform their obligations under the contract within 60 days and let debtors cancel the contract until midnight of 5th day after signing.
Colorado	12-14.5-101	Credit repair clinics must inform debtors of their rights under the Fair Credit Reporting Act, be bonded, accurately represent what they can and cannot do and let debtors cancel the contract until midnight of 5th day after signing.
Connecticut	36-435l	Credit repair clinics must inform debtors of their rights under the Fair Credit Reporting Act, be bonded and accurately represent what they can and cannot do.
Delaware	6-2401 et seq.	Credit repair clinics must inform debtors of their rights under the Fair Credit Reporting Act, be bonded, accurately represent what they can and cannot do and let debtors cancel the contract until midnight of 3rd day after signing.
District of Columbia	28-4601 et seq.	Credit repair clinics must inform debtors of their rights under the Fair Credit Reporting Act, be bonded and accurately represent what they can and cannot do.
Florida	817.704 et seq.	Credit repair clinics must inform debtors of their rights under the Fair Credit Reporting Act, be bonded, accurately represent what they can and cannot do and let debtors cancel the contract until midnight of 5th day after signing.
Georgia	16-9-59	Credit repair clinics are prohibited.
Hawaii	481B-12	Credit repair clinics are prohibited.
Illinois	815 ILCS 605/6	Credit repair clinics must inform debtors of their rights under the Fair Credit Reporting Act, be bonded and accurately represent what they can and cannot do.
Indiana	24-5-15-7	Credit repair clinics must inform debtors of their rights under the Fair Credit Reporting Act, be bonded, accurately represent what they can and cannot do and let debtors cancel the contract until midnight of 3rd day after signing.
Iowa	538A.1	Credit repair clinics must inform debtors of their rights under the Fair Credit Reporting Act, be bonded, accurately represent what they can and cannot do and let debtors cancel the contract until midnight of 3rd day after signing.
Kansas	50-1103	Credit repair clinics must be bonded and accurately represent what they can and cannot do.
Louisiana	9:3573.7	Credit repair clinics must inform debtors of their rights under the Fair Credit Reporting Act, be bonded, accurately represent what they can and cannot do and let debtors cancel the contract until midnight of 5th day after signing.

State	Code Section	State Laws Regulating Credit Repair Clinics
Maine	9-A-10-101 et seq.	Credit repair clinics must inform debtors of their rights under the Fair Credit Reporting Act, be bonded and accurately represent what they can and cannot do.
Maryland	14-1905 et seq.	Credit repair clinics must inform debtors of their rights under the Fair Credit Reporting Act, be bonded, accurately represent what they can and cannot do and let debtors cancel the contract until midnight of 3rd day after signing.
Massachusetts	93-68C et seq.	Credit repair clinics must inform debtors of their rights under the Fair Credit Reporting Act, be bonded, accurately represent what they can and cannot do and let debtors cancel the contract until midnight of 3rd day after signing.
Michigan	23.1195 (91) et seq.	Credit repair clinics must inform debtors of their rights under the Fair Credit Reporting Act, be bonded, accurately represent what they can and cannot do and let debtors cancel the contract until midnight of 5th day after signing.
Minnesota	332.52 et seq.	Credit repair clinics must inform debtors of their rights under the Fair Credit Reporting Act, be bonded, accurately represent what they can and cannot do and let debtors cancel the contract until midnight of 5th day after signing.
Missouri	407.638	Credit repair clinics must inform debtors of their rights under the Fair Credit Reporting Act, be bonded and accurately represent what they can and cannot do.
Nebraska	45-807 et seq.	Credit repair clinics must inform debtors of their rights under the Fair Credit Reporting Act, be bonded, accurately represent what they can and cannot do and let debtors cancel the contract until midnight of 3rd day after signing.
Nevada	598.282	Credit repair clinics must inform debtors of their rights under the Fair Credit Reporting Act, be bonded, accurately represent what they can and cannot do, let debtors cancel the contract until midnight of 5th day after signing and cannot collect any money until all promised services are performed.
New Hampshire	359-D:1	Credit repair clinics must inform debtors of their rights under the Fair Credit Reporting Act, be bonded, accurately represent what they can and cannot do and let debtors cancel the contract until midnight of 5th day after signing.
New York	GBL 458-d	Credit repair clinics must inform debtors of their rights under the Fair Credit Reporting Act, be bonded, accurately represent what they can and cannot do, let debtors cancel the contract until midnight of 3rd day after signing and cannot collect any money until all promised services are performed.
North Carolina	66-220 et seq.	Credit repair clinics must inform debtors of their rights under the Fair Credit Reporting Act, be bonded, accurately represent what they can and cannot do and let debtors cancel the contract until midnight of 3rd day after signing.
Ohio	4712.05	Credit repair clinics must inform debtors of their rights under the Fair Credit Reporting Act, be bonded, accurately represent what they can and cannot do and let debtors cancel the contract until midnight of 3rd day after signing.

State	Code Section	State Laws Regulating Credit Repair Clinics
Oklahoma	24-136	Credit repair clinics must inform debtors of their rights under the Fair Credit Reporting Act, be bonded, accurately represent what they can and cannot do and let debtors cancel the contract until midnight of 5th day after signing.
Tennessee	47-18-1003	Credit repair clinics must inform debtors of their rights under the Fair Credit Reporting Act, be bonded, accurately represent what they can and cannot do and let debtors cancel the contract until midnight of 3rd day after signing.
Texas	Bus. & Comm. 18.07	Credit repair clinics must inform debtors of their rights under the Fair Credit Reporting Act, be bonded, accurately represent what they can and cannot do and let debtors cancel the contract until midnight of 3rd day after signing.
Utah	13-21-6	Credit repair clinics must inform debtors of their rights under the Fair Credit Reporting Act, be bonded, accurately represent what they can and cannot do and let debtors cancel the contract until midnight of 5th day after signing.
Virginia	59.1-335.5	Credit repair clinics must inform debtors of their rights under the Fair Credit Reporting Act, be bonded, accurately represent what they can and cannot do, let debtors cancel the contract until midnight of 3rd day after signing and cannot collect any money until all promised services are performed.
Washington	19.134.020	Credit repair clinics must be licensed and cannot collect any money from debtor until all promised services are performed unless clinic has a surety bond for $10,000.
West Virginia	46A-6C-1 et seq.	Credit repair clinics must inform debtors of their rights under the Fair Credit Reporting Act, be bonded, accurately represent what they can and cannot do and let debtors cancel the contract until midnight of 3rd day after signing.
Wisconsin	422.501 et seq.	Credit repair clinics must inform debtors of their rights under the Fair Credit Reporting Act, be bonded, accurately represent what they can and cannot do and let debtors cancel the contract until midnight of 5th day after signing.

■

HELP BEYOND THE BOOK

It takes nearly as much ability to know how to profit by good advice as to know how to act for one's self.

—François de La Rochefoucauld, French writer and moralist, 1613-1680

THIS BOOK GIVES YOU STRATEGIES for coping with your debts. But the suggestions outlined in this book may not be enough—a bill collector might continue to harass you even after you tell her to stop, you might want help in negotiating with your creditors, you might be sued, you may want to sue a creditor or you may decide to file for bankruptcy.

Here are some places to go if you need more information or advice than this book provides:

Law library. In a law library, you can research in more depth a specific issue raised in this book.

Lawyer. A lawyer can provide you with information, legal advice or legal representation.

Typing service. A typing service can help you use this book and other self-help law materials. A typing service can also act as a "legal secretary" if you need documents prepared for you and filed in court. Typing services, however, cannot give legal advice, but they charge far less than lawyers for their services.

Credit counselor. Credit counselors can help you negotiate with your creditors and set up systems to manage your finances.

Before discussing each of these in more detail, here's a general piece of advice: Make all decisions yourself. By reading this book you've taken the responsibility of getting information necessary to make informed decisions about your legal and financial affairs. If you decide to get help from others, apply this same self-empowerment principle—shop around until you find an advisor who values your competence and intelligence, and recognizes your right to make your own decisions.

A. Law Libraries

OFTEN, YOU CAN HANDLE A LEGAL PROBLEM yourself if you're willing to do some research in a law library. The trick is in knowing what types of information you can find there. Sometimes, what you need to know isn't written down. For instance, if you want to know whether the local small claims court has Saturday or evening hours, you probably won't find out by going to the law library. You'll need to call the small claims court clerk.

At the same time, some questions that can be answered at the law library may be answered more efficiently elsewhere. If, for example, you want to know whether a bill collector is allowed to sue in small claims court, your state statutes would have the answer. But making a telephone call to the small claims court clerk is usually a better approach.

The library can help you, however, find a law and any court interpretations of it. For example, in the library you can read the Fair Debt Collection Practices Act, find out that harassment by collection agencies is illegal, and then read court cases that have decided what types of behavior constitute harassment by a bill collector.

Here's what you should find in an average law library:

- explanations by lawyer-experts of most aspects of debtors' rights law

- the text of the major federal consumer credit and debt laws, such as the Fair Credit Reporting Act and the Fair Debt Collections Practices Act

- published court opinions interpreting both federal and state laws affecting consumers, and

- forms and written guidance for filing a lawsuit in court.

Here, briefly, are the basic steps to researching a legal question. For more detailed, but user-friendly, instructions on legal research, see *Legal Research: How to Find and Understand the Law*, by Elias and Levinkind (Nolo Press).

1. Find the Law Library

To do legal research, you need to find a law library that's open to the public. Public law libraries are often housed in county courthouses, public law schools and state capitals. If you can't find one, ask a public library reference librarian, court clerk or lawyer.

2. If You Want to Find a Relevant Statute

Statutes passed by Congress and state legislatures are referred to throughout this book, in footnotes and charts. To find a federal statute, you need to look in a multi-volume set of books known as the United States Code (U.S. Code), which is organized into 50 numbered titles. Title 15 contains the Consumer Credit Act; Title 11 contains the Bankruptcy Act.

The U.S. Code is published in three ways. One is simply the U.S. Code itself. The other two, U.S. Code Annotated (published by West Publishing Co.) and U.S. Code Service (published by Lawyers Co-op/Bancroft-Whitney), contain the statutes and clarifying materials. The statutes are the same in both publications; the accompanying material, however, varies. Some libraries carry only one of these publications; larger libraries carry both.

To read a federal statute, find the U.S. Code Annotated or U.S. Code Service in your law library, locate the title you need, turn to the section number and read. If you already have a proper reference to the statute—called the citation—finding the statute is straightforward. If you don't have a citation, you can find it by referring to the General Index to the Code you're using.

After you read the statute in the hardcover book, turn to the back of the book. There should be an insert pamphlet (called a pocket part) for the current or previous year. Look for the statute in the pocket part to see if it has been amended or if additional cases interpreting the statute have been decided since the hardcover volume was published.

Finding and reading a state statute is similar to finding and reading a federal one. Like federal codes, state codes are divided into titles—most states divide their titles by number; a few states divide them by subject, such as the civil code, consumer code and finance code. Once you read a state statute, be sure to check the pocket part. If the volume has no pocket part, look on the shelf for a separately-bound supplement before assuming there's no update. If you have trouble locating any statute, use the index accompanying the state code or ask a librarian for help.

3. Go Beyond the Statute

If you want to find the answer to a legal question, rather than simply look up a statute, or you want to find, read and understand cases that interpret the statute or otherwise shed light on your problem, you will need some guidance in basic legal research techniques. Good resources—in addition to Nolo's *Legal Research* book—that may be available in your law library are:

- *Legal Research Made Easy: A Roadmap Through the Law Library Maze*, by Nolo Press and Robert Berring (Legal Star Video)

- *The Legal Research Manual: A Game Plan for Legal Research and Analysis*, by Christopher and Jill Wren (A-R Editions)

- *Introduction to Legal Research: A Layperson's Guide to Finding the Law*, by Al Coco (Want Publishing Co.)

- *How to Find the Law*, by Morris Cohen, Robert Berring and Kent Olson (West Publishing Co.).

4. Use Background Resources

If you want to research a legal question but don't know where to begin, several resources are available on consumers' and debtors' rights issues. The best all-around sources are the publications of the National Consumer Law Center. Their very thorough and annually updated volumes include the following titles:

- *Consumer Bankruptcy Law and Practice*
- *Consumer Class Actions*
- *Equal Credit Opportunity Act*
- *Fair Credit Reporting Act*
- *Fair Debt Collection*
- *Repossessions*
- *Sales of Goods and Services*
- *Truth in Lending*
- *Unfair and Deceptive Acts and Practicess,* and
- *Usury and Consumer Credit Regulation.* (Usury is another word for illegally high interest rates.)

Unfortunately, not all law libraries have these volumes. You may need to call several law and public libraries until you find a library that does carry them.

Another good treatise is Dee Pridgen's *Consumer Credit and the Law.* Many law libraries carry this loose-leaf volume, which is published by Clark Boardman Callaghan. Topics covered include consumer loans, default, repossession, foreclosures, collection agencies, getting sued, credit and ATM cards, credit bureaus, restrictions on garnishments and door-to-door sales. *Consumer Credit and the Law* has very detailed analyses of its topics, and includes several case citations for each subject.

B. Lawyers and Typing Services

AS A GENERAL RULE, you should get an attorney involved in your situation if the dispute is of high enough value to justify the attorney's fees. For example, if a you owe a creditor $1,200, but the goods were defective and you don't feel you should have to pay, and an attorney will cost $800, you're probably better off handling the matter yourself, even though this increases the risk that the creditor will win. If, however, you owe $10,000 and the

attorney will cost $1,000, hiring the attorney may make sense.

1. What Lawyers Can Do for You

There are three basic ways a lawyer can help you:

Consultation and advice. A lawyer can analyze your situation and advise you on your best plan of action. Ideally, the lawyer will describe all your alternatives so you can make your own choices—but keep on your toes. Many lawyers will subtly steer you in the direction the attorney wants you to go, often the one that nets the attorney the largest fee.

Negotiation. The lawyer can help you negotiate with your creditors. Lawyers often possess negotiating skills, especially if they negotiate a lot in their practice. If the creditor has an attorney, that attorney may be more apt to settle with your lawyer than with you. And an attorney's letterhead itself lets a creditor know you are serious about settling.

Representation. If you are sued or want to sue, especially if you have a good defense or a claim of your own against the creditor, you may want to hire a lawyer to represent you. This, however, could get expensive, so be sure you want to be represented by a lawyer before you hire one. You also may consider hiring a lawyer to assist you if you decide to file for bankruptcy. While most bankruptcies are routine and debtors can often represent themselves when armed with a good self-help book, some cases get complex and need the involvement of a bankruptcy lawyer.

2. How to Find a Lawyer

Here are several ways to find a lawyer:

Legal Aid. Legal Aid offices are partially funded by the federal Legal Services Corporation and offer legal assistance in many areas, especially for people with debt problems. To qualify for Legal Aid, you must be low income—that is, your household income cannot exceed 135 times the federal poverty level. To find a Legal Aid office, look in your local phone book.

Legal clinic. Many law schools sponsor legal clinics and provide free legal advice to consumers. Some legal clinics have the same income requirements as Legal Aid offices—others offer free services to low to moderate-income people.

Personal referrals. This is the most common approach. If you know someone who was pleased with the services of a lawyer, call that lawyer first. If that lawyer doesn't handle debtor's rights matters or can't take your case, he may recommend someone else. Be careful, however, when selecting a lawyer from a personal referral. That a lawyer performed satisfactorily in one situation doesn't guarantee she'll do so in your case.

Type of Lawyer to Look for

Most lawyers have expertise—or at least focus their practice—in just a few areas of law. In looking for a lawyer, you'll want to find one who works in particular areas of the law, depending on your problem:

- back taxes—tax lawyer

- child support or alimony—family (or domestic relations) lawyer

- bankruptcy—bankruptcy lawyer

- consumer debts—business or commercial lawyer

- warranty or fraud claim against a creditor—consumer protection lawyer

- eviction—landlord-tenant lawyer

- mortgage problems—real estate or business lawyer.

Group legal plans. Some unions, employers and consumer action organizations offer group plans to their members or employees, who can obtain comprehensive legal assistance free or for low rates. If you're a member of such a plan, check with it first for a lawyer.

Prepaid legal insurance. Prepaid legal insurance plans offer some services for a low monthly fee and charge more for additional or different work. Participating lawyers may use the plan as a way to get clients who are attracted by the low-cost, basic services, and then sell them more expensive services. If the lawyer recommends an expensive course of action, get a second opinion before you agree.

But if a plan offers extensive free advice, or you can use the lawyer to write several letters to your hounding creditors, your initial membership fee may be worth the consultation you receive or the letters the lawyers write. You can always join a plan for a specific service and then not renew.

There's no guarantee that the lawyers available through these plans are of the best caliber. Check out the plan carefully before signing up. Ask about the plan's complaint system, whether you get to choose your lawyer and whether or not the lawyer will represent you in court.

Consumer organizations. Many national or local consumer organizations can recommend an attorney who handles debtor's rights cases. In some large urban areas, consumer advocates publish guides of consumer-oriented legal organizations and/or lawyers. Check the library to see if it has such a guide.

Lawyer referral panels. Most county bar associations will give out the names of attorneys who practice in your area. But bar associations often fail to provide meaningful screening for the attorneys listed, which means those who participate may not be the most experienced or competent.

3. What to Look for in a Lawyer

No matter what approach you take to finding a lawyer, here are three suggestions on how to make sure you have the best possible working relationship.

First, fight the urge you may have to surrender your will and be intimidated by a lawyer. You should be the one who decides what you feel comfortable doing about your legal and financial affairs. Keep in mind that you're hiring the lawyer to perform a service for you; shop around if the price or personality isn't right.

Second, you must be as comfortable as possible with any lawyer you hire. When making an appointment, ask to talk directly to the lawyer. If you can't, this may give you a hint as to how accessible he is.

If you do talk directly to the lawyer, ask some specific questions. Do you get clear, concise answers? If not, try someone else. If the lawyer says little except to suggest that he handle the problem—with a substantial fee—watch out. You're talking with someone who doesn't know the answer and won't admit it, or someone who pulls rank on the basis of professional standing. Don't be a passive client or hire a lawyer who wants you to be one. If the lawyer admits to not knowing an answer, that isn't necessarily bad. In most cases, the lawyer must do some research.

Also, pay attention to how the lawyer responds to your having considerable information. If you've read this book, you're already better informed about debtors rights' laws than most clients are. Many lawyers are threatened when the client knows too much—or, in some cases, anything.

Once you find a lawyer you like, make an hour-long appointment to discuss your situation fully. Your goal at the initial conference is to find out what the lawyer recommends and how much it will cost. Go home and think about the lawyer's suggestions. If they don't make complete sense or if you have other reservations, call someone else.

Finally, keep in mind that the lawyer works for you. Once you hire a lawyer, you have the absolute right to switch to another—or to just fire the lawyer and handle the matter yourself—at any time, for any reason.

4. How Much Lawyers Charge

If all you want is a consultation with an attorney to find out where you stand and what options you have, the lawyer should not charge more than $100 per hour. Some charge as little as $75 an hour, while others charge as much as $175 an hour. But any lawyer willing to work with people with debt problems is taking advantage of a debtor if he charges much more than $100 per hour.

If you want the lawyer to do some negotiating, his fee could pile up. A letter doesn't take that long to write, however, and as long as you are clear about what you want the lawyer to do and not do, you can keep the bill low.

If you're sued by a creditor and hire a lawyer to represent you, the lawyer's fee will probably add up fast. A few lawyers might represent you for a flat fee, for example $500, but most charge by the hour. If you have a claim against a creditor and might win damages—for example, if a bill collector posted your name throughout the town as a "deadbeat"—the lawyer might take your case on a contingency fee basis. That means the lawyer gets paid only if you win your case. If you don't win, the lawyer doesn't get a cent. Obviously, lawyers tend to take only those cases they think they have a good chance of winning on contingency.

If you plan to hire a lawyer to help you file for bankruptcy, expect to pay between $350 to $1,000. Many bankruptcy attorneys let you pay in installments. Also, the attorney must report his fee to the bankruptcy court for approval. The court can make the attorney justify the fee if it's high. This rarely happens, however, because attorneys know what local bankruptcy judges will allow and set their fees accordingly.

One final word: No matter what reason you hire a lawyer for, at whatever fee, be sure the lawyer puts the fee arrangement in writing and you sign it. If the lawyer doesn't mention a written fee agreement, ask about one. If you hire a lawyer to help you with your debt problems, you don't want the financial arrangement to be misunderstood so that the lawyer's fee just becomes another debt you can't or you refuse to pay.

5. Typing Services

Although you can probably handle your debt problems and the re-establishment of your credit yourself, you may want someone to assist you. One place to turn is a typing service. Typing services—and paralegals who do consumer advocacy—cannot give legal advice or represent you on legal matters, but they can do the following:

- identify the credit reporting agencies (credit bureaus) in your area and explain how to work with them

- assist you in negotiating with your creditors

- assist you in getting incorrect, outdated and ambiguous information removed from your credit file

- assist you in writing letters to creditors, collection agencies, government agencies and others

- provide assistance if you file for bankruptcy, such as:

  —helping you through rough spots in completing the forms

  —typing your forms

  —filing the forms with the court, and

  —providing basic information about local procedures and requirements.

a. Compared to Consumer Credit Counseling Service

Typing services differ from Consumer Credit Counseling Service, referred to as CCCS. (See Section C, below.) CCCS is a nonprofit organization funded by the major creditors and thus works with you to pay off all your debts in full. By contrast, typing services (and paralegals who do consumer advocacy) work for you, not your creditors. You decide what steps to take and you must gather the information necessary to implement your decisions.

b. Choosing a Typing Service

In selecting a typing service, you must separate the good (honest and competent) from the bad (dishonest and/or incompetent). Most good typing services will provide you with a written contract that describes the services they plan to provide, states the total price you will be charged and explains their complaint procedure and refund policy.

Here are some things to look for when choosing a typing service.

- *An established or recommended service.* Few typing services stay in business unless they provide honest and competent services. A recommendation from a social service agency, friend, court clerk or lawyer is probably a good place to take your business.

- *Reasonable fees.* The fee should be based on the amount of work a task requires, the specialized nature of the task and reasonable overhead. For example, if the task is straightforward and takes just 30 minutes of typing, the fee should reflect the rate charged by basic typing services with similar overhead—about $10 a page or $20 an hour.

- *Honest marketing.* There are no miracle cures for debt and credit problems. Avoid credit repair clinics (see Chapter 12) that advertise quick fixes. Look for marketing that emphasizes the self-help nature of the business.

- *Reliance on quality self-help publications.* Good typing services provide ready access to reliable self-help materials, either for free or at a reasonable price.

- *Trained staff.* One indication of whether or not people are committed to providing good services is if they have undertaken skills training. Appropriate training is available through independent paralegal associations and continuing education seminars.

C. Consumer Credit Counseling Service

CONSUMER CREDIT COUNSELING SERVICE (CCCS) is a nonprofit organization set up and sponsored by major creditors such as department stores, credit card companies and banks, and overseen by volunteer creditors and consumer advocates. CCCS can produce a decent result for free or a low price.

To use CCCS to help you pay your debts, you must have some disposable income. A CCCS counselor contacts your creditors to let them know that you've sought CCCS assistance and need more time to pay. Based on your income and debts, the counselor, with your creditors, decides on how much you pay. You then make one or two direct payments each month to CCCS, which in turn pays your creditors. A CCCS counselor can often get wage garnishments revoked and interest and late charges dropped. For example, Citicorp waives minimum payment and late charges—and may freeze interest assessments—for customers undergoing credit counseling.

CCCS may, if allowed by state law, charge you a monthly fee up to $50—but averaging $9—for setting up a repayment plan. CCCS also helps people make monthly budgets, and if allowed by state law, charges a one-time fee of about $20. If you can't afford the fee, CCCS will waive it.

CCCS has more than 1,000 offices, located in every state. Look in the phone book to find the one nearest you or contact the main office at 8611 2nd Avenue, Suite 100, Silver Spring, MD 20910, (800) 388-2227.

Participating in a CCCS plan is somewhat similar to filing for Chapter 13 bankruptcy. (See Chapter 10.) Working with CCCS has one advantage: no bankruptcy will appear on your credit record.

But CCCS also has two major disadvantages when compared to Chapter 13 bankruptcy, and many people feel the disadvantages outweigh the advantages. First, if you miss a payment, Chapter 13 protects you from creditors who would start collection actions. A CCCS plan has no such protection and any one creditor can pull the plug on your CCCS plan. Also, a CCCS plan usually requires that your debts be paid in full. In Chapter 13 bankruptcy, you're only required to pay the value of your nonexempt property, which can mean that you pay only a small fraction (as low as 0%) of your unsecured debts.

In some parts of the country, retailers—including Dayton-Hudson—will offer or reinstate credit for people who successfully complete a CCCS repayment program.

Critics of CCCS are quick to point out that individual CCCS offices retain a portion of the money collected for creditors. They claim that CCCS counselors cannot be objective in counseling debtors to file for bankruptcy if they know the office won't receive any funds. Despite this criticism, most CCCS counselors pride themselves on giving objective and complete advice.

D. Free or Cheap Information

WE HAVE TRIED TO BE COMPREHENSIVE in this book. Due to space limitations, however, some topics were only touched on briefly. More consumer credit information is available from government agencies and nonprofit organizations, often for free or low cost. All you have to do is ask, and occasionally send along a few dollars. Where the publications listed below correspond to a certain chapter in this book, we've indicated the chapter.

1. Federal Government Publications

A few federal government agencies publish pamphlets and booklets which give you an overview of your rights.

Federal Trade Commission. The FTC has the most extensive list of credit and consumer publications of any federal agency, all free. To get copies, write FTC, Public Reference, 6th and Pennsylvania Avenue, NW, Washington, DC 20580 (or write a regional office listed in Chapter 12, Section B7). These are some of the publications available:

- *Automatic Debit Scams* (Chapter 6)
- *Building a Better Credit Record* (Chapter 12)
- *Businessperson's Guide to Federal Warranty Law*—although written for a businessperson, this booklet has much information to benefit consumers (Chapter 2)
- *Buying and Borrowing: Cash In On the Facts* (Chapter 6)
- *Car Ads: Low Interest Loans and Other Offers*
- *Choosing and Using Credit Cards* (Chapter 6)
- *Consumer Guide to Vehicle Leasing*
- *Cosigning a Loan* (Chapter 6)
- *Credit and Charge Card Fraud* (Chapter 6)
- *Credit and Older Americans* (Chapter 12)
- *Credit Billing Errors? Use FCBA—Fair Credit Billing Act* (Chapter 6)
- *Credit Practices Rule* (Chapter 6)
- *Credit Repair Scams* (Chapter 12)
- *Dance Studios* (Chapter 2)
- *Door-to-Door Sales* (Chapter 2)
- *Electronic Banking* (Chapter 6)
- *Equal Credit Opportunity* (Chapter 12)
- *Escrow Accounts for Home Mortgages*
- *Fair Credit Billing* (Chapter 6)
- *Fair Credit Reporting* (Chapter 12)
- *Fair Debt Collection* (Chapter 5)
- *Fix Your Own Credit Problems and Save Money* (Chapter 12)
- *Franchise and Business Opportunities*
- *General Motors Consumer Mediation/Arbitration Program* (Chapters 2, 9)

- *Getting a Loan: Your Home as Security* (Chapter 3)
- *Health Spas: Exercise Your Rights* (Chapter 2)
- *Home Equity Credit Lines* (Chapter 3)
- *How to Write a Wrong: Complain Effectively and Get Results* (Chapter 2)
- *Layaway Purchase Plans* (Chapter 2)
- *Lost or Stolen: Credit and ATM Cards* (Chapter 6)
- *Mortgage Money Guide: Creative Financing for Home Buyers*
- *Scoring for Credit* (Chapter 6)
- *Second Mortgage Financing* (Chapter 3)
- *Service Contracts* (Chapter 2)
- *Shopping by Mail* (Chapter 2)
- *Shopping by Phone and Mail* (Chapter 2)
- *Solving Credit Problems* (Chapter 12)
- *Unordered Merchandise* (Chapter 2)
- *Vehicle Repossession* (Chapter 4)
- *Warranties* (Chapter 2)
- *Women and Credit Histories* (Chapter 12).

Federal Deposit Insurance Corporation. The FDIC publishes a few consumer credit booklets, all free. To get copies, write FDIC, 550 17th Street, N.W., Washington, DC 20429 (or write a regional office listed in Chapter 6, Section D). Here's some of what you can request:

- *Consumer Information: For Your Protection*
- *Equal Credit Opportunity and Age* (Chapter 12)
- *Equal Credit Opportunity and Women* (Chapter 12)
- *Fair Credit Billing* (Chapter 6)
- *Fair Credit Reporting Act* (Chapter 12)
- *How the Equal Opportunity Act Affects You* (Chapter 12)
- *Truth In Lending* (Chapter 6)
- *Your Insured Deposit.*

Federal Reserve Board. Several federal reserve banks publish consumer credit periodicals, all free. To get copies, write the Washington, DC, office or the regional federal reserve bank listed after the publication. Addresses are in Chapter 6, Section D. These are some of the Federal Reserve Board publications:

- *Alice in Debitland: Consumer Protections and the Electronic Fund Transfer Act* (Chapter 6—Washington)

- *Annual Percentage Rate Tables* (Chapter 6—Washington)

- *Arithmetic of Interest Rates* (New York or Chicago)

- *Check Rights* (Boston)

- *Consumer Credit Terminology Handbook* (Chapters 6, 12—New York)

- *Consumer Education Catalogue* (Boston)

- *Consumer Handbook of Credit Protection Laws* (Washington)

- *Consumer Handbook on Adjustable Rate Mortgages* (Washington)

- *Credit Guide* (Chicago)

- *Fair Credit Billing* (Chapter 6—Washington)

- *How the Equal Credit Opportunity Act Affects You* (Chapter 12—Philadelphia)

- *How to Establish and Use Credit* (Chapter 12—Philadelphia)

- *How to File a Consumer Credit Complaint* (Chapter 2—Washington)

- *If You Use a Credit Card* (Chapter 6—Washington)

- *If You Borrow to Buy Stock* (Washington)

- *Rule of 78s: What May Happen When You Pay Off a Loan Early—The Fair Debt Collection Practices Act* (Chapter 5—Philadelphia)

- *United States Treasury Securities: Basic Information* (Dallas)

- *What Truth-in-Lending Means to You* (Chapter 6—Washington)

- *When Your Home is On the Line: What You Should Know About Home Equity Lines of Credit* (Chapter 3—Washington)

- *Your Credit Rating* (Chapter 12—Philadelphia).

2 State Government Information

Many state consumer protection offices have publications describing consumer credit and protection laws specific to where you live. To obtain these publications, and to keep abreast of laws as they are enacted, call or write your state consumer protection office, ask for their publications and ask to be placed on its mailing list. Consumer protection offices also often accept complaints against collection agencies, credit bureaus and many other businesses with which you may be having a problem.

State	Phone Number	State Consumer Protection Offices
Alabama	(205) 242-7334 (800) 392-5658	Consumer Assistance, Office of Attorney General, 11 South Union Street, Montgomery, AL 36130 (collection agencies, credit bureaus, general consumer complaints)
Alaska	(907) 465-3600	Office of the Attorney General, P.O. Box K—State Capitol, Juneau, AK 99811-0300 (the Consumer Protection Section was eliminated in budget cuts in 1989; if you write or call this office, you can be sent a four-page letter listing various state, federal and private consumer protection agencies and organizations which may be of assistance)
Arizona	(602) 255-4421 (800) 544-0708	State Banking Department, Consumer Affairs, 2910 North 44th Street, Suite 310, Phoenix, AZ 85018 (collection agencies)
	(602) 542-5763 (800) 352-8431	Consumer Information and Complaints, Office of Attorney General, 1275 West Washington Street, Phoenix, AZ 85007 (credit bureaus, general consumer complaints)
Arkansas	(501) 682-2341 (800) 482-8982	Advocacy Division of Attorney General's Office, 200 Tower Building, 323 Center Street, Little Rock, AR 72201 (collection agencies, credit bureaus, general consumer complaints)
California	(916) 445-1254 (800) 952-5210	Department of Consumer Affairs, Consumer Assistance Office, 400 R Street, Room 1040, Sacramento, CA 95814 (general consumer complaints)
	Chapter 12, Section B7	Federal Trade Commission (collection agencies, credit bureaus)
Colorado	(303) 866-5304 (800) 332-2071	Collection Agency Board, Office of Attorney General, 1525 Sherman Street, 5th Floor, Denver, CO 80203 (collection agencies)
	(303) 866-5189 (800) 332-2071	Consumer Protection Unit, Office of Attorney General, 1525 Sherman Street, 5th Floor, Denver, CO 80203 (credit bureaus, general consumer complaints)
Connecticut	(203) 566-4560	Department of Banking, Consumer Credit Division, 44 Capitol Avenue, Hartford, CT 06106 (collection agencies, credit bureaus)
	(203) 566-1170	Department of Consumer Protection, 165 Capitol Avenue, Hartford, CT 06106 (general consumer complaints)
Delaware	(302) 577-3250	Department of Justice, Consumer Protection Unit, 820 North French Street, 4th Fl., Wilmington, DE 19801 (collection agencies, credit bureaus, general consumer complaints)
District of Columbia	(202) 727-7076	Department of Consumer and Regulatory Affairs, 614 H Street, NW, Room 106, Washington, DC 20001 (collection agencies, credit bureaus, general consumer complaints)
Florida	(904) 488-2226 (800) 435-7352	Division of Consumer Services, Department of Agriculture and Consumer Services, 218 Mayo Building, Tallahassee, FL 32399 (collection agencies, credit bureaus, general consumer complaints)
Georgia	(404) 651-8600	Governor's Office of Consumer Affairs, 2 Martin Luther King Jr. Drive, Suite 356, Atlanta, GA 30334 (collection agencies, credit bureaus, general consumer complaints)

State	Phone Number	State Consumer Protection Offices
Hawaii	(808) 587-3222	Regulated Industries Complaint Office, Department of Commerce and Consumer Affairs, 828 Fort Street, Room 600A, Honolulu, HI 96813 (collection agencies)
	(808) 586-2630	Office of Consumer Protection, Dept. of Commerce and Consumer Affairs, 828 Fort Street, Room 600B, Honolulu, HI 96813 (credit bureaus, general consumer complaints)
Idaho	(208) 334-2945	State Department of Finance, 700 West State Street, Statehouse Mail, Boise, ID 83720-0031 (collection agencies)
	(208) 334-2424 (800) 432-3545	Consumer Protection Division, Office of Attorney General, 700 West Jefferson Street, P.O. Box 83720, Boise, ID 83720-0010 (credit bureaus, general consumer complaints)
Illinois	(217) 782-9011 (800) 252-8666	Consumer Protection Division, Office of Attorney General, 500 South Second Street, Springfield, IL 62706 (collection agencies, credit bureaus, general consumer complaints)
Indiana	(317) 232-0093	Securities Division, Secretary of State, 302 West Washington, Room E-111, Indianapolis, IN 46204-2270 (collection agencies)
	(317) 232-6330 (800) 382-5516	Consumer Protection Division, Office of Attorney General, Indiana Gov't Center South, 5th Floor, 402 West Washington, Indianapolis, IN 46204-2270 (general consumer complaints)
	Chapter 12, Section B7	Federal Trade Commission (credit bureaus)
Iowa	(515) 281-5926	Consumer Protection Division, Office of Attorney General, 1300 East Walnut, 2nd Floor, Des Moines, IA 50319 (collection agencies, credit bureaus, general consumer complaints)
Kansas	(913) 296-3751 (800) 432-2310	Consumer Protection Division, Office of Attorney General, 301 West Tenth, Topeka, KS 66612 (collection agencies, credit bureaus, general consumer complaints)
Kentucky	(502) 573-2200 (800) 432-9257	Consumer Protection Division, Office of Attorney General, P.O. Box 2000, Frankfort, KY 40602-2000 (collection agencies, credit bureaus, general consumer complaints)
Louisiana	(504) 342-9638	Consumer Protection Section, Office of Attorney General, P.O. Box 94095, Baton Rouge, LA 70804-9095 (collection agencies, credit bureaus, general consumer complaints)
Maine	(207) 582-8718 (800) 332-8529	Bureau of Consumer Credit Protection, State House, Station No. 35, Augusta, ME 04333-0035 (collection agencies, credit bureaus, general consumer complaints)
Maryland	(410) 333-6330	Complaint Department, Commissioner of Consumer Credit, 501 St. Paul Place, 13th Floor, Baltimore, MD 21202 (collection agencies)
	(410) 528-8662	Consumer Protection Division, Office of Attorney General, 200 St. Paul Pl., Baltimore, MD 21202-2022 (credit bureaus, general consumer complaints)
Massachusetts	(617) 727-8400	Consumer Protection Division, Dept. of Attorney General, 131 Tremont Street, Boston, MA 02111 (collection agencies, credit bureaus, general consumer complaints)

State	Phone Number	State Consumer Protection Offices
Michigan	(517) 373-9153	Department of Commerce-BOP, Enforcement Division, P.O. Box 30018, Lansing, MI 48909 (collection agencies)
	(517) 373-1140	Consumer Protection Division, Office of Attorney General, P.O. Box 30213, Lansing, MI 48909 (credit bureaus, general consumer complaints)
Minnesota	(612) 296-2488 (800) 657-3602	State Commerce Department, Enforcement Division, 133 East 7th Street, St. Paul, MN 55101 (collection agencies)
	(612) 296-3353 (800) 657-3787	Citizen Assistance Center, Office of Attorney General, 1400 NCL Tower, 445 Minnesota Street, St. Paul, MN 55101 (general consumer complaints)
	Chapter 12, Section B7	Federal Trade Commission (credit bureaus)
Mississippi	(601) 359-4230	Consumer Protection Division, Office of Attorney General, P.O. Box 22947, Jackson, MS 39225 (collection agencies, credit bureaus, general consumer complaints)
Missouri	(314) 751-3463 (800) 722-3321	Division of Finance, P.O. Box 716, Jefferson City, MO 65102 (collection agencies)
	(314) 751-3321 (800) 392-8222	Consumer Protection Division, Office of Attorney General, P.O. Box 899, Jefferson City, MO 65102 (credit bureaus, general consumer complaints)
Montana	(406) 444-4312	Consumer Affairs Unit, Dept. of Commerce, 1424 Ninth Avenue, Helena, MT 59620 (collection agencies, credit bureaus, general consumer complaints)
Nebraska	(402) 471-2008	Secretary of State, Collection Agency Board, 2300 State Capitol Building, Lincoln, NB 68509-4608 (collection agencies)
	(402) 471-2682	Consumer Protection Division, Office of Attorney General, 2115 State Capitol Building, P.O. Box 98920, Lincoln, NB 68509-8920 (general consumer complaints)
	Chapter 12, Section B7	Federal Trade Commission (credit bureaus)
Nevada	(702) 486-4120	Financial Institution Division, State Mail Room Complex, Las Vegas, NV 89158 (collection agencies)
	(702) 486-7355	Consumer Affairs Division, State Mail Room Complex, Las Vegas, NV 89158 (credit bureaus, general consumer complaints)
New Hampshire	(603) 271-3641	Consumer Protection Bureau, Department of Justice, 33 Capitol Street, Concord, NH 03301 (collection agencies, credit bureaus, general consumer complaints)
New Jersey	(201) 504-6200	Division of Consumer Affairs, 124 Halsey Street, Newark, NJ 07102 (credit bureaus, general consumer complaints)
	Chapter 12, Section B7	Federal Trade Commission (collection agencies)

State	Phone Number	State Consumer Protection Offices
New Mexico	(505) 827-7100	Financial Institution Division, Office of Attorney General, P.O. Box 25101, Santa Fe, NM 87504 (collection agencies, credit bureaus)
	(505) 827-6910 (800) 678-1508	Consumer Protection Division, Office of Attorney General, P.O. Drawer 1508, Santa Fe, NM 87504 (general consumer complaints)
New York	(518) 474-8583	Consumer Protection Board, 99 Washington Avenue, Albany, NY 12210 (collection agencies, credit bureaus, general consumer complaints)
North Carolina	(919) 733-7741	Consumer Protection Section, Office of Attorney General, Department of Justice, P.O. Box 629, Raleigh, NC 27602 (collection agencies, credit bureaus, general consumer complaints)
North Dakota	(701) 224-2253	Department of Banking and Financial Institutions, 600 East Boulevard, Bismarck, ND 58505 (collection agencies, credit bureaus)
	(701) 224-3404 (800) 472-2600	Consumer Protection Division, Office of Attorney General, 600 East Boulevard, Bismarck, ND 58505 (general consumer complaints)
Ohio	(614) 466-4986 (800) 282-0515	Consumer Protection Division, Office of Attorney General, State Office Tower, 30 East Broad Street, 25th Floor, Columbus, OH 43215-3428 (collection agencies, credit bureaus, general consumer complaints)
Oklahoma	(405) 521-4274	Consumer Affairs Division, Office of Attorney General, 4545 North Lincoln, Suite 260, Oklahoma City, OK 73105-3498 (collection agencies, credit bureaus, general consumer complaints)
Oregon	(503) 378-4320	Financial Fraud, Department of Justice, 1162 Court Street, NE, Salem, OR 97310 (collection agencies, credit bureaus, general consumer complaints)
Pennsylvania	(717) 787-9707 (800) 441-2555	Bureau of Consumer Protection, Office of Attorney General, Strawberry Square, 14th Floor, Harrisburg, PA 17120 (collection agencies, credit bureaus, general consumer complaints)
Rhode Island	(401) 277-2104	Consumer Protection Division, Department of Attorney General, 72 Pine Street, Providence, RI 02903 (collection agencies, credit bureaus, general consumer complaints)
South Carolina	(803) 734-9452 (800) 922-1594	Department of Consumer Affairs, P.O. Box 5757, Columbia, SC 29250 (collection agencies, credit bureaus, general consumer complaints)
South Dakota	(605) 773-4400	Division of Consumer Affairs, Office of Attorney General, State Capitol Building, 500 East Capitol, Pierre, SD 57501 (collection agencies, credit bureaus, general consumer complaints)
Tennessee	(615) 741-4737 (800) 342-8385	Division of Consumer Affairs, Department of Commerce and Insurance, 500 James Robertson Parkway, 5th Floor, Nashville, TN 37243-0600 (collection agencies, credit bureaus, general consumer complaints)
Texas	(512) 463-2070	Consumer Protection Division, Office of Attorney General, P.O. Box 12548, Austin, TX 78711 (collection agencies, credit bureaus, general consumer complaints)

State	Phone Number	State Consumer Protection Offices
Utah	(801) 530-6601	Division of Consumer Protection, Department of Business Regulation, 160 East 300 South, P.O. Box 45804, Salt Lake City, UT 84145-0804 (general consumer complaints)
	Chapter 12, Section B7	Federal Trade Commission (collection agencies, credit bureaus)
Vermont	(802) 656-3183 (800) 649-2424	Consumer Assistance, Office of Attorney General, 104 Morrill Hall, University of Vermont, Burlington, VT 05405 (collection agencies, credit bureaus, general consumer complaints)
Virginia	(804) 786-2042 (800) 552-9963	Office of Consumer Affairs, Department of Agriculture and Consumer Services, P.O. Box 1163, Richmond, VA 23209 (collection agencies, credit bureaus, general consumer complaints)
Washington	(206) 464-6684 (800) 551-4636	Consumer Resource Center, Office of Attorney General, 900 Fourth Avenue, Room 2000, Seattle, WA 98164 (collection agencies, credit bureaus, general consumer complaints)
West Virginia	(304) 558-8986 (800) 368-8808	Consumer Protection Division, Office of Attorney General, 812 Quarrier Street, LNS Building, 6th Floor, Charleston, WV 25301 (collection agencies, credit bureaus, general consumer complaints)
Wisconsin	(608) 266-1852	Consumer Protection Agency, Department of Justice, 123 West Washington Avenue, Room 150, Madison, WI 53707 (collection agencies, credit bureaus, general consumer complaints)
Wyoming	(307) 777-7841	Consumer Affairs Division, Office of Attorney General, 123 State Capitol Building, Cheyenne, WY 82002 (collection agencies, credit bureaus, general consumer complaints)

3. Publications of Nonprofit Organizations

Several nonprofit organizations publish consumer credit booklets and brochures. Although most of the publications cost a few dollars, they are well worth the price.

American Bar Association. For $3, you can get a copy of the ABA Public Education Division's 48-page booklet, *Your Legal Guide to Consumer Credit.* Write ABA, 750 N. Lake Shore Drive, Chicago, IL 60611.

Bankcard Holders of America. BHA, an organization that helps bankcard holders become informed consumers, publishes several brochures and lists. One is noted in Chapter 12 , Section G3. Others include:

- *College Students and Credit*
- *Consumer Credit Rights*
- *Credit Card Fraud* (Chapter 6)
- *Credit Cards—What You Don't Know Can Cost You* (Chapter 6)
- *Credit Cards and Seniors* (Chapters 6, 12)
- *Credit Repair Clinics: Consumers Beware* (Chapter 12)
- *Establishing Credit for the First Time* (Chapter 12)
- *Getting Out of Debt*
- *How to Re-Establish Good Credit* (Chapter 12)
- *Managing Family Debt*
- *Secured Credit Cards: Selecting the Best One For You* (Chapter 12)
- *Solving Your Credit Card Billing Questions* (Chapter 6)
- *Traveling with Your Credit Card* (Chapter 6)
- *Understanding Credit Bureaus* (Chapter 12)
- *Women's Credit Rights* (Chapter 12)

BHA costs $24 per year to join. Once you're a member, all consumer publications are free. Otherwise, most brochures cost around $1. For membership information or to obtain any publications, write BHA, 524 Branch Drive, Salem, VA 24153, or call (800) 638-6407.

International Credit Association. ICA is a trade organization of credit professionals (people who lend money and manage credit bureaus). For $2, you can obtain a copy of ICA's 48-page booklet, *How to Use Consumer Credit Wisely.* Write ICA, 243 North Lindbergh Blvd., St. Louis, MO 63141. ■

GLOSSARY

This glossary defines certain terms that appear frequently in this book.

Arrears
Arrears is a general term used to describe any loan payment or debt that is past due. It's most often used to describe back-owed child support.

Balloon payment
A balloon payment is a final lump sum payment on an installment contract, such as a mortgage or car loan, which is larger than the earlier payments.

Bankruptcy
Bankruptcy is a legal proceeding in which you are relieved from paying your debts. There are two kinds of bankruptcies for individuals—Chapter 7 and Chapter 13. In Chapter 7 bankruptcy, you may be required to give up some property in exchange for the erasure of your debts. In Chapter 13 bankruptcy, you don't have to give up any property, but you must pay off a portion of your debts over three to five years. At the end of the three-to five-year period, the balance of what you owe is wiped out.

Collateral
Collateral is property pledged as security for repayment of a secured debt.

Cosigner
A cosigner is a person who signs her name to a loan agreement or credit application. If the primary debtor does not pay, the cosigner is fully responsible for the loan or debt. Many people use cosigners to qualify for a loan or credit card. By using a cosigner (and making regular payments), however, the primary debtor does not improve her credit rating.

Credit rating
A credit rating is the point system used by a credit bureau to indicate a person's payment history.

Credit repair
Credit repair refers to the steps a person takes to get outdated and incorrect information removed from a credit file. Credit repair can also include removing negative information from a file. A credit repair company refers to a questionable for-profit business that charges substantial money and claims to clean up credit files.

Default judgment
If you are sued and you do not file papers in response to the lawsuit within in the time allowed, the plaintiff (the person who sued you) can ask the court to enter a default judgment against you. When a default judgment is entered, you have lost the case. You can try to get the default judgment set aside, but it can be difficult to do so.

Deficiency balance	A deficiency balance is the difference between the amount you owe a creditor who has foreclosed on your house or repossessed an item of personal property, and the amount that the sale of the property brings in.
Discharge	When a bankruptcy court erases your debts, it is called a discharge.
Exempt property or exemption	The items of property you are allowed to keep if a creditor gets a judgment against you or you file for bankruptcy are called your exempt property or exemptions.
Foreclosure	Foreclosure is the right of a mortgage lender or other creditor with a lien on your house, such as the IRS or a construction worker you didn't pay, to force the sale of your house in order to recover what you owe.
Guarantor	A guarantor is a person who pledges to repay a loan or debt in the event the primary debtor does not pay. Many people use guarantors to qualify for a loan or credit card. By using a guarantor (and making regular payments), the primary debtor can improve her credit rating.
Installment contract	An installment contract is a written agreement to pay for goods or services purchased, in payments of principal and interest, at regularly scheduled intervals.
Judgment	A judgment is the decision issued by a court at the end of a lawsuit. If you are sued and either don't file papers in response within in the time allowed or file papers but eventually lose the case, the plaintiff (the person who sued you) will get a judgment. To attach your wages or put a lien on your property, virtually all creditors need a court judgment.
Judgment creditor	A creditor who has sued you and obtained a court judgment is called a judgment creditor.
Judgment debtor	Once a creditor sues you and gets a court judgment, you may be referred to as a judgment debtor.
Judgment proof	If you don't own any nonexempt property or earn any income that can be taken by a creditor to pay a debt in the event a creditor sues you and gets a judgment, you are considered to be judgment proof.
Lien	A lien is a notice a creditor attaches to your property that tells the world that the creditor claims you owe him money. If a creditor puts a lien on your property, you won't be able to sell it without paying off the creditor. This is because the lien makes the property's "title" (ownership history) cloudy and a new owner won't buy property if the title is unclear.
Necessities	Necessities are articles needed to sustain life, such as food, clothing, medical care and shelter.

Nonexempt property The items of property you are not allowed to keep if a creditor gets a judgment against you and puts a lien on your property, or you file for bankruptcy, are called your nonexempt property.

Open-ended account An open-ended account is one which has no fixed date by which you must pay off the balance, though you often have to make a minimum payment each month. Credit card, department store and gasoline accounts are all examples of open-ended charges.

Post-judgment interest Post-judgment interest is interest on a court judgment that a creditor may add from the time the judgment is entered in the court clerk's record until you pay it.

Pre-judgment attachment A pre-judgment attachment is a legal procedure which lets an unsecured creditor tie up property before obtaining a court judgment. The attachment freezes the property—you can't sell it, spend it (in the case of money) or give it away. If the creditor wins the lawsuit, the property covered by the attachment can be used to pay him.

Pre-judgment interest Pre-judgment interest is the interest a creditor is entitled to collect under a loan agreement or contract before obtaining a court judgment.

Prepayment penalty A prepayment penalty is a fee imposed by some lenders in the event you pay off a loan early and the lender doesn't earn all the interest the lender anticipated earning. The penalty is usually a percentage of the balance paid off early.

Secured credit card A secured credit card is a credit card you can obtain by depositing some money into a savings account while you have no access to that account. The money you deposit is security for your paying the charges you make on the card. If you don't pay, the bank deducts the money from your account.

Secured creditor A secured creditor is a creditor owed a secured debt—that is, a debt linked to a specific item of property (collateral). If you don't pay the debt, the secured creditor can take the collateral.

Secured debt A secured debt is linked to a specific item of property, such as a house or car, called collateral. The collateral guarantees payment of the debt. If you don't pay, the creditor is entitled to take the property designated as the collateral.

Security agreement A security agreement is the contract you sign when you take out a secured loan. The agreement specifies precisely what property (collateral) can be taken by the creditor if you default.

Security interest A security interest is the right of a secured creditor to take your property in the event you default.

Statute of limitation	A statute of limitation is the legal length of time a creditor has to sue you after you default on a loan or debt.
Unsecured creditor	A creditor who is owed an unsecured debt is called an unsecured creditor. If you don't pay, for most debts an unsecured creditor's only recourse is to sue you, obtain a court judgment, and then attach your wages or put a lien on your property.
Unsecured debt	A debt that is not secured is called an unsecured debt. An unsecured debt is not linked to any specific item of property. That means that if you don't pay the debt, the creditor usually must sue you in court, get a judgment, and then attach your wages or put a lien on your property in order to get paid.
Wage assignment	A wage assignment is a method of voluntarily paying off a debt whereby when you are paid, a sum of money is deducted from your pay check and sent on to the creditor before you ever see that money. Under federal law, a wage assignment is not allowed in consumer loans unless you have the power to revoke the assignment.
Wage attachment	A wage attachment is a method of involuntarily paying off a debt whereby when you are paid, a sum of money is deducted from your pay check and sent on to the creditor before you ever see that money. Wage attachments are a common method used to collect court judgments and back-owed child support.
Wage withholding	A wage withholding is used to collect child support. After a court orders you to pay child support, your employer is notified of the court order. At each pay period, your employer withholds a portion of your pay and sends it on to the custodial parent.

STATE AND FEDERAL EXEMPTION CHARTS

Alabama
All law references are to Alabama Code.

ASSET	EXEMPTION	LAW PROVIDING EXEMPTION
homestead	Real property or mobile home to $5000; property cannot exceed 160 acres (husband & wife may double)	6-10-2
	Must record homestead declaration before attempted sale of home	6-10-20
insurance	Annuity proceeds or avails to $250 per month	27-14-32
	Disability proceeds or avails to an average of $250 per month	27-14-31
	Fraternal benefit society benefits	27-34-27
	Life insurance proceeds or avails if beneficiary is insured's spouse or child	6-10-8
	Life insurance proceeds or avails if beneficiary is wife of insured	27-14-29
	Life insurance proceeds or avails if clause prohibits proceeds from being used to pay beneficiary's creditors	27-15-26
	Mutual aid association benefits	27-30-25
miscellaneous	Property of business partnership	10-8-72(b)(3)
pensions	Judges (only payments being received)	12-18-10(a), (b)
	Law enforcement officers	36-21-77
	State employees	36-27-28
	Teachers	16-25-23
personal property	Books	6-10-6
	Burial place	6-10-5
	Church pew	6-10-5
	Clothing needed	6-10-6
	Family portraits or pictures	6-10-6
public benefits	Aid to blind, aged, disabled, AFDC	38-4-8
	Coal miners' pneumoconiosis benefits	25-5-179
	Crime victims' compensation	15-23-15(e)
	Southeast Asian War POWs' benefits	31-7-2
	Unemployment compensation	25-4-140
	Workers' compensation	25-5-86(b)
tools of trade	Arms, uniforms, equipment that state military personnel are required to keep	31-2-78
wages	Greater of 75% of your weekly net earnings or 30 times the federal minimum wage per week —judgment creditor	6-10-7
	Minimum 75% of earned but unpaid wages—bankruptcy	6-10-7
wild card	$3000 of any personal property, except life insurance (*In re Morris*, 30 B.R. 392 (N.D. Ala. 1983))	6-10-6

Alaska

All law references are to Alaska Statutes.

ASSET	EXEMPTION	LAW PROVIDING EXEMPTION
homestead	$54,000 (joint owners may each claim portion, but total can't exceed $54,000)	9.38.010
insurance	Disability benefits	9.38.015(b), 9.38.030(e)(1), (5)
	Fraternal benefit society benefits	21.84.240
	Insurance proceeds for personal injury, to extent wages exempt (bankruptcy judge may authorize more—9.38.050(a))	9.38.030(e)(3)
	Insurance proceeds for wrongful death, to extent wages exempt	9.38.030(e)(3)
	Life insurance or annuity contract loan value to $10,000	9.38.017, 9.38.025
	Life insurance proceeds if beneficiary is insured's spouse or dependent, to extent wages exempt	9.38.030(e)(4)
	Medical, surgical or hospital benefits	9.38.015(a)(3)
miscellaneous	Alimony, to extent wages exempt	9.38.030(e)(2)
	Child support payments made by collection agency	9.38.015(b)
	Liquor licenses	9.38.015(a)(7)
	Permits for limited entry into Alaska fisheries	9.38.015(a)(8)
	Property of business partnership	9.38.100(b)
pensions	Elected public officers (only benefits building up)	9.38.015(b)
	ERISA-qualified benefits deposited more than 120 days before being sought by judgment creditor or filing bankruptcy	9.38.017
	Judicial employees (only benefits building up)	9.38.015(b)
	Public employees (only benefits building up)	9.38.015(b), 39.35.505
	Teachers (only benefits building up)	9.38.015(b)
	Other pensions, to extent wages exempt (only payments being received)	9.38.030(e)(5)
personal property	Books, musical instruments, clothing, family portraits, household goods & heirlooms to $3000 total	9.38.020(a)
	Building materials	34.35.105
	Burial plot	9.38.015(a)(1)
	Health aids needed	9.38.015(a)(2)
	Jewelry to $1000	9.38.020(b)
	Motor vehicle to $3000; vehicle's market value can't exceed $20,000	9.38.020(e)
	Personal injury recoveries, to extent wages exempt	9.38.030(e)(3)
	Pets to $1000	9.38.020(d)
	Proceeds for lost, damaged or destroyed exempt property	9.38.060
	Wrongful death recoveries, to extent wages exempt	9.38.030(e)(3)
public benefits	Adult assistance to elderly, blind, disabled	47.25.550
	AFDC	47.25.395
	Alaska longevity bonus	9.38.015(a)(5)
	Crime victims' compensation	9.38.015(a)(4)
	Federally exempt public benefits paid or due	9.38.015(a)(6)
	General relief assistance	47.25.210
	45% of permanent fund dividends	43.23.065
	Tuition credits under an advance college tuition payment contract	9.38.015(a)(9)
	Unemployment compensation	9.38.015(b), 23.20.405
	Workers' compensation	23.30.160
tools of trade	Implements, books & tools of trade to $2800	9.38.020(c)
wages	Weekly net earnings to $350; for sole wage earner in a household, $550; if you don't receive weekly, monthly or semi-monthly pay, can claim $1400 in cash or liquid assets paid in any month; for sole wage earner in household, $2200	9.38.030(a), (b), 9.38.050(b)
wild card	None	

Arizona

All law references are to Arizona Revised Statutes unless otherwise noted.
Note: Doubling is permitted for noted exemptions by § 33-1121.01.

ASSET	EXEMPTION	LAW PROVIDING EXEMPTION
homestead	Real property, an apartment or mobile home you occupy to $100,000; sale proceeds exempt 18 months after sale or until new home purchased, whichever occurs first (husband & wife may not double)	33-1101
	Must record homestead declaration before attempted sale of home	33-1102
insurance	Fraternal benefit society benefits	20-881
	Group life insurance policy or proceeds	20-1132
	Health, accident or disability benefits	33-1126(A)(3)
	Life insurance cash value to $1000 per dependent ($5000 total) (husband & wife may double)	33-1126(A)(5)
	Life insurance cash value to $2000 per dependent ($10,000 total)	20-1131(D)
	Life insurance proceeds to $20,000 if beneficiary is spouse or child (husband & wife may double)	33-1126(A)(1)
miscellaneous	Minor child's earnings, unless debt is for child	33-1126(A)(2)
	Property of business partnership	29-225
pensions	Board of regents members	15-1628(I)
also see wages	ERISA-qualified benefits deposited more than 120 days before being sought by judgment creditor or filing bankruptcy	33-1126(B)
	IRAs	*In re Herrscher*, 121 B.R. 29 (D. Ariz. 1990)
	Firefighters	9-968
	Police officers	9-931
	Public safety personnel	38-850(C)
	Rangers	41-955
	State employees	38-762
personal property	2 beds & living room chair per person; 1 dresser, table, lamp, bedding per bed; kitchen table; dining room table & 4 chairs (1 more per person); living room carpet or rug; couch; 3 lamps; 3 coffee or end tables; pictures, paintings, drawings created by debtor; family portraits; refrigerator; stove; TV, radio or stereo; alarm clock; washer; dryer; vacuum cleaner to $4000 total	33-1123
husband & wife may double all personal property exemptions		
	Bank deposit to $150 in one account	33-1126(A)(7)
	Bible; bicycle; sewing machine; typewriter; burial plot; rifle, pistol or shotgun to $500 total	33-1125
	Books to $250; clothing to $500; wedding & engagement rings to $1000; watch to $100; pets, horses, milk cows & poultry to $500; musical instruments to $250; prostheses, including wheelchair	33-1125
	Food & fuel to last 6 months	33-1124
	Motor vehicle to $1500 ($4000, if disabled)	33-1125(8)
	Prepaid rent or security deposit to $1000 or 1-1/2 times your rent, whichever is less, in lieu of homestead	33-1126(C)
	Proceeds for sold or damaged exempt property	33-1126(A)(4), (6)
public benefits	Unemployment compensation	23-783
	Welfare benefits	46-208
	Workers' compensation	23-1068
tools of trade	Arms, uniforms & accouterments you're required to keep	33-1130(3)
	Farm machinery, utensils, seed, instruments of husbandry, feed, grain & animals to $2500 total (husband & wife may double)	33-1130(2)
	Teaching aids of teacher	33-1127
	Tools, equipment, instruments & books (except vehicle driven to work) to $2500	33-1130(1)
wages	Greater of 75% of your weekly net earnings or 30 times the federal minimum wage per week —judgment creditor	33-1131
	Minimum 75% of earned but unpaid wages, pension payments—bankruptcy	33-1131
wild card	None	

Arkansas

In bankruptcy, you may claim these exemptions or the federal bankruptcy exemptions.
All law references are to Arkansas Code Annotated unless otherwise noted.

ASSET	EXEMPTION	LAW PROVIDING EXEMPTION
homestead *choose option 1 or 2, not both*	1. For head of family: real or personal property used as residence, to an unlimited value; property cannot exceed 1/4 acre in city, town, village, or 80 acres elsewhere. If property is between 1/4-1 acre in city, town or village, or 80-160 acres elsewhere, to $2500; no homestead may exceed 1 acre in city, town or village, or 160 acres elsewhere (husband & wife may not double, *In re Stevens*, 829 F.2d 693 (8th Cir. 1987))	Constitution 9-3, 9-4, 9-5; 16-66-210, 16-66-218(b)(3), (4)
	2. Real or personal property used as residence, to $800 if single; $1250 if married	16-66-218(a)(1)
insurance	Annuity contract	23-79-134
	Disability benefits	23-79-133
	Fraternal benefit society benefits	23-74-403
	Group life insurance	23-79-132
	Life, health, accident or disability cash value or proceeds paid or due (limited to the $500 exemption provided by §§ 9-1 and 9-2 of the Arkansas Constitution, *In re Holt*, 97 B.R. 997 (W.D. Ark. 1988).)	16-66-209
	Life insurance proceeds if clause prohibits proceeds from being used to pay beneficiary's creditors	23-79-131
	Life insurance proceeds or avails if beneficiary isn't the insured	23-79-131
	Mutual assessment life or disability benefits to $1000	23-72-114
	Stipulated insurance premiums	23-71-112
miscellaneous	Property of business partnership	4-42-502
pensions	Disabled firefighters	24-11-814
	Disabled police officers	24-11-417
	Firefighters	24-10-616
	IRA deposits to $20,000 if deposited over 1 year before being sought by judgment creditor or filing for bankruptcy	16-66-218(b)(16)
	Police officers	24-10-616
	School employees	24-7-715
	State police officers	24-6-202, 24-6-205, 24-6-223
personal property	Burial plot to 5 acres, in lieu of homestead option 2	16-66-207, 16-66-218(a)(1)
	Clothing	Constitution 9-1, 9-2
	Motor vehicle to $1200	16-66-218(a)(2)
	Wedding bands; any diamond can't exceed 1/2 carat	16-66-218(a)(3)
public benefits	Aid to blind, aged, disabled, AFDC	20-76-430
	Crime victims' compensation unless seeking to discharge debt for treatment of injury incurred during the crime	16-90-716(e)
	Unemployment compensation	11-10-109
	Workers' compensation	11-9-110
tools of trade	Implements, books & tools of trade to $750	16-66-218(a)(4)
wages	Earned but unpaid wages due for 60 days; in no event under $25 per week	16-66-208, 16-66-218(b)(6)
wild card	$500 of any personal property if married or head of family; else $200	Constitution 9-1, 9-2; 16-66-218(b)(1), (2)

All law references are to California Code of Civil Procedure unless otherwise noted.

ASSET	EXEMPTION	LAW PROVIDING EXEMPTION
homestead	Real or personal property you occupy including mobile home, boat, stock cooperative, community apartment, planned development or condo to $50,000 if single & not disabled; $75,000 for families if no other member has a homestead (if only one spouse files, may exempt one-half of amount if home held as community property and all of amount if home held as tenants in common, *In re McFall,* 112 B.R. 336 (9th Cir. B.A.P. 1990)), $100,000 if 65 or older, or physically or mentally disabled; $100,000 if 55 or older, single & earn under $15,000 or married & earn under $20,000 & creditors seek to force the sale of your home; sale proceeds exempt for 6 months after received (husband & wife may not double)	704.710, 704.720, 704.730
	May file homestead declaration	704.920
insurance	Disability or health benefits	704.130
	Fidelity bonds	Labor 404
	Fraternal unemployment benefits	704.120
	Homeowners' insurance proceeds for 6 months after received, to homestead exemption amount	704.720(b)
	Life insurance proceeds if clause prohibits proceeds from being used to pay beneficiary's creditors	Ins. 10132, Ins. 10170, Ins. 10171
	Matured life insurance benefits needed for support	704.100(c)
	Unmatured life insurance policy loan value to $4000 (husband & wife may double)	704.100(b)
miscellaneous	Business or professional licenses, except liquor licenses (708.630)	695.060
	Inmates' trust funds to $1000 (husband and wife may not double)	704.090
	Property of business partnership	Corp. 15025
pensions	County employees	Gov't 31452
	County firefighters	Gov't 32210
	County peace officers	Gov't 31913
	Private retirement benefits, including IRAs & Keoghs	704.115
	Public employees	Gov't 21201
	Public retirement benefits	704.110
personal property	Appliances, furnishings, clothing & food needed	704.020
	Bank deposits from Social Security Administration to $500; $750 for husband and wife	704.080
	Building materials to $1000 to repair or improve home (husband and wife may not double)	704.030
	Burial plot	704.200
	Credit union shares (exempt against judgment creditors only)	Financial 14864
	Health aids	704.050
	Jewelry, heirlooms & art to $2500 total (husband and wife may not double)	704.040
	Motor vehicles to $1200, or $1200 in auto insurance if vehicle lost, damaged or destroyed (husband and wife may not double)	704.010
	Personal injury causes of action	704.140(a)
	Personal injury recoveries needed for support; if receiving installments, at least 75%	704.140(b), (c), (d)
	Wrongful death causes of action	704.150(a)
	Wrongful death recoveries needed for support; if receiving installments, at least 75%	704.150(b), (c)
public benefits	Aid to blind, aged, disabled, AFDC	704.170
	Financial aid to students	704.190
	Relocation benefits	704.180
	Unemployment benefits	704.120
	Union benefits due to labor dispute	704.120(b)(5)
	Workers' compensation	704.160
tools of trade	Tools, implements, materials, instruments, uniforms, books, furnishings, equipment, vessel, motor vehicle to $2500 total; to $5000 total if used by both spouses in same occupation (cannot claim motor vehicle under tools of trade exemption if claimed under motor vehicle exemption)	704.060
wages	Earnings needed for support (exempt against judgment creditors only)	706.051
	Greater of 75% of your weekly net earnings or 30 times the federal minimum wage per week —judgment creditor	704.050
	Public employees vacation credits; if receiving installments, at least 75%	704.113
	75% of wages paid within 30 days of filing for bankruptcy	704.070
wild card	None	

California—System 2

California System 2 exemptions are available only in bankruptcy. Then, you may choose the exemptions offered by either System 1 or System 2.

All law references are to California Code of Civil Procedure unless otherwise noted.

Note: Married couples may not double any exemptions (*In re Talmadge,* 832 F.2d 1120 (9th Cir. 1987); *In re Baldwin,* 70 B.R. 612 (9th Cir. B.A.P. 1987))

ASSET	EXEMPTION	LAW PROVIDING EXEMPTION
homestead	Real or personal property, including coop, used as residence to $7500; unused portion of homestead may be applied to any property	703.140 (b)(1)
insurance	Disability benefits	703.140 (b)(10)(C)
	Life insurance proceeds needed for support of family	703.140 (b)(11)(C)
	Unmatured life insurance contract accrued avails to $4000	703.140 (b)(8)
	Unmatured life insurance policy other than credit	703.140 (b)(7)
miscellaneous	Alimony, child support needed for support	703.140 (b)(10)(D)
pensions	ERISA-qualified benefits needed for support	703.140 (b)(10)(E)
personal property	Animals, crops, appliances, furnishings, household goods, books, musical instruments & clothing to $200 per item	703.140 (b)(3)
	Health aids	703.140 (b)(1)
	Burial plot to $7500, in lieu of homestead	703.140 (b)(9)
	Jewelry to $500	703.140 (b)(4)
	Motor vehicle to $1200	703.140 (b)(2)
	Personal injury recoveries to $7500 (not to include pain & suffering or pecuniary loss)	703.140 (b)(11)(D, E)
	Wrongful death recoveries needed for support	703.140 (b)(11)(B)
public benefits	Crime victims' compensation	703.140 (b)(11)(A)
	Public assistance	703.140 (b)(10)(A)
	Social security	703.140 (b)(10)(A)
	Unemployment compensation	703.140 (b)(10)(A)
	Veterans' benefits	703.140 (b)(10)(B)
tools of trade	Implements, books & tools of trade to $750	703.140 (b)(6)
wages	None	
wild card	$400 of any property	703.140 (b)(5)
	Unused portion of homestead or burial exemption, of any property	703.140 (b)(5)

Colorado

All laws references are to Colorado Revised Statutes.

ASSET	EXEMPTION	LAW PROVIDING EXEMPTION
homestead	Real property, mobile home or manufactured home (mobile or manufactured home if loan incurred after 1/1/83) you occupy to $30,000; sale proceeds exempt 1 year after received.	38-41-201, 38-41-201.6, 38-41-203, 38-41-207
	Spouse or child of deceased owner may claim homestead exemption	38-41-204
	House trailer or coach used as residence to $3500	13-54-102(1)(o)(I)
	Mobile home used as residence to $6000	13-54-102(1)(o)(II)
insurance	Disability benefits to $200 per month; if receive lump sum, entire amount exempt	10-8-114
	Fraternal benefit society benefits	10-14-122
	Group life insurance policy or proceeds	10-7-205
	Homeowners' insurance proceeds for 1 year after received, to homestead exemption amount	38-41-209
	Life insurance avails to $5000	13-54-102(1)(l)
	Life insurance proceeds if clause prohibits proceeds from being used to pay beneficiary's creditors	10-7-106
miscellaneous	Property of business partnership	7-60-125
pensions *also see wages*	ERISA-qualified benefits, including IRAs	13-54-102(1)(s)
	Firefighters	31-30-412, 31-30-518
	Police officers	31-30-313, 31-30-616
	Public employees	24-51-212
	Teachers	22-64-120
	Veterans	13-54-102(1)(h), 13-54-104
personal property	1 burial plot per person	13-54-102(1)(d)
	Clothing to $750	13-54-102(1)(a)
	Food & fuel to $300	13-54-102(1)(f)
	Health aids	13-54-102(1)(p)
	Household goods to $1500	13-54-102(1)(e)
	Jewelry & articles of adornment to $500 total	13-54-102(1)(b)
	Motor vehicles used for work to $1000; to $3000 to get medical care, if elderly or disabled	13-54-102(j)(I), (II)
	Personal injury recoveries, unless debt related to injury	13-54-102(1)(n)
	Pictures & books to $750	13-54-102(1)(c)
	Proceeds for damaged exempt property	13-54-102(1)(m)
	Security deposit	13-54-102(1)(r)
public benefits	Aid to blind, aged, disabled, AFDC	26-2-131
	Crime victims' compensation	13-54-102(1)(q), 24-4.1-114
	Unemployment compensation	8-80-103
	Veterans' benefits for veteran, spouse or child if veteran served in war	13-54-102(1)(h)
	Workers' compensation	8-42-124
tools of trade	Horses, mules, wagons, carts, machinery, harness & tools of farmer to $2000 total	13-54-102(1)(g)
	Library of professional to $1500 or stock in trade, supplies, fixtures, machines, tools, maps, equipment & books to $1500 total	13-54-102(1)(i), (k)
	Livestock & poultry of farmer to $3000	13-54-102(1)(g)
wages	Greater of 75% of your weekly net earnings or 30 times the federal minimum wage per week —judgment creditor	13-54-104
	Minimum 75% of earned but unpaid wages, pension payments—bankruptcy	13-54-104
wild card	None	

Connecticut

ASSET	EXEMPTION	LAW PROVIDING EXEMPTION
homestead	Real property, including mobile or manufactured home, to $75,000	52-352b(t)
insurance	Disability benefits paid by association for its members	52-352b(p)
	Fraternal benefit society benefits	38a-637
	Health or disability benefits	52-352b(e)
	Life insurance proceeds if clause prohibits proceeds from being used to pay beneficiary's creditors	38a-454
	Life insurance proceeds or avails	38a-453
	Unmatured life insurance policy loan value to $4000	52-352b(5)
miscellaneous	Alimony, to extent wages exempt	52-352b(n)
	Child support	52-352b(h)
	Farm animals and livestock feed reasonably required to run farm partnership in which at least 50% of all partners are members of same family	52-352d
	Property of business partnership	34-63
pensions	ERISA-qualified benefits, to extent wages exempt (only payments being received)	52-352b(m)
	Municipal employees	7-446
	Probate judges & employees	45-29o
	State employees	5-171, 5-192w
	Teachers	10-183q
personal property	Appliances, food, clothing, furniture & bedding needed	52-352b(a)
	Burial plot	52-352b(c)
	Health aids needed	52-352b(f)
	Motor vehicle to $1500	52-352b(j)
	Proceeds for damaged exempt property	52-352b(q)
	Residential utility & security deposits for 1 residence	52-352b(l)
	Wedding & engagement rings	52-352b(k)
public benefits	Aid to blind, aged, disabled, AFDC	52-352b(d)
	Crime victims' compensation	52-352b(o), 54-213
	Social security	52-352b(g)
	Unemployment compensation	31-272(c), 52-352b(g)
	Veterans' benefits	52-352b(g)
	Vietnam veterans' death benefits	27-140i
	Wages from earnings incentive program	52-352b(d)
	Workers' compensation	52-352b(g)
tools of trade	Arms, military equipment, uniforms, musical instruments of military personnel	52-352b(i)
	Tools, books, instruments & farm animals needed	52-352b(b)
wages	Greater of 75% of your weekly net earnings or 30 times the federal minimum wage per week —judgment creditor	52-361a(f)
	Minimum 75% of earned but unpaid wages—bankruptcy	52-361a(f)
wild card	$1000 of any property	52-352b(r)

Delaware

All law references are to Delaware Code Annotated unless otherwise noted.

Note: In bankruptcy, a single person may exempt no more than $5000 total in all exemptions; a husband & wife may exempt no more than $10,000 total (10-4914).

ASSET	EXEMPTION	LAW PROVIDING EXEMPTION
homestead	None, however, property held as tenancy by the entirety may be exempt against debts owed by only one spouse	*In re Hovatter*, 25 B.R. 123 (D. Del. 1982)
insurance	Annuity contract proceeds to $350 per month	18-2728
	Fraternal benefit society benefits	18-6118
	Group life insurance policy or proceeds	18-2727
	Health or disability benefits	18-2726
	Life insurance proceeds if clause prohibits proceeds from being used to pay beneficiary's creditors	18-2729
	Life insurance proceeds or avails	18-2725
miscellaneous	Property of business partnership	6-1525
pensions	Kent County employees	9-4316
	Police officers	11-8803
	State employees	29-5503
	Volunteer firefighters	16-6653
personal property	Bible, books & family pictures	10-4902(a)
	Burial plot	10-4902(a)
	Church pew or any seat in public place of worship	10-4902(a)
	Clothing, includes jewelry	10-4902(a)
	Pianos and leased organs	10-4902(d)
	Sewing machines	10-4902(c)
public benefits	Aid to aged, disabled, AFDC, general assistance	31-513
	Aid to blind	31-2309
	Unemployment compensation	19-3374
	Workers' compensation	19-2355
tools of trade	Tools, implements & fixtures to $75 in New Castle & Sussex Counties; to $50 in Kent County	10-4902(b)
wages	85% of earned but unpaid wages	10-4913
wild card	$500 of any personal property, except tools of trade, if head of family	10-4903

District of Columbia

In bankruptcy, you may claim these exemptions or the federal bankruptcy exemptions. All law references are to District of Columbia Code unless otherwise noted.

ASSET	EXEMPTION	LAW PROVIDING EXEMPTION
homestead	None, however, property held as tenancy by the entirety may be exempt against debts owed by only one spouse	*Estate of Wall*, 440 F.2d 215 (D.C. Cir. 1971)
insurance	Disability benefits	35-522
	Fraternal benefit society benefits	35-1211
	Group life insurance policy or proceeds	35-523
	Life insurance proceeds if clause prohibits proceeds from being used to pay beneficiary's creditors	35-525
	Life insurance proceeds or avails	35-521
	Other insurance proceeds to $200 per month, maximum 2 months, for head of family; else $60 per month	15-503
miscellaneous	Property of business partnership	41-124
pensions	Judges	11-1570(d)
also see wages	Public school teachers	31-1217, 31-1238
personal property	Beds, bedding, radios, cooking utensils, stoves, furniture, furnishings & sewing machines to $300 total	15-501(a)(2)
	Books to $400	15-501(a)(8)
	Clothing to $300	15-501(a)(1), 15-503(b)
	Cooperative association holdings to $50	29-1128
	Family pictures	15-501(a)(8)
	Food & fuel to last 3 months	15-501(a)(3), (4)
	Residential condominium deposit	45-1869
public benefits	Aid to blind, aged, disabled, AFDC, general assistance	3-215.1
	Crime victims' compensation	3-407
	Unemployment compensation	46-119
	Workers' compensation	36-317
tools of trade	Library, furniture, tools of professional or artist to $300	15-501(a)(6)
	Mechanic's tools; tools of trade or business to $200	15-501(a)(5), 15-503(b)
	Motor vehicle, cart, wagon or dray, & horse or mule harness to $500	15-501(a)(7)
	Seal & documents of notary public	1-806
	Stock & materials to $200	15-501(a)(5)
wages	Greater of 75% of your weekly net earnings or 30 times the federal minimum wage per week —judgment creditor	16-572
	Minimum 75% of earned but unpaid wages, pension payments—bankruptcy	16-572
	Non-wage (including pension) earnings for 60 days to $200 per month for head of family; else $60 per month	15-503
wild card	None	

Florida

ASSET	EXEMPTION	LAW PROVIDING EXEMPTION
homestead	Real or personal property including mobile or modular home to unlimited value; property cannot exceed 1/2 acre in municipality or 160 contiguous acres elsewhere; spouse or child of deceased owner may claim homestead exemption	222.01, 222.02, 222.03, 222.05, Constitution 10-4
	May file homestead declaration	222.01
	Property held as tenancy by the entirety may be exempt against debts owed by only one spouse	*In re Avins,* 19 B.R. 736 (S.D. Fla. 1982)
insurance	Annuity contract proceeds; does not include lottery winnings	222.14; *In re Pizzi,* 153 B.R. 357 (S.D. Fla. 1993)
	Death benefits payable to a specific beneficiary, not the deceased's estate	222.13
	Disability or illness benefits	222.18
	Fraternal benefit society benefits, if received before 10/1/96	632.619
	Life insurance cash surrender value	222.14
miscellaneous	Alimony, child support needed for support	222.201
	Damages to employees for injuries in hazardous occupations	769.05
	Property of business partnership	620.68
pensions	County officers, employees	122.15
also see wages	ERISA-qualified benefits	222.21(2)
	Firefighters	175.241
	Highway patrol officers	321.22
	Police officers	185.25
	State officers, employees	121.131
	Teachers	238.15
personal property	Any personal property to $1000 (Husband & wife may double)	Constitution 10-4; *In re Hawkins,* 51 B.R. 348 (S.D. Fla. 1985)
	Health aids	222.11
	Motor vehicle to $1000	222.11
public benefits	Crime victims' compensation unless seeking to discharge debt for treatment of injury incurred during the crime	960.14
	Public assistance	222.201
	Social security	222.201
	Unemployment compensation	222.201, 443.051(2), (3)
	Veterans' benefits	222.201, 744.626
	Workers' compensation	440.22
tools of trade	None	
wages	100% of wages for heads of family up to $500 per week either unpaid or paid and deposited into bank account for up to 6 months	222.11
	Federal government employees pension payments needed for support & received 3 months before filing for bankruptcy or being sought by judgment creditor	222.21
wild card	See personal property	

All law references are to the Official Code of Georgia Annotated, *not* to the Georgia Code Annotated.

ASSET	EXEMPTION	LAW PROVIDING EXEMPTION
homestead	Real or personal property, including coop, used as residence to $5000; unused portion of homestead may be applied to any property	44-13-100(a)(1)
insurance	Annuity & endowment contract benefits	33-28-7
	Disability or health benefits to $250 per month	33-29-15
	Fraternal benefit society benefits	33-15-20
	Group insurance	33-30-10
	Industrial life insurance if policy owned by someone you depended on, needed for support	33-26-5
	Life insurance proceeds if policy owned by someone you depended on, needed for support	44-13-100(a)(11)(C)
	Unmatured life insurance contract	44-13-100(a)(8)
	Unmatured life insurance dividends, interest, loan value or cash value to $2000 if beneficiary is you or someone you depend on	44-13-100(a)(9)
miscellaneous	Alimony, child support needed for support	44-13-100(a)(2)(D)
pensions	Employees of non-profit corporations	44-13-100(a)(2.1)(B)
	ERISA-qualified benefits	18-4-22
	Public employees	44-13-100(a)(2.1)(A), 47-2-332
	Other pensions needed for support	18-4-22, 44-13-100(a)(2)(E), 44-13-100(a)(2.1)(C)
personal property	Animals, crops, clothing, appliances, books, furnishings, household goods, musical instruments to $200 per item, $3500 total	44-13-100(a)(4)
	Burial plot, in lieu of homestead	44-13-100(a)(1)
	Health aids	44-13-100(a)(10)
	Jewelry to $500	44-13-100(a)(5)
	Lost future earnings needed for support	44-13-100(a)(11)(E)
	Motor vehicles to $1000	44-13-100(a)(3)
	Personal injury recoveries to $7500	44-13-100(a)(11)(C)
	Wrongful death recoveries needed for support	44-13-100(a)(11)(B)
public benefits	Aid to blind	49-4-58
	Aid to disabled	49-4-84
	Crime victims' compensation	44-13-100(a)(11)(A)
	Local public assistance	44-13-100(a)(2)(A)
	Old age assistance	49-4-35
	Social security	44-13-100(a)(2)(A)
	Unemployment compensation	44-13-100(a)(2)(A)
	Veterans' benefits	44-13-100(a)(2)(B)
	Workers' compensation	34-9-84
tools of trade	Implements, books & tools of trade to $500	44-13-100(a)(7)
wages	Greater of 75% of your weekly net earnings or 30 times the federal minimum wage per week —judgment creditor	18-4-20, 18-4-21
	Minimum 75% of earned but unpaid wages for private & federal workers—bankruptcy	18-4-20, 18-4-21
wild card	$400 of any property	44-13-100(a)(6)
	Unused portion of homestead exemption, of any property	44-13-100(a)(6)

Hawaii

In bankruptcy, you may claim these exemptions or the federal bankruptcy exemptions.
All law references are to Hawaii Revised Statutes unless otherwise noted.

ASSET	EXEMPTION	LAW PROVIDING EXEMPTION
homestead	Head of family or over 65 to $30,000; all others to $20,000; property cannot exceed 1 acre. Sale proceeds exempt for 6 months after sale.	36-651-91, 36-651-92, 36-651-96
	Property held as tenancy by the entirety may be exempt against debts owed by only one spouse	*Security Pacific Bank v. Chang,* 818 F.Supp. 1343 (D. Ha. 1993)
insurance	Annuity contract or endowment policy proceeds if beneficiary is insured's spouse, child or parent	24-431:10-232(b)
	Disability benefits	24-431:10-231
	Fraternal benefit society benefits	24-432:2-403
	Group life insurance policy or proceeds	24-431:10-233
	Life or health insurance policy for spouse or child	24-431:10-234
	Life insurance proceeds if clause prohibits proceeds from being used to pay beneficiary's creditors	24-431:10-D:112
miscellaneous	Property of business partnership	23-425-125
pensions	ERISA-qualified benefits deposited over 3 years before being sought by judgment creditor or filing bankruptcy	36-651-124
	Firefighters	7-88-169
	Police officers	7-88-169
	Public officers & employees	7-88-91, 36-653-3
personal property	Appliances & furnishings needed	36-651-121(1)
	Books	36-651-121(1)
	Burial plot to 250 square feet plus tombstones, monuments & fencing on site	36-651-121(4)
	Clothing	36-651-121(1)
	Housing down payments for home in state project	20-359-104
	Jewelry & articles of adornment to $1000	36-651-121(1)
	Motor vehicle to wholesale value of $1000	36-651-121(2)
	Proceeds for sold or damaged exempt property; sale proceeds exempt only 6 months	36-651-121(5)
public benefits	Public assistance paid by Dept. of Health Services for work done in home or workshop	20-346-33
	Unemployment compensation	21-383-163
	Unemployment work relief funds to $60 per month	36-653-4
	Workers' compensation	21-386-57
tools of trade	Tools, implements, books, instruments, uniforms, furnishings, fishing boat, nets, motor vehicle & other personal property needed for livelihood	36-651-121(3)
wages	Unpaid wages due for services of past 31 days; after 31 days, 95% of 1st $100, 90% of 2nd $100, 80% of rest	36-651-121(6), 36-652-1
	Prisoner's wages held by Dept. of Public Safety	20-353-22
wild card	None	

Idaho

All law references are to Idaho Code.

ASSET	EXEMPTION	LAW PROVIDING EXEMPTION
homestead	Real property or mobile home to $50,000; sale proceeds exempt for 6 months	55-1003, 55-1113
	Must record homestead exemption for property that is not yet occupied	55-1004
insurance	Annuity contract proceeds to $350 per month	41-1836
	Death or disability benefits	11-604(1)(a), 41-1834
	Fraternal benefit society benefits	41-3218
	Group life insurance benefits	41-1835
	Homeowners' insurance proceeds to amount of homestead exemption	55-1008
	Life insurance proceeds if clause prohibits proceeds from being used to pay beneficiary's creditors	41-1930
	Life insurance proceeds or avails for beneficiary other than the insured	11-604(d), 41-1833
	Medical, surgical or hospital care benefits	11-603(5)
miscellaneous	Alimony, child support needed for support	11-604(1)(b)
	Liquor licenses	23-514
	Property of business partnership	53-325
pensions	ERISA-qualified benefits	55-1011
also see wages	Firefighters	72-1422
	Police officers	50-1517
	Public employees	59-1317
	Other pensions needed for support; payments can't be mixed with other money	11-604(1)(e)
personal property	Appliances, furnishings, books, clothing, pets, musical instruments, 1 firearm, family portraits & sentimental heirlooms to $500 per item, $4000 total	11-605(1)
	Building materials	45-514
	Burial plot	11-603(1)
	Crops cultivated by debtor on maximum 50 acres, to $1000; includes water rights of 160 inches	11-605(6)
	Health aids needed	11-603(2)
	Jewelry to $250	11-605(2)
	Motor vehicle to $1500	11-605(3)
	Personal injury recoveries needed for support	11-604(1)(c)
	Proceeds for damaged exempt property for 3 months after proceeds received	11-606
	Wrongful death recoveries needed for support	11-604(1)(c)
public benefits	Aid to blind, aged, disabled, AFDC	56-223
	Federal, state & local public assistance	11-603(4)
	General assistance	56-223
	Social security	11-603(3)
	Unemployment compensation	11-603(6)
	Veterans' benefits	11-603(3)
	Workers' compensation	72-802
tools of trade	Arms, uniforms & accouterments that peace officer, national guard or military personnel is required to keep	11-605(5)
	Implements, books & tools of trade to $1000	11-605(3)
wages	Greater of 75% of your weekly net earnings or 30 times the federal minimum wage per week (currently $127.50)—judgment creditor	11-207
	Minimum 75% of earned but unpaid wages, pension payments—bankruptcy	11-207
wild card	None	

ASSET	EXEMPTION	LAW PROVIDING EXEMPTION
homestead	Real or personal property including a farm, lot & buildings, condo, coop or mobile home to $7500; sale proceeds exempt 1 year from sale (husband & wife may double)	735-5/12-901, 735-5/12-906 (*First National Bank v. Mohr*, 515 N.E.2d 1356 (App. Ct. Ill. 1988))
	Spouse or child of deceased owner may claim homestead exemption	735-5/12-902
insurance	Fraternal benefit society benefits	215-5/299.1a
	Health or disability benefits	735-5/12-1001(g)(3)
	Homeowners proceeds if home destroyed, to $7500	735-5/12-907
	Life insurance, annuity proceeds or cash value if beneficiary is insured's child, parent, spouse or other dependent	215-5/238
	Life insurance policy if beneficiary is insured's spouse or child	735-5/12-1001(f)
	Life insurance proceeds if clause prohibits proceeds from being used to pay beneficiary's creditors	215-5/238
	Life insurance proceeds needed for support	735-5/12-1001(f), (g)(3)
miscellaneous	Alimony, child support needed for support	735-5/12-1001(g)(4)
	Property of business partnership	805-205/25
pensions	Civil service employees	40-5/11-223
	County employees	40-5/9-228
	Disabled firefighters; widows & children of firefighters	40-5/22-230
	ERISA-qualified benefits	735-5/12-1006
	Firefighters	40-5/4-135, 40-5/6-213
	General assembly members	40-5/2-154
	House of correction employees	40-5/19-117
	Judges	40-5/18-161
	Municipal employees	40-5/7-217(a), 40-5/8-244
	Park employees	40-5/12-190
	Police officers	40-5/3-144.1, 40-5/5-218
	Public employees	735-5/12-1006
	Public library employees	40-5/19-218
	Sanitation district employees	40-5/13-808
	State employees	40-5/14-147
	State university employees	40-5/15-185
	Teachers	40-5/16-190, 40-5/17-151
personal property	Bible, family pictures, school books & needed clothing	735-5/12-1001(a)
	Health aids	735-5/12-1001(e)
	Motor vehicle to $1200	735-5/12-1001(c)
	Personal injury recoveries to $7500	735-5/12-1001(g)(4)
	Proceeds of sold exempt property	735-5/12-1001
	Title certificate for boat over 12 feet long	652-45/3A-7
	Wrongful death recoveries needed for support	735-5/12-1001(h)(2)
public benefits	Aid to aged, blind, disabled, AFDC	305-5/11-3
	Crime victims' compensation	735-5/12-1001(h)(1)
	Restitution payments on account of WWII relocation of Aleuts and Japanese Americans	735-5/12-1001(12)(h)(5)
	Social security	735-5/12-1001(g)(1)
	Unemployment compensation	735-5/12-1001(g)(1), (3)
	Veterans' benefits	735-5/12-1001(g)(2)
	Workers' compensation	820-305/21
	Workers' occupational disease compensation	820-310/21
tools of trade	Implements, books & tools of trade to $750	735-5/12-1001(d)
wages	Greater of 75% of your weekly net earnings or 30 times the federal minimum wage per week—judgment creditor	740-170/4
	Minimum 85% of earned but unpaid wages—bankruptcy	740-170/4
wild card	$2000 of any personal property	735-5/12-1001(b)
	Includes wages	*In re Johnson*, 57 B.R. 635 (N.D. Ill. 1986

Indiana

ASSET	EXEMPTION	LAW PROVIDING EXEMPTION
homestead *also see wild card*	Real or personal property used as residence to $7500 (homestead plus personal property—except health aids—can't exceed $10,000, 34-28-1(c))	34-2-28-1(a)(1)
	Property held as tenancy by the entirety may be exempt against debts incurred by only one spouse	34-2-28-1(a)(5)
insurance	Fraternal benefit society benefits	27-11-6-3
	Group life insurance policy	27-1-12-29
	Life insurance policy, proceeds, cash value or avails if beneficiary is insured's spouse or dependent	27-1-12-14
	Life insurance proceeds if clause prohibits proceeds to be used to pay beneficiary's creditors	27-2-5-1
	Mutual life or accident proceeds	27-8-3-23
miscellaneous	Property of business partnership	23-4-1-25
pensions	Firefighters	36-8-7-22, 36-8-8-17
	Police officers (only benefits building up)	10-1-2-9, 36-8-8-17
	Public employees	5-10.3-8-9
	Public or private retirement benefits	34-2-28-1(a)(6)
	Sheriffs (only benefits building up)	36-8-10-19
	State teachers	21-6.1-5-17
personal property *also see wild card*	Health aids	34-2-28-1(a)(4)
	$100 of any intangible personal property, except money owed to you	34-2-28-1(a)(3)
public benefits	Crime victims' compensation unless seeking to discharge debt for treatment of injury incurred during the crime	12-18-6-36
	Unemployment compensation	22-4-33-3
	Workers' compensation	22-3-2-17
tools of trade	National guard uniforms, arms & equipment	10-2-6-3
wages	Greater of 75% of your weekly net earnings or 30 times the federal minimum wage per week (currently $127.50)—judgment creditor	24-4.5-5-105
	Minimum 75% of earned but unpaid wages—bankruptcy	24-4.5-5-105
wild card	$4000 of any real estate or tangible personal property	34-2-28-1(a)(2)

Iowa

All law references are to Iowa Code Annotated.

ASSET	EXEMPTION	LAW PROVIDING EXEMPTION
homestead	Real property or an apartment to an unlimited value; property cannot exceed 1/2 acre in town or city, 40 acres elsewhere	499A.18, 561.2, 561.16
	May record homestead declaration	561.4
insurance	Accident, disability, health, illness or life proceeds or avails to $15,000, paid to surviving spouse, child or other dependent	627.6(6)
	Employee group insurance policy or proceeds	509.12
	Life insurance proceeds to $10,000, acquired within 2 years of being sought by judgment creditor or filing for bankruptcy, paid to spouse, child or other dependent	627.6(6)
	Life insurance proceeds if clause prohibits proceeds from being used to pay beneficiary's creditors	508.32
miscellaneous	Alimony, child support needed for support	627.6(8)(d)
	Liquor licenses	123.38
	Property of business partnership	544.25
pensions	Disabled firefighters, police officers (only payments being received)	410.11
	Federal government pension (only payments being received)	627.8
also see wages	Firefighters	411.13
	Peace officers	97A.12
	Police officers	411.13
	Public employees	97B.39
	Other pensions needed for support (only payments being received)	627.6(8)(e)
personal property	Appliances, furnishings & household goods to $2000 total	627.6(5)
	Bibles, books, portraits, pictures & paintings to $1000 total	627.6(3)
	Burial plot to 1 acre	627.6(4)
	Clothing to $1000 plus receptacles to hold clothing	627.6(1)
	Health aids	627.6(7)
	Motor vehicle, musical instruments & tax refund to $5000 total, no more than $1000 from tax refund	627.6(9)
	Rifle or musket; shotgun	627.6(2)
	Wedding or engagement rings	627.6(1)
public benefits	Adopted child assistance	627.19
	AFDC	627.6(8)(a)
	Local public assistance	627.6(8)(a)
	Social security	627.6(8)(a)
	Unemployment compensation	627.6(8)(a)
	Veterans' benefits	627.6(8)(b)
	Workers' compensation	627.13
tools of trade	Farming equipment; includes livestock, feed to $10,000 (can't include car, *In re Van Pelt*, 83 B.R. 617 (S.D. Iowa 1987))	627.6(11)
	Non-farming equipment to $10,000 (can't include car, *In re Van Pelt*, 83 B.R. 617 (S.D. Iowa 1987))	627.6(10)
wages	Greater of 75% of your weekly net earnings or 30 times the federal minimum wage per week —judgment creditor	642.21
	Minimum 75% of earned but unpaid wages, pension payments—bankruptcy	642.21
wild card	$100 of any personal property, including cash	627.6(13)

Kansas

ASSET	EXEMPTION	LAW PROVIDING EXEMPTION
homestead	Real property or mobile home you occupy or intend to occupy to unlimited value; property cannot exceed 1 acre in town or city, 160 acres on farm	60-2301, Constitution 15-9
insurance	Fraternal life insurance benefits	40-414(a)
	Life insurance forfeiture value if file for bankruptcy over 1 year after policy issued	40-414(b)
	Life insurance proceeds if clause prohibits proceeds from being used to pay beneficiary's creditors	40-414(a)
miscellaneous	Liquor licenses	41-326
	Property of business partnership	56-325
pensions	Elected & appointed officials in cities with populations between 120,000 & 200,000	13-14,102
	ERISA-qualified benefits	60-2308(b)
	Federal government pension needed for support & paid within 3 months of being sought by judgment creditor or filing for bankruptcy (only payments being received)	60-2308(a)
	Firefighters	12-5005(e), 14-10a10
	Judges	20-2618
	Police officers	12-5005(e), 13-14a10
	Public employees	74-4923, 74-49,105
	State highway patrol officers	74-4978g
	State school employees	72-5526
personal property	Burial plot or crypt	60-2304(d)
	Clothing to last 1 year	60-2304(a)
	Food & fuel to last 1 year	60-2304(a)
	Funeral plan prepayments	16-310(d)
	Furnishings & household equipment	60-2304(a)
	Jewelry & articles of adornment to $1000	60-2304(b)
	Motor vehicle to $20,000; if designed or equipped for disabled person, no limit	60-2304(c)
public benefits	AFDC, general assistance, social welfare	39-717
	Crime victims' compensation	74-7313(d)
	Unemployment compensation	44-718(c)
	Workers' compensation	44-514
tools of trade	Books, documents, furniture, instruments, equipment, breeding stock, seed, grain & stock to $7500 total	60-2304(e)
	National Guard uniforms, arms & equipment	48-245
wages	Greater of 75% of your weekly net earnings or 30 times the federal minimum wage per week —judgment creditor	60-2310
	Minimum 75% of earned but unpaid wages—bankruptcy	60-2310
wild card	None	

Kentucky

All law references are to Kentucky Revised Statutes.

ASSET	EXEMPTION	LAW PROVIDING EXEMPTION
homestead	Real or personal property used as residence to $5000; sale proceeds exempt	427.060, 427.090
insurance	Annuity contract proceeds to $350 per month	304.14-330
	Cooperative life or casualty insurance benefits	427.110(1)
	Fraternal benefit society benefits	427.110(2)
	Group life insurance proceeds	304.14-320
	Health or disability benefits	304.14-310
	Life insurance policy if beneficiary is a married woman	304.14-340
	Life insurance proceeds if clause prohibits proceeds from being used to pay beneficiary's creditors	304.14-350
	Life insurance proceeds or cash value if beneficiary is someone other than insured	304.14-300
miscellaneous	Alimony, child support needed for support	427.150(1)
	Property of business partnership	362.270
pensions	Firefighters, police officers	67A.620, 95.878, 427.120, 427.125
	IRAs	*In re Worthington,* 28 B.R. 736 (W.D. Ky. 1983)
	State employees	61.690
	Teachers	161.700
	Urban county government employees	67A.350
	Other pensions	427.150(2)(e), (f)
personal property	Burial plot to $5000, in lieu of homestead	427.060
	Clothing, jewelry, articles of adornment & furnishings to $3000 total	427.010(1)
	Health aids	427.010(1)
	Lost earnings payments needed for support	427.150(2)(d)
	Medical expenses paid & reparation benefits received under motor vehicle reparation law	304.39-260
	Motor vehicle to $2500	427.010(1)
	Personal injury recoveries to $7500 (not to include pain & suffering or pecuniary loss)	427.150(2)(c)
	Wrongful death recoveries for person you depended on needed for support	427.150(2)(b)
public benefits	Aid to blind, aged, disabled, AFDC	205.220
	Crime victims' compensation	427.150(2)(a)
	Unemployment compensation	341.470
	Workers' compensation	342.180
tools of trade	Library, office equipment, instruments & furnishings of minister, attorney, physician, surgeon, chiropractor, veterinarian or dentist to $1000	427.040
	Motor vehicle of mechanic, mechanical or electrical equipment servicer, minister, attorney, physician, surgeon, chiropractor, veterinarian or dentist to $2500	427.030
	Tools, equipment, livestock & poultry of farmer to $3000	427.010(1)
	Tools of non-farmer to $300	427.030
wages	Greater of 75% of your weekly net earnings or 30 times the federal minimum wage per week —judgment creditor	427.010(2), (3)
	Minimum 75% of earned but unpaid wages—bankruptcy	427.010(2), (3)
wild card	$1000 of any property	427.160

ASSET	EXEMPTION	LAW PROVIDING EXEMPTION
homestead	Property you occupy to $15,000; cannot exceed 160 acres on 1 tract, or on 2 or more tracts if there's a home on 1 tract and field, garden or pasture on others (husband & wife may not double)	20:1
	Spouse or child of deceased owner may claim homestead exemption; spouse given home in divorce gets homestead	
insurance	Fraternal benefit society benefits	22:558
	Group insurance policies or proceeds	22:649
	Health, accident or disability proceeds or avails	22:646
	Life insurance proceeds or avails; if policy issued within 9 months of filing, exempt only to $35,000	22:647
miscellaneous	Property of minor child	13:3881A(3), Civil 223
pensions	Gratuitous payments to employee or heirs whenever paid	20:33(2)
	ERISA-qualified benefits if contributions made over 1 year before being sought by judgment creditor or filing for bankruptcy	13:3881D(1), 20:33(4)
personal property	Arms, military accouterments, bedding, linens & bedroom furniture, chinaware, glassware, utensils, silverware (non-sterling), clothing, family portraits, musical instruments, heating & cooling equipment, living room & dining room furniture, poultry, fowl, 1 cow, household pets, pressing irons, sewing machine, refrigerator, freezer, stove, washer & dryer	13:3881A(4)
	Cemetery plot, monuments	8:313
	Engagement & wedding rings to $5000	13:3881A(5)
public benefits	Aid to blind, aged, disabled, AFDC	46:111
	Crime victims' compensation	46:1811
	Unemployment compensation	23:1693
	Workers' compensation	23:1205
tools of trade	Tools, instruments, books, pickup truck (maximum 3 tons) or non-luxury auto & utility trailer, needed to work	13:3881A(2)
wages	Greater of 75% of your weekly net earnings or 30 times the federal minimum wage per week —judgment creditor	13:3881A(1)
	Minimum 75% of earned but unpaid wages—bankruptcy	13:3881A(1)
wild card	None	

All law references are to Maine Revised Statutes Annotated.

ASSET	EXEMPTION	LAW PROVIDING EXEMPTION
homestead	Real or personal property (including cooperative) used as residence to $12,500; if debtor over age 60 or physically or mentally disabled, $60,000 (joint debtors may double)	14-4422(1)
insurance	Annuity proceeds to $450 per month	24-A-2431
	Disability or health proceeds, benefits or avails	14-4422(13)(A)&(C) 24-A-2429
	Fraternal benefit society benefits	24-A-4118
	Group health or life policy or proceeds	24-A-2430
	Life, endowment, annuity or accident policy, proceeds or avails	14-4422(14)(C), 24-A-2428
	Life insurance policy, interest, loan value or accrued dividends for policy from person you depended on, to $4000	14-4422(11)
	Unmatured life insurance policy, except credit insurance policy	14-4422(10)
miscellaneous	Alimony & child support needed for support	14-4422(13)D
	Property of business partnership	31-305
pensions	ERISA-qualified benefits	14-4422(13)E
	Judges	4-1203
	Legislators	3-703
	State employees	5-17054
personal property	Animals, crops, musical instruments, books, clothing, furnishings, household goods, appliances to $200 per item	14-4422(3)
	Balance due on repossessed goods; total amount financed can't exceed $2000	9-A-5-103
	Burial plot in lieu of homestead exemption	14-4422(1)
	Cooking stove; furnaces & stoves for heat	14-4422(6)A&B
	Food to last 6 months	14-4422(7)A
	Fuel not to exceed 10 cords of wood, 5 tons of coal or 1000 gallons of petroleum	14-4422(6)C
	Health aids	14-4422(12)
	Jewelry to $750; no limit for 1 wedding & 1 engagement ring	14-4422(4)
	Lost earnings payments needed for support	14-4422(14)E
	Military clothes, arms & equipment	37-B-262
	Motor vehicle to $2500	14-4422(2)
	Personal injury recoveries to $12,500, not to include pain & suffering	14-4422(14)D
	Seeds, fertilizers & feed to raise & harvest food for 1 season	14-4422(7)B
	Tools & equipment to raise & harvest food	14-4422(7)C
	Wrongful death recoveries needed for support	14-4422(14)B
public benefits	AFDC	22-3753
	Crime victims' compensation	14-4422(14)A
	Social security	14-4422(13)A
	Unemployment compensation	14-4422(13)A&C
	Veterans' benefits	14-4422(13)B
	Workers' compensation	39-67
tools of trade	Boat not exceeding 5 tons used in commercial fishing	14-4422(9)
also see personal	Books, materials & stock to $5000	14-4422(5)
property	1 of each type of farm implement needed to harvest & raise crops	14-4422(8)
wages	Greater of 75% of your weekly net earnings or 30 times the federal minimum wage per week —judgment creditors only (no bankruptcy wage exemption)	14-3127
wild card	Unused portion of homestead exemption to $6000 of animals, crops, musical instruments, books, clothing, furnishings, household goods, appliances, tools of the trade and personal injury recoveries	14-4422(15)
	$400 of any property	14-4422(15)

All law references are to Annotated Code of Maryland unless otherwise noted.

ASSET	EXEMPTION	LAW PROVIDING EXEMPTION
homestead	None, however, property held as tenancy by the entirety may be exempt against debts owed by only one spouse	*In re Sefren,* 41 B.R. 747 (D. Md. 1984)
insurance	Disability or health benefits, including court awards, arbitration awards & settlements	Courts & Jud. Proceedings 11-504(b)(2)
	Fraternal benefit society benefits	48A-328, Estates & Trusts 8-115
	Life insurance or annuity contract proceeds or avails if beneficiary is insured's dependent, child or spouse	48A-385, Estates & Trusts 8-115
	Medical benefits deducted from wages	Commercial 15-601.1
miscellaneous	Property of business partnership	Corporation 9-502
pensions	Deceased Baltimore police officers (only benefits building up)	73B-49
	ERISA-qualified benefits, except IRAs	Courts & Jud. Proceedings 11-504(h)
	State employees	73B-17, 73B-125
	State police	88B-60
	Teachers	73B-96, 73B-152
personal property	Appliances, furnishings, household goods, books, pets & clothing to $500 total	Courts & Jud. Proceedings 11-504(b)(4)
	Burial plot	23-164
	Health aids	Courts & Jud. Proceedings 11-504(b)(3)
	Lost future earnings recoveries	Courts & Jud. Proceedings 11-504(b)(2)
public benefits	AFDC, general assistance	88A-73
	Crime victims' compensation	26A-13
	Unemployment compensation	Labor & Employment 8-106
	Workers' compensation	Labor & Employment 9-732
tools of trade	Clothing, books, tools, instruments & appliances to $2500; can't include car (*In re Chapman,* 68 B.R. 745 (D. Md. 1986))	Courts & Jud. Proceedings 11-504(b)(1)
wages	Earned but unpaid wages, the greater of 75% or $145 per week; in Kent, Caroline, & Queen Anne's of Worcester Counties, the greater of 75% of actual wages or 30 times the federal minimum wage per week	Commercial 15-601.1
wild card	$5500 of any property	Courts & Jud. Proceedings 11-504(b)(5), (f)

Massachusetts

ASSET	EXEMPTION	LAW PROVIDING EXEMPTION
homestead	Property you occupy or intend to occupy to $100,000; if over 65 or disabled, $200,000 (joint owners may not double)	188-1, 188-1A
	Must record homestead declaration before filing bankruptcy	188-2
	Spouse or child of deceased owner may claim homestead exemption	188-4
	Property held as tenancy by the entirety may be exempt against non-necessity debts	209-1
insurance	Disability benefits to $400 per week	175-110A
	Fraternal benefit society benefits	176-22
	Group annuity policy or proceeds	175-132C
	Group life insurance policy	175-135
	Life or endowment policy, proceeds or cash value	175-125
	Life insurance annuity contract which says it's exempt	175-125
	Life insurance policy if beneficiary is married woman	175-126
	Life insurance proceeds if clause prohibits proceeds from being used to pay beneficiary's creditors	175-119A
	Medical malpractice self-insurance	175F-15
miscellaneous	Property of business partnership	108A-25
pensions	ERISA-qualified benefits	235-34A, 246-28
also see wages	Private retirement benefits	32-41
	Public employees	32-19
	Savings bank employees	168-41, 168-44
personal property	Bank deposits to $125; food or cash for food to $300	235-34
	Beds, bedding & heating unit; clothing needed	235-34
	Bibles & books to $200 total; sewing machine to $200	235-34
	Burial plots, tombs & church pew	235-34
	Cash for fuel, heat, water or light to $75 per month	235-34
	Cash to $200 per month for rent, in lieu of homestead	235-34
	Cooperative association shares to $100	235-34
	2 cows, 12 sheep, 2 swine, 4 tons of hay	235-34
	Furniture to $3000; motor vehicle to $750	235-34
	Moving expenses for eminent domain	79-6A
	Trust company, bank or credit union deposits to $500	246-28A
public benefits	AFDC	118-10
	Aid to aged, disabled	235-34
	Unemployment compensation	151A-36
	Veterans' benefits	115-5
	Workers' compensation	152-47
tools of trade	Arms, accouterments & uniforms you're required to keep	235-34
	Boats, fishing tackle & nets of fisherman to $500	235-34
	Materials you designed & procured to $500	235-34
	Tools, implements & fixtures to $500 total	235-34
wages	Earned but unpaid wages to $125 per week	246-28
wild card	None	

Michigan

In bankruptcy, you may claim these exemptions or the federal bankruptcy exemptions.
All law references are to Michigan Compiled Laws Annotated unless otherwise noted.

ASSET	EXEMPTION	LAW PROVIDING EXEMPTION
homestead	Real property including condo to $3500; property cannot exceed 1 lot in town, village, city, or 40 acres elsewhere	559.214, 600.6023 (1)(h), (i), 600.6023 (3), 600.6027
	Spouse or child of deceased owner may claim homestead exemption	
	Property held as tenancy by the entirety may be exempt against debts owed by only one spouse	*SNB Bank & Trust v. Kensey*, 378 N.W.2d 594 (Ct. App. Mich. 1985)
insurance	Disability, mutual life or health benefits	600.6023(1)(f)
	Fraternal benefit society benefits	500.8181
	Life, endowment or annuity proceeds if clause prohibits proceeds from being used to pay beneficiary's creditors	500.4054
miscellaneous	Property of business partnership	449.25
pensions	Firefighters, police officers	38.559(6)
	ERISA-qualified benefits	600.6023(1)(k)
	IRAs	600.6023(1)(l)
	Judges	38.826
	Legislators	38.1057
	Probate judges	38.927
	Public school employees	38.1346
	State employees	38.40
personal property	Appliances, utensils, books, furniture & household goods to $1000 total	600.6023(1)(b)
	Building & loan association shares to $1000 par value, in lieu of homestead	600.6023(1)(g)
	Burial plots, cemeteries; church pew, slip, seat	600.6023(1)(c)
	Clothing; family pictures	600.6023(1)(a)
	2 cows, 100 hens, 5 roosters, 10 sheep, 5 swine; hay & grain to last 6 months if you're a head of household	600.6023(1)(d)
	Food & fuel to last 6 months if you're a head of household	600.6023(1)(a)
public benefits	AFDC	330.1158a
	Crime victims' compensation	18.362
	Social welfare benefits	400.63
	Unemployment compensation	421.30
	Veterans' benefits for Korean War veterans	35.977
	Veterans' benefits for Vietnam veterans	35.1027
	Veterans' benefits for WWII veterans	35.926
	Workers' compensation	418.821
tools of trade	Arms & accouterments you're required to keep	600.6023(1)(a)
	Tools, implements, materials, stock, apparatus, team, motor vehicle, horse & harness to $1000 total	600.6023(1)(e)
wages	60% of earned but unpaid wages for head of household; else 40%; head of household may keep at least $15 per week plus $2 per week per non-spouse dependent; others may keep at least $10 per week	600.5311
wild card	None	

Minnesota

In bankruptcy, you may claim these exemptions or the federal bankruptcy exemptions.
All law references are to Minnesota Statutes Annotated.
Note: Section 550.37(4)(a) requires that certain exemptions be adjusted for inflation on July 1 of even-numbered years. The below exemptions include all changes through July 1, 1994. For additional information, contact the Minnesota Department of Commerce at (612) 296-2297.

ASSET	EXEMPTION	LAW PROVIDING EXEMPTION
homestead	Real property, mobile home or manufactured home to unlimited value; cannot exceed 1/2 acre in city or 160 acres elsewhere	510.01, 510.02, 550.37 subd. 12
insurance	Accident or disability proceeds	550.39
	Fraternal benefit society benefits	64B.18
	Life insurance proceeds if beneficiary is spouse or child of insured to $32,000, plus $8000 per dependent	550.37 subd. 10
	Police, fire or beneficiary association benefits	550.37 subd. 11
	Unmatured life insurance contract dividends, interest or loan value to $6400 if insured is debtor or someone debtor depends on	550.37 subd. 23
miscellaneous	Earnings of minor child	550.37 subd. 15
	Property of business partnership	323.24
pensions	ERISA-qualified benefits needed for support, which do not exceed $48,000 in present value	550.37 subd. 24
	IRAs needed for support, which do not exceed $48,000 in present value	550.37 subd. 24
	Private retirement benefits (only benefits building up)	181B.16
	Public employees	353.15
	State employees	352.96
	State troopers	352B.071
personal property	Appliances, furniture, radio, phonographs & TV to $7200 total	550.37 subd. 4(b)
	Bible, books & musical instruments	550.37 subd. 2
	Burial plot; church pew or seat	550.37 subd. 3
	Clothing (includes watch), food & utensils	550.37 subd. 4(a)
	Motor vehicle to $3200 (up to $32,000 if vehicle has been modified for disability)	550.37 subd. 12(a)
	Personal injury recoveries	550.37 subd. 22
	Proceeds for damaged exempt property	550.37 subds. 9, 16
	Wrongful death recoveries	550.37 subd. 22
public benefits	AFDC, supplemental assistance, general assistance, supplemental security income	550.37 subd. 14
	Crime victims' compensation	611A.60
	Unemployment compensation	268.17 subd. 2
	Veterans' benefits	550.38
	Workers' compensation	176.175
tools of trade	Farm machines, implements, livestock, farm produce & crops of farmers to $13,000 total	550.37 subd. 5
	Teaching materials (including books, chemical apparatus) of public school teacher	550.37 subd. 8
total tools of trade (except teaching materials) can't exceed $13,000	Tools, implements, machines, instruments, furniture, stock in trade & library to $8000 total	550.37 subd. 6
wages	Earned but unpaid wages, paid within 6 months of returning to work, if you received welfare in past	550.37 subd. 13
	Greater of 75% of your weekly net earnings or 30 times the federal minimum wage per week —judgment creditor	571.922
	Minimum 75% of earned but unpaid wages—bankruptcy	571.922
	Wages deposited into bank accounts for 20 days after depositing	550.37 subd. 13
	Wages of released inmates paid within 6 months of release	550.37 subd. 14
wild card	None	

Note: Some courts have held "unlimited" exemptions (such as fraternal benefit society benefits, musical instruments, personal injury recoveries) unconstitutional under the Minnesota Constitution which allows debtors to exempt only a *reasonable* amount of property. See *In re Tveten*, 402 N.W. 2d 551 (Minn. 1987) and *In re Medill*, 119 B.R. 685 (D. Minn. 1990).

Mississippi

All law references are to Mississippi Code.

ASSET	EXEMPTION	LAW PROVIDING EXEMPTION
homestead	Property you occupy unless over 60 & married or widowed, to $75,000; property cannot exceed 160 acres; sale proceeds exempt	85-3-1(b)(i), 85-3-21, 85-3-23
	May file homestead declaration	85-3-27, 85-3-31
insurance	Disability benefits	85-3-1(b)(ii)
	Fraternal benefit society benefits	83-29-39
	Homeowners' insurance proceeds to $75,000	85-3-23
	Life insurance proceeds if clause prohibits proceeds from being used to pay beneficiary's creditors	83-7-5
miscellaneous	Property of business partnership	79-12-49
pensions	ERISA-qualified benefits deposited over 1 year before being sought by judgment creditor or filing bankruptcy	85-3-1(b)(iii)
	Firefighters	21-29-257
	Highway patrol officers	25-13-31
	IRAs deposited over 1 year before being sought by judgment creditor or filing bankruptcy	85-3-1(b)(iii)
	Keoghs deposited over 1 year before being sought by judgment creditor or filing bankruptcy	85-3-1(b)(iii)
	Private retirement benefits to extent tax-deferred	71-1-43
	Police officers	21-29-257
	Public employees retirement & disability benefits	25-11-129
	State employees	25-14-5
	Teachers	25-11-201(1)(d)
personal property	Tangible personal property of any kind to $10,000	85-3-1(a)
	Personal injury judgments to $10,000	85-3-17
	Proceeds for exempt property	85-3-1(b)(i)
public benefits	Assistance to aged	43-9-19
	Assistance to blind	43-3-71
	Assistance to disabled	43-29-15
	Crime victims' compensation	99-41-23
	Social security	25-11-129
	Unemployment compensation	71-5-539
	Workers' compensation	71-3-43
tools of trade	See personal property	
wages	Earned but unpaid wages owed for 30 days—bankruptcy	85-3-4
	100% first 30 days; after 30 days, greater of 75% of your weekly net earnings or 30 times the federal minimum wage per week—judgment creditor	85-3-4
wild card	See personal property	

ASSET	EXEMPTION	LAW PROVIDING EXEMPTION
homestead	Real property to $8000 or mobile home to $1000 (joint owners may not double)	513.430(6), 513.475
	Property held as tenancy by the entirety may be exempt against debts owed by only one spouse	*In re Anderson*, 12 B.R. 483 (W.D. Mo. 1981)
insurance	Assessment or insurance premium proceeds	377.090
	Disability or illness benefits	513.430(10)(c)
	Fraternal benefit society benefits to $5000, bought over 6 months before filing	513.430(8)
	Life insurance dividends, loan value or interest to $5000, bought over 6 months before being sought by judgment creditor or filing for bankruptcy	513.430(8)
	Life insurance proceeds if policy owned by a woman & insures her husband	376.530
	Life insurance proceeds if policy owned by unmarried woman & insures her father or brother	376.550
	Stipulated insurance premiums	377.330
	Unmatured life insurance policy	513.430(7)
miscellaneous	Alimony, child support to $500 per month	513.430(10)(d)
	Property of business partnership	358.250
pensions	Employees of cities with 100,000 or more people	71.207
	ERISA-qualified benefits needed for support (only payments being received)	513.430(10)(e)
	Firefighters	87.090, 87.365, 87.485
	Highway & transportation employees	104.250
	Police department employees	86.190, 86.353, 86.493, 86.780
	Public officers & employees	70.695
	State employees	104.540
	Teachers	169.090
personal property	Appliances, household goods, furnishings, clothing, books, crops, animals & musical instruments to $1000 total	513.430(1)
	Burial grounds to 1 acre or $100	214.190
	Health aids	513.430(9)
	Jewelry to $500	513.430(2)
	Motor vehicle to $1000	513.430(5)
	Personal injury causes of action	*In re Mitchell*, 73 B.R. 93 (E.D. Mo. 1987)
	Wrongful death recoveries for person you depended on	513.430(11)
public benefits	AFDC	513.430(10)(a)
	Social security	513.430(10)(a)
	Unemployment compensation	288.380(10)(l), 513.430(10)(c)
	Veterans' benefits	513.430(10)b
	Workers' compensation	287.260
tools of trade	Implements, books & tools of trade to $2000	513.430(4)
wages	Greater of 75% of your weekly net earnings or 30 times the federal minimum wage per week —judgment creditor	525.030
	Minimum 75% of earned but unpaid wages (90% for head of family)—bankruptcy	525.030
	Wages of servant or common laborer to $90	513.470
wild card	$1250 of any property if head of family, else $400; head of family may claim additional $250 per child	513.430(3), 513.440

All law references are to Montana Code Annotated.

ASSET	EXEMPTION	LAW PROVIDING EXEMPTION
homestead	Real property or mobile home you occupy to $40,000; sale, condemnation or insurance proceeds exempt 18 months	70-32-104, 70-32-201, 70-32-216
	Must record homestead declaration before filing for bankruptcy	70-32-105
insurance	Annuity contract proceeds to $350 per month	33-15-514
	Disability or illness proceeds, avails or benefits	25-13-608(1)(d), 33-15-513
	Fraternal benefit society benefits	33-7-522
	Group life insurance policy or proceeds	33-15-512
	Hail insurance benefits	80-2-245
	Life insurance proceeds if clause prohibits proceeds from being used to pay beneficiary's creditors	33-20-120
	Medical, surgical or hospital care benefits	25-13-608(1)(e)
	Unmatured life insurance contracts to $4000	25-13-609(4)
miscellaneous	Alimony, child support	25-13-608(1)(f)
	Property of business partnership	35-10-502
pensions	ERISA-qualified benefits deposited over 1 year before being sought by judgment creditor or filing bankruptcy in excess of 15% of debtor's yearly income	31-2-106
	Firefighters	19-11-612(1), 19-13-1004
	Game wardens	19-8-805(2)
	Highway patrol officers	19-6-705(2)
	Judges	19-5-704
	Police officers	19-9-1006, 19-10-504(1)
	Public employees	19-3-105(1)
	Sheriffs	19-7-705(2)
	Teachers	19-4-706(2)
	University system employees	19-21-212
personal property	Appliances, household furnishings, goods, animals with feed, crops, musical instruments, books, firearms, sporting goods, clothing & jewelry to $600 per item, $4500 total	25-13-609(1)
	Burial plot	25-13-608(1)(g)
	Cooperative association shares to $500 value	35-15-404
	Health aids	25-13-608(1)(a)
	Motor vehicle to $1200	25-13-609(2)
	Proceeds for damaged or lost exempt property for 6 months after received	25-13-610
public benefits	Aid to aged, disabled, AFDC	53-2-607
	Crime victims' compensation	53-9-129
	Local public assistance	25-13-608(1)(b)
	Silicosis benefits	39-73-110
	Social security	25-13-608(1)(b)
	Subsidized adoption payments	53-2-607
	Unemployment compensation	31-2-106(2), 39-51-3105
	Veterans' benefits	25-13-608(1)(c)
	Vocational rehabilitation to the blind	53-2-607
	Workers' compensation	39-71-743
tools of trade	Implements, books & tools of trade to $3000	25-13-609(3)
	Uniforms, arms, accouterments needed to carry out government functions	25-13-613(b)
wages	Minimum 75% of earned but unpaid wages—bankruptcy	25-13-614
	Greater of 75% of your weekly net earnings or 30 times the federal minimum wage per week —judgment creditor	25-13-614
wild card	None	

Nebraska

All law references are to Revised Statutes of Nebraska.

ASSET	EXEMPTION	LAW PROVIDING EXEMPTION
homestead	$10,000; cannot exceed 2 lots in city or village, 160 acres elsewhere; sale proceeds exempt 6 months after sale	40-101, 40-111, 40-113
	May record homestead declaration	40-105
insurance	Fraternal benefit society benefits to $10,000 loan value	44-1089
	Life insurance or annuity contract proceeds to $10,000 loan value	44-371
miscellaneous	Property of business partnership	67-325
pensions *also see wages*	County employees	23-2322
	ERISA-qualified benefits needed for support	25-1563.01
	Military disability benefits to $2000	25-1559
	School employees	79-1060, 79-1552
	State employees	84-1324
personal property	Burial plot	12-517
	Clothing needed	25-1556
	Crypts, lots, tombs, niches, vaults	12-605
	Food & fuel to last 6 months	25-1556
	Furniture & kitchen utensils to $1500	25-1556
	Perpetual care funds	12-511
	Personal injury recoveries	25-1563.02
	Personal possessions	25-1556
public benefits	Aid to disabled, blind, aged, AFDC	68-1013
	Unemployment compensation	48-647
	Workers' compensation	48-149
tools of trade	Equipment or tools to $1500 (husband & wife may double)	25-1556 (*In re Keller*, 50 B.R. 23 (D. Neb. 1985))
wages	Greater of 75% of your weekly net earnings or 30 times the federal minimum wage per week —judgment creditor	25-1558
	Minimum 85% of earned but unpaid wages or pension payments for head of family; 75% for all others—bankruptcy	25-1558
wild card	$2500 of any personal property, except wages, in lieu of homestead	25-1552

ASSET	EXEMPTION	LAW PROVIDING EXEMPTION
homestead	Real property or mobile home to $95,000 (husband & wife may not double)	21.090(1)(m), 115.010
	Must record homestead declaration before filing for bankruptcy	115.020
insurance	Annuity contract proceeds to $350 per month	687B.290
	Fraternal benefit society benefits	695A.220
	Group life or health policy or proceeds	687B.280
	Health proceeds or avails	687B.270
	Life insurance policy or proceeds if annual premiums not over $1000	21.090(1)(k)
	Life insurance proceeds if you're not the insured	687B.260
miscellaneous	Property of business partnership	87.250
pensions	ERISA-qualified benefits to $100,000	21.090(1)(q)
	Public employees	286.670
personal property	Appliances, household goods, furniture, home & yard equipment to $3000 total	21.090(1)(b)
	Books to $1500	21.090(1)(a)
	Burial plot purchase money held in trust	452.550
	Funeral service contract money held in trust	689.700
	Health aids	21.090(1)(p)
	Keepsakes & pictures	21.090(1)(a)
	Metal-bearing ores, geological specimens, art curiosities or paleontological remains; must be arranged, classified, catalogued & numbered in reference books	21.100
	Motor vehicle to $1500; no limit if vehicle equipped to provide mobility for disabled person	21.090(1)(f), (o)
	One gun	21.090(1)(i)
public benefits	Aid to blind, aged, disabled, AFDC	422.291
	Industrial insurance (workers' compensation)	616.550
	Unemployment compensation	612.710
	Vocational rehabilitation benefits	615.270
tools of trade	Arms, uniforms & accouterments you're required to keep	21.090(1)(j)
	Cabin or dwelling of miner or prospector; cars, implements & appliances for mining & mining claim you work to $4500 total	21.090(1)(e)
	Farm trucks, stock, tools, equipment & seed to $4500	21.090(1)(c)
	Library, equipment, supplies, tools & materials to $4500	21.090(1)(d)
wages	Greater of 75% of your weekly net earnings or 30 times the federal minimum wage per week —judgment creditor	21.090(1)(g)
	Minimum 75% of earned but unpaid wages—bankruptcy	21.090(1)(g)
wild card	None	

All law references are to New Hampshire Revised Statutes Annotated.

ASSET	EXEMPTION	LAW PROVIDING EXEMPTION
homestead	Real property or manufactured housing (if you own the land it's on) to $30,000	480:1
insurance	Firefighters' aid insurance	402:69
	Fraternal benefit society benefits	418:24
	Homeowners' insurance proceeds to $5000	512:21(VIII)
miscellaneous	Child support	161-C-11
	Jury, witness fees	512:21(VI)
	Property of business partnership	304A:25
	Wages of minor child	512:21(III)
pensions	Federally created pension (only benefits building up)	512:21(IV)
	Firefighters	102:23
	Police officers	103:18
	Public employees	100A:26
personal property	Automobile to $1000	511:2(XVI)
	Beds, bedsteads, bedding & cooking utensils needed	511:2(II)
	Bibles & books to $800	511:2(VIII)
	Burial plot, lot	511:2(XIV)
	Church pew	511:2(XV)
	Clothing needed	511:2(I)
	Cooking & heating stoves, refrigerator	511:2(IV)
	Cow, 6 sheep or fleece; 4 tons of hay	511:2(XI), (XII)
	Domestic fowl to $300	511:2(XIII)
	Food & fuel to $400	511:2(VI)
	Furniture to $2000	511:2(III)
	Hog, pig or pork (if already slaughtered)	511:2(X)
	Jewelry to $500	511:2(XVII)
	Proceeds for lost or destroyed exempt property	512:21(VIII)
	Sewing machine	511:2(V)
public benefits	Aid to blind, aged, disabled, AFDC	167:25
	Unemployment compensation	282A:159
	Workers' compensation	281A:52
tools of trade	Tools of your occupation to $1200	511:2(IX)
	Uniforms, arms & equipment of military member	511:2(VII)
	Yoke of oxen or horse needed for farming or teaming	511:2(XII)
wages	Earned by unpaid wages; judge decides amount exempt based on a percentage of the federal minimum wage	512:21(II)
	Earned but unpaid wages of spouse	512:21(III)
wild card	None	

New Jersey

ASSET	EXEMPTION	LAW PROVIDING EXEMPTION
homestead	None	
insurance	Annuity contract proceeds to $500 per month	17B:24-7
	Disability or death benefits for military member	38A:4-8
	Disability, death, medical or hospital benefits for civil defense workers	App. A:9-57.6
	Fraternal benefit society benefits	17:44A-19
	Group life or health policy or proceeds	17B:24-9
	Health or disability benefits	17:18-12, 17B:24-8
	Life insurance proceeds if clause prohibits proceeds from being used to pay beneficiary's creditors	17B:24-10
	Life insurance proceeds or avails if you're not the insured	17B:24-6b
miscellaneous	Property of business partnership	42:1-25
pensions	Alcohol beverage control officers	43:8A-20
	City boards of health employees	43:18-12
	Civil defense workers	App. A:9-57.6
	County employees	43:10-57, 43:10-105
	ERISA-qualified benefits	43:13-9
	Firefighters, police officers, traffic officers	43:16-7, 43:16A-17
	Judges	43:6A-41
	Municipal employees	43:13-44
	Prison employees	43:7-13
	Public employees	43:15A-53
	School district employees	18A:66-116
	State police	53:5A-45
	Street & water department employees	43:19-17
	Teachers	18A:66-51
personal property	Goods & chattels, personal property & stock or interest in corporations to $1000 total	2A:17-19
	Burial plots	8A:5-10
	Clothing	2A:17-19
	Furniture & household goods to $1000	2A:26-4
public benefits	Crime victims' compensation	52:4B-30
	Old-age, permanent disability assistance	44:7-35
	Unemployment compensation	43:21-53
	Workers' compensation	34:15-29
tools of trade	None	
wages	90% of earned but unpaid wages if income under $7500; if income over $7500, judge decides amount that is exempt	2A:17-56
	Wages or allowances received by military personnel	38A:4-8
wild card	None	

New Mexico

In bankruptcy, you may claim these exemptions or the federal bankruptcy exemptions.
All law references are to New Mexico Statutes Annotated.

ASSET	EXEMPTION	LAW PROVIDING EXEMPTION
homestead	Married, widowed or supporting another may claim real property to $30,000 (joint owners may double)	42-10-9
insurance	Benevolent association benefits to $5000	42-10-4
	Fraternal benefit society benefits	59A-44-18
	Life, accident, health or annuity benefits, withdrawal or cash value, if beneficiary is a New Mexican citizen	42-10-3
miscellaneous	Ownership interest in unincorporated association	53-10-2
	Property of business partnership	54-1-25
pensions	Pension or retirement benefits	42-10-1, 42-10-2
	Public school employees	22-11-42A
personal property	Books, health equipment & furniture	42-10-1, 42-10-2
	Building materials	48-2-15
	Clothing	42-10-1, 42-10-2
	Cooperative association shares, minimum amount needed to be member	53-4-28
	Jewelry to $2500	42-10-1, 42-10-2
	Materials, tools & machinery to dig, torpedo, drill, complete, operate or repair oil line, gas well or pipeline	70-4-12
	Motor vehicle to $4000	42-10-1, 42-10-2
public benefits	AFDC, general assistance	27-2-21
	Crime victims' compensation paid before 7/1/93	31-22-15
	Occupational disease disablement benefits	52-3-37
	Unemployment compensation	51-1-37
	Workers' compensation	52-1-52
tools of trade	$1500	42-10-1, 42-10-2
wages	Greater of 75% of your weekly net earnings or 30 times the federal minimum wage per week —judgment creditor	35-12-7
	Minimum 75% of earned but unpaid wages—bankruptcy	35-12-7
wild card	$500 of any personal property	42-10-1
	$2000 of any property, in lieu of homestead	42-10-10

New York

All law references are to Consolidated Laws of New York, Civil Practice Law & Rules, unless otherwise noted.

ASSET	EXEMPTION	LAW PROVIDING EXEMPTION
homestead	Real property including coop, condo or mobile home, to $10,000	5206(a)
	Husband & wife may double	*In re Pearl*, 723 F.2d 193 (2nd Cir. 1983)
insurance	Annuity contract benefits due or prospectively due the debtor, who paid for the contract; if purchased within 6 months of being sought by judgment creditor or filing for bankruptcy & not tax-deferred, only $5000	Insurance 3212(d), Debtor & Creditor 283(1)
	Disability or illness benefits to $400 per month	Insurance 3212(c)
	Life insurance proceeds left at death with the insurance company pursuant to agreement, if clause prohibits proceeds from being used to pay beneficiary's creditors	Estates, Powers & Trusts 7-1.5(a)(2)
	Life insurance proceeds and avails if the person effecting the policy is the spouse of the insured	Insurance 3212(b)(2)
miscellaneous	Alimony, child support needed for support	Debtor & Creditor 282(2)(d)
	Property of business partnership	Partnership 51
pensions	ERISA-qualified benefits needed for support	Debtor & Creditor 282(2)(e), 5205(c)
	IRAs needed for support	Debtor & Creditor 282(2)(e), 5205(c)
	Keoghs needed for support	Debtor & Creditor 282(2)(e), 5205(c)
	Public retirement benefits	Insurance 4607
	State employees	Retirement & Social Security 110
	Village police officers	Unconsolidated 5711-o
personal property	Bible; schoolbooks; books to $50; pictures; clothing; church pew or seat; stoves with fuel to last 60 days; sewing machine; domestic animal with food to last 60 days, to $450; food to last 60 days; furniture; refrigerator; TV; radio; wedding ring; watch to $35; crockery, cooking utensils and tableware needed, to $5000 total (with farm machinery, etc.)	5205(1)-(6), Debtor & Creditor 283(1)
	Burial plot, without structure to 1/4 acre	5206(f)
	Cash, the lesser of either $2500, or an amount, that, with annuity, totals $5000; in lieu of homestead	Debtor & Creditor 283(2)
	Health aids, including animals with food	5205(h)
	Lost earnings recoveries needed for support	Debtor & Creditor 282(3)(iv)
	Motor vehicle to $2400	Debtor & Creditor 282(1)
	Personal injury recoveries to $7500 (not to include pain & suffering)	Debtor & Creditor 282(3)(iii)
	Security deposits to landlord, utility company	5205(g)
	Trust fund principal, 90% of income	5205(c), (d)
	Wrongful death recoveries for person you depended on, needed for support	Debtor & Creditor 282(3)(ii)
public benefits	Aid to blind, aged, disabled, AFDC	Debtor & Creditor 282(2)(c)
	Crime victims' compensation	Debtor & Creditor 282(3)(i)
	Home relief, local public assistance	Debtor & Creditor 282(2)(a)
	Social security	Debtor & Creditor 282(2)(a)
	Unemployment compensation	Debtor & Creditor 282(2)(a)
	Veterans' benefits	Debtor & Creditor 282(2)(b)
	Workers' compensation	Debtor & Creditor 282(2)(c)
tools of trade	Farm machinery, team, food for 60 days, professional furniture, books & instruments to $600 total	5205(b)
	Uniforms, medal, equipments, emblem, horse, arms & sword of military member	5205(e)
wages	90% of earnings from milk sales to milk dealers	5205(f)
	90% of earned but unpaid wages received within 60 days of being sought by judgment creditor or filing for bankruptcy (100% for a few militia members)	5205(d), (e)
wild card	None	

North Carolina

All law references are to General Statutes of North Carolina unless otherwise noted.

ASSET	EXEMPTION	LAW PROVIDING EXEMPTION
homestead	Real or personal property, including coop, used as residence to $10,000; up to $3500 of unused portion of homestead may be applied to any property	1C-1601(a)(1), (2)
	Property held as tenancy by the entirety may be exempt against debts owed by only one spouse	*In re Crouch*, 33 B.R. 271 (E.D. N.C. 1983)
insurance	Employee group life policy or proceeds	58-58-165
	Fraternal benefit society benefits	58-24-85
miscellaneous	Property of business partnership	59-55
pensions	Firefighters & rescue squad workers	58-86-90
	Law enforcement officers	143-166.30(g)
	Legislators	120-4.29
	Municipal, city & county employees	128-31
	Teachers & state employees	135-9, 135-95
personal property	Animals, crops, musical instrument, books, clothing, appliances, household goods & furnishings to $3500 total; may add $750 per dependent, up to $3000 total additional	1C-1601(a)(4)
	Burial plot to $10,000, in lieu of homestead	1C-1601(a)(1)
	Health aids	1C-1601(a)(7)
	Motor vehicle to $1500	1C-1601(a)(3)
	Personal injury recoveries for person you depended on	1C-1601(a)(8)
	Wrongful death recoveries for person you depended on	1C-1601(a)(8)
public benefits	AFDC, special adult assistance	108A-36
	Aid to blind	111-18
	Crime victims' compensation	15B-17
	Unemployment compensation	96-17
	Workers' compensation	97-21
tools of trade	Implements, books & tools of trade to $750	1C-1601(a)(5)
wages	Earned but unpaid wages received 60 days before being sought by judgment creditor or filing for bankruptcy, needed for support	1-362
wild card	$3500 less any amount claimed for homestead or burial exemption, of any property	1C-1601(a)(2)

All law references are to North Dakota Century Code.

ASSET	EXEMPTION	LAW PROVIDING EXEMPTION
homestead	Real property, house trailer or mobile home to $80,000	28-22-02(10), 47-18-01
insurance	Fraternal benefit society benefits	26.1-15.1-18, 26.1-33-40
	Life insurance proceeds payable to deceased's estate, not to a specific beneficiary	26.1-33-40
	Life insurance surrender value to $100,000 per policy, if beneficiary is insured's relative & owned over 1 year before being sought by judgment creditor or filing for bankruptcy; no limit if more needed for support; with ERISA-qualified benefits, IRAs and Keoghs exempt under 28-22-03.1 (except pensions for disabled veterans), total cannot exceed $200,000	28-22-03.1(3)
miscellaneous	Property of business partnership	45-08-02
pensions	Disabled veterans' benefits, except military retirement pay	28-22-03.1(4)(d)
	ERISA-qualified benefits to $100,000 per plan; no limit if more needed for support; with insurance exempt under 28-22-03.1, total cannot exceed $200,000	28-22-03.1(3)
	IRAs to $100,000 per plan; no limit if more needed for support; with insurance exempt under 28-22-03.1, total cannot exceed $200,000	28-22-03.1(3)
	Keoghs to $100,000 per plan; no limit if more needed for support; with insurance exempt under 28-22-03.1, total cannot exceed $200,000	28-22-03.1(3)
	Public employees	28-22-19(1)
personal property	1. All debtors may exempt:	
	Bible, books to $100 & pictures; clothing	28-22-02(1), (4), (5)
	Burial plots, church pew	28-22-02(2), (3)
	Cash to $7500, in lieu of homestead	28-22-03.1(1)
	Crops or grain raised on debtor's tract to 160 acres (64.75 hectares) on 1 tract	28-22-02(8)
	Food & fuel to last 1 year	28-22-02(6)
	Motor vehicle to $1200	28-22-03.1(2)
	Personal injury recoveries to $7500 (not to include pain & suffering)	28-22-03.1(4)(b)
	Wrongful death recoveries to $7500	28-22-03.1(4)(a)
	2. Head of household not claiming crops or grain may claim $5000 of any personal property or:	28-22-03
	Books & musical instruments to $1500	28-22-04(1)
	Furniture, including bedsteads & bedding, to $1000	28-22-04(2)
	Library & tools of professional to $1000	28-22-04(4)
	Livestock & farm implements to $4500	28-22-04(3)
	Tools of mechanic & stock in trade to $1000	28-22-04(4)
	3. Non-head of household not claiming crops or grain, may claim $2500 of any personal property	28-22-05
public benefits	AFDC	28-22-19(3)
	Crime victims' compensation	28-22-19(2)
	Social security	28-22-03.1(4)(c)
	Unemployment compensation	52-06-30
	Vietnam veterans' adjustment compensation	37-25-07
	Workers' compensation	65-05-29
tools of trade	See personal property	
wages	Greater of 75% of your weekly net earnings or 30 times the federal minimum wage per week —judgment creditor	32-09.1-.03
	Minimum 75% of earned but unpaid wages—bankruptcy	32-09.1-.03
wild card	See personal property	

Ohio

All law references are to Ohio Revised Code unless otherwise noted.

ASSET	EXEMPTION	LAW PROVIDING EXEMPTION
homestead	Real or personal property used as residence to $5000	2329.66(A)(1)
	Property held as tenancy by the entirety may be exempt against debts owed by only one spouse	*In re Thomas,* 14 B.R. 423 (N.D. Ohio 1981)
insurance	Benevolent society benefits to $5000	2329.63, 2329.66(A)(6)(a)
	Disability benefits to $600 per month	2329.66(A)(6)(e), 3923.19
	Fraternal benefit society benefits	2329.66(A)(6)(d), 3921.18
	Group life insurance policy or proceeds	2329.66(A)(6)(c), 3917.05
	Life, endowment or annuity contract avails for your spouse, child or dependent	2329.66(A)(6)(b), 3911.10
	Life insurance proceeds for a spouse	3911.12
	Life insurance proceeds if clause prohibits proceeds from being used to pay beneficiary's creditors	3911.14
miscellaneous	Alimony, child support needed for support	2329.66(A)(11)
	Property of business partnership	1775.24, 2329.66(A)(14)
pensions	ERISA-qualified benefits needed for support	2329.66(A)(10)(a)
	Firefighters, police officers	742.47
	Firefighters', police officers' death benefits	2329.66(A)(10)(a)
	IRAs needed for support	2329.66(A)(10)(b)
	Keoghs needed for support	2329.66(A)(10)(b)
	Public employees	145.56
	Public school employees	3307.71, 3309.66
	State highway patrol employees	5505.22
	Volunteer firefighters' dependents	146.13
personal property	Animals, crops, books, musical instruments, appliances, household goods, furnishings, hunting & fishing equipment & firearms to $200 per item, $1500 total ($2000 if no homestead claimed)	2329.66(A)(4)(b), (d)
Note: Jewelry must be counted toward the $1500/$2000 totals	Beds, bedding & clothing to $200 per item	2329.66(A)(3)
	Burial plot	517.09, 2329.66(A)(8)
	Cash, money due within 90 days, bank & security deposits & tax refund to $400 total (spouse without income can't exempt tax refund, *In re Smith,* 77 B.R. 633 (N.D. Ohio 1987))	2329.66(A)(4)(a)
	Cooking unit & refrigerator to $300 each	2329.66(A)(3)
	Health aids	2329.66(A)(7)
	Jewelry to $200 per item (1 item may be to $400)	239.66 (A)(c)(d)
	Lost future earnings needed for support, received during 12 months before filing for bankruptcy or sought by judgment creditor	2329.66(A)(12)(d)
	Motor vehicle to $1000	2329.66(A)(2)
	Personal injury recoveries to $5000 (not to include pain & suffering), received during 12 months before filing for bankruptcy or sought by judgment creditor	2329.66(A)(12)(c)
	Wrongful death recoveries for person debtor depended on, needed for support, received during 12 months before filing for bankruptcy or sought by judgment creditor	2329.66(A)(12)(b)
public benefits	AFDC	2329.66(A)(9)(d), 5107.12
	Crime victim's compensation, received during 12 months before filing for bankruptcy or sought by judgment creditor	2329.66(A)(12)(a), 2743.66
	Disability assistance payments	2329.66(A)(9)(f), 5115.07
	General assistance payments	2329.66(A)(9)(e), 5113.03
	Unemployment compensation	2329.66(A)(9)(c), 4141.32
	Vocational rehabilitation benefits	2329.66(A)(9)(a), 3304.19
	Workers' compensation	2329.66(A)(9)(b), 4123.67
tools of trade	Implements, books & tools of trade to $750	2329.66(A)(5)
	Seal, official register of notary public	2329.66(A)(15), 147.04
wages	Greater of 75% of your weekly net earnings or 30 times the federal minimum wage per week —judgment creditor	2329.66(A)(13)
	Minimum 75% of earned but unpaid wages due for 30 days—bankruptcy	2329.66(A)(13)
wild card	$400 of any property	2329.66(A)(17)

Oklahoma

All law references are to Oklahoma Statutes Annotated.

ASSET	EXEMPTION	LAW PROVIDING EXEMPTION
homestead	Real property or manufactured home to unlimited value; property cannot exceed 1/4 acre. If property exceeds 1/4 acre, may claim $5000 on 1 acre in city, town or village, or 160 acres elsewhere (need not occupy homestead to claim it exempt as long as you don't acquire another)	31-1(A)(1), 31-1(A)(2), 31-2
insurance	Assessment or mutual benefits	36-2410
	Fraternal benefit society benefits	36-2720
	Funeral benefits prepaid & placed in trust	36-6125
	Group life policy or proceeds	36-3632
	Limited stock insurance benefits	36-2510
miscellaneous	Alimony, child support	31-1(A)(19)
	Property of business partnership	54-225
pensions	County employees	19-959
	Disabled veterans	31-7
	ERISA-qualified benefits	31-1(A)(20)
	Firefighters	11-49-126
	Law enforcement employees	47-2-303.3
	Police officers	11-50-124
	Public employees	74-923
	Tax exempt benefits	60-328
	Teachers	70-17-109
personal property	Books, portraits, pictures & gun	31-1(A)(7), (14)
	2 bridles & 2 saddles	31-1(A)(12)
	Burial plots	31-1(A)(4), 8-7
	100 chickens, 10 hogs, 2 horses, 5 cows & calves under 6 months, 20 sheep; forage for livestock to last 1 year (cows must be able to produce milk for human consumption)	31-1(A)(10), (11), (15), (16)
	Clothing to $4000	31-1(A)(8)
	Furniture, health aids, food to last 1 year	31-1(A)(3), (9), (17)
	Motor vehicle to $3000	31-1(A)(13)
	Personal injury, wrongful death & workers' compensation recoveries to $50,000 total; cannot include punitive damages	31-1(A)(21)
public benefits	AFDC	56-173
	Crime victims' compensation	21-142.13
	Social security	56-173
	Unemployment compensation	40-2-303
	Workers' compensation (see personal property)	85-48
tools of trade	Husbandry implements to farm homestead, tools, books & apparatus to $5000 total	31-1(A)(5), (6), 31-1(C)
wages	75% of wages earned in 90 days before being sought by judgment creditor or filing bankruptcy; judge may allow more if you show hardship	12-1171.1, 31-1(A)(18)
wild card	None	

ASSET	EXEMPTION	LAW PROVIDING EXEMPTION
homestead	Real property, mobile home or house boat you occupy or intend to occupy to $25,000 ($33,000 for joint owners); if you don't own land mobile home is on, to $23,000 ($30,000 for joint owners); property cannot exceed 1 block in town or city or 160 acres elsewhere; sale proceeds exempt 1 year from sale, if you intend to purchase another home	23.164, 23.240, 23.250
insurance	Annuity contract benefits to $500 per month	743.049
	Fraternal benefit society benefits	748.225
	Group life policy or proceeds not payable to insured	743.047
	Health or disability proceeds or avails	743.050
	Life insurance proceeds or cash value if you are not the insured	743.046
miscellaneous	Alimony, child support needed for support	23.160(1)(i)
	Liquor licenses	471.301(1)
	Property of business partnership	68.420
pensions	ERISA-qualified benefits	23.170
	Public officers, employees	237.201
	School district employees	239.261
personal property	Bank deposits to $7500; cash for sold exempt property	23.166
	Books, pictures & musical instruments to $600 total (husband & wife may double)	23.160(1)(a)
	Burial plot	65.870
	Clothing, jewelry & other personal items to $1800 total (husband & wife may double)	23.160(1)(b)
	Domestic animals, poultry with food to last 60 days to $1000	23.160(1)(e)
	Food & fuel to last 60 days if debtor is householder	23.160(1)(f)
	Furniture, household items, utensils, radios & TVs to $3000 total	23.160(1)(f)
	Health aids	23.160(1)(h)
	Lost earnings payments for debtor or someone debtor depended on, to extent needed (husband & wife may double)	23.160(1)(j)(C)
	Motor vehicle to $1700 (husband & wife may double)	23.160(1)(d)
	Personal injury recoveries to $7500, not to include pain & suffering (husband & wife may double)	23.160(1)(j)(B)
	Pistol; rifle or shotgun if owned by person over 16, to $1000	23.200
public benefits	Aid to blind	412.115
	Aid to disabled	412.610
	Civil defense & disaster relief	401.405
	Crime victims' compensation (husband & wife may double)	23.160(1)(j)(A), 147.325
	General assistance	411.760
	Injured inmates' benefits	655.530
	Medical assistance	414.095
	Old-age assistance	413.130
	Unemployment compensation	657.855
	Vocational rehabilitation	344.580
	Workers' compensation	656.234
tools of trade	Tools, library, team with food to last 60 days, to $3000 (husband & wife may double)	23.160(1)(c)
wages	Greater of 75% of your weekly net earnings or 30 times the federal minimum wage per week —judgment creditor	23.185
	Minimum of 75% of earned but unpaid wages—bankruptcy	23.185
	Wages withheld in state employee's bond savings accounts	292.070
wild card	$400 of any personal property, however, can't use to increase existing exemption (husband & wife may double)	23.160(1)(k) (*In re Wilson*, 22 B.R. 146 (D. Or. 1982))

Pennsylvania

In bankruptcy, you may claim these exemptions or the federal bankruptcy exemptions.
All law references are to Pennsylvania Consolidated Statutes Annotated unless otherwise noted.

ASSET	EXEMPTION	LAW PROVIDING EXEMPTION
homestead	None, however, property held as tenancy by the entirety may be exempt against debts owed by only one spouse	*Keystone Savings Ass'n v. Kitsock,* 633 A.2d 165 (Pa. Super. Ct. 1993)
insurance	Accident or disability benefits	42-8124(c)(7)
	Fraternal benefit society benefits	42-8124(c)(1), (8)
	Group life policy or proceeds	42-8124(c)(5)
	Insurance policy or annuity contract payments, where insured is the beneficiary, cash value or proceeds to $100 per month	42-8124(c)(3)
	Life insurance annuity policy, cash value or proceeds if beneficiary is insured's dependent, child or spouse	42-8124(c)(6)
	Life insurance proceeds if clause prohibits proceeds from being used to pay beneficiary's creditors	42-8214(c)(4)
	No-fault automobile insurance proceeds	42-8124(c)(9)
miscellaneous	Property of business partnership	15-8341
pensions	City employees	53-13445, 53-23572, 53-39383
	County employees	16-4716
	Municipal employees	53-881.115
	Police officers	53-764, 53-776, 53-23666
	Private retirement benefits if clause prohibits proceeds from being used to pay beneficiary's creditors, to extent tax-deferred; exemption limited to $15,000 per year deposited; no exemption for amount deposited within 1 year of being sought by judgment creditor or filing for bankruptcy	42-8124(b)
	Public school employees	24-8533
	State employees	71-5953
personal property	Bibles, school books & sewing machines	42-8124(a)(2), (3)
	Clothing	42-8124(a)(1)
	Tangible personal property at an international exhibit sponsored by U.S. government	42-8125
	Uniform & accouterments	42-8124(a)(4)
public benefits	Crime victims' compensation	71-180-7.10
	Korean conflict veterans' benefits	51-20098
	Unemployment compensation	42-8124(a)(10), 43-863
	Veterans' benefits	51-20012
	Workers' compensation	42-8124(c)(2)
tools of trade	None	
wages	Earned but unpaid wages	42-8127
wild card	$300 of any property	42-8123

Rhode Island

In bankruptcy, you may claim these exemptions or the federal bankruptcy exemptions. All law references are to General Laws of Rhode Island.

ASSET	EXEMPTION	LAW PROVIDING EXEMPTION
homestead	None	
insurance	Accident or sickness proceeds, avails or benefits	27-18-24
	Fraternal benefit society benefits	27-25-18
	Life insurance proceeds if clause prohibits proceeds from being used to pay beneficiary's creditors	27-4-12
	Temporary disability insurance	28-41-32
miscellaneous	Earnings of a minor child	9-26-4(9)
	Property of business partnership	7-12-36
pensions	ERISA-qualified benefits	9-26-4(11)
	Firefighters	9-26-5
	IRAs	9-26-4(12)
	Police officers	9-26-5
	Private employees	28-17-4
	State & municipal employees	36-10-34
personal property	Beds, bedding, furniture & family stores of a housekeeper, to $1000 total	9-26-4(3)
	Bibles & books to $300	9-26-4(4)
	Body of deceased person	9-26-3
	Burial plot	9-26-4(5)
	Clothing needed	9-26-4(1)
	Consumer cooperative association holdings to $50	7-8-25
	Debt secured by promissory note or bill of exchange	9-26-4(7)
public benefits	Aid to blind, aged, disabled, AFDC, general assistance	40-6-14
	State disability benefits	28-41-32
	Unemployment compensation	28-44-58
	Veterans' disability or survivors' death benefits	30-7-9
	Workers' compensation	28-33-27
tools of trade	Library of professional in practice	9-26-4(2)
	Working tools to $500	9-26-4(2)
wages	Earned but unpaid wages to $50	9-26-4(8)(C)
	Earned but unpaid wages due military member on active duty	30-7-9
	Earned but unpaid wages due seaman	9-26-4(6)
	Earned but unpaid wages if received welfare during year before filing bankruptcy	9-26-4(8)(B)
	Wages of spouse	9-26-4(9)
	Wages paid by charitable organization to the poor	9-26-4(8)(A)
wild card	None	

South Carolina

In bankruptcy, you may claim these exemptions or the federal bankruptcy exemptions. All law references are to Code of Laws of South Carolina.

ASSET	EXEMPTION	LAW PROVIDING EXEMPTION
homestead	Real property, including coop, to $5000 (joint owners may double)	15-41-30(1)
insurance	Benefits accruing under life insurance policy after death of insured, where proceeds left with insurance company pursuant to agreement; benefits not exempt from action to recover necessaries if parties so agree	38-63-50
	Disability or illness benefits	15-41-30(10)(C)
	Fraternal benefit society benefits	38-37-870
	Life insurance avails from policy for person you depended on to $4000	15-41-30(8)
	Life insurance proceeds from policy for person you depended on, needed for support	15-41-30(11)(C)
	Unmatured life insurance contract, except credit insurance policy	15-41-30(7)
miscellaneous	Alimony, child support	15-41-30(10)(D)
	Property of business partnership	33-41-720
pensions	ERISA-qualified benefits	15-41-30(10)(E)
	Firefighters	9-13-230
	General assembly members	9-9-180
	Judges, solicitors	9-8-190
	Police officers	9-11-270
	Public employees	9-1-1680
personal property	Animals, crops, appliances, books, clothing, household goods, furnishings, musical instruments to $2500 total	15-41-30(3)
	Burial plot to $5000, in lieu of homestead (joint owners may double)	15-41-30(1)
	Cash & other liquid assets to $1000, in lieu of burial or homestead exemption	15-41-30(5)
	Health aids	15-41-30(9)
	Jewelry to $500	15-41-30(4)
	Motor vehicle to $1200	15-41-30(2)
	Personal injury recoveries	15-41-30(11)(B)
	Wrongful death recoveries	15-41-30(11)(B)
public benefits	AFDC, general relief, aid to aged, blind, disabled	43-5-190
	Crime victims' compensation	15-41-30(11)(A), 16-3-1300
	Local public assistance	15-41-30(10)(A)
	Social security	15-41-30(10)(A)
	Unemployment compensation	15-41-30(10)(A)
	Veterans' benefits	15-41-30(10)(B)
	Workers' compensation	42-9-360
tools of trade	Implements, books & tools of trade to $750	15-41-30(6)
wages	None	
wild card	None	

South Dakota

All law references are to South Dakota Codified Laws.

ASSET	EXEMPTION	LAW AUTHORIZING EXEMPTION
homestead	Real property (or mobile home larger than 240 square feet at its base and registered in state at least 6 months before being sought by judgment creditor or filing for bankruptcy) to unlimited value; property cannot exceed 1 acre in town or 160 acres elsewhere; sale proceeds to $30,000 (unlimited if you're over age 70 or an unmarried widow or widower) exempt for 1 year after sale (can't exempt gold or silver mine, mill or smelter, 43-31-5)	43-31-1, 43-31-2, 43-31-3, 43-31-4
	Spouse or child of deceased owner may claim homestead exemption	43-31-13
	May file homestead declaration	43-31-6
insurance	Annuity contract proceeds to $250 per month	58-12-6, 58-12-8
	Endowment, life insurance policy, proceeds or cash value to $20,000 (husband & wife may not double, *In re James*, 31 B.R. 67 (D. S.D. 1983))	58-12-4
	Fraternal benefit society benefits	58-37-68
	Health benefits to $20,000	58-12-4
	Life insurance proceeds, held pursuant to agreement by insurer, if clause prohibits proceeds from being used to pay beneficiary's creditors	58-15-70
	Life insurance proceeds to $10,000, if beneficiary is surviving spouse or child	43-45-6
miscellaneous	Property of business partnership	48-4-14
pensions	City employees	9-16-47
	Public employees	3-12-115
personal property	1. All debtors may exempt bible, books to $200, pictures, burial plots, church pew, food & fuel to last 1 year & clothing	43-45-2
	2. Head of family may claim $4000 of any personal property or:	43-45-4, 43-45-5
	Books & musical instruments to $200	43-45-5(1)
	2 cows, 5 swine, 25 sheep with lambs under 6 months; wool, cloth or yarn of sheep; food for all to last 1 year	43-45-5(3)
	Farming machinery, utensils, tackle for teams, harrow, 2 plows, sleigh, wagon to $1250 total	43-45-5(3)
	Furniture, including bedsteads & bedding to $200	43-45-5(2)
	Library & tools of professional to $300	43-45-5(5)
	Tools of mechanic & stock in trade to $200	43-45-5(4)
	2 yoke of oxen, or span of horses or mules	43-45-5(3)
	3. Non-head of family may claim $2000 of any personal property	43-45-4
public benefits	AFDC	28-7-16
	Unemployment compensation	61-6-28
	Workers' compensation	62-4-42
tools of trade	See personal property	
wages	Earned wages owed 60 days before being sought by judgment creditor or filing bankruptcy, needed for support of family	15-20-12
	Greater of 75% of your weekly net earnings or 30 times the federal minimum wage per week —judgment creditor	21-18-51
	Wages of prisoners in work programs	24-8-10
wild card	See personal property	

Tennessee

All law references are to Tennessee Code Annotated unless otherwise noted.

ASSET	EXEMPTION	LAW PROVIDING EXEMPTION
homestead	$5000; $7500 for joint owners	26-2-301
	Life estate	26-2-302
	2-15 year lease	26-2-303
	Spouse or child of deceased owner may claim homestead exemption	26-2-301
	Property held as tenancy by the entirety may be exempt against debts owed by only one spouse	*In re Arango*, 136 B.R. 740, *aff'd*, 992 F.2d 611 (6th Cir. 1993)
insurance	Accident, health or disability benefits for resident & citizen of Tennessee	26-2-110
	Disability or illness benefits	26-2-111(1)(C)
	Fraternal benefit society benefits	56-25-1403
	Homeowners' insurance proceeds to $5000	26-2-304
miscellaneous	Alimony owed for 30 days before being sought by judgment creditor or filing for bankruptcy	26-2-111(1)(E)
	Property of business partnership	61-1-124
pensions	ERISA-qualified benefits	26-2-111(1)(D)
	Public employees	8-36-111
	State & local government employees	26-2-104
	Teachers	49-5-909
personal property	Bible, school books, pictures, portraits, clothing & storage containers	26-2-103
	Burial plot to 1 acre	26-2-305, 46-2-102
	Health aids	26-2-111(5)
	Lost earnings payments for you or person you depended on	26-2-111(3)
	Personal injury recoveries to $7500 (not to include pain & suffering); wrongful death recoveries to $10,000 (you can't exempt more than $15,000 total for personal injury, wrongful death & crime victims' compensation)	26-2-111(2)(B), 26-2-111(2)(C)
public benefits	AFDC	71-3-121
	Aid to blind	71-4-117
	Aid to disabled	71-4-1112
	Crime victims' compensation to $5000 (see personal property)	26-2-111(2)(A), 29-13-111
	Local public assistance	26-2-111(1)(A)
	Old-age assistance	71-2-216
	Social security	26-2-111(1)(A)
	Unemployment compensation	26-2-111(1)(A)
	Veterans' benefits	26-2-111(1)(B)
	Workers' compensation	50-6-223
tools of trade	Implements, books & tools of trade to $750	26-2-111(4)
wages	Greater of 75% of your weekly net earnings or 30 times the federal minimum wage per week —judgment creditor	26-2-106, 26-2-107
	Minimum 75% of earned but unpaid wages, plus $2.50 per week per child—bankruptcy	26-2-106, 26-2-107
wild card	$4000 of any personal property	26-2-102

Texas

ASSET	EXEMPTION	LAW PROVIDING EXEMPTION
homestead	Unlimited; property cannot exceed 1 acre in town, village, city or 100 acres (200 for families) elsewhere; sale proceeds exempt for 6 months after sale (need not occupy when file for bankruptcy if not acquire another home, Property 41.003)	Property 41.001, 41.002
	May file homestead declaration	Property 41.005
insurance	Fraternal benefit society benefits	Insurance 10.28
	Life, health, accident or annuity benefits or monies, including policy proceeds and cash values to be paid or rendered to beneficiary or insured	Insurance 21.22
	Life insurance present value if beneficiary is debtor or debtor's dependent (see note under personal property)	Property 42.002(a)(12)
	Retired public school employees group insurance	Insurance 3.50-4(11)(a)
	Texas employee uniform group insurance	Insurance 3.50-2(10)(a)
	Texas state college or university employee benefits	Insurance 3.50-3(9)(a)
miscellaneous	Property of business partnership	6132b-25
pensions	County & district employees	Government 811.005
	ERISA-qualified government or church benefits, including Keoghs and IRAs	Property 42.0021
	Firefighters	6243e(5), 6243e.1(12), 6243e.2(12)
	IRAs to extent tax-deferred	Property 42.0021
	Judges	Government 811.005
	Keoghs to extent tax-deferred	Property 42.0021
	Law enforcement officers' survivors	6228f(8)
	Municipal employees	6243g, Government 811.005
	Police officers	6243d-1(17), 6243j(20), 6243g-1(23B)
	Retirement benefits to extent tax-deferred	Property 42.0021
	State employees	Government 811.005
	Teachers	Government 811.005
personal property *total includes tools of trade, unpaid commissions, life insurance cash value*	Athletic and sporting equipment, including bicycles; 2 firearms; home furnishings, including family heirlooms; food; clothing; jewelry (not to exceed 25% of total exemption); 1 two-, three- or four-wheeled motor vehicle per member of family or single adult who holds a driver's license (or who operates vehicle for someone else who does not have a license); 2 horses, mules or donkeys and a saddle, blanket and bridle for each; 12 head of cattle; 60 head of other types of livestock; 120 fowl; and pets to $30,000 total ($60,000 for head of family)	Property 42.001, 42.002
	Burial plots	Property 41.001
	Health aids	Property 42.001(b)(2)
public benefits	AFDC	Hum. Res. 31.040
	Crime victims' compensation	8309-1(7)(f)
	Medical assistance	Hum. Res. 32.036
	Unemployment compensation	5221b-13
	Workers' compensation	8308-4.07
tools of trade *see note under personal property*	Farming or ranching vehicles and implements	Property 42.002(a)(3)
	Tools, equipment (includes boat & motor vehicles) & books	Property 42.002(a)(4)
wages	Earned but unpaid wages	Property 42.001(b)(1)
	Unpaid commissions to 75% (see note under personal property)	Property 42.001(d)
wild card	None	

Utah

ASSET	EXEMPTION	LAW PROVIDING EXEMPTION
homestead	Real property, mobile home or water rights to $8000; may add $2000 for spouse & $500 per dependent	78-23-3
	Must file homestead declaration before attempted sale of home	78-23-4
insurance	Disability, illness, medical or hospital benefits	78-23-5(1)(c), (d)
	Fraternal benefit society benefits	31A-9-603
	Life insurance policy cash surrender value to $1500	78-23-7
	Life insurance proceeds if beneficiary is insured's spouse or dependent, as needed for support	78-73-6(2)
miscellaneous	Alimony needed for support	78-23-5(1)(k), 78-23-6(1)
	Child support	78-23-5(1)(f), (k)
	Property of business partnership	48-1-22
pensions	ERISA-qualified benefits	78-23-5(1)(j)
	Public employees	49-1-609
	Other pensions needed for support	78-23-6(3)
personal property	Animals, books & musical instruments to $500 total	78-23-8(1)(b)
	Artwork depicting, or done by, family member	78-23-5(1)(h)
	Bed, bedding, carpets, washer & dryer	78-23-5(1)(g)
	Burial plot	78-23-5(1)(a)
	Clothing (cannot claim furs or jewelry)	78-23-5(1)(g)
	Food to last 3 months	78-23-5(1)(g)
	Furnishings & appliances to $500	78-23-8(1)(a)
	Health aids needed	78-23-5(1)(b)
	Heirloom or other sentimental item to $500	78-23-8(1)(c)
	Personal injury recoveries for you or person you depended on	78-23-5(1)(i)
	Proceeds for damaged exempt property	78-23-9
	Refrigerator, freezer, stove & sewing machine	78-23-5(1)(g)
	Wrongful death recoveries for person you depended on	78-23-5(1)(i)
public benefits	AFDC	17-13-9
	Crime victims' compensation	63-63-21
	General assistance	55-15-32
	Occupational disease disability benefits	35-2-35
	Unemployment compensation	35-4-18
	Veterans' benefits	78-23-5(1)(e)
	Workers' compensation	35-1-80
tools of trade	Implements, books & tools of trade to $1500	78-23-8(2)
	Military property of national guard member	39-1-47
	Motor vehicle to $1500	78-23-8(2)
wages	Greater of 75% of your weekly net earnings or 30 times the federal minimum wage per week —judgment creditor	70C-7-103
	Minimum 75% of earned but unpaid wages—bankruptcy	70C-7-103
wild card	None	

Vermont

In bankruptcy, you may claim these exemptions or the federal bankruptcy exemptions. All law references are to Vermont Statutes Annotated unless otherwise noted.

ASSET	EXEMPTION	LAW PROVIDING EXEMPTION
homestead	Real property or mobile home to $30,000; may also claim rents, issues, profits & out-buildings	27-101
	Spouse of deceased owner may claim homestead exemption	27-105
	Property held as tenancy by the entirety may be exempt against debts owed by only one spouse	*In re McQueen,* 21 B.R. 736 (D. Ver. 1982)
insurance	Annuity contract benefits to $350 per month	8-3709
	Disability benefits that supplement life insurance or annuity contract	8-3707
	Disability or illness benefits needed for support	12-2740(19)(C)
	Fraternal benefit society benefits	8-4478
	Group life or health benefits	8-3708
	Health benefits to $200 per month	8-4086
	Life insurance proceeds if beneficiary is not the insured	8-3706
	Life insurance proceeds for person you depended on	12-2740(19)(H)
	Life insurance proceeds if clause prohibits proceeds from being used to pay beneficiary's creditors	8-3705
	Unmatured life insurance contract other than credit	12-2740(18)
miscellaneous	Alimony, child support needed for support	12-2740(19)(D)
	Property of business partnership	11-1282
pensions	Municipal employees	24-5066
	Self-directed accounts (IRAs, Keoghs) to $10,000	12-2740(16)
	State employees	3-476
	Teachers	16-1946
	Other pensions	12-2740(19)(J)
personal property	Appliances, furnishings, goods, clothing, books, crops, animals, musical instruments to $2500 total	12-2740(5)
	Cow, 2 goats, 10 sheep, 10 chickens; 3 swarms of bees & their honey; feed to last 1 winter; 10 cords of firewood, 5 tons of coal or 500 gallons of oil; 500 gallons of bottled gas; growing crops to $5000; 2 harnesses, 2 halters, 2 chains, plow & ox yoke; yoke of oxen or steers & 2 horses	12-2740(6), 12-2740(9)-(14)
	Jewelry to $500; wedding ring unlimited	12-2740(3), (4)
	Motor vehicles to $2500; bank deposits to $700	12-2740(1), (15)
	Personal injury recoveries for person you depended on	12-2740(19)(F)
	Stove, heating unit, refrigerator, freezer, water heater & sewing machines; lost future earnings for you or person you depended on; health aids	12-2740(8), 12-2740(17), 12-2740(19)(I)
	Wrongful death recoveries for person you depended on	12-2740(19)(G)
public benefits	Aid to blind, aged, disabled, AFDC, general assistance	33-124
	Crime victims' compensation needed for support	12-2740(19)(E)
	Social security needed for support	12-2740(19)(A)
	Unemployment compensation	21-1367
	Veterans' benefits needed for support	12-2740(19)(B)
	Workers' compensation	21-681
tools of trade	Books & tools of trade to $5000	12-2740(2)
wages	Greater of 75% of your weekly net earnings or 30 times the federal minimum wage per week—judgment creditor	12-3170
	Minimum 75% of earned but unpaid wages—bankruptcy	12-3170
	Wages, if received welfare during 2 months before being sought by judgment creditor or filing for bankruptcy	12-3170
wild card	$7000 less any amount of appliances, et al, growing crops, jewelry, motor vehicle & tools of trade, of any property	12-2740(7)
	$400 of any property	12-2740(7)

Virginia

All law references are to Code of Virginia unless otherwise noted.

ASSET	EXEMPTION	LAW PROVIDING EXEMPTION
homestead	$5000 plus $500 per dependent; may also claim rents & profits; sale proceeds exempt to $5000 (husband & wife may double, *Cheeseman v. Nachman*, 656 F.2d 60 (4th Cir. 1981)); unused portion of homestead may be applied to any personal property	34-4, 34-18, 34-20
	May include mobile home	*In re Goad*, 161 B.R. 161 (W.D. Va. 1993)
	Must file homestead declaration before being sought by judgment creditor or filing for bankruptcy	34-6
	Property held as tenancy by the entirety may be exempt against debts owed by only one spouse	*In re Harris*, 155 B.R. 948 (E.D. Va. 1993)
insurance	Accident or sickness benefits	38.2-3549
	Burial society benefits	38.2-4021
	Cooperative life insurance benefits	38.2-3811
	Fraternal benefit society benefits	38.2-4118
	Group life or accident insurance for government officials	51.1-510
	Group life insurance policy or proceeds	38.2-3339
	Industrial sick benefits	38.2-3549
miscellaneous	Property of business partnership	50-25
pensions *also see wages*	City, town & county employees	51.1-802
	ERISA-qualified benefits to $17,500 per year	34-34
	Judges	51.1-102
	State employees	51.1-102
personal property *you must be a householder to exempt any personal property*	Bible	34-26(1)
	Burial plot	34-26(3)
	Clothing to $1000	34-26(4)
	Family portraits and heirlooms to $5000 total	34-26(2)
	Health aids	34-26(6)
	Household furnishings to $5000	34-26(4)(a)
	Motor vehicle to $2000	34-26(8)
	Personal injury causes of action	34-28.1
	Personal injury recoveries	34-28.1
	Pets	34-26(5)
	Wedding and engagement rings	34-26(1)(a)
public benefits	Aid to blind, aged, disabled, AFDC, general relief	63.1-88
	Crime victims' compensation unless seeking to discharge debt for treatment of injury incurred during crime	19.2-368.12
	Unemployment compensation	60.2-600
	Workers' compensation	65.2-531
tools of trade	Horses, mules (pair) with gear, wagon or cart, tractor to $3000, plows (2), drag, harvest cradle, pitchfork, rake, iron wedges (2), fertilizer to $1000 of farmer (you must be a householder)	34-27
	Tools, books and instruments of trade, including motor vehicles, to $10,000, needed in your occupation or education (you must be a householder)	34-26
	Uniforms, arms, equipment of military member	44-96
wages	Greater of 75% of your weekly net earnings or 30 times the federal minimum wage per week —judgment creditor	34-29
	Minimum 75% of earned but unpaid wages, pension payments—bankruptcy	34-29
wild card	Unused portion of homestead, of any personal property	34-13
	$2000 of any property for disabled veterans (you must be a householder)	34-4.1

Washington

In bankruptcy, you may claim these exemptions or the federal bankruptcy exemptions.
All law references are to Revised Code of Washington Annotated.

ASSET	EXEMPTION	LAW PROVIDING EXEMPTION
homestead	Real property or mobile home to $30,000 (no limit if seeking to discharge debt based on failure to pay a state income tax assessed on retirement benefits received while a resident of Washington, 6.15.030)	6.13.010, 6.13.030
	Must record homestead declaration before sale of home if property unimproved or home unoccupied	6.15.040
insurance	Annuity contract proceeds to $250 per month	48.18.430
	Disability proceeds, avails or benefits	48.18.400
	Fire insurance proceeds for destroyed exemption	6.15.030
	Fraternal benefit society benefits	48.36A.180
	Group life insurance policy or proceeds	48.18.420
	Life insurance proceeds or avails if beneficiary is not the insured	48.18.410
miscellaneous	Property of business partnership	25.04.250
pensions	City employees	41.28.200
	ERISA-qualified benefits	6.15.020
	IRAs	6.15.020
	Public employees	41.40.380
	State patrol officers	43.43.310
	Volunteer firefighters	41.24.240
personal property	Appliances, furniture, household goods, home & yard equipment to $2700 total (no limit on any property located within Washington if seeking to discharge debt based on failure to pay a state income tax assessed on retirement benefits received while a resident of Washington, 6.15.025)	6.15.010(3)(a)
	Books to $1500	6.15.010(2)
	Burial plots sold by nonprofit cemetery association	68.20.120
	Clothing, no more than $1000 in furs, jewelry, ornaments	6.15.010(1)
	Food & fuel for comfortable maintenance	6.15.010(3)(a)
	Keepsakes & pictures	6.15.010(2)
	Two motor vehicles to $2500 total	6.15.010(3)(c)
public benefits	Child welfare (AFDC)	74.13.070
	Crime victims' compensation	7.68.070, 51.32.040
	General assistance	74.04.280
	Industrial insurance (workers' compensation)	51.32.040
	Old-age assistance	74.08.210
	Unemployment compensation	50.40.020
tools of trade	Farm trucks, stock, tools, seed, equipment & supplies of farmer to $5000 total	6.15.010(4)(a)
	Library, office furniture, office equipment & supplies of physician, surgeon, attorney, clergy or other professional to $5000 total	6.15.010(4)(b)
	Tools & materials used in another's trade to $5000	6.15.010(4)(c)
wages	Greater of 75% of your weekly net earnings or 30 times the federal minimum wage per week —judgment creditor	6.27.150
	Minimum 75% of earned but unpaid wages—bankruptcy	6.27.150
wild card	$1000 of any personal property (no more than $100 in cash, bank deposits, bonds, stocks & securities)	6.15.010(3)(b)

West Virginia

All law references are to West Virginia Code.

ASSET	EXEMPTION	LAW PROVIDING EXEMPTION
homestead	Real or personal property used as residence to $7500; unused portion of homestead may be applied to any property	38-10-4(a)
insurance	Fraternal benefit society benefits	33-23-21
	Group life insurance policy or proceeds	33-6-28
	Health or disability benefits	38-10-4(j)(3)
	Life insurance payments from policy for person you depended on, needed for support	38-10-4(k)(3)
	Unmatured life insurance contract, except credit insurance policy	38-10-4(g)
	Unmatured life insurance contract's accrued dividend, interest or loan value to $4000, if debtor owns contract & insured is either debtor or a person on whom debtor is dependent	38-10-4(h)
miscellaneous	Alimony, child support needed for support	38-10-4(j)(4)
	Property of business partnership	47-8A-25
pensions	ERISA-qualified benefits needed for support	38-10-4(j)(5)
	Public employees	5-10-46
	Teachers	18-7A-30
personal property	Animals, crops, clothing, appliances, books, household goods, furnishings, musical instruments to $200 per item, $1000 total	38-10-4(c)
	Burial plot to $7500, in lieu of homestead	38-10-4(a)
	Health aids	38-10-4(i)
	Jewelry to $500	38-10-4(d)
	Lost earnings payments needed for support	38-10-4(k)(5)
	Motor vehicle to $1200	38-10-4(b)
	Personal injury recoveries to $7500 (not to include pain & suffering)	38-10-4(k)(4)
	Wrongful death recoveries needed for support, for person you depended on	38-10-4(k)(2)
public benefits	Aid to blind, aged, disabled, AFDC, general assistance	9-5-1
	Crime victims' compensation	14-2A-24, 38-10-4(k)(1)
	Social security	38-10-4(j)(1)
	Unemployment compensation	38-10-4(j)(1)
	Veterans' benefits	38-10-4(j)(2)
	Workers' compensation	23-4-18
tools of trade	Implements, books & tools of trade to $750	38-10-4(f)
wages	Greater of 75% of your weekly net earnings or 30 times the federal minimum wage per week —judgment creditor	38-5A-3
	Minimum 80% of earned but unpaid wages—bankruptcy	38-5A-3
wild card	$400 of any property	38-10-4(e)
	Unused portion of homestead or burial exemption, of any property	38-10-4(e)

Wisconsin

In bankruptcy, you may claim these exemptions or the federal bankruptcy exemptions.
All law references are to Wisconsin Statutes Annotated.

ASSET	EXEMPTION	LAW PROVIDING EXEMPTION
homestead	Property you occupy or intend to occupy to $40,000; sale proceeds exempt for 2 years from sale if you plan to obtain another home (husband and wife may not double)	815.20
insurance	Federal disability insurance	815.18(3)(ds)
	Fire proceeds for destroyed exempt property for 2 years from receiving	815.18(3)(e)
	Fraternal benefit society benefits	614.96
	Life insurance policy or proceeds to $5000, if beneficiary is a married woman	766.09
	Life insurance proceeds held in trust by insurer, if clause prohibits proceeds from being used to pay beneficiary's creditors	632.42
	Life insurance proceeds if beneficiary was dependent of insured, needed for support	815.18(3)(i)(a)
	Unmatured life insurance contract, except credit insurance contract, owned by debtor & insuring debtor, dependent of debtor or someone debtor is dependent on	815.18(3)(f)
	Unmatured life insurance contract's accrued dividends, interest or loan value (to $4000 total in all contracts), if debtor owns contract & insured is debtor, dependent of debtor or someone debtor is dependent on	815.18(3)(f)
miscellaneous	Alimony, child support needed for support	815.18(3)(c)
	Property of business partnership	178.21
pensions	Certain municipal employees	66.81
	Firefighters, police officers who worked in city with population over 100,000	815.18(3)(ef)
	Military pensions	815.18(3)(n)
	Private or public retirement benefits	815.18(3)(j)
	Public employees	40.08(1)
personal property	Burial provisions	815.18(3)(a)
	Deposit accounts to $1000	815.18(3)(k)
	Household goods and furnishings, clothing, keepsakes, jewelry, appliances, books, musical instruments, firearms, sporting goods, animals and other tangible property held for personal, family or household use to $5000 total	815.18(3)(d)
	Lost future earnings recoveries, needed for support	815.18(3)(i)(d)
	Motor vehicles to $1200	815.18(3)(g)
	Personal injury recoveries to $25,000	815.18(3)(i)(c)
	Tenant's lease or stock interest in housing coop, to homestead amount	182.004(6)
	Wages used to purchase savings bonds	20.921(1)(e)
	Wrongful death recoveries, needed for support	815.18(3)(i)(b)
public benefits	AFDC, other social services payments	49.41
	Crime victims' compensation	949.07
	Unemployment compensation	108.13
	Veterans' benefits	45.35(8)(b)
	Workers' compensation	102.27
tools of trade	Equipment, inventory, farm products, books and tools of trade to $7500 total	815.18(3)(b)
wages	Minimum 75% of earned but unpaid wages	815.18(3)(h)
wild card	None	

Wyoming

ASSET	EXEMPTION	LAW PROVIDING EXEMPTION
homestead	Real property you occupy to $10,000 or house trailer you occupy to $6000 (joint owners may double)	1-20-101, 1-20-102, 1-20-104
	Spouse or child of deceased owner may claim homestead exemption	1-20-103
	Property held as tenancy by the entirety may be exempt against debts owed by only one spouse	*In re Anselmi*, 52 B.R. 479 (D. Wy. 1985)
insurance	Annuity contract proceeds to $350 per month	26-15-132
	Disability benefits if clause prohibits proceeds from being used to pay beneficiary's creditors	26-15-130
	Fraternal benefit society benefits	26-29-218
	Group life or disability policy or proceeds	26-15-131
	Life insurance proceeds held by insurer, if clause prohibits proceeds from being used to pay beneficiary's creditors	26-15-133
miscellaneous	Liquor licenses & malt beverage permits	12-4-604
	Property of business partnership	17-13-502
pensions	Criminal investigators, highway officers	9-3-620
	Firefighters, police officers (only payments being received)	15-5-209
	Game & fish wardens	9-3-620
	Private or public retirement funds and accounts	1-20-110
	Public employees	9-3-426
personal property	Bedding, furniture, household articles & food to $2000 per person in the home	1-20-106(a)(iii)
	Bible, school books & pictures	1-20-106(a)(i)
	Burial plot	1-20-106(a)(ii), 35-8-104
	Clothing & wedding rings needed, up to $1000	1-20-105
	Funeral contracts, pre-paid	26-32-102
	Motor vehicle to $2000	1-20-106(a)(iv)
public benefits	AFDC, general assistance	42-2-113
	Crime victims' compensation	1-40-113
	Unemployment compensation	27-3-319
	Workers' compensation	27-14-702
tools of trade	Library & implements of professional to $2000 or, tools, motor vehicle, implements, team & stock in trade to $2000	1-20-106(b)
wages	Earnings of national guard members	19-2-501
	Greater of 75% of your weekly net earnings or 30 times the federal minimum wage per week —judgment creditor	1-15-511
	Minimum 75% of earned but unpaid wages—bankruptcy	1-15-511
	Wages of inmates on work release	7-16-308
wild card	None	

Federal Bankruptcy Exemptions

Married couples may double all exemptions.
All references are to 11 U.S.C. § 522.

Debtors in the following states may select the Federal Bankruptcy Exemptions:

Arkansas	Massachusetts	New Jersey	Rhode Island	Vermont
Connecticut	Michigan	New Mexico	South Carolina	Washington
District of Columbia	Minnesota	Pennsylvania	Texas	Wisconsin
Hawaii				

ASSET	EXEMPTION	SUBSECTION PROVIDING EXEMPTION
homestead	Real property, including coop or mobile home, to $15,000; unused portion of homestead to $7500 may be applied to any property	(d)(1)
insurance	Disability, illness or unemployment benefits	(d)(10)(C)
	Life insurance payments for person you depended on, needed for support	(d)(11)(C)
	Life insurance policy with loan value, in accrued dividends or interest, to $8000	(d)(8)
	Unmatured life insurance contract, except credit insurance policy	(d)(7)
miscellaneous	Alimony, child support needed for support	(d)(10)(D)
pensions	ERISA-qualified benefits needed for support	(d)(10)(E)
personal property	Animals, crops, clothing, appliances, books, furnishings, household goods, musical instruments to $400 per item, $8000 total	(d)(3)
	Health aids	(d)(9)
	Jewelry to $1000	(d)(4)
	Lost earnings payments	(d)(11)(E)
	Motor vehicle to $2400	(d)(2)
	Personal injury recoveries to $15,000 (not to include pain & suffering or pecuniary loss)	(d)(11)(D)
	Wrongful death recoveries for person you depended on	(d)(11)(B)
public benefits	Crime victims' compensation	(d)(11)(A)
	Public assistance	(d)(10)(A)
	Social security	(d)(10)(A)
	Unemployment compensation	(d)(10)(A)
	Veterans' benefits	(d)(10)(A)
tools of trade	Implements, books & tools of trade to $1500	(d)(6)
wages	None	
wild card	$800 of any property	(d)(5)
	$7500 less any amount of homestead exemption claimed, of any property	(d)(5)

Federal Non-Bankruptcy Exemptions

These exemptions are available if you file for bankruptcy and use your state exemptions or if you are pursued by a judgment creditor. All law references are to the United States Code.

ASSET	EXEMPTION	LAW AUTHORIZING EXEMPTION
retirement benefits	CIA employees	50 § 403
	Civil service employees	5 § 8346
	Foreign service employees	22 § 4060
	Military honor roll pensions	38 § 562
	Military service employees	10 § 1440
	Railroad workers	45 § 231m
	Social security	42 § 407
	Veterans' benefits	38 § 3101
	Veterans' medal of honor benefits	38 § 562
survivor's benefits	Judges, U.S. court directors, judicial center directors, Supreme Court chief justice administrators	28 § 376
	Lighthouse workers	33 § 775
	Military service	10 § 1450
death & disability benefits	Government employees	5 § 8130
	Longshoremen & harbor workers	33 § 916
	War risk hazard death or injury compensation	42 § 1717
miscellaneous	Klamath Indians tribe benefits for Indians residing in Oregon	25 § 543, 25 § 545
	Military deposits in savings accounts while on permanent duty outside U.S.	10 § 1035
	Military group life insurance	38 § 770(g)
	Railroad workers' unemployment insurance	45 § 352(e)
	Seamen's clothing	46 § 11110
	Seamen's wages (while on a voyage) pursuant to a written contract	46 § 11111
	75% of earned but unpaid wages; bankruptcy judge may authorize more for low-income debtors	15 § 1673

Index

CATALOG

ESTATE PLANNING & PROBATE

	EDITION	PRICE	CODE
Plan Your Estate	3rd	$24.95	NEST
Make Your Own Living Trust	1st	$19.95	LITR
Nolo's Simple Will Book	2nd	$17.95	SWIL
How to Probate an Estate (California)	8th	$34.95	PAE
Nolo's Law Form Kit: Wills	1st	$14.95	KWL
Write Your Will (audio cassette)	1st	$14.95	TWYW
5 Ways to Avoid Probate (audio cassette)	1st	$14.95	TPRO

BUSINESS & WORKPLACE

	EDITION	PRICE	CODE
Employers Legal Handbook	1st	$29.95	EMPL
The Legal Guide for Starting & Running a Small Business	1st	$22.95	RUNS
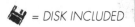 The Legal Guide for Starting & Running a Small Business on Disk—WIN	1st	$24.95	RUNSW1
Your Rights in the Workplace	2nd	$15.95	YRW
How to Write a Business Plan	4th	$21.95	SBS
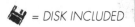 Software Development: A Legal Guide—DOS	1st	$44.95	SFT
Marketing Without Advertising	1st	$14.00	MWAD
Sexual Harassment on the Job	2nd	$18.95	HARS
The Partnership Book	4th	$24.95	PART
The Independent Paralegal's Handbook	3rd	$29.95	PARA
Getting Started as an Independent Paralegal (audio cassette)	2nd	$44.95	GSIP

MONEY MATTERS

	EDITION	PRICE	CODE
How to File for Bankruptcy	5th	$25.95	HFB
Stand Up to the IRS	2nd	$21.95	SIRS
Simple Contracts for Personal Use	2nd	$16.95	CONT
Nolo's Law Form Kit: Power of Attorney	1st	$14.95	KPA
Nolo's Law Form Kit: Personal Bankruptcy	1st	$14.95	KBNK
Nolo's Law Form Kit: Rebuild Your Credit	1st	$14.95	KCRD
Nolo's Law Form Kit: Loan Agreements	1st	$14.95	KLOAN
Nolo's Law Form Kit: Buy & Sell Contracts	1st	$9.95	KCONT

CONSUMER

	EDITION	PRICE	CODE
How to Win Your Personal Injury Claim	1st	$24.95	PICL
Nolo's Pocket Guide to California Law	2nd	$10.95	CLAW
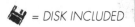 Nolo's Pocket Guide to California Law on Disk	Windows	$24.95	CLWIN
	Macintosh	$24.95	CLM
Nolo's Law Form Kit: Hiring Child Care & Household Help	1st	$14.95	KCHLD
Nolo's Pocket Guide to Consumer Rights	2nd	$12.95	CAG

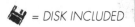 = DISK INCLUDED

TO ORDER CALL 800-992-6656

GOING TO COURT

Represent Yourself in Court	1st	$29.95	RYC
Everybody's Guide to Municipal Court (California)	1st	$29.95	MUNI
Everybody's Guide to Small Claims Court (National)	5th	$18.95	NSCC
Everybody's Guide to Small Claims Court (California)	11th	$18.95	CSCC
Collect Your Court Judgment (California)	2nd	$19.95	JUDG
Fight Your Ticket (California)	5th	$18.95	FYT
How to Change Your Name (California)	6th	$24.95	NAME
The Criminal Records Book (California)	3rd	$19.95	CRIM
Winning in Small Claims Court (audio cassette)	1st	$14.95	TWIN

FAMILY MATTERS

The Living Together Kit	7th	$24.95	LTK
A Legal Guide for Lesbian and Gay Couples	8th	$24.95	LG
Divorce & Money	2nd	$21.95	DIMO
Smart Ways to Save Money During and After Divorce	1st	$14.95	SAVMO
How to Raise or Lower Child Support In California	2nd	$17.95	CHLD
Nolo's Pocket Guide to Family Law	3rd	$14.95	FLD
How to Adopt Your Stepchild in California	4th	$22.95	ADOP
The Guardianship Book (California)	1st	$19.95	GB
How to Do Your Own Divorce in California	19th	$21.95	CDIV
How to Do Your Own Divorce in Texas	5th	$17.95	TDIV
Practical Divorce Solutions	1st	$14.95	PDS

THE NEIGHBORHOOD

Neighbor Law: Fences, Trees, Boundaries & Noise	2nd	$16.95	NEI
Safe Home, Safe Neighborhoods: Stopping Crime Where You Live	1st	$14.95	SAFE
Dog Law	2nd	$12.95	DOG

LANDLORDS & TENANTS

The Landlord's Law Book, Vol. 1: Rights & Responsibilities (California)	4th	$32.95	LBRT
The Landlord's Law Book, Vol. 2: Evictions (California)	5th	$34.95	LBEV
Tenants' Rights (California)	12th	$18.95	CTEN
Nolo's Law Form Kit: Leases & Rental Agreements (California)	1st	$14.95	KLEAS

HOMEOWNERS

How to Buy a House in California	3rd	$24.95	BHCA
For Sale By Owner	2nd	$24.95	FSBO
Homestead Your House	8th	$9.95	HOME
The Deeds Book	3rd	$16.95	DEED

OLDER AMERICANS

Beat the Nursing Home Trap: A Consumer's Guide to Choosing & Financing Long Term Care	2nd	$18.95	ELD
Social Security, Medicare & Pensions	5th	$18.95	SOA

TO ORDER CALL 800-992-6656

Legal Research .... 3rd $19.95 LRES

SOFTWARE

WillMaker 5.0 .... Windows ~~$69.95~~ $48.96 WI5
DOS ~~$69.95~~ $48.96 WI5
Macintosh ~~$69.95~~ $48.96 WM5

Nolo's Personal RecordKeeper 3.0 .... DOS ~~$49.95~~ $34.96 FRI3
Macintosh ~~$49.95~~ $34.96 FRM3

Living Trust Maker 2.0 .... Windows ~~$79.95~~ $55.96 LTWI2
Macintosh ~~$79.95~~ $55.96 LTM2

Patent It Yourself 1.0 .... Windows ~~$229.95~~ $160.96 PYW1

Nolo's Partnership Maker 1.0 .... DOS ~~$129.95~~ $90.96 PAGI1

California Incorporator 1.0 .... DOS ~~$129.00~~ $90.30 INCI

GET 25% OFF YOUR NEXT PURCHASE

Recycle your out-of-date books. It's important to have the most current legal information. Because laws and legal procedures change often, we update our books regularly. To help keep you up-to-date we are extending this special offer. Cut out and mail the title portion of the cover of any old Nolo book with your next order and we'll give you a 25% discount off the retail price of ANY new Nolo book you purchase directly from us. For current prices and editions call us at 1-800-992-6656. This offer is to individuals only.

ORDER FORM

Code	Quantity	Title	Unit Price	Total
			Subtotal	
		California residents add Sales Tax		
		Shipping & Handling ($4 for 1st item; $1 each additional)		
		2nd day UPS (additional $5; $8 in Alaska and Hawaii)		
		TOTAL		

Name

Address

(UPS to street address, Priority Mail to P.O. boxes)

FOR FASTER SERVICE, USE YOUR CREDIT CARD AND OUR TOLL-FREE NUMBERS

Monday-Friday, 7 a.m. to 6 p.m. Pacific Time
Order Line   1 (800) 992-6656
                    in the 510 area code, call 549-1976
General Information 1 (510) 549-1976
Fax your order   1 (800) 645-0895
                    in the 510 area code, call 548-5902

METHOD OF PAYMENT

☐ Check enclosed   ☐ VISA   ☐ Mastercard   ☐ Discover Card
☐ American Express

Account #

Expiration Date

Authorizing Signature

Daytime Phone

MAIL YOUR ORDER WITH A CHECK OR MONEY ORDER MADE PAYABLE TO: NOLO PRESS, 950 PARKER ST., BERKELEY, CA 94710

[Nolo books are]..."written in plain language, free of legal mumbo jumbo, and spiced with witty personal observations."

—ASSOCIATED PRESS

"Well-produced and slickly written, the [Nolo] books are designed to take the mystery out of seemingly involved procedures, carefully avoiding legalese and leading the reader step-by-step through such everyday legal problems as filling out forms, making up contracts, and even how to behave in court."

—SAN FRANCISCO EXAMINER

"...Nolo publications...guide people simply through the how, when, where and why of law."

—WASHINGTON POST

"Increasingly, people who are not lawyers are performing tasks usually regarded as legal work... And consumers, using books like Nolo's, do routine legal work themselves."

—NEW YORK TIMES

"...All of [Nolo's] books are easy-to-understand, are updated regularly, provide pull-out forms...and are often quite moving in their sense of compassion for the struggles of the lay reader."

—SAN FRANCISCO CHRONICLE